D0325856

THE PENTAGON

THE PENTAGON

Politics, Profits and Plunder

By Clark R. Mollenhoff

G. P. PUTNAM'S SONS
NEW YORK

PRINTED IN THE UNITED STATES OF AMERICA

TO

GJORE JEAN

WHOSE HELP WAS INVALUABLE

Contents

THE PENTAGON

1

IF POWER CORRUPTS

"Power tends to corrupt and absolute power corrupts absolutely."—Lord Acton

IF "power tends to corrupt," we should be filled with the greatest apprehension about the power of the Pentagon. Never in the history of our nation has so much power been centralized in the hands of so few men and subject to so few effective checks.

Periodically, an authoritarian trend becomes apparent in the comments or actions of a highly placed civilian official or military officer. But such glimpses of the danger are fleeting, and few take the time to examine the evidence of the total power potential accumulated in the Office of Defense Secretary.

Viewed in its totality, the power centralized in the Office of Defense Secretary could be used to impose a dictatorship on the nation. There are still occasional challenges to the Office of Defense Secretary, but they have appeared to be futile in most instances. Unless there are more effective challenges in the future, accompanied by courageous and persistent dissent, we may have passed the critical point and have already lost the battle against authoritarian government.

Pentagon power has terrorized timid men who are fearful of being identified as dissenters. It has muffled the criticisms of brave men with positions or family responsibilities that made it seem unwise to risk a career setback, loss of a defense contract, loss of a Pentagon research grant, or loss of a politically important military base. Few big-business executives, military officers, members of Congress, or governors are willing to risk the anger of the Secretary of Defense or his most influential assistants.

Even men with financial independence, courage and great prestige can be wary and apprehensive about risking a fight with the colossal multimillion-dollar propaganda machine that is the Pentagon press office. "You can't fight City Hall," and today the realist must recognize that no city hall, no county courthouse, no state capitol has held one tenth of the coercive power now lodged in the Office of Defense Secretary through the power tentacles that reach into the economics, the politics, and the communications network of the entire nation. (See Appendix A for a chart on U.S. military spending 1925–1964.)

Many on the outside—not direct participants in the contest with the Pentagon leadership—are not greatly concerned over the power centralization that has developed. At worst, they regard it as a benevolent dictatorship that is probably necessary to command our military machine in days of space-age warfare.

A different picture emerges for many of those who are directly involved in the struggle with the Office of Defense Secretary and who have tried to dissent. Defense contractors, Congressmen, or high-ranking military officers have been faced with actions they consider arbitrary, arrogant and ruthless.

Yet certain aspects of the Pentagon power are so subtle and so ubiquitous that its pervasiveness is accepted without any extended complaint. We accept it as the inevitable price we must pay for protecting our freedom from foreign enemies. The average citizen gives little thought to the dangers inherent in little reorganizations, little adjustments, little shifts of power which over a period of years have removed most of the effective checks on our huge military watchdog.

The enormity of the Pentagon power is not understood and the danger not recognized for a number of reasons. Predominant is the fact that the daily press is reluctant to take on the job of criticizing those who control the major sources of news at the Pentagon. It is easy to submit to Pentagon news-management pressures when the bait is an occasional exclusive story and comfortable, easy access to the "invitation-only background news conferences" with top Pentagon spokesmen. Only a few of the Pentagon reporters will fight the system and risk the cold and uncooperative treatment handed out to those who are regarded as "unfriendly" or "unsympathetic" to the civilian power structure.

If the daily press does not show the way, magazine writers, columnists and television reporters have difficulty recognizing that a critical problem exists. The work of the courageous few is overwhelmed and inundated by the mass of stories flowing from sycophant journalists who depict key Pentagon civilians as supermen.

As a result, the public is not confronted with the cold facts on Pentagon power, but finds them buried on the back pages while the glories of the heroic civilian bosses saturate the stories on page one.

The punishment of critical or "unfriendly" newsmen has served as an effective weapon to intimidate many bright and normally independent newsmen who must depend upon access to high Pentagon contacts for their livelihood. Defense Secretaries have initiated F.B.I. investigations of reporters for alleged breaches of national security when the stories embarrassed the administration, but the contentions of a security breach were highly questionable.

We assume that such Pentagon-inspired shadowing of reporters is rare, but there are other equally effective means of coercing newsmen or interfering with their contacts. There are efforts to ridicule the tough questioner. There have been attempts by the Defense Secretary to undermine the reporter's standing with his superiors with vague and unsubstantiated charges of "irresponsibility."

Directives are issued which seriously interfere with the freedom of action by any independent newsman. Such an order, written in October, 1962, instructed all civilian and military personnel at the Pentagon to report, before the end of each working day, on all contacts with newsmen and the subjects discussed. That order is still in effect four years later, despite press complaints that it was an obvious effort to pin down sources of unfavorable news stories and to eliminate this channel of dissent.

Effective efforts to discipline and control many of the Pentagon press corps have been used in other areas to coerce and control possible dissenters in Congress, among the highest-ranking military officers, and among the major defense contractors. Existing case studies can demonstrate how this control has been exercised through subtle as well as brutal methods.

Observant individuals will see the manifestations of fear of the Pentagon in many places:

An executive of a major defense contractor called a United States Senator to ask that there be no investigation of a Pentagon decision which robbed his company of a billion-dollar contract. The firm was the low bidder, the product was evaluated as "superior," so there seemed every reason for the corporation executive to want the investigation. He believed his firm had been wronged by a political decision, but he feared to complain because he believed that the Office of Defense Secretary might be vindictive and cut the firm even more severely on future contract negotiations.

A Republican Congressman declined to restate his criticism of the Defense Secretary in a Democratic Administration, and said he feared retaliation in the form of the closing of a military base in his district. He did not feel that he could afford the political repercussions if an opponent hinted that a friendly Democrat could have saved the base and might obtain more defense contracts and other federal funds.

An admiral voiced private apprehension about his career because his answers to a Senate committee revealed his opposition to a major decision by the Office of Defense Secretary. His fears were valid—his Navy career was prematurely ended.

Two Senators with leading roles in critical investigations of a decision by the Defense Secretary found themselves subject to a series of attacks from anonymous Pentagon spokesmen unjustly charging them with base political motivations.

A Democratic lawmaker expressed frustration after the Office of Defense Secretary declined to make pertinent information available to his subcommittee, and later slapped a "secret" classification on a congressional report highly critical of the Defense Department management.

A distinguished military-affairs writer found himself subject to private smears as "irresponsible" by the Office of Defense Secretary after publication of articles critical of military equipment shortages developing as a result of the Vietnam war.

Usually the coercion and the potential for coercion go unnoticed by the public. Of course, there is a general awareness of the tremendous military might embodied in a war machine that includes more than 2,500,000 people, ballistic missiles, a nuclear submarine fleet armed with Polaris missiles, and a Strategic Air Command armed with supersonic planes and the latest in nuclear weapons. And with this destructive power in mind, some political leaders issue periodic warnings of the danger of our military establishment falling into the hands of authoritarian-minded, professional military men. Learned articles and exciting, popular novels such as *Seven Days in May* are based on the theory that we must be alert to the dangers of the military coups so commonplace in other nations.

Periodically, we are assured that the great power of the Pentagon will not be misused by professional military men because our civilian political appointees are guarding against any usurpation of power. Year by year, the civilian power of the Pentagon has been increased and centralized, and nearly always on the theory that the authoritarian-minded and arrogant military brass is being put in its place by the democracy-minded civilians.

President Eisenhower left office warning of the danger of the industrial-military complex in our society. Because he did not spell out the details, his remarks were interpreted widely as another caution against a military or economic coup conducted by a coalition of our big industrial leaders and our uniformed military hierarchy. Some high-level political appointees used the Eisenhower comment as another authority to quote, justifying more civilian action to remove power from the military men so it could be lodged in the hands of civilian political appointees.

While the warning finger was pointed at top-ranking military officers, the political appointees pulled together the power over Pentagon decisions and centralized them in the Office of Defense Secretary. Few noted the consolidation of power even though the Congress continued to grind out annual studies on the "Economic Impact of Federal Procurement" that spelled out the facts and figures of strength lodged in the Pentagon budget. (See Appendix B for a chart on military procurement by the states for 1963, 1964 and 1965.)

Cold facts, in studies that were low key and dull, demonstrated that defense spending, ranging from $40 billion to $60 billion a year, had tremendous political as well as economic impact on the biggest industries in the United States, on the most respected universities and colleges, and on the most influential political leaders. In fact, the more carefully the details of the Pentagon budget are studied, the more apparent it becomes that there are few institutions in our society—industrial, educational or political—not compelled to respect the power of the Pentagon decision-makers.

Edward Kennedy, younger brother of President John F. Kennedy, was elected to the United States Senate in a campaign that claimed he could do more for Massachusetts because of his political connections in Washington. A large number of other Democratic candidates for the United States Senate and House tried to convey the impression that they, too, could be more successful than Republicans in intervening with the Pentagon.

The fear of possible political factors entering into Defense contract decisions is heightened when one examines statistics showing the overwhelming percentage of military contracts that are awarded through the "negotiation" process. This eliminates protections afforded in standard competitive bidding and leaves the contractor at the mercy of the Pentagon negotiator.

In the period from 1951 through fiscal 1965, the Pentagon let contracts worth more than $357 billion. Only 13.7 percent of those contracts, covering $49 billion, were awarded through formally advertised bidding procurement procedures. The remaining $307 billion—a total of 86.3 percent—was handled through negotiated procurement. (See Appendix C for a chart on contracts negotiated and advertised for bids from 1951 through 1965.)

Defense contracts are the life blood of many of the largest corporations in the United States, and the prosperity of a city, congressional district or state can be contingent upon the prosperity of the large corporations, their subsidiaries or their subcontractors. In the case of the large airplane manufacturers, the defense contracts often make up the overwhelming majority of the total business load.

When the Boeing Company, headquartered in Seattle, Washington, lost the TFX warplane contract and had the Dyna-soar program ended, the economy of the whole state of Washington was seriously hurt. The impact of military procurement actions was dramatically demonstrated in the state of Washington where military buying totaled $1,041,581,000 in fiscal 1963, increased slightly to $1,085,696,000 in fiscal 1964 and then plummeted to $545,607,000 in fiscal 1965.

The Boeing Company was low bidder for the multibillion-dollar TFX warplane, but lost out to the Texas-based Convair Division of the General Dynamics Corporation. Significantly, military contracts awarded in Texas climbed steadily from $1,203,123,000 in fiscal 1963, to $1,294,431,000 in fiscal 1964 and on up to $1,446,769,000 in fiscal 1965.

Perhaps Pentagon attitudes toward important political figures from those states were not factors in the decline of Washington and the rise of Texas, but in the political atmosphere where candidates proudly boast that they can deliver the prosperity of big contracts, it is dangerous to assume it is all idle boasting.

Whether rightly or wrongly, it has long been assumed that the political power of Senator Richard Russell and Representative Carl Vinson, both Georgia Democrats, had a great deal to do with the unusual amount of Pentagon money that seemed to flow into that Southern state. Large defense contractors seemed to have an affinity for the state represented by Russell, chairman of the Senate Armed Services Committee and the Senate Appropriations Subcommittee on Defense Spending, and Representative Vinson, chairman of the House Armed Services Committee.

Only California and Texas had more active-duty military personnel than the 93,980 stationed in Georgia at the end of June, 1965. The annual payroll and allowances from this military payroll poured $396,437,000 into Georgia that year. In addition there were 33,563 civilian employees of the Defense Department in Georgia at that time with an estimated annual payroll of $223,527,000. (See Appendix D for a chart on defense personnel, military and civilian, by states for fiscal year 1965.)

But military bases were not the only Pentagon gifts to the home state of the two men who ran the Senate and House Armed Services Committees. The net value of military procurement action in Georgia was $423,290,000 in fiscal 1963, $520,169,000 in fiscal 1964, and a whopping $662,332,000 in fiscal 1965.

Lockheed Aircraft Corporation, with major plants in Georgia, was number one in military prime-contract awards in fiscal 1965 with $1.7 billion—approximately 7.1 percent of the total Defense contracts in the United States.

The Pentagon decisions were a life-and-death matter to Lockheed, and the same was true of General Dynamics Corporation, which held the number-two spot in military prime-contract awards as a result of the huge TFX warplane decision. General Dynamics could boast $1.1 billion in prime military contracts in fiscal 1965, followed by McDonnell Aircraft Corporation with $855 million; General Electric Company with $824 million; North American Aviation Company with $745 million; United Aircraft Corporation with $632 million; American Telephone & Telegraph Company with $587 million and the Boeing Company with $583 million.

Automotive giants, the Ford Motor Company and General Motors Corporation, also had a share of Pentagon business worth protecting. Ford Motor Company and its Philco affiliate ranked twelfth, with military prime-contract awards totaling $312 million, and General Motors had prime-contract awards of $254 million in fiscal 1965. The Chrysler Corporation was far down the list with $80.9 million in fiscal 1965.

There were men in the communications industry who found it disturbing that two of the three major television networks had financial ties to major defense contractors. National Broadcasting Company is owned by Radio Corporation of America, a firm that was only twenty-four places down from the top among defense contractors in fiscal 1965 with $213,900,000. That same year, the American Broadcasting Company announced it was merging with International Telephone & Telegraph, a firm ranked twenty-fifth among defense contractors with $206,700,000 in prime military contracts.

It was obvious that a clever and power-conscious political Administration could use the Pentagon power over defense spending as a means of disciplining major television networks. Such an arrangement had obvious drawbacks in a nation so dependent on the networks for news and public-service programs.

Several of the government-created, not-for-profit corporations ranked among the top one hundred defense contractors on the net value of military prime-contract awards. Aerospace Corporation was listed forty-eighth with $77,500,000; System Development Corporation, sixtieth with $48,900,000; and Mitre Corporation, seventieth with $38,500,000.

The big Pentagon budget has become a handy place for the nation's colleges and universities to find the answer to some of their pressing financial problems, and no doubt the Defense Department grants and contracts provide the means for paying higher salaries and buying better equipment. The arrangement raises long-range questions about how independent a Defense-subsidized academic community will be in analyzing or criticizing the programs or the policies of the men who control the flow of huge subsidies to higher education.

There is no doubt that many of the largest universities have developed a big stake in retaining the cooperative relationship with the Pentagon that will result in renewal of contracts. In fiscal 1965, Johns Hopkins University was awarded $48,500,000 in military prime contracts and Stanford Research Institute had prime contracts totaling $30,700,000.

Massachusetts Institute of Technology rated the top position among recipients of Pentagon research and science education funds for fiscal 1964 with a total of $98,044,000. Johns Hopkins was second with $54,989,000 from Defense for research and science education, and the University of California was in third place with $19,068,000.

Even the $5,852,000 that Harvard received from the Pentagon in fiscal 1964 was substantial, although two other government agencies, the National Institutes of Health and the National Science Foundation, made greater contributions to the total of $37,092,000 in federal funds that Harvard received.

The importance of the impact of Pentagon money on American educational institutions was emphasized by the testimony of Defense Secretary McNamara on March 8, 1966. He told the House Armed Services Committee that "the Department of Defense supports nearly half of all the academic research in the physical sciences and engineering now being done in American universities and colleges." He said that much of the Pentagon money has been concentrated in larger schools, but McNamara revealed plans to broaden the base and bring most of the universities and colleges into the Pentagon orbit.

Many in the academic community may be unaware of the power that Pentagon money could wield in the larger educational institutions, but in the Defense Department itself, power and the centralization of that power in the Office of Defense Secretary is well understood.

Military and civilian payrolls demonstrate the importance of military bases to the economy and the politics of the various states. Also, there are few political leaders—from City Hall to Congress—who do not understand the power potential in the Pentagon purse. The figures for June 30, 1965, show there were 1,041,244 active-duty military personnel in the United States with total annual pay and allowances of $7.7 billion, while the Pentagon also had control over 940,763 civilian employees with a total annual pay of $6.7 billion. Military bases are a vital factor to all political leaders in a state such as California with 212,859 active-duty military personnel and annual pay and allowances of $983,125,000 plus 138,777 civilian Defense Department employees with an annual payroll of more than $1 billion.

The same is true of Texas with 165,099 active-duty military personnel drawing annual pay and allowances of $798 million plus 60,051 civilian Defense Department employees with annual pay of $398 million.

Even in a state such as Iowa, with only 1,445 active-duty military personnel and 630 civilian Defense Department employees, political awareness of the Pentagon power over base closings is a necessity. The military payroll of $8 million and the civilian payroll of $3.7

million may be small in the overall economic picture of Iowa, but the closing of a base or an office can have important economic and political repercussions in the immediate area of the closing.

In the past years, power over military spending was widely scattered through the Defense Department as well as the military-aligned establishment in Congress. Highest-ranking members of the Senate and House Armed Services and Appropriations Committees were men who had a strong, and often dominant, influence over the Defense Department decisions. They were men whose views had to be considered most seriously in opening or closing bases, in awarding contracts, and in adopting general policy on weapons systems.

In that era of more diffused power, the Secretaries of the Army, Navy and Air Force represented an independent force with considerable authority in spending defense funds. That scattered power structure included many career military officers and civilian technical experts who could and did exert an important influence over the awarding of certain types of defense contracts.

A gradual whittling away of the role of the Service Secretaries occurred over more than a dozen years, but the great change came after Defense Secretary McNamara took office in January, 1961. The former Ford executive used all powers granted by the reorganizations of 1947, 1949, 1953 and 1958 to pull more control into the Office of Defense Secretary and away from the three Service Secretaries.

In the first year of the reign of Defense Secretary McNamara, civilian Service Secretaries bitterly resented what they considered an unlawful usurpation of power by the Office of Defense Secretary. If it was not McNamara personally, it was his Assistant Secretaries of Defense or the Deputy Assistant Secretaries of Defense who were actively bypassing the Service Secretaries to deal directly with almost all of the lower levels of authority. Army Secretary Elvis J. Stahr resigned in protest, stating that "more and more, the decisions once made by the Service Secretaries and military chiefs, as individuals, are made by the Secretary of Defense and his staff."

The Army Secretary contended that an unreasonable centralization was taking place, and said he did not believe that such a huge organization as the Pentagon could or should be run by a few people at the top. That view was similar to one expressed by Representative Carl Vinson, the veteran chairman of the House Armed Services Committee, a few years earlier in opposing too tight a centralization in the hands of a few men who he then believed could not possibly have the wisdom for all of the Defense decision-making that would go with the centralization.

Chairman Vinson made a few futile attempts to oppose the authority of Defense Secretary McNamara, and then reconciled himself to a supporting role in a play in which he no longer held his old power. He found it convenient to become an almost fawning booster of McNamara as "the greatest Secretary of Defense in history."

Secretary of the Air Force Eugene Zuckert and Secretary of the Navy John Connally had some of the same early concern that Army Secretary Stahr expressed over McNamara's power play. Zuckert had a legal study made of his authority, and finally concluded the various reorganizations had, in fact, stripped the Service Secretaries of the power to oppose the Defense Secretary effectively. If they could not reconcile themselves to minor roles, resignation was the only practical alternative. Eventually Zuckert and Connally yielded their opposition to the Office of Defense Secretary and accepted a role which in fact made them subordinate to Assistant Secretaries of Defense in many important areas.

At the same time, the Joint Chiefs of Staff found their jurisdiction cut sharply by the same moves that had undercut the Service Secretaries. The Defense Secretary expanded his own office, established common service agencies for intelligence, supply and audit, and the Assistant Defense Secretaries were permitted to wield an even broader authority in the various services.

The old patterns of military service alliances with United States Senators and Representatives tended to deteriorate and become an ineffective check on the Office of Defense Secretary. They could still exchange information, but it was often pointless. Senators and Representatives could no longer deal directly with the power of their friends in the bureaucratic hierarchy of the Army, Navy or Air Force to get things done. The Defense Secretary and his various Assistant Secretaries had become the final authority in matters that formerly had been handled on a lower level.

The Defense Supply Agency and the Defense Intelligence Agency, created in the fall of 1961, provided Defense Department-wide services for purchasing common items and for gathering and evaluating intelligence information. The Assistant Secretary of Defense for Public

Affairs centralized information services to put a stop to the flow of information from the Army, Navy and Air Force not in tune with the plans and programs of the Secretary of Defense.

The Defense Contract Audit Agency was created in 1964 for the purpose of centralizing and improving audit of contracts. In 1965, it was revealed that the Defense Secretary planned that this audit agency should hire more auditors and accountants than the whole General Accounting Office (GAO), which was established by Congress to serve as a financial watchdog by post-auditing all government departments, including Defense.

Some of the GAO reports on Defense Department contracts had been so critical they caused resentment in the Office of Defense Secretary. While Defense Secretary McNamara was establishing the new Defense Contract Audit Agency, his department was suggesting that GAO should tone down the criticism of Defense contracts, and that there should be a new evaluation of the role of GAO. This new evaluation was aimed at eliminating GAO access to some Defense Department records as well as Defense contractor records.

McNamara's office indicated that perhaps the GAO no longer needed to conduct the same type of audits on the Defense Department because of the more thorough audits Defense was now conducting of its own activities. The Defense Secretary expressed the view that it would be "waste and duplication" for the GAO to come in and do the same type of audit on Defense that had been done in the past. The Defense Department paid little attention to a few complaints from Congress that there would be no objective audit if McNamara were permitted to control the audit of McNamara. It was one more step in the centralization of power and the elimination of outside checks.

The whole emphasis of the McNamara administration was centralization and more centralization with the Office of Defense Secretary expanding in size as well as in functions. The result was an end to the diffusion of power and the creation of a centralized structure that put an aggressive and power-conscious Defense Secretary beyond the checks and effective restraints that had existed in the past.

Five years of McNamara had fairly well completed the job:

(1) The authority of the Service Secretaries was cut, and the possibility of effective or meaningful dissent from that source was minimized if not eliminated.

(2) High-ranking military officers had lost their tools for bargaining with Congress. They no longer had the protection of alliances

with independent Service Secretaries and independent congressional leaders that had been necessary for them to be forcefully independent.

(3) Congress found itself ineffective against the centralized power that had been pulled into the Office of Defense Secretary. A condition had been created in which they were more dependent upon the good will of the Defense Secretary than he was upon them.

A unified Congress might have the leverage to overrule a Defense Secretary, but Congress is not unified. The Office of Defense Secretary had used its power over contracts and base closings to alternately pamper and coerce men of influence in the Senate and House. Only a few Senators or Representatives with small political stakes in Pentagon decisions were willing to engage in open criticism of the Pentagon decision-maker.

Even those who had the courage to criticize were fearful of the propaganda power of the Pentagon's centralized press office. The Pentagon press office spoke with one voice, and with a loud voice, in seeking to discredit critics in Congress. The complex statistical data available in the multibillion-dollar department was enough to confuse or overwhelm most critics as well as the press.

All this power was lodged in the hands of the Pentagon decision-maker—Defense Secretary Robert S. McNamara.

The supporters of centralized Pentagon power would list these advantages:

(1) It has eliminated or sharply diminished the political pressure of Congress on Pentagon decisions.

(2) It has stopped much of the public dissent from the military officers and civilian technical experts.

(3) It has cut down the criticism from the General Accounting Office auditors that had been resented by Defense officials as well as many of the big defense contractors. Also, it appeared likely to eliminate some of the GAO audits as "waste and duplication" of the activities of the new Defense Contract Audit Agency.

(4) It put private industry under more direct control of the Office of Defense Secretary and made it less likely that big defense contractors would exhibit any consistent independence in causing problems for the Defense Secretary.

(5) It has eliminated some of the problem of confusing newspaper stories on defense matters. Centralizing the information functions makes it less likely that dissenters will be talking to reporters and raising issues the Defense Secretary's office does not wish to have

raised. By eliminating the Army, Navy and Air Force press functions, a more perfect unification has been achieved, and the press office contends that more information is dispensed than ever before, including extensive statistical studies and high-level backgrounding. All is coordinated so the public will be spared the confusion of conflicting viewpoints.

What this heavily centralized system lacks in the way of checks on the Pentagon power, it gains in the potential for efficiency under one-man rule of the multibillion-dollar military machine. We are told that worries over what such centralized power might do to our system of government over an extended period of time are groundless. It is explained that those who wield the tremendous power with the broadest discretion are men of ability with a devotion to the duty of making the most effective and efficient war machine in history. If the methods seem a little brusque from time to time, it can be excused, for the decision-makers have heavy responsibilities and are intent upon creating bigger and better "cost effectiveness" tools for managing things for us. If we occasionally cannot understand their acts or their explanations, then we can just count ourselves as fortunate that patriotic and devoted men who understand everything have been willing to accept the responsibility for running our complex, power-laden Pentagon.

In the early 1940's, the Pentagon rose out of the 583-acre flat swamp and wasteland south of the Potomac River in Virginia. The cost for the construction of the huge five-sided structure was $49,600,-000, but when the cost of land, 30 miles of access highways, 21 overpasses and bridges and parking space for 10,000 cars was added, the whole project totaled more than $83,000,000.

The fort-like structure with its five concentric rings of corridors contained ten spoke-like corridors as connecting links in what was to be the "world's largest office building" and the nerve center of the United States war machine.

The site of the building and its unusual construction had been the subject of sharp controversy in early 1941 as final plans were taking shape. It was still a subject of controversy on August 11, 1941, the day the prime contract was let, for there were still great divisions among the American people as to how much the United States should be involved with the wars in Asia and Europe. The disaster of Pearl Harbor, December 7, 1941, was still four months away, and even such men as General Brehon Somervell, Army Chief of Engineers, were a bit defensive in explaining the many other purposes for which the Pentagon would be suited when the war clouds had passed over.

The Pentagon was ridiculed in its planning stages as "Somervell's Folly." It remained the subject of jokes long after it was recognized as the efficient structure its designers claimed it would be. It is twice as large as the Merchandise Mart in Chicago, and the corridors in the five floors of five concentric rings total more than seventeen miles in length. Yet it takes no more than six or seven minutes to walk between any two extreme points in the building.

The Pentagon construction was completed on January 15, 1943, but in the early months of World War II there was such pressure for space that the first occupants moved in on April 29, 1942—only eight months after the contract was awarded. It was constructed for what was then the War Department, and served first as a command post for Secretary of War Henry L. Stimson and General George C. Marshall. Although the Navy did not move major activities into the Pentagon until the end of World War II, it was in fact the center of all unified military direction that was improvised in that hectic period.

The unification, or central direction, of the activities of the military operations was largely improvised throughout World War II, for in fact the War Department under Secretary Stimson and the Navy Department under James V. Forrestal were separate and distinct in the law.

While the Pentagon represented the answer to the problem of housing the headquarters for the Departments of the Army and Navy, it did not eliminate the real and imagined administrative weaknesses that were subjects of congressional investigations during World War II and in the years immediately following the war.

President Truman in 1945 asked for unification for purposes of security and economy. In his December 19th message he called for a single Department of National Defense. Under a civilian Secretary, subordinate officials were to include an Under Secretary and Assistant Secretaries for the Army, Navy and Air Force and a single Chief of Staff.

There was strong Navy objection to the proposal, for President Truman had followed in large measure a plan drafted by Lieutenant General J. Lawton Collins. The proposal of General Collins and Air Force General H. H. (Hap) Arnold could have resulted in sharp curtailment of the Navy role through loss of its air and ground functions. The Navy had a powerful supporter in Chairman Carl Vinson (Dem., Ga.) of the House Naval Affairs Committee.

Unification of the defense establishment advanced by stages in the period after World War II, but never won full support in Congress even though it was regarded as essential to eliminate bickering among the services and some duplication and other inefficiencies.

The first big step in 1947 was a compromise. The National Security Act of 1947 provided for a National Military Establishment to replace the War and Navy Departments. This permitted separate administration of the Army, Navy and Air Force with the "general direction, authority, and control" lodged in the first Secretary of Defense, James Forrestal. This legislation also provided that the Joint Chiefs of Staff were to be "the principal military advisors" to the President and the Secretary of Defense.

Two years later, the National Security Act Amendments of 1949 created the Department of Defense, added a Deputy Secretary and three Assistant Secretaries of Defense and established the three military departments as subordinate bodies. The Secretary of Defense was boss, but in a manner that was limited by a certain independence of the Service Secretaries and the members of the Joint Chiefs of Staff in their relations with Congress.

However, greater and greater centralization of power in the Defense Secretary was made possible through a reorganization plan in 1953 and the Defense Department Reorganization Act of 1958.

The 1953 reorganization gave the Defense Secretary the authority to appoint six new Assistant Secretaries of Defense, which created the power and the mechanism to further undercut the independence of the Secretaries of the Army, Navy and Air Force. Also, the Defense Secretary was given the authority to name the Director of the Joint Staff, which in the 1949 reorganization had been expanded from 100 to 210 officers.

The Joint Staff was further expanded in 1958 to 400 officers—a large enough body to create a formidable support for the Office of Defense Secretary in any disputes with the individual services. Also, the act gave the Defense Secretary the authority to consolidate the service and supply functions, which was a more crushing blow to the independence of the Army, Navy and Air Force than was generally realized at the time.

Initially, the Department of Defense was created for the top-level decision-making. It was to be a small, efficient organization, not bogged down in the day-to-day administrative problems of the Army, Navy and Air Force, and capable of making the big decisions and ironing out the squabbles.

For better or for worse, the Pentagon has become the biggest and most centralized bureaucracy in the Free World. Four reorganizations, twenty years of Cold War and brush-fire wars, and eight Defense Secretaries have molded a single-headed military power of structure of massive proportions.

A total of more than 26,000 employees—14,200 civilians and 11,800 military personnel—report for duty at the Pentagon each working day. In addition to the regular Defense Department employees, there are 2,000 to 3,000 others who have offices or business in the mammoth structure. These include the hundreds of writers and commentators for newspapers, radio and television who are assigned to cover the military news. There are the hundreds of shopkeepers and clerks to man the wide variety of business facilities in the Pentagon Concourse that include bookstore, bank, medical and dental clinics, post office, barbershop, clothing stores, laundry and dry cleaning, rail, air and local bus ticket offices, florists, bakery, drugstore, candy store, baggage lockers, Western Union telegraph office, optometrist, photographic store, newsstand, jewelry store, shoe repair and shine shop, mailomats and pharmacy. In addition to these independent concessionaires, the Pentagon has offices for the representatives of foreign government agencies and other United States government agencies who are engaged in liaison work or cooperative ventures with the Defense Department.

It has been estimated by a Defense Department spokesman that between 5,000 and 6,000 outsiders visit the Pentagon each day for business or just plain sight-seeing. Since there is no registration and no requirement for a pass between 7 A.M. and 6 P.M., there is no official count on these visitors. Although the building is under no special security measures during that period, the areas of the building that are regarded as sensitive are under the tightest security precautions on a twenty-four-hour basis. Even the Defense Secretary and members of the Joint Chiefs of Staff must show their credentials and be photographed as they enter such highly sensitive areas as the National Military Command Center, where the highest classified information is on constant display, or the comparable command centers for the military services—the Army War Room, Navy Flag Plot, Air Force Command Post and the Emergency Action Center of the Marine Corps.

From the largest office on the third floor of the "E" ring in the Pentagon, the Secretary of Defense wields an awesome power. It is a power that is far above and beyond the control over what is pictured as the mightiest war machine in history. From the nine-by-five-foot walnut desk that dominates the huge office or from his command post deeper in the Pentagon, the Secretary of Defense has immediate access to the President at all times through a direct telephone line. He has direct contact with the Strategic Air Command headquarters in Omaha, Nebraska, or with the North American Air Defense Command headquarters in Colorado Springs, Colorado. He has direct contact with the fighting ships at sea, or with the planes in the air.

More awesome than his control over the actions of the military force is the power he holds over the spending of a budget of more than $50 billion a year. This is a power that can and does touch nearly every facet of our society, including the business and political community. It is a power that we have been warned should never be permitted to fall into the hands of any authoritarian-minded military man, and there are those who question the wisdom of concentrating such power in the hands of even the best-motivated civilian Secretary of Defense.

When viewed in its totality and in the perspective of history, it is obvious that there are reasons why the political power role of a Defense Secretary can be as terrifying to contemplate as is the military might. Whether it is used or not, the power over the Pentagon budget represents the power to coerce some of the biggest industries, some of the most respected educational institutions, some of the most influential columnists and authors and some of the most powerful members of the Senate and the House.

The fact that the Defense Department is big, complex and difficult to understand does not make the power less real. The naked power is only hidden, camouflaged behind a curtain of polite language and mystifying statistical jargon that often seems designed to confuse rather than clarify.

It is not enough to view the tremendous Pentagon power that exists today only in the light of the political appointees who hold the key offices during any limited period. It is essential that we understand the problem of centralized Pentagon power in the perspective of our history and our political system. I am writing this book to provide that perspective with the examples of the persistent problems that have been with us throughout our history. It would appear that most of these problems will be with us in one form or another as long as we must organize and control a war machine.

Although we have moved from war dominated by horses and small guns into an era of nuclear power and jet aircraft, many of the basic problems have remained. There have been good men and bad men, wise men and foolish men in the highest positions in our military departments. Neither the professional military men nor the civilian political appointees have had a monopoly on brilliance or stupidity. There has been military incompetence and civilian incompetence, military arrogance and civilian arrogance. It is necessary to grasp the entire picture if we are to comprehend what the highly centralized Pentagon power means, or can mean, to our future as a nation.

2

PERSISTENT PROBLEMS

FINANCING, administration and operation of an effective and up-to-the-minute war machine has been a problem since the birth of our nation. Maintenance of the war machine will be increasingly difficult in the future. Survival of a nation, new or old, is contingent upon its ability to finance and organize a force with the destructive capacity to maintain order within the nation and, in cooperation with other nations, to pose a threat to intruders. It will always be so unless there is some fundamental change in the nature of man that eliminates selfish grasping for property and power over other men.

Even if the most optimistic hopes for disarmament or "A Warless World" are fulfilled, there will still be the problem of financing, administering, operating and controlling an effective international police force, with proper concern for the danger that it might become a force for authoritarian control. Those same problems will always remain, regardless of the progress the nations of the world make toward disarmament of individual nations and the settlement of international disputes through some rule of law.

There is a tendency to regard the nuclear age with its complicated weapons systems as so far removed from the past that there is no point in searching our history for guidance to contemporary problems. In fact, there is every reason to reach back and examine our experiences with war and defense for an understanding of the decisions the United States must make in balancing and controlling the power of the Pentagon today and tomorrow.

Throughout our history a series of crises has dramatized and emphasized the perpetual problems that attend the efforts to maintain an effective war machine. A constant struggle has been necessary to achieve the balance required to maintain the civilian control of the military, in accordance with the Constitution, and yet encourage the development and utilization of military experts with a high degree of professional competency.

The goal itself is simple but, as history has pointed out on many occasions, difficult to achieve.

Several primary obstructions to a satisfactory civilian-military balance exist in our defense establishment. First, there is the tendency on the part of the civilian Secretaries to reach decisions that are motivated by their own political aspirations and the short-range political goals of their administrations. Secondly, high-ranking military officers tend to formulate plans on the basis of the needs and goals of past wars rather than new technological developments. Finally, a big bureaucracy tends to become satisfied with itself and impatient with and intolerant of dissenters who rock the boat of complacency.

These attitudes spawn an atmosphere of political favoritism in appointments, promotions and contract awards. The thinkers, the creators and the dissenters who are essential to progress are often crushed or discouraged in their efforts to prod the bureaucracy into changes or effective action.

The problems of a civilian-military balance have arisen so often and in such critical circumstances in the course of our history that they have caused critical comment by highly ranked officials as well as historians. We seldom remember our lessons of the past.

Cases in point, starting in the War of 1812, extending through the

Civil War, the Spanish American War, World War I, World War II, the Korean War and the war in Vietnam, give ample illustration.

During the first years of our Republic all the military functions were centered in one department—the War Department. There were a few frigates in the service of the military, but these were controlled through this one department.[1]

It was not until 1798—in the face of threats of war with France that dramatized the need for a strong, separate navy—that Congress passed legislation establishing the Navy Department.

The Navy moved off to a poor start in its efforts to find the proper balance between civilian control and the needed professional military advice. From 1798 until after the War of 1812, the Navy was under the management of a civilian Secretary who, according to an authoritative military historian, acted "without any assistance or responsible advice from naval officers."

According to the recognized historian, Tracy Barrett Kittredge, "This exclusion of the military element from the control of the Navy made it impossible for the Navy to prepare for war or to fight effectively."

In 1812, just prior to the beginning of the War of 1812, the Navy Department was completely unprepared for war. There were few ships and no drydocks. The only naval establishment that was not in a total state of decay was the one at Washington. Facilities for building, repairing or laying up ships were almost nonexistent.[2]

Because of the war panic, the entire Navy was held in port. It was feared the British naval superiority would completely destroy the fledgling American effort. The dissent of two American naval officers finally resulted in the release of the Navy for duty.

Aside from Perry's Lake Erie command, there was no American fleet. Action was limited to strikes against British trade and a few notable individual victories against single British war vessels. The British landed troops and burned the Capital because the American Navy was powerless to defend the American coast.

In 1815 Congress attempted to correct the imbalance in the administration of the Navy Department. The war had illustrated the pitiful incompetency of exclusively civilian control of a technical military establishment. A Board of Navy Commissioners was established to provide professional assistance and advice to the Secretary. Unfortunately, the act failed to divide the department into civilian and military spheres of responsibility. With no firmly established guidelines, the Board of Commissioners became charged with administration of the civilian branches of the department: supply, ordnance and construction. They were not allowed to assume responsibility for the direction of the military needs of the Navy.

Again in 1842 attempts were made to reorganize the Navy and correct the lack of properly placed military advisers. Various bureaus were established to administer the strictly civilian spheres of the department. But instead of redefining the responsibilities of the Board of Commissioners, the Board was abolished. The Secretary was again left in the position of trying to execute military planning without competent professional help.

Admiral Luce said later of this reorganization:

> No provision was made for any direction of naval operations save by the action of the Secretary, a civilian. The organization was one that could work only while the country was at peace and the military considerations could be neglected. People generally scouted the idea that peace could ever be disturbed. The Civil War rudely dispelled this idle dream and proved the falsity of the theory on which the organization of the Department was based.[3]

The Civil War, with its great demands for men and matériel, again threw the Department of the Navy into confusion. There were no war plans. There were no competent naval officers in positions of responsibility within the department. Secretary of the Navy Gideon Wells related later that he was without military assistance and "in a complete state of isolation." [4]

The emergency created by lack of preparedness resulted in new arrangements hurriedly improvised. Confusion was so great that Lincoln appointed a Confederate naval captain, Samuel Barron, to head the Bureau of Detail. Of course, when the situation became known, the order was rescinded.

With no one to direct operations, the need for some sort of general staff became apparent. After a number of efforts to bring order out of chaos, the position of Assistant Secretary of the Navy was established and filled by a retired naval officer, Gustavus Fox, who took over the military direction of the department. He became, in effect, a chief of naval staff. Temporary boards were established to meet the demands of the war, finally assuming the powers of a general staff. Two long, costly years were lost before reasonably competent military direction was provided. In those two years the Navy tried, in vain, to capture Charleston. They made numerous attempts, confident that they could succeed without the aid of the Army. The department was not without highly competent men, but, as one historian explained it, "the failure was not theirs, but was that of the system, or lack of system, against which they had to struggle." Had the department been organized and directed as a military establishment, many costly delays could have been avoided. Many blunders would not have been made.

Gideon Welles, the Secretary of the Navy, stated in his annual report to the President that "the naval force at the commencement of this administration consisted of 76 vessels, and of these only 42 were in commission." He admitted that there had been no one in the department with the experience or authority to plan or direct military operation, and added, "hence the views of the department were speculative and uncertain." [5]

After the Civil War the effective machinery that had finally been developed was wiped out. The sole military office within the Navy Department, that of the Assistant Secretary, was abolished. According to Admiral Luce, "The lesson of the Civil War was thrown away on us, and the department relapsed into a state looking to the early millennium when war should cease." [6] The Navy Department reverted to its former position: a civilian Secretary with no competent military advisers.

In the thirty years following the Civil War "the impotence of the Navy Department to deal with questions relating to war was made painfully manifest."

In 1873, the Spanish captured the *U.S.S. Virginius* and, after a mock court-martial, executed a number of the crew. War appeared imminent. According to one historian, "The only thing the department could not do, apparently, was go to war. Admiral Porter was called upon for counsel and would probably have been entrusted with the direction of military affairs had war come. But the panic passed, and nothing was done to remedy conditions in the department."

The *U.S.S. Baltimore* was attacked in Valparaiso in 1892. This strain on relations with Chile meant military advice had to be elicited from outside the Navy Department. When the tension passed so did all talk of efficient departmental reorganization.

The Secretaries of the Navy, although civilians, were not blind to the defects in the department. They admitted that the Navy was unprepared to fulfill its primary objective, waging a successful war.

During the Cleveland Administration Secretary of the Navy W. C. Whitney declared in his 1885 report that he doubted if there was a single ship in the Navy at the time that could fight. His pleas for reorganization of the Navy Department were ignored.

Again in 1889, in Benjamin Harrison's Administration, Navy Secretary Benjamin F. Tracy urged reorganization. He pointed out defects that he felt created a state of unpreparedness. Unless changes were forthcoming, he warned, the Navy could not be kept in condition to defend the United States during war. Congress still did not pass the necessary legislation.

War with Spain had been probable for years before the Spanish-American War broke out. During this time no positive action was suggested by the Navy Department. Even in the two months between the sinking of the *Maine* and the declaration of the Cuba blockade, no steps were taken by the department to provide war plans.

"Blithely and confidently the United States embarked on a war it was not prepared to fight." The Regular Army was a scattered force used against Indian uprisings. While the Army had shown great skill in this capacity it was comprised of only 28,000 men with no war experience. "The services of supply, manned by elderly bureaucratic officers, proved incapable of meeting the modest wants of the forces raised during the war."

As in the past the military establishment contained no agency, in either branch, that was prepared to develop war-time strategy.[7]

In 1886 Admiral Luce had promoted the establishment of a Naval War College. Here, for the first time, officers began to study the science of naval warfare. As an exercise the War College, as opposed to the Navy Department, had prepared tentative and unofficial plans for a war with Spain, but their objective had nothing to do with freeing Cuba.

Upon the outbreak of hostilities with Spain, the Navy Department began to improvise a military arm. When the Naval War Board was established it took advantage of the war plans previously drawn up at the War College—the only plans available. They proved sufficient. As Kittredge expressed it:

> Our superiority over the Spanish forces was so soon and so easily established that our war organization and effort suffered no real test.

The story would have been very different had we met an enemy of real strength and efficiency.[8]

The war with Spain had illustrated the need for reform in our defense establishments. Efforts were made to profit from the lessons of the war. During Elihu Root's administration of the War Department it was finally reorganized and given a general staff. But in the Navy Department no action was taken to provide for a staff to direct the technical military operations.

During the Spanish-American War the lack of skill on the part of American gun crews had been a source of severe embarrassment to the country. In the battle of Santiago, for example, less than three percent of the shots fired by the American Navy hit their targets. Fortunately, Spanish marksmanship was even less accurate.

This lack of precision by American fighting men could be traced directly to the methods of sighting available at the time. The sighter was responsible for visually finding his target on the down roll of the ship, then holding his fire until the next down roll so the guns would be as close to sighting position as possible when the shot was fired. But the sighter also had to allow for the interval between the time his firing command was given and executed, therefore pre-timing his command.

Primitive gunsights and the prevailing criteria for target practice contributed to, rather than alleviated, these problems.

As late as September, 1900, target regulations were deficient in the following ways:

Gun crews selected their own range.

No credit was given for rapidity of fire.

Efficiency was rated only on the percentage of hits made, and the gunners did not have to hit the target.

Hits were computed by plotting the course of the shell and seeing if it would have hit a warship in the target position.

No records were kept of firing speed and hits per minute for the various calibre guns.

There was no qualitative comparison of gunners.[9]

The British Navy had been making spectacular progress in gunnery, under Captain Percy Scott, since about 1895. Before 1898, Scott had changed gunnery from an art to a science. His high record of hits was made possible by efficient elevating gears (used for sighting the guns) and telescopic sights with heavy rubber padding. In addition to more efficient range sighting, the device voided the need to move the eye from the sights during firing to avoid serious injury from recoil.

Ironically, the telescopic sights used were an American invention that had been turned down by the U.S. Navy. Bradley A. Fisk of the United States Navy had submitted his invention to the Navy for use in gunnery work, but Robley D. "Fighting Bob" Evans, his commanding officer, rejected the idea as unnecessary and impractical.[10] It was a case of senior officers in a self-satisfied bureaucracy refusing to accept technological advances and new ideas that were available.

Scott drilled his gun crews six days a week with a training device that allowed them to develop sighting accuracy without firing the big guns. His system, a "dotter," consisted of a moving target, scale size, in front of the gun and a pencil attached to the gun with a typewriter action. When the gun was sighted and the trigger pulled, a magnet in the pencil was electrically activated. The metal backing on the moving target attracted the magnet and the pencil marked the target where the shot had hit. By the turn of the century Scott had advanced the practice of continuous action firing to record-shattering heights.

In November 1900 a forty-two-year-old American naval lieutenant, William Sowden Sims,[11] was transferred from his Spanish-American War assignment as security officer for Spain, Russia and Italy. When he stepped on board the newly commissioned *U.S.S. Kentucky* at Gibraltar, it was the first time he had seen an American battleship in three years. The *Kentucky,* then bound for the Pacific, at that time enjoyed a reputation as the ultimate in modern naval construction and design. To Sims, familiar with the latest in European ship design, the *Kentucky* showed engineering and mechanical weaknesses serious enough to impair her battleworthiness.

After discussing his objections with the officers of the *Kentucky* and obtaining their agreement on the ship's deficiencies, he wrote a full report to the Navy Department—which was forwarded through his commanding officer when the *Kentucky* arrived in the Philippines.

Sims' paper[12] on "Arrangement of Magazines, Ammunition Supply and Installation of Battery, *U.S.S. Kentucky*" of February 1, 1901, made the following points:

(1) The machinery used to supply ammunition to the 5-inch guns

was so limited that the guns could not be fired at maximum speed—or as fast as foreign 6-inch guns mounted on board ship.

(2) The design innovation of placing the turrets for the 8-inch guns directly over those of the 13-inch guns caused extremely weak end-on fire because the same mechanism was used to turn the turrets of both guns.

(3) The turrets of the great guns were so large that enemy shells could enter the turrets.

(4) The loading, training and elevating gear, recoil system and ammunition hoist were entirely unprotected and so fully exposed as to invite almost certain destruction.

(5) The open shaft for the shell and powder hoists ran straight from the gun positions to the handling rooms below (adjacent to the powder magazines); any falling spark presented danger of internal magazine explosion such as that Sims had witnessed during the target practice of the Russian ship, *Sissoi Viliki.*

In March, Lieutenant Sims received orders transferring him from the *Kentucky* to the *U.S.S. Monterey* at Canton. While en route, Sims stopped over at Hong Kong and had the good fortune to meet the British captain, Percy Scott. Upon hearing from Scott the efficiency of the new British gunnery methods, Sims asked him to explain his methods of continuous-action firing in detail. Sims saw a tremendous improvement over anything the Americans had been able to accomplish in gunnery up to that point. He sent a full report of his findings to the Navy Department March 15, 1901, on "The Remarkable Record Target Practice *H.M.S. Terrible.*"

In the British method of continuous-action firing Sims also saw added danger in the design problems of the *U.S.S. Kentucky*. After carefully comparing the targets of the *H.M.S. Terrible* with a scale drawing of the *Kentucky,* he sent an additional report to the Navy Department May 19, 1901, with observations on the "Protection of Gun Positions *H.M.S. Canopus* Class (British single great gun turret) Compared with that of the *Kentucky* and *Kearsarge* (sister ship of the *Kentucky*)."

Of the eighty hits scored by the *H.M.S. Terrible* in her record-breaking gun practice, seventy-nine would have been severely damaging hits against the *U.S.S. Kentucky* while against the *H.M.S. Canopus* only thirty-six of the shells would have hit so as to produce serious damage.

A week later Sims received a letter from Captain Stockton of the *Monterey,* through whose hands his latest report had passed on its way to the Navy Department. Stockton expressed his approval of Sims' efforts to bring his views to the attention of his superiors: "We ought to stand in the light and not be afraid of the truth no matter how unsatisfactory. The pathway of the reformer . . . is hard and my experience at the War College leads me to sympathize with you in your efforts and rebuffs." [13]

During the summer of 1901, while Sims was awaiting reply to his papers to the Navy Department, he received for consideration a copy of the "Report of the Board of Construction on a Seagoing Battleship to the Secretary of the Navy" from Rear Admiral F. T. Bowles, the Navy Chief of Construction. Bowles felt that Sims, with his soundly based criticisms of the design of the *Kentucky,* might wish to offer his comments along with those solicited from many high-ranked officers of the Navy before any new plans were adopted. Sims submitted his report in September.

In October Sims had the good fortune to be transferred to the *U.S.S. Brooklyn,* the flagship of the Asiatic Fleet, under the command of Admiral Remey, through whom all of his reports had been forwarded. Remey, favorably impressed with Sims' reports, gave him free reign to try out his ideas on gunnery on board the *Brooklyn.* This involved a great deal of improvisation to compensate for the inferior elevating gear and sights then present on American ships.

Though carrying on his own gunnery practice, Sims was careful to update his report on the British gunnery records, and he submitted a report on the "Record Target Practice *H.M.S. Terrible* for 1901," which carried the following endorsement by Admiral Remey:

> I deem this paper worthy of the most serious attention, recommending that it be considered by the General Board, and also in connection with the plans of ships to be built and building. No well-informed man can deny that our situation is extremely dangerous and it behooves us to spare no effort to attain that state of efficiency which the public and the *majority of the Navy* believe we have already reached. The curse of the Navy is the word improvise.[14]

With no official interest displayed in his reports, Sims decided to sidestep the regular channels of communication and write directly to

President Theodore Roosevelt. This letter, with reference to all his prior reports, was sent November 16, 1901.

Sims knew that his move was unorthodox, and explained to the President:

> The danger of the false impression, that is universal throughout the United States concerning the efficiency of the Navy, appears to me so great, and the need of prompt and radical reform therefore so extremely urgent, that I hope I may not be considered as overstepping the bounds of propriety by inviting your personal attention to the papers indicated in the enclosed memorandum.[15]

While Roosevelt did not at that time agree with Sims' estimates of the preparedness of the Navy, he did order all of Sims' papers collected, reproduced and distributed throughout the Navy for serious consideration before passing final judgment. He also wrote to Sims, expressing his agreement with the propriety of dissent and the need to be ever alert to weakness. The Roosevelt letter of December 12, 1901, to Sims follows:

> My dear Lieutenant Sims:
>
> I value your letter. I think you are unduly pessimistic, as you certainly were at the outset of the Spanish-American War, when, as you may remember, you took a very gloomy view of our vessels even as compared with those of Spain. Nevertheless, I would a hundred fold over that you erred upon the side of thinking us not good enough than of thinking us too good; and many of the suggestions that you have made in the past, both upon the need of improving our gun practice and doing away with or removing faulty construction in our battleships, have been genuinely fruitful.
>
> I thank you for writing me; I shall always be pleased to hear from you, in criticism, or suggestion.[16]

Thus it was only at the intervention of the President that the Navy Department was forced to take under official consideration reports that had been arriving for their attention for almost a year.

With the retirement of Albert P. Niblack from the position of Inspector of Target Practice in 1902, Sims received the Presidential appointment to that position. His six-and-a-half-year tenure was marked by official reluctance to grant the equipment he felt vital to the success of his program.

Sims began receiving reports in February, 1909, that his superiors in the Navy Department planned to court-martial him as soon as Theodore Roosevelt left the Presidency. Obscure clerks in the Navy Department, feeling this was harsh payment for all his efforts to modernize the Navy, told Sims of the conversations they had overheard. Because his fitness reports made no mention of his contributions to the advances adopted in naval design and gunnery, Sims knew his own record could not be used for his defense.

When asked for his advice, President Roosevelt demanded to see the records for himself. There was no mention of Sims' many reports and accomplishments. The President immediately dictated a statement on Sims' contributions for inclusion in his fitness reports. Roosevelt also directed every branch of the Navy Department, from the Office of Secretary Newberry through the Chiefs of the Naval Bureaus, right down to friends and fellow officers of Sims, to prepare complete memoranda of all correspondence and reports from Sims. These were to include full explanations of all positive action taken by the Navy at the recommendation of Sims. Sims discovered that his own list of papers submitted between 1903 and 1907 totaled more than one hundred thirty.

Roosevelt's action killed all talk of a court-martial for Sims.

Sims' efforts and dissent were totally vindicated in 1910 when two efficiency experts visited the *U.S.S. Minnesota*. They declared in their report on continuous action fire: "The synchronization of gun operations, fire control, and engine room was a model exhibition of scientific management—stopwatch work, no waste effort, no lost motion, but every movement standardized and unified to the shortest possible time." [17]

Because of William Sowden Sims, American naval gunners had become the greatest shots in the world. President Roosevelt said in 1909, "Commander Sims has done more for target practice than any other man in the United States. It is chiefly due to him that we shoot as well as we do. It is humiliating to think what poor shots we were during the Spanish War." [18]

Somehow the memory of the humiliation of poor naval marksmanship did not make a permanent enough imprint on the memory of the military establishment, or was not applied properly, if remembered. This lesson on the problem of bureaucratic lethargy was only one of many that have had to be repeated year after year.

3

CORRUPTERS, PACIFISTS AND POLITICIANS

THE operations of the War Department in the Civil War still represent the ultimate example of corruption in American military history. This period illustrates almost everything that can go wrong with the military establishment when under corrupt as well as incompetent political control.

The implements of war at this time were uncomplicated. People were qualified to judge the merits of horses and guns; they were a part of almost every household. A man could comprehend the drain on the Treasury when he heard reports of guns being sold to the government for $35 each. And he could doubt the honesty of such purchases if he had paid only $15 for the same gun for his personal use. He could object to the prices paid for horses that he knew from observation were unfit for the plow let alone the cavalry. Citizens saw these abuses and protested violently, leading to strong congressional investigations into every phase of military procurement.

The problem of corruption in the procurement of horses was a persistent one throughout the Civil War; the following example is an excellent representative case.[1]

In October of 1861, Secretary of War Simon Cameron ordered his Quartermaster, General Meigs, to contract for one thousand horses to be delivered at Huntingdon, Pennsylvania, the Secretary's home state. The price was set at $117 each. This was a high price and should have bought the very best in horseflesh.

Horses began arriving for inspection and selection in November of the same year. The events of that inspection so outraged the citizens of Huntingdon that twenty of the town's most reputable men sent a formal protest to the Quartermaster. After two days of conscientious inspection of all horses presented, the contractors withdrew their animals and announced they would not be submitted until a new inspector was appointed. Within a week the inspections had again been stopped and a third set of inspectors appointed.

Under the new inspectors, the horses were reviewed and accepted for branding with great rapidity. No attempt was made to carry on an honest appraisal of the animals. Openly diseased horses were ordered branded for government use.

Only two days after the arrival of inspectors satisfactory to the contractors, Adin W. Benedict, a Huntingdon lawyer, drew up a letter of protest to Quartermaster General Meigs, who had his own inspector in Huntingdon to investigate within three weeks. He said that all of the allegations were true and expressed his belief that only half of the nine hundred horses accepted were fit for any Army service.

When four hundred of these horses were ordered shipped to Kentucky for a cavalry unit, "many were left on the [Pittsburgh] warf as utterly useless."

Top prices had been paid for the horses accepted at the Huntingdon inspection. Conscientious inspectors who were obtaining full value for every government dollar expended were twice removed to meet the demands and needs of the sellers. Corrupt inspectors paid $117 for horses worth no more than $10 or $20 on the open market and of no value to the cavalry. They passed spavined horses, horses that were windbroken, horses with open sores. They passed one horse that was twenty-nine years old. Their only consistent criteria was that the horse be able to walk.

On this one contract alone, the government was swindled of more than $50,000 of a total expenditure of only slightly more than $100,000.[2]

Outside of the office of Secretary of War, the most shocking disregard for the law and for regular military procedure was in the Western Department, the command of General John Charles Frémont.[3]

In July 1861, Frémont took up his command in St. Louis with a flourish of praise and confidence, acquiring for his quarters a beautiful private residence with an annual rental, paid by the government, of $6,000.

The War Department granted him almost total liberty in purchasing equipment and supplies. General Ripley, the head of the Ordnance Bureau, sent orders to the New York ordnance officer to extend every aid to Frémont for preparing his army.[4] Postmaster General

Montgomery Blair encouraged Frémont to ignore governmental red tape and to operate on his own responsibility.[5]

Frémont, in August, 1861, appointed his civilian Inspector of Horses, John E. Reeside, to the dual position of purchasing agent for horses for the Western Department and informed him that he would be "allowed 2½ percent commission" on all of his purchases.[6]

Frémont operated outside of the offices of the Quartermaster General and the Ordnance Bureau not only on horses, but in the field of guns, construction and financing for his purchases. When the almost-bankrupt federal treasury did not promptly pay for his accounts, he contacted various St. Louis bankers to request loans for the government. The word was also passed that should the requested loans not be forthcoming, Frémont might find it necessary, in his position of military commander, to confiscate the required amounts.[7] In offering contracts he ignored the procedure of bids and paid top prices—often in direct competition with the War Department agents and in most cases well above the prevailing market prices for goods.

Complaints regarding the administration of the Western Department reached Congress and prompted a full congressional investigation. Based on the committee's findings, the House of Representatives, April 30, 1861, passed a resolution asking the Treasury Department to adjust one especially questionable contract for the purchase of five thousand Hall's carbines. When Congressman Lovejoy attempted to amend the resolution to read that this request should in no way be construed as casting doubts on the personal integrity of Frémont, the amendment was defeated.[8]

A special commission was also established to adjust all war claims from contractors to the Western Department. A moratorium was declared on payments of Frémont's accounts until each had been fully investigated.

Frémont's arms purchases began with the war, before his appointment as Commander of the Western Department. In the spring of 1861 Frémont, in Europe in a nonofficial capacity, ordered quantities of foreign arms for delivery to the United States, at the expense of the United States government. Following his appointment to command the Western Department, the guns were forwarded for his use in St. Louis. But when the guns were issued, it was discovered in one regiment alone that only twenty percent of them would even fire.[9]

An Ordnance Bureau officer refused to purchase 25,000 Austrian muskets at $5.50 each because they needed alteration before they could be used. Yet an agent for Frémont purchased these same muskets at $6.50 each—an increased cost to the government of $25,-000 for arms they didn't want to begin with. The government then had to alter the guns before there could be any attempt to use them.

Frémont declared during the investigation that he had found the muskets in question to be a "good substantial arm," [10] preferred by many of the German troops in his command. But the testimony of another officer presented a conflicting opinion. He testified that even after repairs these arms proved unreliable, easily broken and liable to fire at half-cock.[11] At the battle of Belmont, when weapons for the Union forces were in severe shortage, these Austrian muskets were not considered worth removing from their shipping crates.

Frémont's policy of operating outside of government channels led to an example of duplication and extravagance that would, in theory, be impossible within the framework of a well-ordered and scrupulously honest defense establishment.

In April, 1861, Alexander Cummings, an arms agent for Secretary Cameron, purchased 790 Hall's carbines for the War Department at $15 each. In June of the same year these carbines formed part of a lot of 5,000 to 6,000 Hall's carbines sold by Cameron at the recommendation of General Ripley, who considered them valueless. Arthur M. Eastman, an arms dealer, purchased the lot for $3.50 each and, after making inexpensive alterations on them, sold them to Simon Stevens, an acquaintance of Frémont, for $22 each. Frémont approved the purchase for his command with no questions asked.

When this transaction was taken up by the investigating committee, the committee asked if Stevens had in fact been a member of Frémont's staff at this time. According to Frémont, Stevens was not on his staff at the time of the purchase, but did, in fact, later become an aide-de-camp.[12] Frémont explained that he had accepted the carbine purchase because he had used that gun once on a journey and supposed that these were "about what such arms usually are," also explaining, "I am not very familiar with them." [13]

The Contracts Committee saw this whole situation as a problem of placing the blame properly. If Cameron and Ripley were correct in assessing these arms as useless, "the repurchase of the arm is without any possible excuse; if otherwise, the original sale of the arm is utterly indefensible." [14]

In the case of fortifications, Frémont removed construction from the province of the army engineers. Of ten forts to be constructed, one set of five was to be built by the Army at a cost of $60,000. The second half of the job was awarded to one of Frémont's personal friends, who was advanced $85,000 before the contract was even signed. Within six weeks additional advances had brought the total payment to $191,000. The contractor then received from Frémont a contract to complete the five forts then being constructed by the military.[15]

When War Secretary Cameron finally ordered Frémont to discontinue work on the forts, Frémont sent a formal protest to Washington and proceeded with construction. When questioned by a congressional committee he said his authority was his position as "commanding general of that department, carrying on military operations." [16]

Before the investigating committee, General Cullom, an army engineer, testified that the construction of the forts ignored every known principle of military engineering and they were utterly useless for defense. He estimated that if the work had been completed and paid for according to Frémont's contracts, the government would have been swindled out of close to $240,000.[17]

The operations permitted by Frémont were not completely without the knowledge of his staff. His chief quartermaster, McKinstry, was found guilty by a court-martial of twenty-six counts of fraud, based on his own profiteering during the war.[18]

Whether Frémont himself was corrupt, or merely surrounded by unscrupulous officers and associates, is still a matter of historical debate. He allowed speculation and profiteering to thrive. Scandal went unchecked. Conflicts of interest were encouraged. Official orders were ignored. Dissent was disregarded.

But the responsibility for this total lack of adherence to sound governmental procedure must also fall on Frémont's superiors. Cameron's War Department granted Frémont his unique freedoms. The War Department failed to set up proper checks on his activities. The War Department failed to heed responsible criticism of Frémont's administration of the Western Department. Only the right of Congress to investigate, when aggressively pursued, revealed the many irregularities in the Frémont regime.

At the beginning of the Civil War the lack of preparedness in the War Department prevented the department from assuming responsibility for organizing the war effort. A fighting force had to be established and equipped. Frémont was given the authority to act as a regional war department because the War Department itself was unable to exercise its authority efficiently. The emergency step provided the broadest discretion and lacked proper official supervision.

No matter how irresponsible or corrupt Frémont's administration of the Western Department, the War Department created his administration. And the War Department allowed it to thrive.

The problem of Secretary Cameron and procurement for the War Department reached the Supreme Court in one instance. The case of *The Providence Tool Company v. Norris*[19] brought out testimony on Cameron's direct involvement with profiteering middlemen. Early in the war, Norris, acting as the agent for the Providence Tool Company to secure government contracts, arrived in Washington and set out to concentrate "influence at the War Department." He sought out and cultivated those who could be of service in introducing him to highly placed Administration officials. After an influential introduction to Cameron, Norris was successful in obtaining an order from the Secretary for 25,000 muskets at $20 each. While this was not out of line with the prices then being paid by the War Department for arms, it was well above the price in the open market. "Upon being thanked, the Secretary expressed the hope that Norris would make a great deal of money" from the contract. Cameron had usurped the authority of the office of the Quartermaster General in awarding this contract, a move that was typical of his administration.

Unfortunately for Norris a dispute arose with the Tool Company as to the terms of his arrangement with them. Norris claimed that he was to have received $3 for each gun purchased by the government; the company contended that they had agreed to reward him with "liberal compensation" only.

In handing down the decision in favor of the company, Associate Justice Stephen J. Field declared:

> All contracts for supplies should be made with those, and with those only, who will execute them most faithfully, and at the least expense to the Government. Considerations as to the most efficient and economical mode of meeting the public wants should alone control, in this respect, the actions of every department of the Government. No other consideration can lawfully enter into the transaction so far as the Government is concerned. Such is the rule of public policy; and whatever tends to introduce any other element into the transaction is against public policy. That agreements, like the one

under consideration, have this tendency is manifest. They tend to introduce personal solicitation, and personal influence, as elements in the procurement of contracts; and thus directly lead to inefficiency in the public service, and to unnecessary expenditures of public funds.[20]

Still another example of the direct forays of Secretary of War Cameron into the province of the Quartermaster General led to the congressional censure of the War Secretary after he had been removed from the Cabinet. On April 30, 1862, the House of Representatives passed the following resolution:

Resolved, That Simon Cameron, late Secretary of War, . . . has adopted a policy highly injurious to the public service, and deserves the censure of the House.[21]

From the outbreak of World War I until American entrance into the war, disagreement existed on the question of American preparedness. Foremost proponents of preparedness included former President Theodore Roosevelt, General Leonard Wood, and Secretary of War Newton D. Baker. Opponents held stronger positions in the Wilson Cabinet. In addition to Wilson himself, the Cabinet included active pacifists, Secretary of State William Jennings Bryan and Secretary of the Navy Josephus Daniels.

As soon as the war in Europe broke out, General Leonard Wood, a brilliant and highly respected member of the professional Army, became concerned with America's lack of preparation for the possibility of entering the war. Without the consent of the War Department he began actively supporting college military training. He also backed the establishment of summer camps for reserve training. In the latter he was actively encouraged by former President Roosevelt.

When word reached Wilson, the Commander-in-Chief of the Army, that his military policy was under attack by the best-known officer of the day, he instructed the Secretary of War to issue a reprimand to Wood. Since Secretary Baker, a recent convert to preparedness, agreed with Wood's estimation of American military strength, the reprimand was written in the Secretary's own hand and delicately worded. Wood continued to receive half-hearted reprimands and orders to stop creating public controversy until after the United States entered the war.[22]

Opposition from Roosevelt was easier to deal with. Since he had been defeated by Wilson in the 1912 election, Roosevelt's encouragement of war preparation was termed politically motivated.

In 1915 the *Baltimore Sun* carried a report that the General Staff of the Army was preparing plans for a war with Germany. When the report reached Wilson, he ordered Assistant Secretary of War Breckenridge to investigate the report. If the story was true, Breckenridge was directed to "relieve every officer of the General Staff and order him [*sic*] out of Washington." General Tasker H. Bliss explained that the Army War College, in strategy exercises, had gone over plans for war with every major power in the world, including Germany. Secretary of War Baker told Wilson that these were just "war games," and told the military to go ahead with their games, but to keep them out of the papers.[23]

Fortunately this incident did not occur in the Navy Department under Josephus Daniels. During the clamor for preparedness Daniels had efficiently muzzled his admirals, who decried the Navy's weakened condition. Even after the United States had entered the war, Daniels clung to his pacifist ideas. More than one naval officer, when requesting active duty, was told the Navy Secretary would sign his orders "the day after an armistice is declared." [24]

The sinking of the *Lusitania* shocked the country. Americans began to consider the possibilities of entering the war against Germany. Wilson turned the crisis into a diplomatic emergency. Protests were sent to the German government. Secretary of State Bryan objected that the protests were too strong, and resigned. Once outside the Cabinet Bryan became the acknowledged leader and spokesman for pacifist groups in the country. By timing his first speech to coincide with the public release of the second *Lusitania* note, he seriously injured Wilson's attempt to stand up for American rights. Critics of the President claimed that the rift with Bryan proved Wilson did not have the backing of the country.[25]

As the 1916 election approached Wilson realized that he would have to modify his stand on preparedness or risk losing the votes of the large numbers of Americans who were beginning to fear that Germany was going to force American entrance into the war.

In December, 1915, Wilson recommended that Congress increase the standing Army to 140,000 men and add a reserve force of 400,000, which would be trained for two months each year for three years. "At all times, until war actually came, the majority sentiment of

Congress was against preparedness, or reluctantly assented to a smaller preparedness than even Wilson thought desirable."

But even in this request, Wilson was careful to declare that he felt these modest increases in the Army were necessary for "defense" rather than possible participation in the European war.[26]

Shortly thereafter, the Assistant Secretary of the Navy, Franklin D. Roosevelt, requested permission to recall all naval vessels then in the Caribbean and equip them for the war that was becoming more imminent daily. Wilson himself blocked this attempt to decrease the glaring Navy deficiencies.[27]

When the war began in Europe the regular American Army numbered only 92,000 men. Of these approximately 25,000 were available for emergency war use. The rest were either engaged in the Coast Artillery defense or stationed overseas in American possessions and protectorates where they were needed. The National Guard could hardly be considered a capable fighting force. Training consisted of only twenty-four drills a year, including summer camp. Time and intensive training would be needed before this second line of defense could be considered ready for active duty.[28]

Once America entered the war almost five million men were enrolled in the armed forces. Over two million of them served overseas.[29] This tremendous mustering of manpower was considerably simpler than organizing strategy and providing for supplies and matériel.

Efforts to create a war machine comparable to that developed by the Allied and Central powers during the preceding three years of the war were plagued with tremendous difficulties. The whole official policy of the Wilson Administration had to be turned one hundred eighty degrees. Large segments of the population, whole areas in some instances, had to be rallied to the cause.

The General Staff received no request from the President for war plans. Plans had to be improvised without official objectives. General John J. Pershing, in France as Commander of the A.E.F., had to assume the responsibility for on-the-spot planning because he received no specific direction from Washington.

Pershing's greatest struggle was with the Army supply bureaus, which proved incapable of meeting the needs of a modern war machine. The General Staff finally had to take over direction of supply activities to move matériel on the way to the front.[30]

Early efforts to facilitate industrial mobilization proved frustrating. The War Industries Board was established in July, 1917, to provide the needed coordination that two previous boards had failed to achieve. The two first chairmen of the W.I.B., who were not given the authority to put their recommendations into effect, resigned in disgust.

During the winter of 1917-18 the total mobilization problem became so bad that the Senate staged an investigation. The report charged that the military establishment "has almost stopped functioning . . . because of inefficiency in every bureau and in every department of the Government." [31]

April, 1918, saw the War Industries Board reorganized under the leadership of Bernard Baruch. Baruch had the power to coordinate government purchasing and establish construction and manufacturing priorities. Under his control the board was able to provide impressive quantities of needed war matériel that comprised America's ultimate contribution to the Allied war effort.

Other emergency boards were established to help regulate the acquisition of a wide range of needed equipment. There were boards for aircraft production, naval construction, fuel supplies and foodstuffs.

Shortly after the end of the war a subcommittee of the Senate Naval Affairs Committee conducted two full-scale investigations into the war-time administration of the Navy Department under the pacifist, Secretary Josephus Daniels.[32]

One investigation charged Daniels with willful neglect of the needs of the Navy as a fighting force between 1913 and the time of American entrance into World War I and with allowing his own pacifist beliefs to obstruct the conduct of the war at sea by the Navy Department. This first investigation was composed of much highly technical testimony, not easily understood by the general public.

The other investigation, of Daniels' methods of making medal awards after the war, dealt with something much closer to the man in the street, something he could comprehend.

At the outset of World War I, the Navy Department had an extremely limited system of awards for bravery and valor. Those American sailors fighting alongside the British saw their Allies being rewarded for service that for them went unrecognized.

In 1917, the British government requested permission from the American government to make medal awards to Americans engaged in the same conflicts that resulted in awards to the Allied sailors.

Admiral William S. Sims wrote at once to Washington urging the passage of whatever legislation was necessary to allow these awards to Americans by foreign powers.

During the congressional hearings on this bill, Secretary of the Navy Daniels advised the committee that it was not the wish of his department that the bill be passed. The legislation was passed over his objections in July, 1918. Daniels held off until February, 1919, before recognizing the bill and allowing its application.[33]

At the same time many people began to complain of the lack of sufficient recognition by the American government to her own military personnel for meritorious conduct. Three months after the armistice, a bill was finally passed authorizing naval medals: the Distinguished Service Medal, the Medal of Honor, the Navy Cross, and a Letter of Commendation.

In March, 1919, four months after the armistice, Daniels first requested recommendations for awards for commanding officers of the Navy.

During the same month Daniels appointed a Board of Awards, composed of retired naval personnel from the noncombatant branches of the service to sit in review of the recommendations and advise him. None of the board members had been involved in the war, and they were in no position to judge the relative merits of any of the recommendations. Daniels then dissolved the board in October, 1919, before the majority of recommendations had even been received.[34]

Daniels submitted, without qualifications, his list of awards in his official report to the President for 1919. As soon as the list was published many of the highest-ranked men in the Navy notified Daniels that they intended to refuse their honors. They felt his list did a grave disservice to the whole principle of medals.

Professional naval opposition to Daniels' list was based on several main points. Fully half the recommendations by commanding officers had been completely rejected by Daniels without so much as a request for further information. Many men had received awards arbitrarily higher or lower than those requested by their commanding officers. Six hundred and eleven men who had received no recommendation for a medal by their commanding officers had been added to the list of award recipients by Secretary Daniels himself. More than two-thirds of the medals awarded had been selected on the basis of Josephus Daniels' personal judgment.

The most shocking abuse to the principles behind military honors was Daniels' decision to grant higher awards to American naval officers who had lost their ships to German torpedoes than to officers who had successfully met and defeated the enemy. By bestowing this honor on men who had acted as Daniels felt was becoming to the American Navy in defeat, he had created a higher reward for failure than for success.[35]

The clamor of the public and the press at these revelations led directly to the Senate investigation of Daniels' policies. When questioned by the committee he tried to escape criticism by the belated excuse that his official listing of medal recipients was only tentative. When blasted for ignoring recommendations Daniels chose to exclude mention of the various commanding officers and justified his action in the following letter to Senator Page, Chairman of the Senate Naval Affairs Committee:

> . . . The award of medals is a function of the executive branch of the Government and is at the discretion of the President.
>
> Furthermore, I desire to emphasize the fact that this Board of Awards was established by my order and its recommendations were only for the information of the Secretary of the Navy. This Board, therefore, did not have any statutory authority, its recommendations were not final, and the executive was authorized to act as if no boards had been constituted. There is nothing to prevent the Secretary of the Navy departing from the recommendations of this Board, when in his opinion this should be done.[36]

The Senate committee found, in its report of March 7, 1920, that not only did Daniels have no real comprehension of the purpose of awards, he was opposed to them and used them primarily to reward his own loyal political underlings—making other awards only where their obvious omission might have caused an even louder cry of public consternation.

Of Daniels' tenure as Secretary of the Navy the historian Kittredge has concluded:

> He ruled as a despot, ruthlessly crushing opposition . . . while publicly parading himself as an ardent democrat; from 1913 to 1917 he enforced a policy of pacifism upon the Navy; in consequence he prevented any real preparedness for the war; [he deceived] the coun-

try . . . by declaring . . . that the Navy was ready . . . for any emergency.

He repeatedly made false statements—perhaps inspired by lack of understanding rather than by intent to deceive,—to the country, to Congress and to the President, concerning the Navy and its conditions; he made incorrect assertions, officially and in writing, to the United States Senate [investigating committees]; he gave testimony under oath before the Senate Committee which was completely at variance with the testimony of other witnesses, and with the facts established by the evidence of official records.[37]

Despite his valiant attempts to confuse the issues during the Senate investigations, Secretary of the Navy Josephus Daniels, in 1920, was censured by the United States Senate.

The Daniels investigations were only two of the many issues Congress examined with a critical eye after the fighting stopped.

Throughout World War I there were Republican charges of widespread corruption in the heavy buying that took place in connection with the prosecution of the war by the Democratic Administration. Most of the charges were aimed at contracts for troop quarters, contracts for ships and airplanes and contracts for munitions and other war supplies; and there was strong public distrust for the manner in which the Wilson Administration spent more than $22 billion on the war, exclusive of the amount loaned to the Allies.

When the Republicans moved into a position of control in Congress, there was considerable discussion of the allegations of "thievery" in the war contracts. There was a pledge by Representative Nicholas Longworth, a Republican, to investigate these matters thoroughly, and there was evidence that excessive prices were paid for horses and that there were indications of ridiculous overbuying of many items.

It was a Republican, Charles G. Dawes, who had headed the supply procurement division in France, and the investigations naturally required his testimony. The able and articulate Dawes emerged the most effective defender of the Wilson Administration both because of his Republicanism and because of his ability under fire.

When questioned about the evidence of bad buying practices, Dawes exploded:

"Sure we paid. We didn't dicker. Why, man alive, we had to win the war. We would have paid horse prices for sheep if sheep could have pulled artillery to the front. Oh, it's all right now to say we bought too much vinegar and too many cold chisels, but we saved the civilization of the world. Damn it all, the business of an army is to win the war, not to quibble around with a lot of cheap buying. Hell and Maria, we weren't trying to keep a set of books, we were trying to win the war!" [38]

In a nation still proud of its victory in World War I, and unfamiliar with the conditions that existed in Europe at the time the purchases were made, it was not an unreasonable explanation. The Dawes formula of mixing strong doses of patriotism with the urgency of war needs proved successful then, as it has many times since then, in taking some of the fire out of the charges of war profiteering and corruption. However, it did not stop the Republicans in Congress from directing the Attorney General to establish a "Bureau of War Transactions" for the purpose of centralizing an extensive criminal investigation to try to obtain indictment of any persons involved in illegal actions, and civil investigations aimed at recovery of any government funds that were obtained by fraud or otherwise illegally.

The Republican Attorney General, Harry M. Daugherty, later reported, "I found no reason to bring indictments against a single one whom I was urged to prosecute." There were civil suits brought that resulted in recovery of about $8,500,000.[39]

Although Daugherty said he had conducted a "thorough investigation," the record of the Harding Administration and the role of Daugherty in a number of scandalous circumstances is not reassuring relative to the quality or the integrity of the investigations he directed into the allegations of war corruption or any other matter.

It should be noted that even in the first year of the Harding Administration in 1921, two Cabinet officers—Secretary of Interior Albert B. Fall and Secretary of Navy Edwin Denby—set the stage for the sale of the Navy oil reserves. This sale of the Navy oil reserves to private oil interests, the Teapot Dome scandal, resulted in a large payoff to Secretary of Interior Fall, who became the first Cabinet officer to be convicted of a crime and sent to federal prison.

Even by the time Attorney General Daugherty was starting his investigations of allegations of corruption in the purchasing in World War I, the Harding Administration was under fire for scandalous conduct and Daugherty had become the key figure in trying to whitewash the Teapot Dome affair and scandals that enveloped Harding's Ohio Gang.

Certainly, the role of Charles G. Dawes as the top purchasing agent in Europe did not hurt his political career. The Ohio Republican was named as the Vice-Presidential candidate on the ticket with Calvin Coolidge in 1924, and was elected.

As the investigations of World War I contracts came to a close, the Army Department and the Navy Department became embroiled in a new controversy that was to change radically the purchasing practices as well as the military tactics of all future wars. The central figure in the controversy was General Billy Mitchell, and his dramatic, unorthodox fight to prove the superiority of air power became one of the great classic stories of the United States military services. As Billy Mitchell shook the bureaucracy of the Army Department and the Navy Department through a defiance of the system, he also set the stage for the ascendancy of air power with its problems of expensive new weapons systems that were to prove far beyond the comprehension of the average citizen.

4

THE ORDEAL OF GENERAL BILLY MITCHELL

GENERAL William Lendrum "Billy" Mitchell, the Army's most outspoken proponent of strong, aggressive development of the potential of air power, did not learn to fly until he was thirty-six, in the early years of World War I. Stationed in Washington with the General Staff, he took flying lessons from the Curtiss Company of Newport News, Virginia, on his off-duty hours. This was an advanced age to begin dabbling in such a dangerous pastime.[1]

When the United States entered the war, Mitchell, then a colonel, led American flyers in the use of this novel military machine, and in the spring of 1917 became the first American to fly over enemy lines.[2] At the close of the war, Billy Mitchell was appointed assistant to the Chief of the Army Air Service, General Charles T. Menoher, with the associated rank of brigadier general.

Following the "war to end war" the dominant military opinion did not favor aggressive development of air power as either an offensive or defensive branch of the military. Few officers of rank or responsibility in the Army or Navy had any experience in flying. There was no unified command for the development of air power. Both the Army and Navy were responsible for the strategic implementation of air power and resources within the framework of their own military spheres.

As early as 1920 Mitchell began to campaign actively for a strong air force, stressing the bombing potential of airplanes in war. Public interest was aroused when he went so far as to predict that planes could defeat battleships. The Navy charged Mitchell was boasting, and flatly refused to consider the possibility that his claims might be true.

Pacifist Secretary of the Navy Josephus Daniels was so confident in the power of the Navy destroyers that he offered to command a ship against live aerial attack from Mitchell. Mitchell was willing, and flyers from all over the country volunteered to join Mitchell in this duel to the death.[3] Fortunately for Daniels, it never came to pass; this could have been the most dramatic of his many wrong judgments as Secretary of the Navy.

Mitchell requested permission to prove his boast by bombing tests on captured German war vessels; these ships had been turned over to the government at the close of the war for study, with the proviso that they be destroyed by August, 1921. Mitchell asked only to sink ships already slated for destruction, but the Navy, under Secretary Daniels, would not release the ships.[4]

Congress, faced with a new Administration and new budget requests, wanted the opportunity to judge the validity of Mitchell's boast, and joined with the press to prod a reluctant agreement from the new Navy Secretary, Edwin Denby, to permit joint Army-Navy bombing exercises in April, 1921.

Denby, like his predecessor, doubted the value of air power, and resented any belittlement of naval superiority.

Denby reserved the right to establish all ground rules for the summer bombing exercises. Mitchell realized the rules would be weighted in favor of Navy tradition, but he had no choice—this was his only opportunity to prove the value of air power. Mitchell was presented with the Navy regulations for the bombings, which he was required to sign. Five target ships would be anchored fifty miles from the coast. They were a captured German submarine, the obsolete *U.S.S. Iowa,* a German destroyer, the cruiser *Frankfort,* and the superdreadnaught, the *Ostfriesland.* Runs against the first four ships would be limited to 600-pound bombs. Against the *Ostfriesland,* Mitchell's Army flyers would be allowed one run with 1,000-pound bombs, and only two direct hits with unlimited-size weapons. At the end of World War I, the 1,000-pound bomb was the largest in use. Between April and July of 1921, the Army Ordnance Bureau developed a supply of 2,000-pound bombs at Mitchell's request. This bomb remained the largest in the American arsenal through the first year of World War II.

As Mitchell had feared, the Navy restrictions were designed to limit the efficiency of his aerial bombers. An anchored ship was more difficult to hit than a moving target; in actual warfare, an enemy vessel would be loaded with ammunition, which a strategically placed but not crippling hit would explode. Combat would restrict fire power only to the capacity of the planes involved, and the drama of an air-sea battle would be lost in a month of off-again-on-again exercises. Mitchell accepted the Navy rules. He was determined to have a chance.

The Army gave Mitchell full support for the naval bombing games. Flyers were assembled from all over the country. Mitchell's final force numbered over one thousand of the best flyers and aviation mechanics in the country. He inspired strong loyalty in his men, who were already devout believers in air power. Training hours were long and continued under the worst of flying conditions. Bombing practice became a way of life.

The air corps of the Army and Navy managed to sink the first four vessels with little difficulty other than official interference. The real challenge to Mitchell's boast was the *Ostfriesland,* which the Navy claimed was "unsinkable."

Early on the morning of July 21, 1921, the Navy called off the scheduled attack games against the *Ostfriesland* because of cloudy weather. Official explanation was that the bombers would not be able to locate the target. When Mitchell did not receive his orders to start his run, he ordered his planes to proceed to the target and be ready when the Navy decided to begin. When Mitchell arrived he found the Atlantic Fleet abandoning the target area. However, the weather began to clear, and the fleet with its cargo of diplomats, congressional and Cabinet members, and foreign air attachés reassembled for the attacks against the *Ostfriesland.*

The morning run against the *Ostfriesland* was limited by the Navy Department to 1,000-pound bombs. When the first direct hit was scored, the Navy signaled that their judges wished to go aboard and inspect the damage. Before Mitchell's pilots could respond to the visual signal, a total of five bombs had been dropped, scoring three direct hits. The Army aviators were directed to proceed to their land base and await further orders. Rather than dump their remaining cargo of live bombs far out at sea, the loaded planes, without direct orders from Mitchell, proceeded to rid themselves of their unwanted weight close enough for the mighty Atlantic Fleet to feel the shock of the underwater detonations.

The Navy judges announced that though the *Ostfriesland* had sustained direct hits during this bomb run, she was still capable of reaching a home port under her own steam. The hull remained watertight. Pilots in Mitchell's command contended that from their aerial vantage point it was easy to determine that, though still afloat, the *Ostfriesland* had suffered debilitating damage.

Before the afternoon run, Mitchell was informed by the Navy that his planes could embark upon their unlimited power run with only three bombs. Mitchell replied that he was proceeding as per prior agreement—with sufficient bombs to score two direct hits. In attacking the *Ostfriesland,* Mitchell was not concerned with direct hits. He had planned his assault strategy around a "water hammer," the water pressure that results from high-force detonation below the water line, because he was well aware that direct hits would not cause damage serious enough to sink the *Ostfriesland.* His two direct hits would be used to demonstrate that his command could make direct contact with the target.

Mitchell's bombers approached the target with seven 2,000-pound bombs. The first three bombs were successfully detonated below the water line, inflicting severe strain upon the hull of the *Ostfriesland.* The fourth, a direct hit, managed to do visible damage to the superstructure. The fifth bomb, again, exploded below the water line, and the *Ostfriesland's* bow lifted perpendicular to the water. As she began to glide slowly beneath the waves a sixth bomb found its mark. This direct hit punctuated the end of the *Ostfriesland.*

With six bombs and twenty-one minutes, Billy Mitchell had made good his boast of months before. He had sunk the unsinkable queen of the German Navy.

Immediate reaction was varied. The Army was proud to take

credit for Mitchell's accomplishment. Some men in the official Navy party actually wept. They saw the sinking of the *Ostfriesland* as a threat to the future of the Navy and feared that naval life and tradition were in danger of becoming extinct.[5]

As soon as the shock of Mitchell's victory over bureaucratic and military reactionaries began to wear off, the Navy embarked on a public campaign to undercut Mitchell's support. They carefully explained that German design was not so sound as originally believed, and that an unarmed ship could not prove the strategic worth of Mitchell's policies. The *Ostfriesland* herself, they claimed, had been damaged during the war and though repaired had been allowed to fall into a state of decay since the armistice.

Mitchell sought to pursue his advantage and fanned the flames of the controversy with his articles and speeches. In the ensuing hassle, Mitchell's immediate superior resigned and was replaced by Major General Mason Patrick. When Navy Secretary Denby continued his protests against Mitchell and the publicity he had aroused, Secretary of War John W. Weeks ordered Mitchell to submit all statements and articles to the War Department for prepublication clearance.[6] The Defense establishment chose to ignore the full significance of the power of concentrated aerial bombing, which Mitchell had proved. Rather than concentrate on development of this new weapon, halfhearted attempts were made to devise antiaircraft defenses for ships and the coast artillery.

In 1923 and 1924 Mitchell honeymooned with his second wife in the Orient while on assignment to inspect Pacific Air Service activities. On his return in July of 1924 he submitted a full report on the military posture of the Pacific Fleet, and the advanced use of air power by the Japanese. He also noted the ease with which the Japanese could hopscotch across the Pacific by island bases.

When asked about the report in Washington, General Patrick said that it had no immediate applicability, but might prove of "extreme value" to the department in ten or fifteen years.[7] Fifteen years later was 1939.

When he failed to gain official sanction for his recommendation of a separate air force and a unified department of national defense, Mitchell set out to present his ideas to the public. He seized every chance to speak on the subject, and when offered the opportunity, wrote a series of five articles that appeared in *The Saturday Evening Post* from December, 1924 through March, 1925.

Mitchell circumvented War Secretary Weeks' attempt to censor his outspoken dissent against official air policy by going directly to President Coolidge for permission to publish this series. The President tried to remain aloof from the whole question. He refused to read the articles and told Mitchell that he didn't care what he published as long as Mitchell received the consent of his superiors. Mitchell interpreted this to mean he needed only the approval of General Patrick. Patrick later denied that Mitchell had ever received his permission.[8]

The explosive Mitchell articles set off highly unfavorable reaction among the upper echelon at the War Department. Secretary Weeks claimed that the series and Mitchell's equally critical speeches had stretched his patience to the limit. He requested permission from the President not to reappoint Mitchell to his position as Assistant to the Chief of the Army Air Service, which was granted.

As a result, in March, 1925, Mitchell reverted to his former rank of colonel. He was further chastised by being transferred from Washington to Fort Sam Houston in San Antonio, Texas. In exile, he was fairly successfully muzzled by location if nothing else.

While Mitchell had been actively seeking public support for dynamic air force development, the nation was horrified by three major military air tragedies.

On October 4, 1924, the Army and Navy had staged an interservice air race, the Pulitzer Cup Race, at Wright Field in Ohio. During the final race an Army Curtiss Racer crashed and burned, killing the pilot, Captain Burt Skeel.[9]

On September 1, 1925, the Navy began a flight to Hawaii in an effort to show up the Army's recent round-the-world flight. Three planes were to take part, two Navy built PN-9's and a Boeing PB-1. Only the two Navy planes took off on schedule; the Boeing plane was grounded with engine trouble. One of the Navy planes broke down three hundred miles out from the California coast. The second PN-9 was lost 1,600 miles out, even though the Navy had stationed patrol ships every two hundred miles along the course. It was not until nine days later that Commander John Rodgers and his starving crew were located and towed to safety.[10]

On September 2 of the same year, the Navy blimp *Shenandoah* left her hangar in Lakehurst, New Jersey, on maneuvers that were to take her over several Midwestern states. The next day, in Ohio, the *Shenandoah* ran into a severe storm. The craft split in two, killing the commanding officer, Commander Zachary Lansdowne, and thirteen members of his crew.

In the investigation that followed, the Navy Department cited orders granting Lansdowne the authority to postpone the flight if weather conditions made it advisable. But Captain G. W. Steele of the Lakehurst base submitted the copy of a request from Lansdowne to the Navy Department to delay the flight for at least a week. Communication from the Navy Department ordered the flight to proceed as originally scheduled.[11]

On September 5, 1925, Colonel Billy Mitchell called representatives of three San Antonio papers and of the Associated Press and gave them a full statement of his views[12] on the causes for these recent air tragedies. He carefully explained that his opinion had been requested "from all parts of the country" and that he had developed his views "after mature deliberation."

Mitchell charged that "these accidents are the direct result of the incompetency, criminal negligence and the almost treasonable administration of the national defense by the Navy and War Departments," and, "in their attempts to keep down the development of aviation into an independent department, separate from the Army and Navy and handled by aeronautical experts, and to maintain the existing systems, they have gone to the utmost lengths."

He further declared, "All aviation policies, schemes and systems are dictated by the nonflying officers of the Army and Navy who know practically nothing about it. The lives of the airmen are being used merely as pawns in their hands.

"The airmen themselves are bluffed and bulldozed so that they dare not tell the truth, in the majority of cases, knowing full well that if they do they will be deprived of their future career, sent to the most out-of-the-way places to prevent their telling the truth, and deprived of any chance for advancement unless they subscribe to the dictates of the nonflying bureaucratic superiors. These either distort facts or openly tell falsehoods about aviation to the people and to the Congress."

Mitchell felt the air-race disaster was caused "by an arrangement between the Navy and Army that the Navy should take the races one year and the Army should take them the next year, thereby equalizing propaganda, not service. Instead of building new airplanes our men were given the old crates to fly at those terrific speeds. Of course, they came to pieces, as they were designed for only one race two years before. This was done in spite of the fact that we had sufficient money to build new ships according to entirely advanced patterns and new safety factors."

As for the *Shenandoah,* Mitchell couldn't understand why the Navy was holding maneuvers "over the mountains."

Mitchell's charges raised an immediate furor. Acting Secretary of the Navy, Curtis D. Wilbur, had already presented his interpretation of the disasters to the press. "In view of . . . the failure of the Hawaiian flight and the *Shenandoah* disaster we have come to the conclusion that the Atlantic and Pacific are still our best defenses. We have nothing to fear from enemy aircraft that is not on this continent." [13]

Rear Admiral William A. Moffett, Chief of the Navy's Bureau of Aeronautics, tried to launch an effective counteroffensive. He cried "red." "The revolutionary methods of the communists [*sic*] have been invoked to overcome the opposition of loyal men who have sought to thwart the ambition of unscrupulous self-seekers," Admiral Moffett slapped at Mitchell. "The ambitions of these selfish men are as unbounded as their methods are unscrupulous. Their tactics are those of the demagogue. They like to pose as eagles soaring aloft with keen eye for the country's defense. They have really played the part of vultures swooping down on their prey once it is down." [14]

Lieutenant Commander Sidney Ballon, also of the Navy, replied to Mitchell through a paper for the Naval Institute Proceedings thus: "An anchored battleship with no means of defense is sunk . . . and the word goes out at once that the battleship is obsolete." He carefully explained that the war had proved the value of the battleships "indisputable" and added that "the bombing plane is by nature a raider. . . . No raiding operation ever severed a line of sea communications." He concluded with the American philosophy for military preparation: "Wars, whether on land or sea, will be won in the future as they have been in the past by the comparatively slow but irresistible force which is able to move from one strategic position to another. . . . On land this force is the Infantry; on sea it is the battleship. The airplane is not of this type." [15]

The War Department did not immediately state its response. Secretaries and chiefs were busy going over Mitchell's statement to see if he were liable for a general court-martial.

In a speech before an insurance convention in San Antonio on September 15, Colonel Mitchell clarified his earlier statement. He said in part, "We [flying officers] insist that our Nation be not held back in its progress, and we insist that our air power no longer be farmed out as an orphan in the asylums of the Army and Navy; that it take a seat in equality beside those ancient services with one common overlord in a department of national defense. . . ." [16]

While the War Department was trying to decide whether to call for a general court-martial of Mitchell, he was summoned to Washington to testify before the National Air Board. President Coolidge had ordered a full investigation of American air preparedness when the furor over Mitchell's statement broke out. He established the Board in an attempt to reach some conclusions before Congress reconvened and to avoid the possibility of a congressional investigation into what he considered his province, the executive department.[17]

Billy Mitchell presented testimony before the Board for two days. The first day he read into the proceedings several chapters of his recent book, *Winged Defense*. By so doing, he lost the chance for the publicity he was seeking. It was not until his second day as a witness that he began answering questions from the Board. By then the public had decided he was only reading "dull" testimony and failed to follow his second, more outspoken day as a witness. He again called for independent administration for the air force and the establishment of a unified department of national defense. The committee report, in November, 1925, recommended against Billy Mitchell's proposals.[18]

Court-martial proceedings against Colonel William Mitchell began on October 28, 1925. As the War Department did not wish the Mitchell trial to become a cause célèbre, the building selected for the hearings was an old one no longer used by the Army, even for a warehouse. Mitchell arrived for the hearings in the new roll-collar uniform of the air service, with more medals than any of the officers sitting in judgment on him. The officials of the court wore olive-drab rather than the customary full-dress uniforms.[19]

Mitchell was tried on charges of insubordination and conduct prejudicial to proper military discipline. His lawyer tried to challenge the jurisdiction of the court. He pleaded that the hearing was a violation of Mitchell's right of free speech. The court responded that they did have the authority because Mitchell had made his statements as a member of the armed services, not as a private citizen. Had Mitchell resigned before making his inflammatory charges, the court would indeed have been without validity.

The high point in the Mitchell trial came when Admiral Sims appeared for the defense. Sims had come out of retirement to support Mitchell's views that an invading fleet could be destroyed by an aggressively organized and land-based air force.[20]

Mitchell was not being tried on the validity of his views, but on his charges against the military high command. Mitchell was found guilty of the charges against him on December 17, 1925.

Mitchell had resorted to extreme language in his September 5th statement, almost necessitating a court-martial, in order to present his case to the American people. He had remained in the service in an attempt to criticize and correct from within the deficiencies he saw, refusing to choose the sanctuary of resignation. By forcing a court-martial, he could have been evicted from the service and freed to express his opinions before investigating committees and the public. Instead, he received an extremely light sentence—suspension from his rank for five years, without pay or allowances. President Coolidge reinstated his allowances and granted him half pay. But this sentence kept Mitchell under the command of those with whom he disagreed and barred him from becoming a martyr.[21]

Mitchell resigned from the Army on January 29, 1926. He withdrew from Washington and became a gentleman farmer in nearby Virginia. During his retirement he continued to campaign for a separate and strong air force.

Billy Mitchell never lived to see his proposals accepted. He died in 1936, before America began her build-up for World War II. During World War II, when the truth of Mitchell's prophecies had become painfully clear and America was fighting for her very existence by the principles Mitchell laid down during his career, he was officially vindicated. In 1942 he was honorably restored to the service and granted the posthumous rank of major general. Much later his dream for a separate air force command in a single department of defense became a reality.

The court-martial trial of General Billy Mitchell did more than dramatize the fight of the enthusiastic air-power supporters against the more traditional forces in the Army and Navy. It was a trial that included the participation of two other military men who will always rank with the great iconoclasts of United States military history. Admiral Sims' appearance for the defense was as a witness in behalf of defiance of the system as personified by Billy Mitchell. Among those Army officers who took part in the court-martial proceedings was

Douglas MacArthur, whose later record as a colorful tradition-breaker spanned World War II and the Korean War.[22]

Even the color and the issue of the Billy Mitchell case were not enough to stir the American public or Congress with the full significance of the development of the airplane as an important military machine. Although there was recognition of air power, it remained a relatively small budget item until just prior to World War II. But, of course, air power was not the only aspect of the United States military establishment that was permitted to fall into disrepair until World War II was nearly upon us.

There are many reasons why the warnings by Billy Mitchell for a strong military posture went unheeded. The nation was intent upon peace again and disillusioned with the failure of World War I to bring about a stable world. Many Americans were swayed by the anti-League members of Congress who argued that isolation was the only way to avoid further crass entanglements in foreign problems. Investigations by the Nye Committee increased public disaffection with the war when it reported on the tremendous profits made by munitions manufacturers.

The onslaught of the Depression caused most Americans to become almost totally concerned with their domestic problems. President Franklin Roosevelt, who had tried in vain to strengthen the Navy prior to World War I, was blocked by domestic emergencies from developing strong military preparations for more than the first four years of his Administration.

At the Geneva disarmament conference in May, 1933, the official United States policy was directed toward greater disarmament. To facilitate this policy the country was prepared to agree to collective security measures and consultation with other nations in the face of any threats to the peace.

Hitler withdrew Germany from the conference and the League of Nations in October, 1933, refusing to have any limits placed on his rights to establish the German military posture.

Shortly after this Roosevelt sought large appropriations from Congress to bring the Navy up to full treaty strength. Isolationists, among others, were shocked by his request for $1 billion for naval expansion and $100 million for annual replacements. Advocates of a large navy backed Roosevelt since there had been no ships commissioned during Hoover's tenure.

President Roosevelt also planned to use $238 million granted for emergency relief for the construction of thirty-two ships. He argued that this would flood money into the economy in all parts of the country; a total of 85 percent was to be spent for salaries. However, in early 1934 Congress acted to block the use of public-works money on Navy building.

The Vinson-Trammel Act, passed by Congress in March of 1934, did authorize immediate construction of four cruisers. It also provided for a long-range program of development to bring the Navy up to treaty strength by 1942. Unfortunately Congress did not provide sufficient funds to implement the Act.

Roosevelt, a strong Navy man, battled public opinion and congressional objection to his desires for a strong American military posture almost to the day the United States entered the war.[23]

Even after receiving some appropriations from Congress the total American military expenditure for 1933 was only $784 million—17 percent of the budget. By 1937 the military expenditure had risen to over a billion, but had dropped to 15 percent of the total federal budget.[24]

In May, 1938 after Hitler had annexed Austria, the President was able to obtain a 20-percent increase in naval appropriations, although this modest request met with strong opposition from congressional isolationists, who argued that the Navy was then larger than at any previous time in history.

Poland was invaded in September, 1939. President Roosevelt immediately explained to Congress that the 1935 embargo act would aid Hitler rather than the Allies and requested modification. He wanted to assure sufficient quantities of American arms to England and France. The isolationist Senator Borah of Idaho, claiming "superior sources of information," asserted "there would be no war." Congress took no action.[25]

Representative Carl Vinson sponsored a new four-year program for naval expansion. In November, 1939, Congress granted $1,300,000,000 to implement the second Vinson Naval Act.

During the relative inactivity of the "Phony War" (the winter of 1939-40) the President made only moderate requests for armaments increases by Congress. The House Appropriation Committee cut $12 million for an air base in Alaska and authorized construction of only 57 of the 496 airplanes the President had recommended. By the time the bill reached the Senate for action, it had been made obsolete by events in Europe.

Hitler invaded Denmark and Norway during the spring of 1940. In the face of this action Congress quickly granted the additional billion defense dollars Roosevelt desired. At the same time the President set a goal of at least 50,000 airplanes a year. Roosevelt adopted Billy Mitchell's plan for an air armada to form a major force in the American defenses.

Through June, 1940, Roosevelt had requested armaments increases from Congress more than four times. The total, reluctantly appropriated in 1938 and 1939, was less than $2 billion. As late as 1939 defense spending still amounted to only 15 percent of the budget. In the face of the spreading Nazi terror, Congress had increased Army and Navy appropriations only 50 percent during the two-year period ending June 30, 1940.[26]

President Roosevelt was very much aware of the growing danger signs in Europe and the Orient. However, Congress still contained many isolationists and as late as the month before Pearl Harbor polls showed that only 20 percent of the American population favored a declaration of war against Germany.

American nonintervention feeling was divided into two widely differing philosophies. William Allen White organized the Committee to Defend America. The White Committee favored strong aid to the Allies, because its members felt that England and France were again defending American democracy. "We can help by sending planes, guns, munitions, food," stated the Committee's advertisement. "We can help to end the fear that American boys will fight and die in another Flanders, closer to home. . . ." [27]

The America First Committee was formed by a Yale student, R. Douglas Stuart, Jr., and headed by the Chicago businessman, General Robert E. Wood. Colonel Charles Lindbergh, General Hugh Johnson and Senators Wheeler and Nye contributed their positions and oratorical powers. In April, 1941, Lindbergh stated the policy of the America First Committee: "We should not enter a war unless we have a reasonable chance of winning. . . . I do not believe that our American ideals, and our way of life, will gain through an unsuccessful war," he said and added, "I know that the United States is not prepared to wage war in Europe sucessfully at this time. . . ." When later in the same month Lindbergh called for England and France to accept a negotiated peace, he incurred the wrath of the President. Lindbergh resigned from the Army Air Force in response to Roosevelt's charges that he was "an appeaser and a defeatist." [28]

The views of the White Committee and the America First Committee expressed the feelings of many Americans before the United States entered the war. Roosevelt struggled against this reluctance to become involved in another "foreign war" as he tried to prepare the United States for the war that he believed was becoming inevitable.

Opposition dissolved December 7, 1941, among the falling bombs over Pearl Harbor.

5

PEARL HARBOR—CAUGHT NAPPING

IN his annual report on December 6, 1941, Secretary of Navy Frank Knox boasted: "I am proud to report that the American people may feel fully confident in their Navy. In my opinion, the loyalty, morale and technical ability of the personnel are without superior. On any comparable basis, the United States Navy is second to none." [1]

There was some justification for this optimistic report, for the Navy had made substantial progress in building a fleet to defend the interests of the United States. Unfortunately the mental attitudes of the highest military officials had not reached an equal state of readiness. There were alerts, there were warnings, but there was a failure to realize that this was a critical period in which no "business as usual" or "politics as usual" attitudes could be tolerated.

Lieutenant General Walter C. Short, Commander of the Hawaiian Department, attended an Army benefit dinner the evening of December 6. Admiral Husband E. Kimmel, Commander of the Pacific Fleet, took the evening off for a visit with an old classmate. Admiral Harold R. Stark, Chief of Naval Operations, attended a performance of *The Student Prince* in Washington. General George C. Marshall, Chief of the Army General Staff, could not recall where he spent the evening but he was up bright and early on December 7 to take his usual Sunday-morning horseback ride and arrived late at the War Department. It was little wonder that the Naval Intelligence unit in Washington made no effort to alert such junior naval officers as John F. Kennedy, who drove off to Griffith Stadium to attend a football game between the Washington Redskins and the Philadelphia Eagles. He was riding home from that game when he heard the news of the Japanese attack on Pearl Harbor.

The sneak air raid on Pearl Harbor caught the American military establishment asleep, and so devastated the Pacific Fleet that the country had to do more than simply prepare for war. It was necessary to repair for war the equipment that Secretary of Navy Knox had planned to use as the foundation of war operations. Pearl Harbor cost the United States the immediate retaliatory force of 188 planes, all eight battleships in the harbor, three cruisers, three destroyers, and the lives of 2,323 men.[2]

Only four months before Pearl Harbor, Congress extended the first peacetime draft in history, by a scant margin of one vote, making it possible to boost the Army to 1,600,000 men. Pearl Harbor provided the shock and fear to bring unified action, and from that moment the figures on mobilization were impressive. From a total of 4,500 ships of all sizes just before Pearl Harbor, the Navy grew to more than 91,000 ships by the end of 1945. The Army Air Force entered the war with only 9,000 planes, of which a mere 1,100 were in service. By the end of the war the United States had 72,000 planes in the skies. During the war more than 15,000,000 men and women served in the armed forces. The 10,420,000 in the Army included 2,300,000 in what was then the Army Air Corps. There were 3,883,520 in the Navy; 599,693 in the Marines; and 241,902 in the Coast Guard.[3]

Industrial mobilization in America was equally astounding. In 1941, the American war production was only $8,400,000,000. During 1942, the total rose to $30,200,000,000, and the contracts awarded that year came to more than $100,000,000,000. Annual plane production rose from 5,865 in 1939 to a peak of 96,369 in 1944. Total wartime production of planes was 274,941. Merchant-ship construction was only 1,000,000 tons in 1940, but swelled to provide a wartime aggregate of 55,239,000 tons.

American munition concerns turned out 15,300,000 rifles, carbines and side arms and close to three million machine guns. More than 4,200,000 tons of artillery shells were manufactured, along with 41,600,000 rounds of small-arms ammunition.

The war toll on America's natural resources was staggering. Providing matériel consumed over 7,500,000,000 barrels of oil, more than

3,000,000,000 net tons of coal and 16 trillion cubic feet of natural gas. The United States federal budget rose from an average of $8,000,000,000 during the 1930's to a wartime maximum of $98,303,000,000 in 1945.[4] The total spending for the war years was more than $321,000,000,000. The gross national debt increased from $49,000,000,000 before America entered the war to $259,000,000,000 by mid-1945. The total expenditure in World War II was twice as much as the whole federal government spent from 1789 to 1941.

The fact that the United States was not a battlefield made it possible for this nation to mobilize its industry in record time despite the "confusion and chaos, incompetence and momentary failure, political intrigue and personal vendetta" that prevailed in the first months.[5]

The experiences and mistakes of World War I had made it obvious to many in government that there would be a need for complete organization of the economy for effective mobilization. However, the necessary planning and action were never achieved despite periodic interest in mobilization of industry in the event of another major conflict. Unfortunately, the Congress left intact the provisions of the National Defense Act of 1916, which called for a Council of National Defense with powers that were purely advisory.

In 1920, Congress passed another National Defense Act, which placed the legal responsibility for procurement and industrial mobilization planning in the Office of the Assistant Secretary of War. This legislation proved to be only the starting point for "two decades of continuous shuffling and reshuffling of administrative responsibilities." The Council of National Defense remained as a holdover from the 1916 legislation, and the Assistant Secretary of War ran into conflicts with other units in the War Department.

When the Office of Assistant Secretary of War submitted new plans in 1929, they were criticized as being too inflexible and were revised into what became the mobilization plan of 1930. Three formal revisions followed in 1933, 1936 and 1939.[6]

Most of the interest in industrial mobilization plans was confined to those engaged in the planning until 1938, and then the deterioration in international relations caused greater general interest on the subject. Much of the public awareness at that time could be traced to the zealous efforts of the then Assistant Secretary of War Louis A. Johnson, who constantly wrote and spoke on the subject of mobilization.

After Johnson's Planning Branch of the War Department and the

Army-Navy Munitions Board had coordinated their efforts on a plan, President Franklin Roosevelt appointed a War Resources Board to review the plan and advise on revision. The War Resources Board appointed on August 9, 1939, was headed by E. R. Stettinius, chairman of the board of U.S. Steel. Other members included W. S. Gifford, president of American Telephone & Telegraph Co.; Karl T. Compton, president of the Massachusetts Institute of Technology; H. G. Moulton, president of Brookings Institution; John Lee Pratt, a director of the General Motors Corporation; General Robert E. Wood, chairman of Sears, Roebuck & Co.; and J. M. Hancock, an industrial banker.

The report, known as the Stettinius report, gave general endorsement to the 1939 plans of the Army-Navy Munitions Board. The War Resources Board stated that any effective mobilization plan had to include the following five principles:

(1) There should be a minimum number of agencies reporting to the President.

(2) Capable executive personnel to man the war agencies should be selected who could win the confidence of their associates in industry.

(3) The status quo of all groups within the economy should be maintained; there should be no seeking special advantage.

(4) The power of authority of all wartime agencies should be covered by appropriate and well-defined statutes or Executive Orders so as to avoid overlapping of jurisdiction and subsequent conflicts of authority.

(5) The choice between a superagency to control all other subagencies, or a limited number of agencies each exercising a delegated war power with provision for coordination among themselves using the President only as a final arbiter in event of major disagreement, should be resolved in favor of the latter course.[7]

To implement these principles, the War Resources Board suggested a central agency for coordinating America's productive capacity with Army, Navy and civilian requirements. This agency, to be known as the War Resources Administration, was to be divided into seven divisions: Raw Materials and Manufactures Division, Facilities Division, Priorities Division, War Trade Division, Power and Fuel Division, Transportation Division, and Technological and Research Division. Also, the War Resources Administration was to coordinate six independent agencies: Public Relations Board, Selective Service Administration, War Labor Administration, War Finance Administration, War Food Administration, and Price Control Authority.

This plan, approved by major figures in American industry, was regarded by some as "the synthesis of all the mobilization planning undertaken in the two decades between the two world wars." [8]

"However, the industrial mobilization plan was never invoked before or during World War II," a Senate committee commented in a critical analysis in 1948.

"Without attempting to assess responsibility for this situation, the committee feels it is significant from the point of view of our future national defense to mention three principal contributing factors:

"1. The gradual nature of our economic involvement in World War II was undoubtedly primarily responsible for the failure to invoke the industrial mobilization plan according to schedule.

"2. Public opinion prior to the outbreak of war was sharply divided as to the role this country should play in the European conflict.

"3. Congress had never repealed the National Defense Act of 1916 setting up the advisory council method of defense organization; it never gave legislative sanction to the industrial mobilization plan revision of 1939, and it failed to remove or suspend such restrictive legislation as, for example, the competitive bidding system."

Bernard M. Baruch, the veteran adviser to American Presidents, declared that the United States suffered an enormous waste in time, lives and resources by not implementing the 1939 plans.

"Because of our foot dragging and fumbling, because of our inability to apply corrective methods when they were clearly indicated —the war cost us, unnecessarily, thousands of lives, extra billions of dollars, and months of time. This is my firm conviction based upon an intimate association which is demonstrable."

"My experience in two world wars," Baruch told a Senate committee, "the aftermaths, and the endeavors to make a lasting peace make me marvel at the regularity with which errors are repeated. One of the errors that most frequently recurs is failure to study and understand the records of past experience. . . . The armed services had an M-day plan, which would have saved precious lives and the wasted wealth, but they were not permitted to put it into effect. We were told this was a different kind of war, and none of that 'old World War stuff' was wanted. No matter whether you use 'old or new stuff,' you always want trained men, maintenance, materials, money and morale." [9]

While James Forrestal, Secretary of the Navy and later the first Secretary of Defense, found the War Resources Board planning to be generally meritorious, he was not so certain that the failure to implement that 1939 plan had caused such serious delays. He found that the plan had shortcomings.

"Whether or not the 1939 plan, with its limitations, would have been better than the steps that were actually taken is a matter of conjecture on which various people had, and still have, differing opinions," Forrestal said. "One thing is clear: The steps that were taken gave us a tremendous outpouring of ships, planes, and guns and thereby gave us the means with which we won the war. That was not Washington alone or labor alone or industry alone; it was the country and not any one segment of it." [10]

Forrestal declared that President Franklin Roosevelt was one of the few people who recognized the depth and extent of the effort the United States would have to make in tapping its total power in World War II, and that the President took the country as far as he could in preparations in the light of public opinion that existed prior to Pearl Harbor.

Even before Pearl Harbor, Roosevelt recognized that the Navy Department and War Department were not properly housed for the coordination and cooperation that would be needed if the United States became involved in the war. Worse physical installations for carrying on a war would have been difficult to imagine. The War Department was located in the woefully inadequate Munitions Building. The Navy Department was crowded into the old Navy Main Building.[11] The growing military establishment required additional, enlarged facilities.

The prime contract for a centralized military headquarters was awarded on August 11, 1941, with plans for an unusual five-sided structure composed of five concentric rings and five stories in height. It was to be called the Pentagon, and it was designed to try to provide a huge efficient building capable of housing the entire Washington headquarters for our military operations.

Construction started on the day the contract was awarded. The first occupants moved into the building eight months later, before it was completed. The construction was finished on January 15, 1943, at a total cost of $49,600,000 for the building, with land, parking and other facilities bringing the total project to $83,000,000.

It was important to have a building in which to centralize the operations of the bulging military establishment, but it was equally important that there be provisions for a congressional check on the billions of dollars in spending that went with the buildup of the greatest military machine in the history of the world.

Senator Harry S. Truman, a Missouri Democrat, had served in the infantry in France in World War I. He had viewed the waste, inefficiency and profiteering that accompanied the big war spending spree in the period between 1916 and 1919. Early in 1941, the 57-year-old Missouri Senator urged the establishment of a special Senate committee to investigate national defense spending. The billions appropriated, and yet to be appropriated, for defense purposes made it apparent that there was the greatest danger of fraud and profiteering of the type that had hampered war efforts in the Civil War and World War I.

Regular standing committees of Congress were already in existence, but it would have been unusual if these committees had provided the aggressive and independent check on the military departments that was needed. Too often there was an overly close relationship between the military departments and the regular standing committees. The relationship was often so cozy that important members of a standing committee lost their role as independent observers and became conspirators with high civilian and military officials in a manner that was detrimental to the best interests of military preparedness. Rarely is this problem discussed on the floor of the House or Senate because it reflects upon members of those august bodies, but it is a reality that has periodically created unwholesome conditions in defense buying. It did, in fact, contribute to outright corruption in World War II, and to many well-recognized examples of favoritism since then.

When Senator Harry S. Truman asked for establishment of the special Senate committee he could not have imagined the broad pattern of mismanagement, corruption and political pressures that it would uncover. It is doubtful if the special committee would have been authorized if there had been any realization that before the investigation was over it would produce evidence of conflicts of interest involving the House, the Senate, a Democratic governor, and persons close to the White House.

Approval of the resolution was given on March 1, 1941, and

Senator Truman was named as the first chairman of what was officially the Special Committee Investigating the National Defense Program. Initially, the committee had seven members, but in October, 1941, the number was increased to ten. Broad jurisdiction granted it the necessary power to investigate programs "for the procurement and construction of supplies, vessels, plants, camps, and other articles and facilities in connection with national defense."

Senator Truman served as chairman of the committee from its inception until August 11, 1944, when he resigned after having been selected as the Democratic Vice-Presidential nominee. The work of the Missouri Democrat as chairman of the war investigating committee brought him the national reputation that catapulted him into the Vice-Presidency and ultimately into the Presidency. Senator James M. Mead (Dem., N.Y.) followed Truman as chairman of the committee. When Mead resigned in October, 1946, after having been nominated as Democratic candidate for the governorship of the State of New York, the chairmanship went briefly to Senator Harley M. Kilgore (Dem., W. Va.).

In the last two years of its existence, the war investigating committee was under Republican control as a result of a Republican sweep in the 1946 election. The chairman was Senator Owen Brewster (Rep., Me.), but the most arduous work was done by a subcommittee headed by Senator Homer Ferguson (Rep., Mich.) after Brewster became involved in political brawling that made it unthinkable for him to participate in some of the investigations.

6

WAR CONTRACTS—MAYOR CURLEY AND COMMANDER CORRIGAN

THE earliest investigations by the Truman committee demonstrated that corrupters of the military establishment may come from such diverse sources as professional confidence men, the political influence-peddlers of a city political machine or the ranks of Annapolis graduates.

In the spring of 1941, James George Fuller lounged in the quiet and solitude of a Washington, D.C., jail and let his mind dwell on increased military spending required by lend lease and the deteriorating conditions in Europe. If government spending policies ran true to form, Fuller reasoned there was opportunity to "enlarge upon the future with cool determination." [1]

Other men saw the potential for a financial killing as the war clouds grew darker in early 1941, but few of them carried the great handicap of a fifteen-year criminal record from the past and a 720-day jail term that encroached upon the future of Jim Fuller. Certainly the chairman of the House Military Affairs Committee and a shrewd money-grabbing Senator from Mississippi were in a position to mix politics and war contracts for personal profit. Also, it took no great stretch of the imagination for a couple of young Naval Academy graduates to see how they could turn their connections with a management consultant firm into a lucrative device for profiteering on war contracts.

Imagination and daring were required for Jailbird Jim Fuller to accomplish his potential as a war profiteer. A persuasive and hard-working confidence man, he believed he could succeed with the plans he was making to cash in on big defense spending. He had faith in the laxity of the United States military bureaucracy.

Only twenty-four days after the Senate established the Truman war investigating committee Fuller wrote a letter from the jail to renew old political contacts as a first step in his schemes to skim off war profits.

Fuller's letter of March 24, 1941, was to Marshall James Fitzgerald, a Boston politician who had toiled long and hard to advance the interests of the flamboyant Massachusetts politician James M. "Big Jim" Curley. Admitting frankly that he was writing from the jail, Fuller explained: "Suffice to say that I was hamstrung for the machinations of several others who . . . when the hour of accounting arrived . . . played the coward with true talent and left old Jim Fuller to pay the piper for the dance which had been nourished by their own selfish desires.

"However, one may not regret . . . what has been an act of destiny," Fuller continued. "I am convinced that even by this paradoxical crowning of thornes [*sic*] I have been immeasurably blessed . . . for here, in the quiet and even solitude of a place remote from the hustle and bustle and conflicting emotions of the affairs of men one may view the past and enlarge upon the future with cool detachment . . . selecting with more than usual care the instruments by which to make the future more secure and the past less lamentable."

With references to his political work "in the Bay State . . . at Chicago and beyond" on behalf of "Big Jim" Curley, Fuller wrote in grand terms of the great scheme he had in mind that was interrupted by the clanging of the jail door. He asked Fitzgerald to visit him at the jail to discuss these plans, which he described as a "great patriotic accomplishment for which I still have high hopes." The major objective was to contact "Big Jim" Curley, then the Democratic National Committeeman from Massachusetts.

Fitzgerald, who then had a Washington office, visited Fuller at the District of Columbia jail at 200 Nineteenth Street, S.E., and with others helped make the arrangements to obtain Fuller's release and provide the persuasive con man with money to pay off some bad checks and get his big business deals moving.

In late July, or early August, Fitzgerald introduced Fuller to Governor Curley in the lobby of the Hotel Mayflower, an important step in Fuller's plans for the activities of a new firm he was organizing, called Engineers Group, Inc. Curley later said he was unaware of Fuller's criminal record at the time, but the question of whether he knew or not was of little consequence in the total picture. While many men with big names in politics would have cautiously made inquiry, or would have shied away from business dealings with a jailbird, "Big Jim" Curley had never been too fussy about his associates as long as they could help advance his political career or his private fortunes. He certainly couldn't have been sensitive about someone with a jail term, for Curley had served a short jail term in 1904 when he was convicted of impersonating a civil service applicant by agreeing to take a civil service examination for one of his political cronies.

The Boston voters had never held that conviction against the loquacious Irishman, for he had served three terms as Mayor of Boston, one term as Governor, and two terms in the United States House of Representatives.

Jim Fuller, the promoter, and Curley, the political wheelhorse, took to each other immediately. Fuller had big ideas for Engineers Group, Inc., and he wanted Governor James M. Curley to serve as president.

Fuller explained the aluminum shortage at that time created by the sinking of ships from West Africa was harmful to the war effort, and emphasized that the rapid development of the Kalunite deposits in

Utah would be most "patriotic." It was essential to move in with a large number of prominent men and grab control of the Kalunite deposits that were not being properly exploited, Fuller said.

Within a period of a few weeks, Curley as president of Engineers Group, Inc., and several other prominent or respected lawyers and businessmen were providing the cover and credentials for the grandiose schemes of Jim Fuller. It is still unclear how much these men knew about the range of Fuller's activities, but their backing was a masterful accomplishment for a fellow who only a few months earlier had been locked in a cell in a Washington jail with a term that seemed likely to last for two years.

Fuller used the names of his influential officers and directors to convey the impression that Engineers Group, Inc., could deliver war contracts for a fee. He produced false financial statements for clients to indicate that the firm had assets of about $250,000 when it was actually operating on a shoestring budget. Thousands of dollars were enticed from clients anxious to be awarded war contracts. When the contracts were not delivered or when clients complained, Fuller pacified them with letters from his prominent associates. Clients were kept on a string for weeks and months with explanations that the completion of the contract had been delayed through some bureaucratic snarl, and that all would be put in order as soon as Mr. Fuller was able to straighten it out with his special talent. Such client complaints made Fuller's juggling act appear unsteady to officials, including Curley, the firm president.

Early in 1942, Hugh A. Fulton, chief counsel for the Truman war investigating committee, received reports about Engineers Group, Inc. Preliminary investigations by the Truman war investigating committee disclosed the unsavory background of Jim Fuller, and this alone was reason for digging much deeper. More evidence piled up relative to the shoddy manner in which he was dealing in the defense contract area, and documentary evidence came to light reflecting unfavorably upon Curley and others.

Letters and other documents uncovered by the Truman war investigating committee indicated that Curley and Donald Wakefield Smith, formerly an attorney for the National Labor Relations Board, had willingly taken a part in some of Fuller's transactions that were considered to be highly questionable.

* * *

When the hearings opened on April 22, 1942, Rayford W. Alley, a New York lawyer, was the first witness to make public the complaints of his clients, who had made payments of $21,000 to Engineers Group, Inc. The money was paid directly to Fuller, but the contracts were not produced. After weeks of waiting, Alley said he became concerned about whether his clients could get their money refunded. It was then he learned for the first time of Fuller's long criminal record.

Alley demanded to see the books of Engineers Group, Inc., and when he was finally permitted to examine them he found that "none of this money had been kept in trust; it had been siphoned out, and I found that they had collected about $60,000 and as far as I could tell had not performed on a single contract." [2]

The New York lawyer said that he talked with Governor Curley on several occasions at the Hotel Mayflower, and that when he complained of lack of action Curley assured him it was only "because of delays" in the government agencies.[3]

The courtly Governor Curley testified after Alley, and expressed a great desire to straighten out the record on his relations with Fuller and his title as president of Engineers Group, Inc. He said he first met Fuller at the Hotel Mayflower while in the company of his old political friend, Marshall Fitzgerald.

"At that time Mr. Fitzgerald did not intimate, nor at any time, that Mr. Fuller had just been released from jail," Curley said.

Curley related that Fuller had explained his plans for controlling Kalunite, and of the organization of a group of prominent men for the syndicate.

"I agreed to lend my name to that transaction," Curley explained. "He agreed . . . that he [*sic*] had just loaned my name to the syndicate for entirely patriotic motives. At no time was there offered or discussed or expected to receive any profits out of the Kalunite transactions. I understood that I was to be nominally president of the Engineers Group, Inc. . . . However, at no time was any action taken by me as president of that group, although I did understand it would use my name as president.

"At no time did I put any money into the group, nor did I ever take any money out of it, or receive any of its funds," Curley insisted. "I had nothing to do with any of the business transacted by the group, and until November, 1941, did not even know that Engineers Group, Inc., had any other business than the syndicate to acquire Kalunite."

The 67-year-old politician pictured himself as thoroughly naïve and innocent of the war contract deals until November, 1941. At that time, Curley said he had heard a conversation in the office that made him curious, and upon inquiry "learned that the Engineers Group was offering engineering services to persons who were seeking federal contracts." Upon receiving this information, Curley said, he submitted his resignation. However, the committee counsel and committee members grilled him about a delay of more than a month before he actually resigned, as well as other dealings with Fuller that seemed inconsistent with the disillusionment he claimed. They also pointed out that it seemed unusual that Curley had "destroyed all letters" dealing with Engineers Group, Inc., activities.

As Governor Curley was questioned by Counsel Fulton, he insisted he was unaware of Jim Fuller's criminal record, and relied upon the fact that many respectable people were members of the board of directors. Curley reeled off a dozen names of the board of directors and officers to demonstrate that "there was quite a respectable group deceived with me." [4]

"Have you seen the Federal Bureau of Investigation report on Mr. Fuller?" Committee Counsel Fulton said as he passed it to Curley.

"No, I have not," Curley replied. As he glanced at the lengthy document he added: "All I can say is that it is unfortunate I didn't see that before I saw Mr. Fuller."

The F.B.I. report on Fuller was made a part of the committee record by Chairman Truman "so that there will be nobody else deceived by Mr. Fuller."

"He [Fuller] was pretty busy," Curley volunteered.

"There is everything from grand larceny to forgery, false pretenses, intoxication, disorderly conduct, conspiracy to commit forgery, confidence games . . . and then numerous minor offenses," Counsel Fulton summarized it.

"I want to say this for him," Curley said. "I think he was one of the most interesting and best-informed men that I have ever met. He could discuss any subject, from chemistry to art, and discuss them intelligently and fully."

Although at that time Curley denied any political dealings around the war-contract operations of Engineers Group, Inc., there were letters and memoranda that refreshed his memory on some other transactions with another Boston political figure. He admitted that a James F. (Jerry) Fitzgerald had called on the Navy relative to a contract for the West Paint Co., Charlestown, Massachusetts. The firm had later received a $67,000 contract.

With a little prodding, Curley admitted that he had probably called an official of the paint company to try to obtain a political contribution of $5,000 or $6,000 for this intercession.

"What basis would you have for asking a contribution on a contract which somebody obtained through intercession?" Fulton asked.

"I suppose I simply called him up and told him Mr. Fitzgerald had got him a contract for $67,000 and wanted to know if they wanted to contribute to a campaign fund," Curley explained. "They said they had bid ten cents a gallon below the market price and couldn't make any contribution. That is the whole story."

"Did Mr. Fitzgerald often send memorandums like that to you, suggesting this or that party might do some political work, and make a contribution?" asked Senator Joseph Ball, the Minnesota Republican.

"No, no," Curley replied. "But if he did, as a rule, I tore them up."

"You didn't tear this one up?" Ball commented wryly.

"I should have," Curley replied and then tried to cover his slip. "It doesn't make any difference anyway, it had no value."

"Do you remember burning those papers?" Ball asked, referring to the indication of destruction of all of Curley's correspondence with Engineers Group, Inc.

"That is right; I never keep any," Curley replied.

Letters and memoranda written by others contradicted Curley's insistence that he knew little of what Fuller was doing as an influence-peddler. Copies of letters purported to have been written by Curley might have had forged signatures, he declared, and insisted that he had no recollection of having written them. He testified that he had received no money from Fuller or Engineers Group, Inc., but there were a number of checks and other transactions that seemed inconsistent with the story Curley told.

The Truman committee forwarded the cases of James Curley, Jim Fuller and their associates to the Justice Department for further investigation and prosecution. However, as is too often the case, there was a long delay between the investigation and jailing of Curley and Fuller.

In the same year as his appearance before the Senate Committee, Curley was elected to Congress where he served from January 3, 1943 until January 3, 1947. He did not run for reelection to Congress in 1946, but was elected for another term as Mayor of Boston despite conviction on fraud charges arising out of the operations of Engineers Group, Inc.—and a sentence of eighteen months in a federal prison.

War was over by the time Curley went to prison at Danbury, Connecticut, on June 27, 1947. His penalty was lightened by executive clemency, and he continued to draw his salary as mayor through the five months he was actually in the federal prison.

Harry S. Truman, as chairman of the war investigating committee, first exposed Curley, but President Harry S. Truman, the political figure preparing for the 1948 election, granted the executive clemency to the Boston Irish rogue politician that resulted in his release from prison on November 27, 1947. Curley served less than one third of the eighteenth-month sentence.[5]

The experience of Jim Curley was hardly one to discourage future war criminals—those politicians or military men who might be inclined to sell out the nation's interests for political advantage or for personal enrichment. However, there were some who did not need the example of Jim Curley to make them take a chance at profiteering on the edge of war contracts. John D. Corrigan and Robert H. Wells, two graduates of the United States Naval Academy at Annapolis, should have been impressed with the best of Navy tradition and should have set the highest standards as businessmen or as Navy officers. Somehow the lessons and traditions were lost on Corrigan and Wells.

In early 1944, the Truman war investigating committee was advised of complaints that a number of firms dealing with the Navy had been persuaded to pay "consulting fees" to a firm in which Navy Commander John D. Corrigan held an interest. Inquiries revealed that the firm, operating under the name of Corrigan, Osborne and Wells, had received more than $300,000 in such fees from six important Navy contractors.

It was alleged that these contractors had hired the Corrigan, Osborne and Wells firm immediately following inspection visits to their plants by Commander Corrigan. Sharpest criticism of production accomplishments was included in Commander Corrigan's reports. As a result of conversations with the Naval Commander the contractors each decided that it was probably advisable to hire the private engineering and managing firm of Corrigan, Osborne and Wells to iron out their difficulties. Inspection problems miraculously vanished when the Corrigan, Osborne and Wells firm was hired.

Committee Counsel Hugh Fulton compiled a list of the Navy contractors that had found it advantageous to retain the Corrigan firm. The largest amount was the $104,800 from Carl L. Norden, Inc., of Elmira, New York, developer and producer of the Norden bombsight.

Danly Machine Specialists Company, of Chicago, had paid $84,200 in consulting fees to the Corrigan firm. Others included: J. S. Thorne and Company, Philadelphia, $18,306; Bell & Howell, Lincolnwood, Illinois, $29,115; Farrand Optical Company, Woodlawn, New York, $15,705; American Cystoscope Maker, Inc., Brooklyn, New York, $30,690; Edgemoor Iron Works, Wilmington, Delaware, $12,150; and Downington Manufacturing Company, Downington, Pennsylvania, $24,405.[6]

The hearings developed the fact that Corrigan and Wells were in the Naval Reserve when the war broke out. They started the firm in 1941, and though the name Osborne was merely tossed in the middle because Corrigan and Wells thought it added something to the sound, it was really only a two-man show. The firm flourished from the moment Corrigan went back on active duty in 1942.

When Wells testified on May 26, 1944, that "Commander Corrigan has not been a member of our firm since his volunteer entry into the Navy over two years ago," testimony on the same day revealed that records showed Corrigan was still receiving a salary of $1,000 a month from the company while on active duty.[7]

F. C. Wappler, an official with American Cystoscope, testified that Corrigan had inspected the American plant and had threatened him with Navy seizure if they did not hire the Corrigan, Osborne and Wells firm.

Corrigan admitted that he had sent classified Navy documents to his company, to aid the company in its efforts to land consulting business with Navy contractors. In a September 13, 1942, letter to David Armour, of Corrigan, Osborne and Wells, Commander Corrigan had written:

"After you have looked this [list] over and taken whatever data you want off it, will you be kind enough to see that it is destroyed by fire. You will notice at the top that it says 'Restricted,' which means that it is not for general distribution.

"But do yourself and your country a service and sell these people in here a job and then proceed to get them the results that you gave Danly."[8]

In the midst of the hearings in May, 1944, Chairman Truman and Ferguson called for a Navy court-martial of Corrigan, and the record of the Senate hearings was sent to the Navy and the Justice Department for further investigation and prosecution.

On December 19, 1944, Commander Corrigan and two officials of Carl L. Norden, Inc.—Theodore H. Barth and Ward B. Marvielle—were indicted for "conspiring to defraud the government" by restricting production of the vital Norden bombsight to the Norden company. Another indictment was returned the same day against Corrigan and Wells, which charged that they conspired to defraud the government of Corrigan's impartial services.

The case against Corrigan and Wells did not go to trial until November, 1946. Testimony from former employees of Corrigan, Osborne and Wells was important. James F. Gough, a former employee, testified that he left the firm in March, 1944, because of his disgust with the way "business was coming in the back door." He testified that he saw volumes of Navy contracts in the company's offices in New York, and told the court that they were marked "restricted" and "Navy property." Dave Armour, a key official in the firm, declared that the letter of instructions he received with directions to burn it helped him decide to leave his job.

There was testimony from a number of officials of businesses that hired the Corrigan, Osborne and Wells firm about the role of Corrigan in bringing what they considered "pressure" upon them to hire the management firm. William F. Hamilton, an accountant with the Federal Bureau of Investigation, testified that Corrigan had received $35,232 in cash from the Corrigan, Osborne and Wells firm in the period between June 8, 1942, and the spring of 1944 while Corrigan was in the Navy. The F.B.I. accountant testified there were profits of $75,606 that could be traced directly to Corrigan's influence.[9]

The short defense witness list was highlighted by testimony by Navy Captain William W. Juvenal, one of Corrigan's former classmates at Annapolis. Captain Juvenal identified a report he made in recommending a promotion for Corrigan, and the defense stressed that the report credited Corrigan with saving the government "millions of dollars in production costs."[10]

The first trial ended in a hung jury.[11]

The second trial was a repetition of much of the same testimony in May and June of 1947, but there was some significant additional evidence. Admiral T. D. Ruddock testified that at the time Corrigan was appointed to procurement and inspection duties, he was told he must sever all connections with his management consultant firm or run the risk of seeming to have a conflict of interest. Although Corrigan denied the appointment carried such a condition, the jury returned a verdict of guilty. Corrigan was sentenced to eighteen months in federal prison and was fined $5,000, and Wells was sentenced to one year and one day. The company was fined $10,000. Both Corrigan and Wells served a part of their prison terms while appealing the convictions.

On May 28, 1948, the United States Court of Appeals for the Second Circuit in New York upset the convictions of Corrigan and Wells on grounds that there had been technical errors in admitting some testimony into evidence. In remanding the case for a new trial, the Court of Appeals stated there was sufficient evidence to uphold a conviction, but that some additional evidence had been improperly presented before the jury.[12]

Since Corrigan and Wells had already served a substantial part of the prison sentence, the Justice Department did not take the case to trial a third time. The government dropped the other indictment against Corrigan, Wells and the officials of Carl L. Norden, Inc. It was reasoned that since Corrigan and Wells had already paid a heavy penalty, and several witnesses had died, little point would be served in seeking a conviction. Also, by that time the Criminal Division of the Justice Department had its hands full with other more explosive investigations arising out of the questionable handling of military procurement.

7

SENATOR BILBO AND CONGRESSMAN MAY

IT is often necessary for small-businessmen and even some big-businessmen to go to their Congressmen for help in doing business with the big bureaucracies of the federal government. Occasionally it takes a congressional inquiry to jar the bureaucracy into action or explanation on a long-pending matter. In the confusion of wartime industrial expansion, there is even more need for an occasional congressional prod to assure fair treatment for a constituent.

At best, there is a rather fine line between what is proper inquiry by a member of the House or Senate, and an intercession that amounts to undue pressure and influence-peddling. The problem is magnified many times when it involves Senators or Representatives who are chairmen of key committees with appropriation, legislative or investigative power over the agency they are contacting. There must be restraint, for a simple telephone call or letter can be interpreted as political pressure. Particularly, intervention must be avoided in any instance where the Senator or Representative appears to have any direct or indirect personal financial interest.

If there is any financial transaction between the lawmaker and those he helps with government business, it throws deep suspicion around the entire transaction and raises serious questions of "conflict of interest" law violations. The work of the Senate war investigating committee focused attention on two major cases dramatizing all the subtle aspects of the problem of congressional "conflict of interest."

In the fall of 1946, the Senate Special Committee for the Investigation of the Defense Program received information that Senator Theodore G. Bilbo, of Mississippi, had received large sums of money from war contractors. Reports indicated that in addition to money, Senator Bilbo had accepted large gifts of personal property as well as improvements to real estate he owned.

Chief Counsel George Meader directed the preliminary field investigation, which indicated that at least some of the allegations against the veteran Mississippi Senator were probably true. Evidence was presented to the committee on November 18, 1946. Chairman Harley Kilgore (Dem., W. Va.) appointed a three-member subcommittee to pursue the matter, with Senator James M. Mead (Dem. N.Y.) as chairman. Other members were Senator James M. Tunnell (Dem., Del.) and Senator Homer Ferguson (Rep., Mich.). Less than a week later, the subcommittee held its first closed hearing and then announced that public hearings would start on December 12.

This was a touchy investigation involving a member of the Senate club, and the subcommittee proceeded with caution. Bilbo demanded and received notification of the nature of the allegation, and was advised that the committee would be willing to subpoena any witnesses he suggested for first-hand information, at committee expense. Forrest Jackson, attorney for Senator Bilbo, notified the committee it should go ahead with its witnesses as Senator Bilbo had no witnesses to suggest.

Because of the inflammatory and highly controversial positions Senator Bilbo assumed on race issues, the subcommittee took great pains to explain that the investigation was limited to Senator Bilbo's relations with war contractors and was not to be concerned with issues of racial or religious minority groups. Nor would this committee probe allegations of campaign-expenditure irregularities made against Senator Bilbo in connection with the 1946 campaign. A Senate Committee to Investigate Senatorial Campaign Expenditures was already involved in a study of those matters.

Testimony was clear and undisputed that Senator Bilbo had assisted a number of contractors in obtaining national defense construction contracts in his home state of Mississippi. There was the cost-plus-fixed-fee contract for the Camp Jackson Army Air Base near Jackson, Mississippi, by the M. T. Reed Construction Company at a total cost of $2,639,983.84. Bilbo had also helped several other firms land the $1,731,129.75 contract for construction of the cantonment at Key Field, near Meridian, Miss. Those involved in the joint venture were A. B. Friend, Volz Construction Company, Rock City Construction, and Flint-Jordan Construction Company. Another joint venture involved J. A. Jones Construction Company, B. L. Knost and Newton & Glenn Company.

In all there were more than a dozen contracts involved in the hearings, with the total amount exceeding $25,000,000.[1]

Testimony and documents before the committee showed that during the same period of time Bilbo was helping the contractors, they were being generous with him. The Mississippi Senator accepted a $1,900 Cadillac sedan, at least $500 in home furnishings and a $6,658 construction job on his estate at Poplarville, Mississippi that included an artificial lake, a swimming pool and a new coat of paint for the house.

Although the contractors had billed Senator Bilbo for the improvements made as early as 1941 and 1942, the records showed that as of late 1946 the Senator had paid only $200 on the paint job.

Also, in those early war years, Senator Bilbo had permitted Michael T. Morrissey, a war contractor, to take a loss of $48,043.28 in connection with the operations of Senator Bilbo's farm.[2]

In late 1942, Senator Bilbo received $30,000 from three of the war contractors for whom he had interceded. The money was claimed to be campaign contributions to an informal committee for the costs of a primary campaign for Wall Doxey, a candidate for the Democratic nomination for the United States Senate in Mississippi.

Between February, 1943, and the end of August, 1945, Senator Bilbo collected $27,501 from war contractors and others to build a church parsonage for the Juniper Grove Baptist Church at Poplarville, Miss. The parsonage was on land owned by Bilbo. At least $7,300 of this money came from war contractors who had been aided by Bilbo.

Senator Bilbo contended that there was no relationship between the money and the favors he received from war contractors and the services he performed for them in connection with contracts. He maintained he was merely doing what any Senator or Representative would do in assisting his constituents in obtaining and performing war contracts. The Senate committee was unwilling to accept the theory of Senator Bilbo and his lawyer.

In its report on the Bilbo matter, the Senate committee stated that there would be no impropriety if Senator Bilbo had merely helped a constituent. "The impropriety of Senator Bilbo's actions consists in the acceptance of gifts, services and political contributions from the same contractors whom he aided." [3]

The Senate committee stated that the evidence relative to the Cadillac, the home furnishings and the improvements on Bilbo's land "were not bona fide transactions in the ordinary course of business" but were in fact a "subterfuge to conceal" the payments and services rendered to Bilbo.

With regard to the large campaign contributions, the committee pointed out that "the donation and solicitation of political contributions from Government contractors while they are negotiating or performing such contracts is prohibited by a Federal criminal statute (Title 18, Sec. 61m-1, U.S.C.).

"In some instances the war contractors in making political contributions and in making improvements on Senator Bilbo's estate, sought to charge the cost of such contributions and services as expenses on their books," the report continued.[4] "Twenty thousand dollars of the F. T. Newton political contribution of $25,000 was originally charged directly to war contracts on the books of Newton & Glenn. These entries were changed on their books only after disallowance either by their own auditors or by Government agents. Five thousand dollars of this $25,000 was never located on the contractors' books."

The committee was equally critical of circumstances under which the parsonage, partially constructed with funds from war contractors, remained in Bilbo's name a full two years after it was completed. At best, the parsonage was Senator Bilbo's personal philanthropic enterprise, and "it was improper for him to utilize the aid he had given the war contractors as a means of inducing them to contribute substantial amounts to his personal charities, administered solely by him."

Senator Bilbo, a member of a four-man committee collecting funds for Wall Doxey's campaign, was, in his own words, a good "collector" of campaign funds, and he admitted that he had solicited the $5,000 collected from B. L. Knost and the $25,000 from F. T. Newton.

The committee pointed out that on July 19, 1940, Congress had passed the law to prohibit campaign contributions by defense contractors "to remove or at least minimize, one source of corruption in politics.

"It was precisely this sort of activity [involving Bilbo and his collection of campaign money] in connection with the national defense program which the Senate created this committee to investigate and expose," the committee stated.[5]

In examining the law in Title 18, Section 61m-1 of the United States Code, the committee concluded that there was an important loophole: "It has been impressed upon the committee that the statute is limited in its application to those who contribute funds and those who knowingly solicit funds, but is silent as to those who knowingly accept or receive illegal contributions."

Senator Bilbo took the witness stand before the committee on December 19, 1946. At the beginning of his forty-one-page refutation of the charges against him, the Senator was confident and appeared almost jaunty. During Bilbo's testimony regarding his campaign-contribution solicitations, Senator Ferguson warned him of the penalties involved in such offenses—five years in prison and a fine of up to $5,000 for illegal contributions of $5,000 or more. Ferguson also commented on the fact that Bilbo had voted against passage of the 1940 law and snapped at the witness, "I hope you don't think that just because you voted against the law you don't have to obey it."[6]

Bilbo had a great deal of difficulty in trying to "recollect" his nefarious business dealings when subjected to the direct questioning of the committee.

By the end of his six hours before the committee Bilbo was a broken man, lisping as a result of a mouth operation that kept him from wearing his lower plate and raging at his former secretary, Edward P. Terry, for testifying against him.

Terry, he declared, was worse than Judas Iscariot, Benedict Arnold and Brutus. His was a plea for mercy, as he contended that the testimony against him only showed that he was "a very poor man and heavily involved in debt." As was expected, the Mississippi Democrat tried to blame all his difficulties on the Communists and Negroes who he said were his enemies.

When the Eightieth Congress opened on January 4, 1947, the seating of Bilbo was disputed; Senator Homer Ferguson, the Michigan Republican, read the report of the Senate committee on Bilbo's activities.[7]

The conclusion was that Bilbo "used his high office as United States Senator for his personal gain in his dealings with war contractors." Although there was no recommendation for action, the Republicans were joined by a group of Northern Democrats in opposition to seating the cantankerous and corrupt Mississippi Senator. However, no action was to be taken pending the return of Bilbo, who was suffering from cancer. Bilbo left Washington vowing to fight for his Senate seat, "till Hell freezes over. If I live I'll be back with my fighting clothes on." [8]

The showdown never came, for Bilbo died on August 21, 1947, without ever attempting to resume his seat.

Those United States Senators and Representatives who are members of the committees dealing with military affairs are in a strong position to pressure the civilian political appointees as well as the career military officials at the Pentagon. And, it is a recognized fact of life in Washington that the men who rule as chairmen of the military affairs committees and the appropriations subcommittees dealing with defense spending often receive unusual consideration when they make requests or even make suggestions. High military officers and civilian political bosses frequently give fawning attention to these powerful chairmen, and find reasons for loading their political areas with military bases and defense contracts.

Andrew Jackson May, a tough country lawyer from the mountains of eastern Kentucky, had been in Congress for ten years when World War II started. His seniority gave the sixty-five-year-old Kentucky man the chairmanship of the House Military Affairs Committee, with all the prestige and influence that went with that job in wartime America. It was his duty, as it was the duty of the special Truman war investigating committee, to keep an eye on the operations of the military departments, to question and to challenge—to make certain that the best judgment was going into military decisions and the government was getting its money's worth in defense spending.

Throughout World War II, wily Andy May ran his House Military Affairs Committee with a tough hand, and he gave the impression of a man dedicated to a strong defense system for the United States with only a normal amount of concern for getting the Pentagon to take care of folks back in his district. It was not until the war was over that the spotlight of the Senate war investigating committee started to focus on some of Chairman May's financial dealings with war contractors.

On July 2, 1946, the Senate committee heard testimony that May, as Chairman of the House Military Affairs Committee, had brought pressure on the Army to award war contracts to a combine that included nineteen Illinois manufacturers. Earlier, testimony indicated that this combine had been engaged in "war profiteering." Major General J. H. Campbell, Jr., Chief of Army Ordnance, testified that May had contacted him by phone in an effort to receive favored consideration for the combine. Campbell had taken the time to have a transcription made of the conversation. It was read into the hearing proceedings.[9]

Senator James M. Mead, the New York Democrat who had become chairman of the investigating committee, was outraged at the testimony of profiteering by Dr. Henry M. Garsson and his brother, Murray Garsson, a former Labor Department employee—the key figures in the combine. There was testimony that the combine received more than $78,000,000 in war contracts, and that the four top officials in the combine had voted themselves salaries of $1,380,000 in less than four years.

Under pressure of the testimony by Army officers that linked him to the Garsson operations, May felt compelled to go before the Senate committee in a closed session on July 4. When the testimony was made public three days later, it disclosed that May admitted acting as an agent for Cumberland Lumber Company, in his home town of Prestonsburg, Kentucky. The Kentucky Congressman, then seventy-one years of age, admitted that he had endorsed checks from the Garsson combine munitions firm, but denied that he had made any money in the financial transactions with the Garsson empire. May denied that he was head of the Garsson-owned Cumberland Lumber Company, despite the fact that he had endorsed one check as "A. J. May, President."

Evidence continued to pile up against May and the Garsson combine. The Garsson empire was accused of reaping $3,520,000 in "excessive profits," and there was evidence that the Pentagon was charged for the expensive gifts and the lavish entertainment for high military and civilian officials. At a time when the nation was at war, a major general and at least four other high-ranking officers received military orders to attend a wedding party for Dr. Henry Garsson's daughter in New York. The Garsson combine picked up the tab for the costs for the officers and for Congressman May, who also attended.

As a member of the House, May normally would have been considered outside of the reach of a Senate subpoena, but this time the Senate war investigating committee took the unusual step of issuing a subpoena for a House member. While Congress was in session, May could ignore the subpoena, but under the pressure of public criticism he agreed to appear on July 25.

Representative May, in the middle of an election campaign, reported that he had suffered a heart attack and could not appear. He submitted an unsworn statement that was rejected by Chairman Mead. On July 26, May's personal physician, Dr. Henry M. Lowden, appeared before the committee and explained that testimony from the Congressman would be delayed for ten days to two weeks because of his heart attack. Chairman Mead replied that rather than adjourn for the summer, the committee would reconvene "whenever Mr. May is able to appear." May said that he would testify before the Senate committee either at his home in Kentucky or in Washington after he had recovered from his heart attack.[10]

Regardless of the fact that May avoided testimony prior to the 1946 election, the impact of the war scandals was sufficient to turn the voters in his home district against him. He was defeated in his bid for reelection.

May was indicted on a charge of accepting a bribe from the Garsson empire, and the Garsson brothers were indicted on "conspiring to defraud the Government of May's services through bribery." Among those giving testimony in the trial were Secretary of War Robert P. Patterson and General Dwight D. Eisenhower, both of whom had been approached by May on behalf of companies in the Garsson combine.

On July 3, 1947—just a year after the case broke open—former Congressman May and the Garssons were sentenced to terms of eight months to two years in the federal penitentiary. May wept as the jury pronounced the verdict, but later told reporters, "I'm still not daunted, we'll appeal it." [11]

May's appeal failed, and two years later, on December 5, 1949, the former Kentucky Congressman was ordered by the courts to begin serving his term. Only nine months and thirteen days later, May was released from prison. The justification was his advanced age, his "poor physical condition," and his "outstanding institutional record."

In June, 1952, the Kentucky Court of Appeals restored the seventy-seven-year-old lawyer's right to practice in the courts of his home state. On December 25, 1952, President Truman granted May a full pardon that restored his citizenship rights. President Truman took this action only a month before he was to leave the White House and turn the government over to a Republican Administration.[12]

Through this series of events, Andy May, a man who sold out his important governmental responsibility in wartime, was restored to his full rights of citizenship, drew a lifetime government pension of $280 a month, and was able to practice law in his home town of Prestonsburg, Kentucky, until he died on September 6, 1959, at the age of eighty-four.

The Garssons did not fare as well. They served twenty-month prison terms, and it took a court order to permit Henry Garsson to regain his engineering license. He went into business as a consulting engineer in New York. Murray Garsson, penniless and homeless, died in a ward at New York's Bellevue Hospital in 1957.

Even before May and the Garsson brothers began serving their prison terms for fraudulent wartime activity, public attention was diverted by major investigations involving exposure of other military scandals. Republicans had taken control of the Senate war investigating committee, and they were eagerly pursuing evidence of mismanagement and misdoings that cast shadows as far as the White House.

8

HOWARD HUGHES—WHITE HOUSE CONNECTION

TESTIMONY concerning party girls and high living on a wartime expense account focused public attention on the investigations of Major General Bennett E. Meyers and the highly questionable circumstances under which some contracts were awarded to the enterprises of Howard Hughes, the millionaire industrialist. But the record of those hearings by the Special Committee Investigating the National Defense Program contained much more important lessons about the price the United States taxpayers paid for the decisions of unqualified political appointees who combined with lax and corrupt military officials to force the signing of war contracts.

Assuming that the Republican-controlled Congress that dominated the investigating committee in 1947 perhaps had some political incentive for the investigations of the multimillion-dollar contracts for the Hughes-Kaiser flying boat and the Hughes photo-reconnaissance plane, nevertheless the unusual circumstances under which both were let demanded that questions be raised. Normal procedural safeguards were avoided, and the two projects were kept going by pouring in additional millions long after it was apparent that both contracts were "failures as war contracts."

Opinions of qualified technical experts were disregarded. Views of qualified military men were discarded. Under the weight of political "pressures" other high military men were convinced that it was wise to change their views and do as the politically appointed Cabinet and sub-Cabinet officers directed. As a result millions of dollars of tax money were wasted on projects that stood little chance of being useful for war, and only slight chance of being of experimental value.

The chairman of the war investigating committee was then Senator Owen Brewster (Rep., Me.), but he assigned the Hughes investigation to a subcommittee headed by Senator Homer Ferguson (Rep., Mich.). Other members of that subcommittee were Senator Joseph R. Mc-

Carthy (Rep., Wis.), Senator George W. Malone (Rep., Nev.), Senator Carl A. Hatch (Dem., N. Mex.) and Senator Herbert R. O'Conor (Dem., Md.). The chief counsel was William P. Rogers, who later became Attorney General in the Eisenhower Administration.

As Chairman Ferguson opened the hearing on November 5, 1947, he noted that ten months earlier the committee was told "that approximately $40,000,000 in public funds had been expended or committed in contracts to obtain a number of large flying boats and a photo-reconnaissance plane which were to be built by the Hughes Tool Company.

"No flyable planes were completed for use during the war," Chairman Ferguson pointed out and added: "The flying boat and the photo-reconnaissance projects did involve departures from normal wartime procurement channels." [1] As the testimony developed, Chairman Ferguson's comments about irregular procurements proved to be an understatement.

* * *

Howard R. Hughes, millionaire industrialist and airplane enthusiast, established the Hughes Aircraft Company, at Culver City, California, as a division of Hughes Tool Company. Initially, the Hughes Aircraft Company was started in 1933 for the purpose of manufacturing airplanes, but it operated on a small scale and built its first single-engine racing plane, the D-1, in 1935.

In 1939, Hughes started work on the second plane, a two-engined, twin-boomed interceptor, which was to be known as the D-2. However, Hughes Aircraft, engaged primarily in aircraft design and experimentation, had never produced airplanes on a commercial scale up to 1942, when he started to work on an $18,000,000 flying boat project in cooperation with Henry J. Kaiser. The highly controversial $21,000,000 contract for one hundred one photo-reconnaissance planes came a year later, in October, 1943.

* * *

By the spring of 1942, the German submarine activity had caused shipping loss tonnage that exceeded the United States shipbuilding production rate. A huge cargo-carrying plane seemed to be the answer, and the War Production Board, then chaired by Donald Nelson, appointed a committee to suggest a means of providing more cargo planes without substantially interfering with the production of combat planes.

Industrialist-politician Henry J. Kaiser took an immediate interest in the idea, suggesting mass production of 70-ton cargo planes and the design of a 200-ton cargo plane. His grandiose plan called for production of five hundred of the 200-ton cargo planes, which were much larger than any plane then contemplated.

In the face of the huge shipping losses, the big Kaiser project caught the public imagination, for Kaiser also suggested the work be done in shipyards then idle because of an inadequate supply of steel plate.

Although recognized authorities in the airplane industry rejected the Kaiser project, he tried to sell the Roosevelt Administration on a large contract with a big public relations push. He produced no detailed plans of the project for the Army, Navy, or the War Production Board, and there were no specific designs for the proposed plane that this so-called industrial genius wanted the government to buy.

In a conversation with Glenn L. Martin, president of the Glenn L. Martin Company, Kaiser declared that he "would go to high places and get the order" despite the objections from the Army and Navy and other high officials who would normally have made the decision on such a project. Martin told Kaiser he wanted no part of it, and would not help Kaiser in trying to override the regular Army and Navy channels.[2]

Kaiser's next effort to sell the idea to Donald Nelson, chairman of the War Production Board, ran into the objections of three prominent aircraft manufacturers who were named to a committee to help advise Nelson. The meeting broke up with no decision, and it was at this point that Kaiser talked with Howard Hughes, suggested a joint project and went back to Donald Nelson for another try.

On September 10, 1942, Nelson approved a production contract for the huge flying boat, which provided that Kaiser-Hughes would build three prototypes and design a plant capable of producing one cargo plane a day. While the War Department and Navy Department still objected to the project, they agreed two days later to make engines and other equipment available for the project.

In a highly unusual procedure, the War Production Board directed that the Defense Plant Corporation issue the letter of intent on the three flying boats at a cost not to exceed $18,000,000. It was the only contract of this type let through the Defense Plant Corporation, and that corporation had no real supervisory control over the project under the arrangements. The designs and engineering were to be approved by the National Advisory Committee for Aeronautics and the Civil Aeronautics Administration.

Kaiser's big public relations campaign paid off, and in October, 1942, the Kaiser-Hughes project moved forward in the face of the opposition "from the armed services, the Joint Chiefs of Staff, and many experts in the War Production Board and the aircraft industry." [3]

No date for completion of the three planes was stated in the contract, even though the initial letter of intent had limited the liability of the Defense Plant Corporation for advancing funds for two years, and stated that the three planes would be completed by October, 1944.

The largest plane built up to that time was the 70-ton flying boat, the Martin Mars, and the Kaiser-Hughes plane was to have essentially three times that capacity. Initially, Kaiser had proposed a twin-boom high-wing flying boat, and this was the general concept included in the contract. However, as the first plane was put into construction it became a single-fuselage flying boat, far in excess of 200 tons, with a 320-foot wing span, a 200-foot length, and a tail five stories high. The power came from eight 3,000-horsepower engines, and it was designed to carry 700 soldiers with full equipment.[4]

The Kaiser-Hughes flying-boat project proceeded with practically no government supervision and little objection, despite the fact that nearly every aspect of the initial agreement was violated at some step. In the first place, the project was a drain on manpower, which was critically short on the West Coast. Officials of the Defense Plant Corporation contended they had only limited authority in supervising construction of the facilities for the plane production and the disbursement of funds. They were given to understand that Hughes had "sole decision" as to design, materials, and methods of construction. The Civil Aeronautics Administration considered its responsibility limited to seeing that the plane met the type-certification requirement at the time it was ready to fly. The National Advisory Committee for Aeronautics assumed only the responsibility to test models of the plane.

When the War Production Board reviewed the progress on the flying boat in October, 1943, they found the cost estimates had gone up and the airplane was to be much heavier than they had been told. After one year of work, the first flying boat was only five percent complete, but nearly $10,000,000 had been spent. If the plane was to have any value in connection with plans of the General Staff, it was essential that it be completed by the fall of 1944.

There was unanimous agreement that the continuance of the project "was not desirable from a technical standpoint and it was decided that unless the armed services objected, to cancel the project." Technical experts from the Army and Navy found the wooden construction was "excessively heavy and unreliable" and concluded that the Martin Mars was a much better plane than this flying boat would ever be.[5]

The National Advisory Committee for Aeronautics stated bluntly that "continuance of this project of constructing the HK flying boat of wood serves no useful purpose in the interest of advancing the American aviation art." Also an assistant to the Secretary of Commerce went beyond the war needs, and commented: "It is difficult to see that this airplane is likely to have real utility in postwar commercial air transportation."[6]

War Production Board Chief Nelson asked Jesse H. Jones, then Secretary of Commerce and Federal Loan Administrator, to cancel the contract in early February, 1944, but wanted Kaiser-Hughes to submit a proposal for developing the flying boat in metal. On February 16, 1944, Jones notified Nelson that the contract was canceled and the new proposal requested. He told Nelson that $13,500,000 had been spent on the project, and that Hughes estimated that completion of just one plane would cost an additional $6,500,000.

Despite the pessimistic outlook for the circumstances, Hughes balked at switching to a metal plane as requested. Nelson and Charles E. Wilson, Executive Vice Chairman of the War Production Board, assumed the contract was ended. Wilson was surprised some weeks later to learn that Secretary of Commerce Jones had ordered Nelson to reinstate the flying boat contract on March 27, 1944.

Jones, a friend of Hughes, stopped to see President Roosevelt following the Cabinet meeting on February 18, 1944, and told him Nelson had instructed him to cancel the contract on the advice of technical experts and military men. It was on orders from Roosevelt that Jones went back to Nelson and stated that construction on the wooden flying boat should be continued.[7] Kaiser was left out of the second contract, which called for only one flying boat for the $18,000,000. The contract also provided for the Reconstruction Finance Corporation to pay $500,000 for moving the plane to Long Beach, California, and $1,000,000 for the actual flight testing.

The views of technical aviation experts and the professional military men were constantly disregarded in this project in favor of the views of political figures, including friends of Kaiser and Hughes, who could always find reasons for spending more millions of tax money. A project that was initially to cost the government $18,000,000 for three planes ended as a project that cost $19,615,970.44 for one plane that was the thorough failure the experts had predicted.[8]

The investigation developed evidence of "poor management and resultant waste" that compounded the problems in this project. "Although top management at the plant was changed several times, efficiency was never achieved," the Senate war investigating committee found. "Much of the delay and waste was attributable to Hughes' insistence upon retaining personal control of the operation yet failing to devote proper attention to the project." The flying boat project violated almost all of the rules that should have been learned from failures in earlier wars.

The Hughes photo-reconnaissance plane, the F-11, provided an even more shocking spectacle of mismanagement of defense spending with overtones of corruption. Again there was the familiar pattern of disregard for the proper contract procedures, and the intervention of important political figures. Also, in this instance there were examples of corruption and laxity on the part of high Army officers.

Through his personal flying feats, Howard Hughes had established a reputation in the aviation field; when World War II approached he was eager to get into the field of military aircraft production. In September, 1939, his company started work on the two-engine wooden interceptor plane that he hoped to sell to the military services. There were negotiations in early 1940 as the Air Force showed interest in his D-2 plane. However, as the months moved on, Hughes changed his plane from an interceptor into a five-place medium bomber, and in the spring of 1941, he redesigned it as a two-place fighter.

The combination of the distracting design changes, plus the extreme secrecy with which Hughes surrounded his work, caused the Air Force to lose interest. The Matériel Command opposed the use of wood in the plane, and in January, 1942, the Chief of the Experimental Engineering Section of the Matériel Division recommended that the Air Corps discontinue its interest in any Hughes project, noting in his statement:

"It is the opinion of this office that this [Hughes Aircraft] plant is a hobby of the management and that the present project now being engineered is a waste of time and that the facilities, both in engineering personnel and in equipment, are not being used to the full adtange of this [war] emergency." [9]

In the face of that conclusion, only six months later Hughes was advised that Wright Field was interested in recommending the purchase of the D-2 for $500,000. Hughes wasn't interested in a sale then, and decided to wait until he had flown the plane, at which time he would seek reimbursement for the $3,000,000 he claimed he had spent on the development.

Failing through the normal channel, the Hughes firm then started working on Hughes' old friend, Secretary of Commerce Jesse Jones. Russell Birdwell, doing public relations work for Hughes, prepared a fancy brochure praising the potential of the D-2 and sent it to Jones, who presented it to President Roosevelt. Only a few days later on July 7, 1942, President Roosevelt sent a memorandum to General H. H. Arnold, then Commanding General of the Air Force. He enclosed the information received from Jones, and a pointed question: "What is there in this?"

The next day, General Arnold informed President Roosevelt that the Air Force was carrying on negotiations with Hughes, and that if the plane was successfully flight-tested they might buy the plane and absorb the development costs. That seemed to end it, for there was no government activity for almost a year when the United States had an urgent need for a higher speed and longer-range photo-reconnaissance plane than was then available.

In late June, 1943, General Arnold indicated to his staff that the Air Force would probably have to buy the Hughes D-2 for use as the photo-reconnaissance plane they needed, and negotiations were opened.

The Air Force, which had given no earlier indications of any great need for a photo-reconnaissance plane, suddenly found this to be a vital project in the summer of 1943. Colonel Elliott Roosevelt, who had commanded the photo-reconnaissance unit in the North African theater, and Lieutenant Colonel Karl L. Prolifka, who had considerable combat experience in the Pacific, were summoned to Washington by the Air Force. A group of a half dozen officers under Colonel Roosevelt made an inspection trip in August, 1943, which included a visit to the Hughes plant and inspection of the Hughes plane.

The report by Colonel Roosevelt recommended immediate procurement of the Hughes plane, and he stated that Hughes would have to have the reconnaissance plane ready for flight-testing in five months. The report also stated that Hughes had advised Colonel Roosevelt's group that he would be willing to include penalty clauses in the contract to insure prompt delivery.

There was little coordination between Colonel Roosevelt and the Air Force division that normally directed buying policies. Even as Colonel Roosevelt was on his inspection tour and concluding that the Hughes plane was just what was needed, Major General Oliver P. Echols, then Chief of Matériel Maintenance and Distribution, wrote a memorandum to the Chief of Air Staff expressing "grave doubts" about the advisability of building any high-performance airplane out of plywood.

General Echols recommended against any actions that would favor the Hughes plane, and added that the Hughes photo-reconnaissance plane "has not progressed favorably to date and . . . shows so little promise in the future." The same opposition to the Hughes plane was expressed by Brigadier General B. W. Chidlaw, who followed Echols as Chief of the Matériel Division of Maintenance and Distribution.

Nevertheless, after General Arnold directed General Echols to take steps to contract with Hughes for the photo-reconnaissance plane, General Echols sent back a memorandum on September 3, 1943, strongly advising against the Hughes plane.

A few days earlier, on August 21, Colonel Roosevelt was appointed Chief of the Reconnaissance Branch, Requirements Division, Air Force Headquarters. On September 3, in this new capacity, he issued the written military characteristics for a photo-reconnaissance plane that fit the Hughes plane in detail. It was not the accepted procedure, for in normal channels officers had been working independently on another set of characteristics for a long-range, high-speed, high-altitude photo-reconnaissance plane with requirements the Hughes plane could not meet.

The plans prepared by Colonel Roosevelt were marked "special" and were given precedence over the plans that came through regular channels. A reluctant General Echols did as he was directed and ordered one hundred Hughes planes, but he included in the order the statement that General Arnold has issued oral instructions for this procurement following a recommendation from Colonel Roosevelt.[10]

On October 11, 1943, the Air Force issued the "letter of intent" to Hughes Aircraft for production of one hundred one photo-reconnaissance planes, including one skeleton plane for static tests. It was a cost-plus-fixed-free arrangement with an estimated cost of $48,555,000 exclusive of a fixed fee not to exceed four percent. It called for delivery of a flyable plane in one year, with ten planes a month after that and full delivery by September, 1946.

The plane was designated as the F-11, but the actual contract was not signed for ten months. There were extensive negotiations on details, with a $70,274,666.86 fixed-price contract as the end result, but with no satisfactory explanation for this $22,000,000 price increase. Furthermore, there was failure at some point in the negotiation to include the penalty clauses that had been regarded as so important to insure prompt delivery. In addition to this highly favorable modification, Hughes was insisting that the government also reimburse him for the $3,300,000 he claimed he had spent on developing the D-2, his forerunner to the F-11.

Again, career military men and technical experts balked at giving Hughes the extra $3,300,000. But another high-ranking military officer recommended giving most of the money to Hughes—Major General Bennett E. Meyers, then the Deputy Chief of Staff for Matériel, Maintenance and Distribution at Wright Field. In this variation from normal procedures, it was agreed to pay Hughes $1,900,000 of the $3,300,000 he asked.[11]

Even after General Meyers approved the contract for the Air Force on May 13, 1944, there were objections to the way the development costs were handled. The protest came from Brigadier General Albert J. Browning, Special Representative of the Under Secretary of War, who declined to sign the contract because of the irregular procedures and the high cost of the planes.

Under Secretary of War Robert P. Patterson ordered General Browning to approve the F-11 contract after receiving a memorandum from General Arnold personally advising him there was urgent military need for the F-11 and that the contract should be placed at once. It was the only time in his wartime experience as special assistant to Patterson that he was directed in writing to approve a contract, General Browning explained later.[12]

After the contract was finally signed, Hughes still continued to tinker with the plane design, changing it several times, engaging in disputes with his plant managers, and personally involving himself in administrative and personnel problems that created "chaotic" conditions. The position of general manager had a rapid turnover, and on one occasion there was a mass resignation of twenty-one engineers.

Hughes did not meet the production schedules, but there was no penalty clause in the contract. When the war ended in 1945, there had still been no delivery on the F-11 that had been so urgently needed in 1943. The Air Force negotiated a termination settlement with Hughes on April 26, 1946, with the net amount set at $8,642,242. A later General Accounting Office audit disclosed that Hughes Aircraft was overpaid by $326,333.26, although no fraud existed. Under the Contract Settlement Act of 1944, the government could not make a legal demand for the overpayment unless fraud was involved.

It was not until July 7, 1946, that the F-11 made its initial test flight, with Howard Hughes, as the test pilot. The plane crashed as a result of a malfunctioning of a propeller, but the Air Force investigators concluded that the accident could have been avoided if Hughes had followed test-flight instructions.

Although the long-awaited F-11 was completely demolished in the crash, the Army, for bookkeeping purposes and in accordance with contract provisions, accepted delivery in January, 1947.[13] The second F-11 was test-flown by Hughes and accepted in March, 1948. In all, the government had expended or committed approximately $22,000,000 on the F-11 and had received one static model, one pile of junk, and one plane. Even though it might have had some value as a postwar experimental plane, the F-11 was a failure as a war project.

The Air Force had to share the responsibility with Hughes Aircraft for this failure, for there was adequate evidence of submission to forces other than the judgment of experts and the best pricing procedures.

"There is no doubt that a feeling existed among certain Air Force officers that pressures from sources outside the Air Force influenced this project," the Senate war investigating committee concluded.[14] This is shown by the Air Force record in which various officers as well as Assistant Secretary Lovett made direct references to the "pressure" and "outside pressure" involved in the project. The "unusual circumstances" surrounding this award "included the part played by Colonel Elliott Roosevelt."

The lavish spending practices of John W. Meyer, a public relations specialist for Hughes, was another of the unusual circumstances criticized by the Senate war investigating committee. The General Accounting Office audit of the Hughes Tool Company from 1941 through 1946 disclosed that the free-wheeling Johnny Meyer spent at least $169,661.17 on a wide range of entertainment for military officers and public officials, including party girls. There were additional large expenses incurred by Meyer and other Hughes representatives at hotels and nightclubs; they were billed directly to the company and could not be traced to individual expense accounts.

Hughes contended that there was prejudice against him in the military services, and that it was necessary to entertain lavishly and extend hospitality to Air Force officers in order to overcome this. Hughes said he took Meyer off a public relations job for the Hughes movie interests and directed him to launch the big spending campaign to create better relations with government officials. At the request of the Hughes Aircraft Company, Meyer was granted a draft deferment on several occasions during the war on grounds that in negotiating war contracts he was performing duties essential to the national defense.

The war investigating committee was critical of Hughes for lavishly entertaining officials with whom his firms did business, and was equally critical of those officials who accepted entertainment from the Hughes representatives. The committee pointed out that General Arnold on March 27, 1942, had issued instructions warning that acceptance of gratuities or casual entertainment by Army Air Force officers could "seriously impair public confidence."

"Obviously Hughes was not the only war contractor who spent money on Government officials during the war period in order to gain favor," the committee stated. "The committee is aware that many war contractors sought to curry favor with and influence the decisions of Government officials by this means. This practice ranged from innocently tendered, inexpensive luncheons to lavish entertainment, expensive gifts, and promises of high-paying positions by which contractors intended to influence public officials. . . . Procurement agencies should do everything within their power to prevent such practices and it should be established policy to take prompt and drastic action against those officials who accept such benefits."

The war investigating committee's study of the role of Major General Benny Meyers provides us with a classic example of laxity and corruption at the highest level in the military procurement area. As Deputy Chief of Staff for Matériel, Maintenance and Distribution, he was on the highest policy level in the Air Force purchasing organization. He signed the F-11 contract with Hughes, and took a number of other actions that were highly beneficial to the Hughes interests.

The Republican majority report on the investigation of the two controversial Howard Hughes contracts was signed by Senator Owen Brewster, of Maine, chairman of the full committee; Senator Homer Ferguson, of Michigan, chairman of the subcommittee; Senator Joseph R. McCarthy, of Wisconsin; Senator John J. Williams, of Delaware; Senator George W. Malone, of Nevada; and Senator Harry P. Cain, of Washington.

The four Democratic members of the war investigating committee wrote a minority report that challenged what they called "inference and innuendo" in the majority report "implying grave wrongdoing not expressly charged." The four Democrats signing the minority report were Senator Carl A. Hatch, of New Mexico; Senator Claude Pepper, of Florida; Senator J. Howard McGrath, of Rhode Island; and Senator Herbert R. O'Conor, of Maryland.

The Democrats resented the implications of questionable activity on the part of Hughes or of high officials of the Roosevelt Administration, and declared "it is unfortunate" that the Republican-controlled committee "selected the Hughes contracts as the only one [*sic*] to be investigated among all the Government's wartime contracts for aircraft.

"Of the many billions of dollars spent by the Government for airplanes in the war, the Hughes and Hughes-Kaiser contracts amounted to approximately $40,000,000 or only a fraction of one percent," the minority members said critically. "While it is true that no airplanes were delivered by Hughes in time for combat service, it is also true from evidence submitted that the Government bought and paid for 61 other types of planes at a cost of hundreds of millions of dollars that likewise never saw combat service. None of these contracts has been made the subject of an investigation." [15]

The Democrats objected to the inclusion of comments on the corrupt role of General Benny Meyers in his dealings with the Meyers-created Aviation Electric Corporation and Bleriot Lamarre, the firm's treasurer, in a manner that did not specifically absolve Howard Hughes of wrongdoing. "In the report on the Howard Hughes investigation there should have been no reference whatever concerning General Meyers and his activities, except those connected with Hughes or his companies," they contended.[16] "There is absolutely nothing in the evidence that discloses any fraud, corruption or wrongdoing [*sic*] on the part of Howard Hughes or his associates.[17]

"There was no political pressure brought to bear in the letting of the contracts for either the photo-reconnaissance airplane or the flying boat," the minority claimed, in an effort to remove the unfavorable reflections on the Roosevelt Administration. There was also the Democratic contention that there was no evidence of "excessive profits" for Hughes and that in fact Hughes claimed he spent "some $7,000,000 of his own money, for which he was not reimbursed."

The Republicans answered the Democrats in another special report that pointed out that investigations had covered "numerous" aircraft contracts, and had been critical in at least a half-dozen cases.[18] With regard to the element of "political pressure" the Republicans cited a recorded telephone conversation between General Benny Meyers and Robert Lovett, the Secretary of War for Air, that was a part of the evidence. Lovett, speaking of the F-11 contract, had said:

"Benny, my own feeling is that I never like any of these projects that are gone into under outside pressure. You can never bring the outside pressure up in your defense."

The Republicans commented, "Obviously, Mr. Lovett would not have made that statement if it were not true. There are many other similar statements in the testimony."

The Republicans challenged the contention that Hughes had spent $7,000,000 of his own money, and declared that records of the Bureau of Internal Revenue and the Hughes Tool Company, available to all committee members, "indicate that during the war years the Hughes companies made a profit of over $15,500,000."

The Democratic contention that Hughes was guiltless was termed "inaccurate" by the Republican majority. "The record of the public hearings clearly indicates that discussions of a corrupt nature took place between General Meyers and Mr. Hughes and his [Hughes'] lawyer during the negotiation of the F-11 contract.

"Mr. Hughes testified that General Meyers tried to obtain $200,000 from him while the Hughes contract was in the process of negotiation in order to speculate in war bonds," the Republicans related. "Mr. Hughes also testified that Meyers' proposition was that if the bonds went up, Meyers was to take all the profit. Obviously this was a corrupt offer and Mr. Hughes must have known it to be such. Notwithstanding this corrupt offer, Hughes subsequently enlisted the assistance of General Meyers in connection with an important transaction concerning the motion picture *The Outlaw,* which Hughes produced. . . . Certainly it would not have been proper to exclude all evidence about General Meyers' important part in the Hughes contract merely because Meyers had also been dishonest in the case of other war contracts." [19]

The Republicans reasoned that although Hughes contended the wrongdoing was all on the part of General Meyers, Hughes did not disclose the information of the corrupt offer in his first appearances and later did so in a most reluctant manner. Although it was difficult to arrive at a determination of the truth between conflicting stories told by Hughes and Meyers as to who had initiated the corrupt conversations, the Republicans concluded that both Hughes and General Meyers were wrong in not admitting such conversations took place.

"The majority believes that Hughes should have promptly made a full disclosure of the activities of General Meyers to the Commanding General of the Air Force or the Department of Justice at the time of their alleged occurrence in 1944," the report said. "Any war contractor is at least morally obligated to report promptly corrupt or fraudulent propositions made to him by Government procurement officials. Unless this is done a corrupt public official may continue without detection in places of high trust to the serious detriment of his Government and his country."

There was no controversy over the fact that General Meyers, the highest Air Force procurement officer, operated in a corrupt manner and continued to do so even after the curtain had been pulled down on World War II. Although the exposure of the role of General Meyers came too late to avoid his corruptive influence on spending in that war, it dramatized the fact that corruption does creep into high places. It pointed up some serious weaknesses in the military investigations controlled within the chain of command.

9

BENNY MEYERS—A CORRUPT GENERAL

IF there was one man who really made advance preparations for World War II, it was Bennett E. Meyers, who became a major general in charge of Air Force Procurement. As early as 1939 and 1940, Benny Meyers, then a major and a colonel, was planning financial investments that could be working for him while he did his bit for the United States war effort.

Even as a major and lieutenant colonel, Benny Meyers lived in a fashion that seemed beyond his means. As early as 1940, there were reports made to Major General Oliver P. Echols, Assistant Chief of the Matériel Division, in charge of Wright Field, Dayton, Ohio, that Benny Meyers had some interest in a firm known as Aviation Electric Corporation, in Dayton, Ohio.

Meyers, then administrative assistant to General Echols, explained he merely had made a little loan to a friend who was in Aviation Electric Corporation, and that ended it. Neither the Army inspector general's office nor any of the Air Corp policing units made an investigation.[1]

That was the year Meyers persuaded an old acquaintance, Bleriot H. Lamarre, to drop a $40-a-week job in the aircraft industry on the West Coast to return to Dayton to take a $38-a-week job as treasurer of Aviation Electric Corporation. Part of the deal was that Mrs. Lamarre, formerly a secretary to Benny Meyers at Dayton, would return to a job with the Army Air Corps at Wright Field.

Promise of great opportunity lured Lamarre to Aviation Electric, for the firm had a $20,000 contract for 1940 and Meyers was acquainted with many executives of big aircraft corporations who might be persuaded to give subcontracts to Aviation Electric. Although 1940 was a financial flop, Benny Meyers took a $30,000 loss and came back the next year with a $164,000 contract with Bell Aircraft that netted a whopping profit of $95,000.

While the country was stepping up its preparation for war, Lieutenant Colonel Meyers was boosted to the rank of colonel and transferred to Washington with more responsibilities over a $2-billion aircraft procurement program. Funds from the now-flourishing Aviation Electric made it possible for Colonel Meyers to live in the fashion to which he wished to become accustomed.

Colonel and Mrs. Meyers moved into an apartment at 2400 Sixteenth Street after spending $10,000 on new furniture and decorating. Aviation Electric paid the bills. Aviation Electric also paid the $825 bill for air-conditioning equipment for the apartment, and $700 for a Magnavox radio.

The surprise raid on Pearl Harbor meant Colonel Meyers had to move rapidly to prepare himself for the war. The government had slapped a January 1, 1942, deadline on the purchase of new cars without a priority. Colonel Meyers bought a new blue 1942 Fleetwood Cadillac sedan in the last week of December, and because Aviation Electric paid for it with a $2,995.70 check, he kept his brown 1939 Cadillac for a second car.[2] While wartime Americans were struggling with gasoline rationing, General Benny Meyers and his wife drove their Cadillacs on government gasoline from Bolling Field. The nation was only in the process of getting ready for a long war, but the foresighted Benny Meyers was well prepared.

Meyers' activities, his high living standards and the reports of his stock interests did not go without notice, but the Army Air Corps had neither the proper type of organization nor the proper inclination to do the thorough investigations that would have flushed the Benny Meyers operation in the first war years.

In the latter part of 1942, rumors surfaced concerning stock speculation on the part of high-ranking Air Force procurement officers in aircraft and aircraft accessory companies. When this came to the attention of top Air Force officials, they recognized there was a problem but not what kind of problem. Colonel William P. Nuckols, of the Air Force Bureau of Public Relations, viewed it as a public relations problem, and the whole emphasis was on steps to counteract the unfavorable public reaction the rumors were creating. To counter the bad publicity, Colonel Nuckols recommended that procurement officers in responsible positions be ordered to report their stock holdings in aircraft companies.

This was a good first step, but it hardly took care of the problem without investigative follow-through. There was none. Several procurement officers, including the then General Meyers, were ordered to make a report concerning their stock holdings to the Chief of the

Air Staff. The Air Force merely received the reports and filed them. Neither the Bureau of Public Relations nor the Air Force top command questioned Meyers or any of the other officers about the rumors. There was no report to the Air Inspector or any other Air Force investigative unit. The Public Relations group created good will for the Air Force, with a whitewash. A preliminary investigation at that time would have revealed that General Meyers' report on his stock holdings was false. Meyers had substantial stock holdings in aircraft companies doing business with the Air Force, but did not report this as he was required to do. Instead he filed a false report and transferred the stock to an account held in his wife's maiden name, Ila Rae Curnutt.[3]

General Meyers breezed through the war in high style, impressing other officers with his purchase of as much as $50,000 in war bonds, and accumulating large amounts of cash deposited in his or his wife's bank account. On one occasion he kept at least $43,000 in cash in his Pentagon safe prior to placing it in a safe-deposit box.[4] However, nothing prompted the Air Force office of inspector general to do the much-needed investigation until months after General Meyers had applied for and received a disability pension in the summer of 1945.

In exposing the story of the activities of Benny Meyers, Committee Counsel William P. Rogers and Assistant Counsel Francis Flanagan had the help of two men who were doing their first major job on a Senate investigation and who were to become legendary figures later in many equally spectacular probes. Senator John J. Williams, the Delaware Republican, was serving his first year in the Senate, and Carmine Bellino, the former F.B.I. accountant, was beginning a career that would range over a dozen major investigations in the next twenty years.

Senator Williams and Bellino took a leading role in developing the records showing that Meyers had been paid a total of $190,970 by Aviation Electric through a number of payments to his father-in-law, to his wife, and through payments for expensive furniture and decorating between 1940 and 1946.

Some of the most damaging testimony against Meyers was given by Bleriot Lamarre, who served as "treasurer" and later as "president" of Aviation Electric. He said the firm was owned by Meyers, explained the efforts to hide Meyers' role, and testified that he had lied at an executive session of the committee on directions from Meyers.[5]

General Meyers admitted he had helped establish Aviation Electric, but said he did it to help Lamarre and his wife, who he claimed had been his "girlfriend" for five years with Lamarre's full knowledge. He testified that Lamarre and his wife had been gone from the Dayton area for about six months when he organized the Aviation Electric "to get Mrs. Lamarre back to Dayton."

Lamarre took the witness chair a day later to insist his story on Meyers' ownership of Aviation Electric was true, to defend his wife, and to charge the General with "a smear campaign against myself, [and] my wife.

"It is my sincere hope that this committee will make General Meyers crawl out of this room on his belly like the snake that he is," Lamarre concluded.

General of the Army H. H. Arnold was a sad man as he appeared before the Senate committee on November 22, 1947, to try to explain the circumstances that had permitted Benny Meyers to escape detection for six years.

"The press of the Nation has been filled for days with evidence developed by your committee of gross misconduct by a high-ranking officer of the Army Air Force," General Arnold said regretfully. "The evidence and the rumors and innuendo that go with it reflect on the 3,000,000 men and women who served in the Air Force, on the vital part they played in the war, and, perhaps, on the future of the Air Force as the foundation stone of our national security. . . . The old Air Corps, the Army Air Force, and now the United States Air Force have never condoned and never will condone such conduct as is indicated by the evidence, regardless of ability, position, or rank.

"If, to our regret, we of the Air Force did not find a rotten apple in our barrel, we are grateful that others have done so. If we were at fault in not finding it, we must admit our fault. But we can say with all the force and sincerity at our command that we were straining every nerve to prepare for and win the war. We thought we had reason to rely on the integrity as well as ability of men entrusted with high responsibility."

He pointed out that General Meyers and other officers "gave me their word that their investments and their only investments were as stated and were disposed of as stated.

"Rightly or wrongly, after these reports, I believed that these officers, including General Meyers, were and would continue free of taint of personal interest," General Arnold said. He then lashed out directly at the story told by Meyers:

"General Meyers had the effrontery to state [before the committee], that, after making his report he verbally disclosed the full facts to me and perhaps to General Stratemeyer; that he received the approval of one or both of us to his continued indirect holdings; that he made what he calls verbal arrangements with his superior officers; and that I told him that the matter of sale of stocks was one of his own judgments," General Arnold explained. "These statements I brand as absolute falsehoods, as does General Stratemeyer."

General Arnold admitted that the Air Force did not give proper attention to the "anonymous letter" alleging improper activities on the part of General Meyers, but he pointed out instances where a president of the New York Stock Exchange and many high officials of the legislative branch and executive branch had gone undetected in crime for long periods of time.

"Mistakes are inevitable in big organizations like the Army, Navy, and Air Force," General Arnold stated, reaching for perspective. "The services must learn from each error and be ever watchful against repetition. But nothing in the career of one man can or should be permitted to take the meaning from the wartime sacrifice and effort of the Air Force men and women." [6]

Chairman Ferguson broke in to comment that protection of the honest officials and the honesty of the system requires, "bad apples must be removed at the earliest possible date so other apples will not be destroyed.

"I just want to say that as you have said, this committee has found in its own Legislative Halls the need for exposure," Ferguson continued.

"If we go back just a short time, this committee had the duty, while it was unpleasant . . . to expose the actions of the chairman of the Military Affairs Committee of the House, Mr. May, in war contracts. It also brought to light the acts of Senator Bilbo from Mississippi, and he was stopped at the door of the Senate and not seated in the last session."

As Chairman Ferguson stressed the need for honest and aggressive investigations and "equal justice" to persons of all ranks, in closing the hearings, he pointed up the many conflicting stories that were told by witnesses under oath that raised serious questions of perjury. "No court, no committee, no nation can survive if perjury is the common thing in hearings," the Senator said. The record of testimony by

General Meyers was ordered forwarded to the Justice Department for study for possible prosecution.

Meyers was indicted on a charge of subornation of perjury for persuading Lamarre to lie to the committee in his first appearance, and Lamarre was indicted on a charge of perjury. On March 12, 1948, Meyers was convicted of subornation of perjury and was sentenced to twenty months to five years in the federal penitentiary. Lamarre, who entered a plea of guilty to perjury, was given a suspended sentence because he cooperated with the committee and told the truth in his later appearances.

When the committee made its report on April 14, 1948, it concluded that there was "a complete lack of coordination within the War Department among the several groups authorized to conduct investigations of misconduct.[7]

"This resulted in a confused, haphazard method of investigation," the committee stated. "The Air Force was put on notice on several occasions that General Meyers was conducting himself in a manner detrimental to the service. Obviously some forceful action should have been taken promptly."

The committee declared that "investigations involving misconduct of personnel should be removed from the chain of command in all branches of the armed services.

"Procurement officers and members of their immediate family should be required periodically to file sworn statements of their net worth, showing in detail their stock holdings and all other financial interest," the committee suggested.

The committee was highly critical of the attitude that "when a high-ranking officer is involved, no action is taken and no disclosure is made on the theory that it would impair the morale of the service."

It commended the view that "the higher the rank and the more important the responsibility of the officer involved, the greater is the effort at detection and the more vigorous and severe the exposure. . . . Any other course will result in serious loss of public confidence. If maladministration or corruption is allowed to exist within a procurement organization, its function may be seriously impaired or completely disrupted. . . . All procurement personnel must be made aware that corrupt or unethical practices will be punished promptly and severely, regardless of rank or position."

The committee declared that the Air Force was "put on notice" as early as 1940 that Meyers had "a personal interest in a company which was engaged in the business of manufacturing electrical devices to be used in planes purchased by the Government.

"There is no excuse for the failure to make an investigation under such circumstances," the committee said.[8]

The "glaring weaknesses" in the investigative system were pinpointed by the testimony of Major General Junious W. Jones, the Air Inspector General. "He [Jones] testified that during the war period he heard rumors concerning alleged corruption involving General Meyers from another general officer," the committee stated. "He said he took no action in the matter because the informant was unfriendly to Meyers and that the information involved a future fraudulent scheme. General Jones was unable to explain why he failed to question the informant for details."[9]

The failure of the investigative system within the Air Force is further illustrated by the manner in which an anonymous letter concerning alleged illegal activities on the part of General Meyers was handled. This anonymous letter dated June 22, 1945, addressed to the Federal Bureau of Investigation, stated that General Meyers held stock in companies with which he was doing business as a government procurement officer and was also engaged in other irregular activities. The Federal Bureau of Investigation promptly forwarded the letter to the War Department for appropriate action in accordance with existing procedures. This letter reached the office of General Arnold, where it was referred to the general files by Colonel Jacob Smart, special assistant to General Arnold, with no action or investigation of any kind. The Air Force furnished no satisfactory explanation to the committee as to why nothing was done. Not until May 1947, after the Air Force had learned that the committee was making an investigation into the activities of General Meyers, did it show any interest in the letter.

General Jones, in an effort to excuse the Air Force's failure to take some action, testified that he considered it to be a "crackpot letter," not worthy of investigation. It is of interest to note that the Chief of the War Frauds Section, Criminal Division, Department of Justice, testified before the committee that in his opinion the letter set forth sufficient specific facts to warrant an investigation. A diligent investigation of the charges made in the anonymous letter would have disclosed General Meyers' financial dealings in the summer of 1945, prior to his retirement.

The committee accused the Air Force of trying "to conceal" the existence of the letter from congressional investigators, and reporting on several different occasions that no such letter existed. To demonstrate the willful cover-up, the committee quoted from a memorandum of May 7, 1947, from Colonel John H. Price, the executive officer, to General Jones:

"Today, Central Files forwarded a copy of an anonymous letter which had been referred to the Air Inspector and indicated by an initial at the bottom of the R & R that this matter was referred to the 'Front Office' and that they had indicated no action to be taken and had forwarded it to Files over the initials of Col. Jacob E. Smart.

"This anonymous letter seemed to have a bearing on this matter; however, I am reluctant to recommend showing it to the Brewster committee or of even referring it to General Osborne in view of the fact that no action was taken by this headquarters. It is, of course, quite possible that this is exactly the information that the Brewster committee is checking on; on the other hand, it is possible that they know nothing of this letter and are hitting from some other source." [10]

The committee declared that "the officers responsible for the concealment of this information from a congressional committee rendered a disservice to the Air Force. This attempt at concealment is a serious reflection on the ability and the desire of the Air Force to clean up its own house."

In 1942, the Air Force established an investigation under William M. O'Dwyer, a New York Democratic political figure who had served as a county judge and as district attorney of Kings County, New York. O'Dwyer was given the rank of brigadier general, and was assigned directly to General Echols to investigate procurement matters. This unit never investigated the Meyers rumors, and it was disbanded in June, 1944.

About the only official to be praised by the Senate committee was the then Secretary of the Air Force W. Stuart Symington, who took "prompt action" to revamp the entire investigative system of the Air Force by removing investigations involving misconduct from the chain of command.

The committee had found that under the chain of command operations in existence during World War II, the commanders exercised control over investigations "which might well involve themselves or at least have a reflection upon their ability as commanding officers.[11]

"This system of placing investigative personnel within the chain of command exists not only in the Air Force, but in the other branches of the armed services," the committee found. "Under this system there is bound to be a tendency to cover up or whitewash particularly in those cases reflecting on or involving commanding officers and others of high rank."

Air Secretary Symington, later elected to the United States Senate, brought in a former F.B.I. agent, Joseph Carroll, gave him the rank of lieutenant general, and established the investigations office outside the chain of command, reporting directly to the Air Secretary.

This was one of many reforms taking place in the military establishment as a result of investigations that demonstrated the organizational weaknesses contributing to mistakes, inefficiencies and corruption in World War II. The major "reform" was the National Security Act of 1947, a strong step toward a "unification" of the armed services under James V. Forrestal, the first Secretary of Defense.

10

REORGANIZATION AND QUESTIONABLE ECONOMY

THE investigation of the Pearl Harbor disaster and the work of the Senate war investigating committee continued to emphasize the lack of preparedness for World War II and the improvisation that had been so necessary in our war effort in the first years.

In his final report to the Secretary of the Army, General Eisenhower commented: "Despite the time cushion afforded us by our allies, and the industrial tooling and experience gained through lend-lease orders, improvisation characterized much of our initial war effort. A magnificent national unity carried us through, but greater efficiency in prior planning would have saved much more time and money." [1]

Similar criticism of the lack of planning was voiced by Bernard Baruch when he appeared before the Senate war investigating committee. "Faltering step by faltering step we moved toward controls, but those controls were never sufficient and far-reaching enough," Baruch testified. "If they had been applied immediately, many lives would have been saved, our casualties lowered, and billions of dollars saved."

In its final report the Senate war investigating committee declared that "the greatest weakness of a democracy in this connection is its repugnance to an idea of another war.

"Because the thought of a war is so repugnant in a democracy, a natural aversion arises to any adequate preparation for it until an emergency arises," the committee stated. "Even then, unless we have been attacked, any act, such as putting an industrial mobilization plan into effect, may cause great public resentment."

General Eisenhower urged Congress to use the period after World War II for the thoughtful consideration of legislation needed to "assure the necessary mobilization of men, production plants, and materials that constitute total defense.

"Legislation on the books, ready for application in emergency, is the first essential in the political sphere of security," Eisenhower said. "In this regard many Americans will object that legislation for total mobilization may invite peacetime regimentation. These fears are idle. Legislative danger to our way of life is most likely to appear in a wave of hysterical measures hastily improvised to meet a war crisis. But in the immediate future, deliberately, in full and open debate, seeking information from all sources, the Congress can enact laws that will assure both the maximum conversion of the Nation to defense in time of need and complete safeguards against damage to our democratic system." [2]

The war investigating committee in its final report declared that we achieved our military strength despite "hesitation, procrastination, delay, conflict, and confusion in the management of war production." The committee pointed out that we might not have the same opportunities for the next time, and warned: "The alternative [to sound mobilization planning] may well mean complete destruction." [3]

Reorganization of the military establishment was regarded as an integral part of any really effective mobilization planning, and a wide range of legislative proposals was submitted within a few months after World War II to assure better coordinated planning.

The need for new laws dealing with Pentagon organization had been apparent for years. President Roosevelt had ordered the creation of a Joint Chiefs of Staff in World War II to coordinate military planning. The Joint Chiefs operated without the authority of law or executive order, with Admiral William D. Leahy serving as the President's personal Chief of Staff and Chairman. General George C. Marshall represented the Army, General H. H. Arnold the Air Force and Admiral Ernest King the Navy.[4]

The Pearl Harbor disaster and the continuing stream of evidence of friction, duplication and mismanagement provided the impetus for some statutory reorganization of the military service. However, there were sharply conflicting views on the form the proposed reorganization should take. The Army Air Force wanted equal status with the Army and the Navy. The Navy feared that if the military establishment was divided into land, sea and air missions, this would threaten naval aviation and Navy control of the Marine Corps.

The first hearings on postwar military policy before a House committee in 1944 crystallized the views of the Army, Navy and Air Force. Secretary of War Henry L. Stimson said it was "essential" that a single Department of Defense be created. The same view was expressed by Under Secretary of War Robert Patterson, who was later to succeed Stimson as Secretary of War. James Forrestal, who had succeeded Frank Knox as Secretary of the Navy, indicated that he still had the matter under study and was "not prepared to say that the Navy believes that the consolidation into one department is desirable."

Within a few months, Forrestal had become firmly opposed to the unification plans favored by General Douglas MacArthur and General Dwight D. Eisenhower. Admiral Chester Nimitz and Admiral William Halsey favored the plans at their inception but later supported the opposition expressed by their Cabinet representative.[5] Forrestal, Ferdinand Eberstadt and Admiral J. O. Richardson formed the core of the opposition to a single Defense Secretary with strong authority.

When the Senate Military Affairs Subcommittee opened hearings in October, 1945, General Marshall and General Arnold and Secretary of War Patterson called for a tight "unification" under a single Defense Secretary.

Forrestal and Eberstadt brought forth an alternative reorganization that called for three military departments, and no overall head. This plan provided for coordination of State Department and military service through a National Security Council. Forrestal emphasized the need for integration of diplomatic military policy, and rejected the importance of a single Defense Chief.

The War Department revealed a plan, drafted by Lieutenant General J. Lawton Collins, to provide a single Secretary of the Armed Forces and a single military Chief of Staff, over subordinate Chiefs for the Navy, Army and Air Force. General Arnold went further, and asked "ruthless" elimination of all traditional service divisions, branches and weapons.

Over the Navy objections, President Truman accepted the Army view as the Administration plan and asked for a single Department of National Defense and a single Chief of Staff. The plan President Truman endorsed would have eclipsed the Navy, for the Defense Secretary and Under Secretary would have been above the three Assistant Secretaries for Army, Navy and Air Force.

Legislation following the general outline of the Army thinking was voted out of the Senate Military Affairs Committee in April, 1946, but was referred to the Senate Naval Affairs Committee where Navy objections were dramatized. Forrestal declared that the Army plan would endanger the functioning of the entire military establishment. His major point of objection was the creation of a Supreme Chief of Staff over all the armed forces to serve under a single Secretary of Defense. The Navy Secretary declared this would open the way for an "ambitious" officer in that post to mold military, and "possibly national policy to suit his ends." [6]

Forrestal criticized the plans to deny Cabinet status to the present Secretaries of War and Navy. He contended that the organizational plan of the proposed plan would be "illogical administratively" and create "cross currents of authority and in some cases vacuums of authority."

One of his major complaints centered on the fact that only the Secretary of Defense "would have statutory access to the Bureau of the Budget, the President and Congress." He declared that the Truman Administration bill would concentrate control to the point that it would lead to "devitalization and unbalance" in research, logistics, training and intelligence.[7]

Charles E. Wilson, president of General Electric Company, questioned the wisdom of concentrating all the power of the military establishment in one Secretary of Defense. "I am convinced that it is utterly impossible for one man to determine policies, coordinate widely different activities and at the same time personally administer the business," the veteran business leader and wartime government administrator said. "It seems inevitable to me that the institution of . . . Secretary of Common Defense . . . is bound to create an inflexible one-way street which will be both undemocratic and inefficient in its operation." [8]

In the deadlock over reorganization, President Truman directed Secretary of War Patterson and Secretary of Navy Forrestal to iron out their differences. The Army accepted the Navy proposal for a Central Intelligence Agency, a National Security Council, and three autonomous departments under one Defense Secretary. The Navy still insisted that the Defense Secretary should be only a "coordinator" while the Army wanted to vest him with full authority to control the Army, Navy and Air Force.

Stalling by Navy partisans in the Naval Affairs Committee permitted Forrestal the time for more negotiation, and he used it to good advantage. The plan announced by President Truman in January, 1947, provided for a Secretary of Defense who had authority to set "common policies," and independent secretaries of Army, Navy and Air Force. The service mission assured a role for the Marine Corps and naval aviation.

When the National Security Act of 1947 was signed into law it stated that its purpose was to provide the service with "authoritative coordination and unified direction under civilian control but not to merge them." [9]

While the Defense Secretary was to supervise and coordinate the budget estimates for the Bureau of the Budget, the service secretaries retained a right to appeal directly to the President or to the Director of the Budget. The Joint Chiefs of Staff was established by law; it included the Chief of Staff to the Commander in Chief, and the Chiefs of Staff for the Army, Navy and Air Force.

That law provided that the Joint Chiefs would be "the principal military advisers" to the President and Secretary of Defense, but it limited the staff to one hundred officers to be drawn on an equal basis from the three services. It also provided for the National Security Council as a military-diplomatic coordinating unit, and a Central Intelligence Agency, which would be limited to correlating and evaluating intelligence relating to national security. It was barred from police powers, subpoena power or internal security functions.

Navy Secretary Forrestal, the man who fought hardest against a "unification," was named by President Truman as the first Secretary of Defense on July 26, 1947. The job was first offered to Patterson, but the War Secretary insisted on going ahead with plans to retire. Under the new legislation, John L. Sullivan was named Secretary of the Navy, Kenneth Royal became Secretary of the Army, and W. Stuart Symington was named as Secretary of the Air Force.

Major General Alfred M. Gruenther was named as Director of the Joint Staff; General Carl Spaatz as Air Force Chief of Staff; Admiral Louis E. Denfeld as Chief of Naval Operations; and General Omar N. Bradley as Army Chief of Staff.

It was not the "unification" that had been pushed by the Army and Air Force two and three years earlier, but it did seem to provide the framework for better coordination of military, diplomatic and intelligence functions than had existed in the past. Forrestal said the reorganization would proceed by "evolution, not revolution."

Reorganizing the military establishment was not the only major problem at the Pentagon. The need to keep American military might at a reasonable state of readiness was recognized. The Pentagon believed in a Universal Military Training concept to provide a steady source of trained military manpower over an extended period of time. Legislation was needed for the proper control and development of nuclear explosives and nuclear power. Development of air power and sea power must continue to replace the old and often obsolete weapons of World War II.

The Air Force had its seventy-group plan, and wanted 1,850 new planes as a starter. The Navy wanted a super-carrier. The Army wanted a broad range of new weapons. President Truman, preparing for his first election campaign as the Presidential candidate, wanted a balanced budget, and he sliced the defense spending budget to $11.3 billion and limited new appropriations to $9.3 billion. Army requests for new weapons and the Navy plan for a super-carrier were wiped out. The Air Force budget was cut to half the new planes requested.

Congress did not restore the budget for the Navy carrier, but the arguments to boost Air Force spending were persuasive enough to win a half-victory. It was argued that President Truman's cuts were "extremely detrimental to an already impoverished Air Force." [10] In addition there were warnings that increases in plane orders were essential to save the vital aircraft industry suffering from hard times in the aftermath of the war.

Requests of military leaders for greater defense spending were rejected as they had been in earlier years, but in 1948 those favoring increased spending received an unexpected assist. The possibility of armed hostility was brought back with some dramatic force when the Communist coup in Czechoslovakia was followed by serious Communist threats in Italy and Greece and the blockade of West Berlin.

President Truman presented a total budget of $39.7 billion for fiscal 1949 that included $11 billion for defense and $7 billion for foreign aid. Congress took things into its own hands in the face of international developments, and boosted the defense budget to $14.1 billion. Two men usually classed as among the most economy-minded —Representative Clarence Cannon (Dem., Mo.) and John Taber (Rep., N.Y.)—were among those prodding the Congress to provide adequate defense funds. Representative Taber, chairman of the House Appropriations Committee, told the House, "This is not a time for cheese-paring on the expansion and modernization of equipment for the front line of the national defense. The country is in dire peril."

It took all the force President Truman and Defense Secretary Forrestal could muster to keep the Defense Department spending below the $15 billion level the President contended was the maximum the nation could afford. Forrestal, who had been a major figure in limiting the power of the Secretary of Defense, found his role as a "coordinator" of policy to be frustrating and difficult in fighting Air Force and Navy demands for more spending. Air Force pressure for the seventy-group Air Force was growing stronger rather than subsiding, and the Navy was becoming more and more restive under the budget restraints and policies that indicated the Navy might be slated for a lesser role.

In closing the book on its work in early 1948, the Senate war investigating committee found reason for concern that the United States was again drifting back into some of the same patterns of negligence that characterized the period between World War I and World War II.

"More drastic and carefully considered legislation to eliminate unfair profits from war is imperative," the committee warned. "Confidence in the system of free enterprise can be preserved in no other way. Capitalism's capacity for self-discipline faces its supreme test."

It warned again that a prompt and effective mobilization of our entire economy was essential in the event of war, and that the needed steps had not been taken. "In reviewing the history of our mobilization planning efforts in two World Wars, the committee has observed that the lessons learned from experience in controlling our national economy during World War I were largely disregarded when similar problems confronted us in World War II," the committee stated. "Only belatedly in World War II did we put into effect many of the organizational principles embodied in our industrial mobilization plans.

"The American people must realize that in another war this Nation may at once become not only an arsenal but also a battlefield. The committee believes that the prompt and effective mobilization of our economy in time of war is of such vital importance to the security of this country that it demands the constant attention and bipartisan consideration of the Congress and the executive branch of the Government." [11]

With the memories of the scandals and the profiteering of World War II still fresh in the record, the Senate war investigating committee stressed the need for vigilance and added that "new techniques must constantly be developed to take unfair profits out of war and out of preparation for war.

"In this era of total war, consideration may well be given to universal [military] service to assure that each shall do his proper part in defense of his country, and to eliminate unjust enrichment," the committee suggested.

The pressures on the Defense Secretary were enormous. On the one hand, there were the military men with their demands for more spending for planes, ships and guns. With them were the war industries—particularly the airplane and ship industries—insisting that more spending was needed to keep them in a healthy state of readiness for war. On the other side were men like Representative George Mahon (Dem., Tex.), who warned that "nothing would please a potential enemy better than to have us bankrupt our country and destroy our economy by maintaining over a period of years complete readiness for armed conflict."

There were sincere men on all sides of the arguments for increasing and for cutting the Defense Department budget, and there was a sincere man trying to grasp control of the huge Pentagon and achieve the "balanced forces" concept that was the middle ground. James Forrestal had questioned whether it was wise to place authority for the entire Defense Department in the hands of any one man, and such an experienced man as Charles E. Wilson had said it was "utterly impossible for one man" to determine policies, coordinate a wide variety of activities and also administer the business of the Pentagon.

At some point in early 1949, Defense Secretary Forrestal started to break under the strain of the job. He was fifty-seven years of age at the time, and had been in Washington for nine years after twenty-eight years with the Wall Street firm of Dillon, Read & Company, where he had started as a bond salesman a year after graduation from

Princeton. He was president of Dillon, Read & Company in early 1940 when he agreed to go to Washington to serve as one of six special assistants to President Roosevelt. In August of 1940, he became the first Under Secretary of the Navy with the responsibility for procurement and matériel, and he became Secretary of the Navy upon the resignation of Frank Knox. The strain of the Defense Secretary job was apparent to friends of Forrestal for weeks before his resignation in March, 1949.

Louis A. Johnson, a West Virginia Democrat, was sworn in as Defense Secretary on March 28, 1949—just five days prior to the time Forrestal entered the U. S. Naval Hospital at Bethesda, Maryland, to be treated for nervous exhaustion. The reports on Forrestal's condition indicated he was gaining weight and was improving in general health, but the optimism was not well-founded.

At one A.M. on May 22, the former Defense Secretary climbed out a window of an adjacent hospital room and took his own life. President Harry Truman declared that Forrestal was "as truly a casualty of war as if he had died on the firing line." [12] He received a military hero's burial at Arlington National Cemetery.

The pressure of major and minor irritation that had been building up under Forrestal exploded in the face of the new Defense Secretary, Louis Johnson. President Truman was trying to impose an arbitrary $15-billion limit on annual defense spending, but costs were rising for more complicated weapon systems. If the Air Force was to get the new B-36's it needed for the Strategic Air Command, then the Navy and Army would be required to accept increasingly smaller slices of the $15 billion defense pie. However, Air Force enthusiasts were setting their sights much higher than the forty-eight-group limit envisioned by President Truman, and were whipping up support for a seventy-group Air Force. This pressure of the Air Force for major reliance on strategic air power was fought by the Army and the Navy, but somehow Air Force views were receiving more attention. There were Army arguments that a ground war in Europe was the greatest threat. The Navy viewed a modern carrier fleet with Marines as ideally suited for the strategic bombing and mobile tactical ground support necessary for effective control in any area of the world.

Only a few weeks after Johnson became Defense Secretary, he cancelled the $189,000,000 super-carrier, the *United States*. The Navy had laid the keel for the 65,000-ton ship only two months earlier. The action was taken on the advice of Army and Air Force members of the Joint Chiefs of Staff, and without notification to Navy Secretary Sullivan or Admiral Louis A. Denfield, the Chief of Naval Operations. Sullivan resigned in protest, and was replaced as Navy Secretary by Francis P. Matthews, who was more inclined to accept the wishes of the Defense Secretary.

Navy anger swelled as the service was hit by two more substantial cuts in quick succession. The Defense Secretary ordered a cutback of 135,000 civilian employees, and 76,000 of them were to be Navy employees. Plans were announced to cut the Navy carrier groups from fourteen to six, and to place four of the Navy's large carriers in the mothball fleet.

Navy efforts to discredit the Air Force and Defense Secretary Johnson backfired in a manner that disclosed the most irresponsible tactics. Cedric Worth, a former scenario writer attached to the Navy Department, wrote an anonymous memorandum that was distributed to several members of Congress, including Representative James E. Van Zandt (Rep., Penn.). The Pennsylvania Republican, a Navy partisan, used the memorandum as the basis for a House speech asking a congressional investigation of "ugly disturbing rumors" that Johnson had been a director of Consolidated Vultee, the manufacturer of the B-36. He also hinted that there was evidence of an arrangement for Air Secretary Symington to bow out as soon as the B-36 funds were approved to take a job heading a large aircraft "combine" that involved executives of Consolidated Vultee. The rumors were denied by Symington and Johnson, and the House investigation exposed the nature of the Worth memorandum. The committee found no evidence of political influence or corruption in the decision to purchase the B-36.[13]

There were sincere differences of opinion between high-ranking officers of the Army, Navy and Air Force, but there were certainly many questionable tactics in the heat of the public relations battle. In big defense contract decisions there was often the pressure of political contributions and the influence of political friends in and out of government. There was the real problem of keeping the aircraft industry in a healthy state, but there was also the need to be wary that the nation did not spend itself into bankruptcy in buying too many weapons that would soon be obsolete.

Although there were men of good motives on both sides of nearly every issue, there were also men who would let personal vanity, politics or personal profits weigh heavily in their thinking. It was not unusual that in the fight for survival tactics were used that were far beneath the dignity we should expect of our highest military leaders. In the light of the experiences of history, it was not unreasonable that one might have deep suspicions about the motivations of high military officers or high civilian political appointees.

The Navy is being "nibbled to death," Captain John G. Crommelin, Jr., declared in an unusual press-conference attack on the Army, the Air Force and the civilian leadership in the Pentagon. Captain Crommelin recognized that his outburst meant the end of his military career, but he believed he should sacrifice career to force a congressional inquiry into what he considered to be serious deterioration in the U. S. defense posture.

As a naval pilot attached to the Joint Staff, Crommelin had viewed the interservice battle from the inside, and he knew his position was in line with the views of most high-ranking naval officers, including the Chief of Naval Operations, Admiral Denfeld.

Crommelin received immediate public backing from retired Fleet Admiral William Halsey, who also asked others to support the outspoken Navy captain. Admiral Denfeld, Admiral Arthur W. Radford, then commander of the Pacific Fleet, and Vice Admiral Gerald F. Bogan gave general endorsement to Crommelin's complaint by writing to Navy Secretary Matthews.[14]

The "revolt of the Admirals" did touch off a congressional inquiry and did focus public attention on Navy complaints about overreliance on the B-36. General Omar Bradley, Chairman of the Joint Chiefs of Staff and a leading spokesman for the Truman Administration, charged that the admirals had done "infinite harm" with the revolt. He declared that the Navy had opposed "unification" from the outset, and said there was no time for "fancy Dans" who were unwilling to cooperate.

When the hearings were over, the revolt was squelched. Navy Secretary Matthews forced the firing of Admiral Denfeld as Chief of Naval Operations, and Denfeld, Bogan and Crommelin retired within a year. Only Admiral Radford and the then Captain Arleigh Burke survived to advance and fight other battles over budgets and defense posture.

The National Security Act of 1947 had not created the smooth-functioning National Military Establishment, and there was more tinkering to tighten the system in 1949. The National Security Act of 1949 changed the name of the National Military Establishment to the Defense Department, and the power of the Secretary of Defense was expanded. The 1949 Act created a Deputy Secretary of Defense and three Assistant Secretaries of Defense. The service secretaries were dropped from the National Security Council and were replaced by the Vice President. The service secretaries were indirectly cut in stature in many other ways although the law still authorized either the service secretaries or the members of the Joint Chiefs of Staff to take the initiative in presenting recommendations to Congress without clearing with the Defense Secretary.

The power of the Defense Secretary and the Joint Staff was augmented by increasing the number of officers on the Joint Staff from one hundred to two hundred ten. This made the Joint Staff less reliant upon the services. Also, the law provided for implementation of the Hoover Commission recommendations for an overhaul of military budget and accounting procedures. The law provided for a comptroller in the Defense Department, and each of the services was provided with a comptroller to provide uniform accounting and budgetary operations, inventory controls, and, it was hoped, better general management.

Defense Secretary Johnson praised the 1949 reorganization, which he claimed would eliminate waste and duplications and would make it possible for him to save at least $1 billion a year. It was a mighty promise and a popular tune in late 1949, but events of the next year were to raise serious questions about the wisdom of some of the economy measures of the Louey Johnson regime.[15]

11

THE FIVE-PERCENTERS

THE sharp drop in military spending at the end of World War II, instead of eliminating the problems of fraud and political influence, placed an even greater premium on obtaining a defense contract. Firms that had little trouble getting a piece of an $80 billion-a-year defense pie in 1944 were in a mad scramble in 1948 for a small piece of a $10.9 billion budget. The impact of this competition was illustrated by the interservice fights in the period after World War II when the aircraft, shipbuilding, and arms industries worked through the services and through sympathetic congressional sources to try to get a bigger piece of the defense dollar. Within the airplane industry itself there was tough competition as large companies used every trick they knew in what they viewed as a battle for survival.

Special frustrations plagued the small-businessman as actual defense expenditures remained at $11.5 billion in 1949 and $11.9 billion in 1950 before jumping to $19.7 billion in 1951. Many small manufacturers had depended upon subcontracts from the giants of industry, or had relied on receiving contracts in fields unwanted by large firms that had been glutted in the war years. In the aftermath of the war they found they did not know how to procure government contracts and could not afford fulltime Washington representation. In their panic they searched out men reputed to be knowledgeable in the ways of Washington, and effective in producing government contracts for a fee of five or ten percent of the contract.

The Munitions Board reported that small business concerns received only 27.2 percent of the dollar volume of military purchases for the period from July 1, 1948 to June 30, 1949. While these statistics included only the prime contracts, a Senate subcommittee considered the figure significant in the light of the fact that 50 percent of the dollar volume of all manufacturing done in the United States is done by small business firms. The Small Business subcommittee of the Senate Banking and Currency Committee was of the opinion that small business was not getting its fair share of military buying, and was making studies to try to determine how small business could obtain a larger percentage.

Over the years, the bulk of government purchasing had been done through competitive bidding for the purpose of eliminating abuses, stimulating competition, and assuring fair price. However, experiences in World War II indicated that in some cases it was more efficient and economical to negotiate government purchases without bidding, and Congress had written the laws with loopholes to permit negotiated contracts in special cases.

Despite the obvious intent of Congress to have the volume of military purchases made by advertised bidding, the Pentagon had used negotiation in a majority of the cases in the period from 1947 through 1949. The latest statistics available as the investigations started indicated 91 percent of the purchases of the armed services were negotiated. Of this number, 72.3 percent were for purchases under $1,000, which are exempted from bidding. However, of the remaining contracts, approximately 70 percent were negotiated. From a dollar standpoint, 70.2 percent of the total value of military purchases for fiscal 1949 were negotiated. Small business felt it was being squeezed out.[1]

In this atmosphere there emerged in Washington "an unsavory fraternity of individuals who represented to businessmen that they could affect Government decisions by pressure or influence. Although the modus operandi of these men varied sharply, they had one thing in common—they were selling their ability to engage in collusive dealings with Government officials." [2]

In late 1948 and early 1949 the boom in the influence-peddling business became apparent, and the Senate Permanent Investigating Subcommittee was assigned the task of delving into the reports that disreputable figures, including some men reputedly close to the White House, had made a racket out of the "management consultant" business.

Secretary of Defense Johnson had gone on record against the five-percenters after the first complaints of influence-peddling. In a speech in May, 1949, Johnson cautioned there were those "who prostitute the profession of salesmanship [and] seek to convince the small businessman that only by buying through them can he get orders from the Government.

"There is no need for special brokers, for 15-percenters, for 10-percenters, for even five-percenters," the Defense Secretary said. "There is no need for anyone to intervene between small business and the Government to procure Government contracts." [3]

Within a few weeks after the Johnson statement, the *New York Herald Tribune* ran a series of articles on the activities of James V. Hunt, a self-styled "management consultant." The articles disclosed that, even after the warning from the Defense Secretary, Hunt had entered into a written contract with a small-businessman for a $1,000 retainer, $500 a month, and five percent of all business done with the government.

Warnings had done no good, and the Permanent Investigating Subcommittee members agreed that public hearings on some of the influence-peddling would be necessary to dramatize the problem and determine if new federal laws were needed.

The Investigating Subcommittee was chaired by Senator Clyde

Hoey (Dem., N.C.). Other members of the committee were Herbert O'Conor (Dem., Md.), James O. Eastland (Dem., Miss.), John L. McClellan (Dem., Ark.), Joseph R. McCarthy (Rep., Wis.), Karl E. Mundt (Rep., S.Dak.), and Margaret Chase Smith (Rep., Me.).

Chairman Hoey opened the hearings with comments on the importance of "efficiency and . . . economy in government.

"It is important not only that we have good government but that the public have confidence in the integrity and the decency of its Government," Senator Hoey said. "Forces which tend to create the belief that our Government functions with favoritism or by conniving should, if possible, be eliminated. The purpose of all this hearing is to consider the broad question of what safeguards Congress can take to prevent or minimize improper influences." [4]

Even as the subcommittee started its hearings in August, 1949, members recognized the problem as the difficulty of distinguishing between the reputable sales representatives and the spurious influence-peddlers. Defense Secretary Louis Johnson, who appeared as the opening witness before the subcommittee, agreed and pledged the full support of the defense establishment in the elimination of the unnecessary five-percenters. The day after his testimony Johnson directed the Defense Department to open a unified procurement office to which businessmen could turn in their dealings with the government.

The necessity of differentiating between the reputable and the questionable representative was dramatized by the activities of James V. Hunt, a $50-a-day consultant in the War Asset Administration; Albert W. Lewitt, secretary for a United States Senator; and John F. Maragon, a parttime government consultant and crony of White House military aide Major General Harry H. Vaughan.

The subcommittee hearings showed that Hunt, while employed as a consultant to Major General Edmund B. Gregory, head of the War Assets Administration, represented clients and collected fees from them for attempting to locate and purchase property that was held by the War Assets Administration. Hunt's testimony was in conflict with that of his superior. Hunt attempted to justify his conduct on the grounds that General Gregory had approved of it in writing. General Gregory testified he had not approved of this practice and that, had he known Hunt was privately engaged in dealing in surplus property at a time when he was employed by the WAA, he would have dismissed him.

The subcommittee stated that the question of an agreement between General Gregory and Hunt was immaterial, for the practice was wrong whether condoned or not. "This practice does not appear to be illegal under the law as presently written," the Permanent Subcommittee stated. "However, it is wholly indefensible. A person employed by the Government, whether prohibited by law or not, should not engage in private business which is inconsistent in any way with his employment." [5]

Hunt's activities with Major General Alden H. Waitt, Chief of the Chemical Warfare Service, were singled out by the Senate subcommittee as an illustration of high officials who actively assisted five-percenters.

The Deering Milliken Research Trust, a textile research organization of Greenwich, Connecticut, hired Hunt to assist in obtaining research contracts with the government, particularly with the military services. Hunt negotiated with the Chemical Warfare Service, and on a number of occasions contacted Major General Waitt.

The evidence also showed that in March, 1949, General Waitt inserted himself into the negotiations of the technical command of the Chemical Warfare Service at the Edgewood Arsenal and gave specific instructions that the contract be awarded to the Deering Milliken organization.

Major John F. Gay, a liaison officer, testified that General Waitt had asked him to go to the arsenal where the contract was being considered to say "he was interested in seeing that Deering Milliken Corp. have a contract."

The Army major also explained to the subcommittee that General Waitt told him "this organization had influence in the White House that might prove valuable to him later."

The subcommittee did not accept General Waitt's testimony when he admitted telling Major Gay that the company representatives knew all the Washington "big shots" but denied doing it to influence the contract award.

The hearings also brought out the fact that after these negotiations General Waitt personally informed Hunt that the contract would be awarded to Deering Milliken. In turn Hunt wrote a letter to his client stating he had received personal assurance that they would receive the contract. It was all corroborated by diary entries and transcripts of telephone conversations that subcommittee investigators found in Hunt's office.

The Senate subcommittee commented that General Waitt's efforts on behalf of Deering Milliken had to be weighed in the light of other plans he was making to succeed himself as Chief of the Chemical Service, when normally the job would have been passed to another officer. Subcommittee officers found memoranda in Hunt's office that told much of the story. General Waitt had gone to Hunt's office and prepared memoranda for the White House that spoke in glowing terms of his own qualifications and pointed out alleged serious shortcomings in each of the other officers who might be in line for the job. General Waitt admitted that he prepared the memoranda to be submitted by Hunt to General Vaughan, President Truman's military aide. The memoranda were to be used by the President in selecting a new chief for the Chemical Warfare Service.

The subcommittee was highly critical of this underhanded manner in which General Waitt "enlisted the help of Hunt to exert influence with his alleged friends in high places for the purpose of furthering Waitt's military career."

The subcommittee also concluded that the evidence was "clear that Hunt succeeded in influencing General Waitt to give special and unusual consideration to his client because he felt that Hunt could help him in the furtherance of his military career."

It was pointed out that Waitt had filled his own official reports with high praise of many of his fellow officers, but had used the memoranda dictated in Hunt's office to undercut these men with derogatory comments and "to perpetuate himself."

This might have "done serious and unwarranted injury to the lifelong careers of many outstanding officers in the United States Army had it not been exposed in time," the subcommittee stated. "Such an act by a general officer is inexcusable."

On July 16, 1949, in the midst of the first hearings, Secretary of the Army Gordon Gray temporarily suspended General Waitt from his duties pending completion of a full investigation. On September 10, 1949, the Secretary of the Army accepted General Waitt's request that he be retired from the Army.

"It would not be in the best interest of the service for him to continue his duties as Chief of the Chemical Warfare Service," the Army Secretary stated.[6]

Another of Hunt's military contacts fared better. General Herman Feldman, Chief of the Quartermaster Corps, and Hunt became friends as a result of Hunt's service in the Quartermaster Corps in World

War II, and they continued a close relationship after Hunt resigned from government to establish his "consultant" bureau in Washington.

General Feldman was accused of granting favoritism to Hunt, including delivery of a proposed quartermaster expenditure program for clothing and equipage for the fiscal year 1948. In a letter by which he sent the report to Hunt, General Feldman wrote, "Where the information is not considered secret, I consider it advisable that it be considered as between us—confidential."

The Senate subcommittee stated that although the information was not classified "confidential" within the strict meaning of the term, the Army had taken the position that the disclosure of this information by Feldman to Hunt was improper.[7]

There were many other instances showing questionable action by General Feldman and Hunt. In one case, Hunt was paid $5,000 by the Cyclic Chemical Company of Washington, D.C., for just a few hours' work in assisting the firm in returning to the WAA a total of 800,000 surplus aerosol insecticide bombs. The chemical firm had purchased the aerosol bombs and then for months had tried to cancel its contract. All efforts had been unsuccessful until Hunt was hired. He contacted General Feldman and Brigadier General James A. Mollison, a highly ranked official in the WAA, and the contract was cancelled. The Senate subcommittee did not quarrel with the decision, but questioned why there was no action until Hunt was retained.[8]

A letter from General Feldman to Brigadier General Wayne R. Allen, chief administrative officer and purchasing agent for the county of Los Angeles, was introduced by the subcommittee to illustrate that Feldman knew Hunt was peddling his political influence. On November 19, 1947, Feldman wrote General Allen at length, describing Hunt's activities. The subcommittee felt the letter emphasized "the fact that he was a man of influence" and pointed out that "Hunt even had ready entre [*sic*] to the White House." [9]

General Feldman was found to have used "bad judgment" in dealing with Hunt after knowing that Hunt held himself out as an "influence peddler." The subcommittee expressed the hope that the reprimand General Feldman received would make him "more fully aware of the high responsibility of his important office." Although Feldman was temporarily suspended by Army Secretary Gordon Gray for "errors in judgment" he was restored to duty because of his 42 years of service.[10]

Albert W. Lewitt, while employed as a secretary to United States Senator Albert W. Hawkes (Rep., N.J.), in 1945, had held discussions with the former owners of the Lido Beach Hotel, Lido Beach, Long Island, New York, regarding the repurchase of the property, which had been taken over by the Navy during the war.

Lewitt referred the owners to Hunt, and then personally made contact with several government officials in their behalf. After lengthy negotiations the owners repurchased the hotel and Hunt received a fee of approximately $100,000.

"Lewitt, who by this time had left the Government, received $5,000 from Hunt as his share of the fee and an attempt was made to disguise this as a fee for consultation," the Permanent Investigating Subcommittee found.

The former Senate employee made what was described by the subcommittee as "half-hearted" denial that the $5,000 was for his work on the Lido Beach Hotel transaction. The subcommittee then produced the diary maintained by Hunt that "expressly set forth that Lewitt was to get part of Hunt's fee on the Lido Beach deal."

The subcommittee pointed out that under the law the owners of the Lido Beach Hotel were entitled to repurchase the hotel, and were entitled to the help of Lewitt as a government employee to obtain a proper repurchase. However, the subcommittee disapproved the accompanying fee arrangement as "not in the public interest."

The fact that Lewitt did not receive the questionable fees until after he had left the government did not alter the conclusion that the fees were in fact "in payment of acts he performed while employed by the Government." [11]

After Lewitt resigned from government service, he accepted a position with a leather goods trade association as a lobbyist for the repeal of the luxury tax on leather goods. Until the hearings of the Investigations Subcommittee began, Lewitt had not registered as a lobbyist. His correspondence with his clients illustrated that he held himself out to them as an active lobbyist for their interests. His letters also demonstrated one of the favorite techniques of the five-percenters—name dropping:

"I have every reason to believe, from my talks with the chairman of the House Ways and Means Committee, and with the officials of the Treasury Department . . . that there will be some tax relief with regard to luggage. . . ."

In another letter he stated, "I just came from having another visit with the former Speaker of the House, the Honorable Joseph Martin, of Massachusetts. . . . He feels very keenly about this tax on luggage and intends to do everything he possibly can to get some action on this. . . ."

More reassurances were given his clients when he wrote: ". . . As one of my specific assignments . . . I have contacted practically every member of the House Ways and Means Committee, as well as the members of the Joint Committee on Revenue and Taxation."

When questioned under oath, Lewitt admitted that not only had he never discussed the taxes in question with any members of Congress, he had merely forwarded information he found in public sources, available to anyone, in a form he felt would impress his clients.[12]

Little John Maragon, once described by General Vaughan as "a lovable sort of a chap," [13] was persona non grata at the White House after the Senate exposed his activities. Because of his White House connections, Maragon, former Kansas City bootblack, became the most infamous of the influence-peddlers.

In 1945, Maragon, long-time crony of Major General Harry Vaughan, military aide to President Truman, was hired by the State Department, at the instigation of Vaughan, as an administrative assistant to the American mission to observe the Greek elections from November 27, 1945 to March 14, 1946. At Vaughan's request Maragon's participation in this mission was marked "1-D"—of special interest to the President. When he testified before the subcommittee, Vaughan admitted that "the President was not interested in any trip that John Maragon would take or [*sic*], in fact, the President wasn't interested in any detail of Maragon's business or life or anything." [14]

While Maragon was supposedly giving fulltime service to the government, he was employed at a salary of $1,000 a month by the Verley Perfume Company, and actively worked for them across Europe. In addition to this salary, Maragon charged the perfume company for traveling expenses of about $10,000. In fact, his travel had been paid for by the government.

"Such conduct is so reprehensible that no discussion of it is necessary," the subcommittee stated.[15]

While traveling at the discretion of the government, John Maragon was arrested by the authorities for smuggling oils used in the manufacture of perfume into the country.[16]

The Senate subcommittee brought out evidence that Maragon indeed had a close friendship with General Harry Vaughan, had entrée to the White House, and had used his high government friendships to peddle influence. The subcommittee found that "in several instances the evidence showed that General Vaughan or his office personally interceded with Government agencies on behalf of those whom he [Maragon] represented." [17]

At a party for General Vaughan at Milwaukee in October, 1946, Milton Polland met John Maragon, a member of the General's entourage. On the strength of Maragon's reputed influence in Washington, Polland retained him as an agent for the Allied Molasses & Food Industries, which was owned by Pollard's nephew, Harold Ross. During the period of wartime sugar rationing the Agriculture Department had suspended any further molasses dealings by Allied and had sought criminal prosecution of the firm for serious violations of the rationing regulations. Ross needed someone to intervene with the government to restore the firm's allowances.[18]

Shortly after Maragon was retained for the firm, General Vaughan telephoned the Department of Agriculture from his White House office in an effort to have the restrictions against Maragon's client lifted. The former administrator of this section of the department, Herbert Hathorn, recalled the conversation for the subcommittee. He quoted Vaughan as saying, "I discussed this with the Secretary [of Agriculture] before he left town, and I would like to have you do something to remedy this situation.

"He ended up," "Hathorn continued, with a statement that he was very close to the President and that a friend in the White House could mean an awful lot to a man in one of the agencies . . . and also that he could get my job or get a job—my impression was that he inferred that he could help . . . someone in my position or that he could be detrimental to their career in the Government." [19]

Allied Molasses & Food Industries was found to be in further violation of the laws on sugar usage when the case was investigated at this time, and no permit for additional allotments was issued. When questioned about his intercession for Maragon's client, Vaughan was unable to deny that they might have occurred.[20]

In other instances the subcommittee found that "Maragon sought and received favorable consideration in matters pending in Government departments by stressing his friendship and close association with General Vaughan. On several occasions Maragon succeeded in convincing Government officials that he was officially connected with the

White House and at his request they called on him in his suite at the Carlton Hotel to discuss his cases. In some instances Maragon used the telephone facilities of General Vaughan's White House office in the conduct of his personal business.

"These operators go to ingenious lengths to convince businessmen that the day-to-day decisions of Government are based on collusion rather than on merit," the Committee said.[21]

The Senate investigators also implicated Maragon in the highly questionable activity of General Vaughan, who held the position of Coordinator of Veterans' Affairs in the Truman Administration. From his White House post, Vaughan attempted to expedite the application for building materials for the Tanforan race track. Investigators concluded that Vaughan had to know that in obtaining materials for the race track he was reducing the materials available for veterans' housing. Vaughan insisted he wasn't seeking favored treatment but was merely seeking to have the matter decided.

The official query also produced evidence that Maragon and his client, the Verley Perfume Company, were involved in presentation of deep-freeze units to a number of government officials, including General Vaughan and the Truman family.[22] (The Truman family was absolved of any impropriety by the subcommittee. It was reasoned that the practice of sending gifts to the President and the President's acceptance of such gifts was a long-standing custom.)

When the activities of Maragon first came to the attention of the Senate, he was questioned under oath in an executive session. As the investigation proceeded, his testimony appeared to the counsel and the subcommittee members to be inconsistent with other facts that were coming to light. The subcommittee subpoenaed Maragon to return for further questioning in an open hearing. This time, on the advice of counsel, Maragon refused to answer any questions concerning his sources of income or his dealings with the government on grounds that he might incriminate or degrade himself.[23]

On January 3, 1950, John F. Maragon was indicted for perjury by a federal grand jury in the District of Columbia. Because one of the counts of the indictment included nearly all of the testimony concerning Maragon and dealings he had with General Vaughan, the Senate subcommittee investigators decided that they should not pursue these problems further, but leave them to the Justice Department.

While staying out of the matters directly related to the perjury indictment pending against Maragon, the subcommittee commented critically that "there seemed to be general acceptance by the Government officials of the view that when General Vaughan called about some matter pending before that department he represented the President. Consequently more attention was given the matters than would have been the case if it had been known that the President was not concerned and knew nothing about the call." General Vaughan himself "testified that these calls were made by him upon his own authority and without the knowledge or direction of the President, except in rare instances when he made specific calls and advised of the wishes of the President."

The report concluded that the whole pattern of activity made it possible for Maragon to "use the great prestige of the White House for his private advantage." The subcommittee deemed it "incredible" that Maragon was able to get by with his peddling of White House influence for a period of several years.

"This is particularly true because several of his dubious activities of recent years have received attention in the public press" and in light of his 1945 arrest for smuggling, the subcommittee stated.[24]

On April 26, 1950, John Maragon, the man the Senate subcommittee had branded "an outright fixer," was found guilty on two counts of the four-count indictment. Accountant Carmine Bellino was a key witness in establishing that Maragon had committed perjury when he denied the existence of his Texas bank account. He had deposited over $100,000 in this account during the same four-year period in which he claimed he had only $30,000 of income and paid taxes on that amount. The other count upon which a guilty verdict was returned involved the charge that Maragon had perjured himself in denying he was on the salary of the Verley Company when he went to Europe for the government.

The government dropped a charge that Maragon lied in testifying the money he had was "loans" from his mother. He was acquitted on the count charging him with falsely denying that he was paid for representing businesses before government agencies.[25]

Maragon's lawyer, Edward J. Haynes, claimed that the fifty-seven-year-old former bootblack was the "scapegoat" of the investigation and prosecution.[26] General Vaughan was not called as a witness in the trial, although it was conceivable that he could have been an important witness for either the government or the defense. Although Vaughan was the object of severe criticism by the Senate subcommittee, he remained White House military aide until President Truman left office.

Maragon's appeals failed, and on May 25, 1951, he went to prison to serve eight months to two years for lying about his influence-peddling activities.[27]

The Permanent Investigating Subcommittee concluded that the mere existence of an atmosphere in which five-percenters can thrive "tends to destroy good government. Unwatched and unchecked [influence-peddlers] have a pernicious effect on decent government far beyond their number. Around centers of government activity their connivance takes on an air of folklore. Businessmen who would prefer to be honest, in their anxiety to get business are lulled into the easy belief that everybody is cheating and soon conclude that as long as it involves no risk on their part they are willing to pay someone to do a little on their behalf."

But the subcommittee also realized that "integrity in government cannot be attained by legislation or by the promulgation of rules alone. It can be attained only when officials at the top decide that its maintenance is an important task and work toward its success." [28] The subcommittee's investigation disclosed that, to a large extent, the success of a five-percenter was totally dependent upon the gullibility of the businessmen who hired him.

Another important factor in the success of some influence-peddlers was the cooperation they received from public officials, who either intentionally or unintentionally permitted the five-percenters to give the impression of influence. In some cases, the subcommittee found that the influence-peddlers did in fact have influence on high officials that they could, and did, exert on behalf of clients.

"This violates the fundamental concept of decent government," the subcommittee said critically. "A democracy is founded on the principle of equality of treatment for all its citizens. Anyone who equivocates with this premise or who seeks to whittle it down for reasons of politics or profits strikes at the heart of our way of life." [29]

Investigations serve their purpose by reminding employees of their public obligations. In an environment of laxity, one tends to forget his fidelity to public trust.

Throughout the five-percenter hearings it was emphasized that the government had to arrange a service so that a businessman would be able to acquire government contracts without resorting to the influence-peddlers. Until midway through the hearings it was necessary for a prospective seller to canvass some twenty or more government agencies if he desired to find out which agencies were purchasing his product or his services.

The General Services Administration expanded a Federal Supply Inquiry Office in Washington to furnish information and other assistance to prospective government contractors. It did not limit its functions to G.S.A. buying, but gave aid on other agencies including the armed services.

Defense Secretary Johnson instituted a Military Procurement Information Center at the Pentagon. Also, the Defense Department opened nine suboffices in major cities to aid and guide businessmen in their dealings with the various procurement bureaus of the armed services.

The Department of Commerce set up a procurement information service in each of its forty-one field offices, and set up a system for greater cooperation with chambers of commerce in other large cities.

The Commerce Procurement Information Service did not confine itself to dissemination of information about the Commerce Department, but tried to make it a governmentwide service.[30]

Spot-checks of these business information offices for the subcommittee indicated that a fairly effective procedure was in existence before the Senate subcommittee made its final report.

The subcommittee suggested that government procurement agencies establish a "refer list" of persons known to have engaged in illegal or unethical practices. Firms placed on the list would not be disqualified from doing business with the government, but would represent those with whom the government should not do business until it makes certain it is not being defrauded or misled.[31]

In a realistic summation, the Senate subcommittee recognized that the "marked decrease in the activities of five-percenters" may be only temporary. "There is always a tendency to drift back to the old improper practices unless the problem is given constant attention. The new preventive procedures which have been drafted by some of the agencies must not be allowed to stagnate. . . . There must be no let-down in the efforts of responsible Government officials to get the influence peddler out of Government and keep him out." [32]

There was a need for constant reminder of the short duration of most reforms, and within months there were bitter experiences to demonstrate that some other military lessons had not made a deep enough imprint.

12

KOREA—A JOLTING REALITY

IT was five A.M. on Sunday, June 25, 1950 (the evening of the 24th, Washington time) when North Koreans struck at the Republic of Korea. The attack startled the world and shocked the Truman Administration into sharp changes in policy. The year the Korean War started, the United States military might was at its lowest point. In 1945, the total military and civilian personnel in the Department of Defense was 14,751,465—an estimated 21 percent of the entire labor force. By 1950, the total number had dropped to 2,213,410 military and civilian personnel—only 3.4 percent of the total labor force.

The Army was down from 8,267,958 to a mere 593,167. The Air Force, included with the Army in 1945, was only 411,277. The Navy had dropped from 3,380,817 in 1945 to 381,538, and the Marine Corps had fallen from 474,680 to 74,279.[1]

Because the military strength of the United States was at its lowest point since the days before World War II, many compared the surprise attack to December 7, 1941. Senator Alexander Wiley, a high-ranking Republican on the Senate Foreign Relations Committee, called it "another grisly Pearl Harbor." The Wisconsin Republican blamed the State Department for having our military forces withdrawn from Korea, and the Defense Department for our poor state of readiness.[2]

As late as January 10, 1950, Defense Secretary Louis Johnson had assured Congress that a $13.5 billion military budget was adequate. In making that assurance, he also offered the opinion that this level of spending would be sufficient for the next two years.

Although General Dwight D. Eisenhower, as chairman of the Joint Chiefs of Staff, had recommended a $15 billion level, he was only a mild critic of the Truman Administration and no real support for the congressional critics who wanted even greater expenditures. General Eisenhower appeared as a witness before the Senate Appropriations Subcommittee in late March to explain what had been described as his expressions of alarm at the extent of disarmament. General Eisenhower denied having said that "we had destroyed our defense." He said he would be satisfied if another $500 million was added to the military budget for fiscal 1951, praised the economy steps taken by Defense Secretary Johnson, and suggested only that perhaps they had gone a little "too far."

General Eisenhower testified that the forty-eight-group Air Force proposed by President Truman was "a safe minimum," but in the light of increased costs the funds allocated for the Air Force could buy only a forty-two-group force. Even as he was recommending some increased spending, General Eisenhower agreed with Defense Secretary Johnson's comment that war was not imminent. He stressed that there was possible danger to the national economy in spending too much for military purposes.[3]

While many political figures were trying to straddle the issues of economy and military preparedness, the blame for the actual decisions fell on President Truman and his Defense Secretary. Senator Styles Bridges (Rep., N.H.) led a Republican assault on President Truman and Johnson for misleading the nation about its military preparedness. Senator Bourke B. Hickenlooper (Rep., Ia.) demanded an accounting of the $57 billion in military funds appropriated since 1947. He also questioned the actions of Secretary of State Dean Acheson in making statements just prior to the Korean attack that indicated Korea and Formosa were outside the perimeter that the United States would defend.

Senator Robert A. Taft (Rep., Ohio) blamed both Johnson and Acheson, and in a speech at McConnelsville, Ohio, he declared, "We invited the attack in Korea.

"Secretary Acheson announced last winter that we would not defend Korea and Formosa," Taft said, setting the tune that many Republican critics were to follow.[4]

President Truman retained Secretary of State Dean Acheson, but within three months after the outbreak of the Korean War, the man symbolic of the Truman economy measures was dropped from the Cabinet. Johnson resigned as Defense Secretary on September 12. His successor was General George C. Marshall. It was necessary for President Truman to persuade Congress to amend the National Security Act of 1947, which barred the appointment of a career military officer as Defense Secretary within ten years after the officer retired.

General Marshall had served as Chief of Staff in World War II, had been President Truman's special envoy to China in 1945 and 1946, and had served as Secretary of State from 1947 through 1949. To many Democrats he was a hero, and one of the few great men out of World War II. To most Republican political leaders General Marshall was a symbol of the agreements between the Chinese Communists and Nationalist China that some of them regarded as a "sell-out."

The legislation to permit General Marshall to become Defense Secretary was passed after the bitterest of debates in the House and Senate. On the confirmation of General Marshall as Secretary of Defense the vote was 57 to 11. Forty-two Democrats and fifteen Republicans voted for nomination. All those opposed were Republicans.[5]

In addition to replacing the Secretary of Defense, President Truman made many more changes in the top civilian team at the Pentagon in the months just before and after the Korean War started. Robert A. Lovett, who had been Under Secretary of State under General Marshall, became Deputy Secretary of Defense, succeeding Stephen T. Early. Frank C. Pace, an Arkansas Democrat and a government lawyer, was named as Secretary of the Army to follow Gordon Gray. When Stuart Symington resigned as Secretary of the Air Force to become Chairman of the National Security Resources Board, he was replaced by Thomas K. Finletter.

General Walter Bedell Smith was named Director of the Central Intelligence Agency to succeed Rear Admiral Roscoe Hillenhoetter, and Admiral Forrest P. Sherman was confirmed to succeed Admiral Louis E. Denfeld as Chief of Naval Operations. In addition to Sherman, the other members of the Joint Chiefs of Staff were General Omar N. Bradley, chairman; General J. Lawton Collins, Army Chief of Staff; and General Hoyt S. Vandenberg, Air Force Chief of Staff.[6]

While most of the bitter criticism of the Truman Administration's policies had political overtones, many Democrats took part in decrying what they regarded as unwise economy in military matters. Also, informed and experienced men outside the political world found much fault with the way the U. S. military posture had been permitted to deteriorate.

The most sweeping criticism came from Hanson Baldwin, distinguished military analyst for *The New York Times*. On July 9,

1950, he published an extensive study of the "errors" of the Truman Administration, including the failure to equip and train South Koreans properly. Baldwin stated that the Defense Department had overestimated the role of air power and had concentrated on big bombers to the neglect of tactical planes and ground forces. The Truman Administration had also underestimated the role of tanks in Korea, and engaged in major cutbacks in the carrier forces and in Marine units, Baldwin charged. He also raked the poor intelligence.

With the outbreak of war, Senator Lyndon B. Johnson, a young Texan serving on the Senate Armed Services Committee, suggested that a Preparedness Subcommittee be established to concentrate on investigation into the state of readiness of U. S. military forces and on the buying practices of the Pentagon. It was to be a subcommittee similar to the war investigating committee with which President Truman had won his first national recognition.

Members of the Armed Services Committee agreed to establishment of the subcommittee and Senator Johnson was named chairman. He went to work immediately on investigation and reports regarding deficiencies in the operations of the Defense Department's Munitions Board that had failed to arrange for an adequate supply of wool and synthetic and natural rubber.[7]

Senator Johnson, the Texas Democrat, had been a consistent critic of the excessive emphasis on economy in the Defense Department. The outbreak of the Korean War signaled more comments by Senator Johnson denouncing Defense Secretary Johnson and asking for immediate mobilization of 823,000 reserves.

Even as the Truman Administration reversed itself and asked for more money, Senator Johnson contended that more was needed than was being requested. He reported to the Senate on August 23, 1950, that military costs were running as much as ten times higher than costs in World War II. The cost of equipping an infantry division had skyrocketed from $14.5 million in 1944 to $74 million in 1950. Equipment for an armored division had jumped from $30 million to $199 million. Cost for a Navy destroyer had increased from $7 million in 1939 to more than $40 million in 1950. A light tank had cost only $27,000 in 1939, but was up to $225,000 in 1950. Senator Johnson pointed out that a B-17 bomber had cost $300,000 before World War II, while the B-36's coming off the assembly line in 1950 were up to more than $3 million.

Even as Congress was approving a $17-billion emergency appropriation bill in September, 1950, Senator Johnson explained to the Senate that the 4.5 billion allocated to the Air Force would not buy the 5,333 new warplanes it was purported to cover. Prices had already risen to the point that approval of the entire Air Force request would supply money for 750 fewer planes.[8]

The Truman Administration's unwillingness to accept a fifty-eight-group Air Force vanished in the aftermath of the Korean conflict, and within a year Congress had approved funds for a sixty-eight-group Air Force. This type of unified action to increase defense spending and mobilization of the nation took place in nearly every area from the $3-billion stockpiling program to the extension of the Selective Service Act without limitation on the President's power to start induction.

The Strategic and Critical Materials Stockpiling Act of 1946 had authorized the buying of goods that were required for wartime needs, but it had started with only $100 million. The omnibus appropriations bill and the first and second supplemental appropriations bills included large stockpile items.[9]

Senator Johnson was impatient with the slow mobilization pace in 1950, and declared that it was time to get on with full-scale preparedness for war and abandon the "chicken-wire" defenses that were being erected. He pointed out that mobilization costs were $2 billion a month, or about 11 percent of the national income, as compared with the 50 percent of the national income used for national defense in 1942. He predicted that the United States would be involved in heavy mobilization for ten years or more.[10]

While concerning himself and his Preparedness Subcommittee with the total scope of military spending, he did not overlook some of the small cases that dramatized the work of his subcommittee in exposing the type of waste and mismanagement that was easy for the average citizen to understand. In late 1950, he spotlighted the case of a Texas farmer who had reaped a profit of nearly $60,000 out of the gross stupidity found in the Pentagon bureaucracy.

The farmer bought $1,209,600 worth of surplus aircraft computers from the government for $6.89. He then resold them to the Air Force for $63,000. His only major expense item was $4,000 he paid to crate and ship the "surplus" computers to the Air Force.[11]

The profits of the farmer on "surplus" goods was only one of many examples that popped up in the first year of the Korean War to demonstrate that neither the "unification" nor the much-heralded watchfulness of Defense Secretary Johnson had eliminated the wastefulness or the administrative bungling that had been such a problem in World War I and World War II.

Although President Truman had surrounded himself with military men and civilian advisers with high reputations, one man—General Douglas A. MacArthur—dominated the scene during the Korean War. His name, his strategy and his words continued to prevail in the discussions of the Korean War even after his differences with President Truman resulted in the most dramatic "firing" of a general in United States military history.

The legendary General of the Army, MacArthur, had been through the problems of World War I, sat as a judge in the famous court-martial proceedings against General William (Billy) Mitchell, and reached spectacular heights as Supreme Allied Commander in the South Pacific in World War II. He had been Army Chief of Staff as early as 1935, and had retired to the Philippines in 1937 where he served as Field Marshal of the Philippine armed forces.

Recalled to active duty in 1941, MacArthur was forced to flee Manila in the face of a Japanese assault, but plotted and directed the island-hopping strategy that was used to win back the Philippines. In his role as commander of United States occupation forces in Japan, he continued to gain stature as he took a major part in guiding the Japanese people to a more democratic society.

General MacArthur, a seasoned veteran of two world wars, was still stationed in Japan at the outbreak of the Korean War, with command over all United States military forces in that area of the world.

For several months there had been indications of a possible attack below the 38th parallel, which divided North Korea and South Korea. Although he was seventy years old when the North Koreans launched their attack on the South Korean Republic, MacArthur was prepared for the steps necessary to protect American lives and evacuate American citizens from the war area. At the request of the American Ambassador in Seoul, he provided the ships and the air cover for the evacuation of American dependents, and took the initiative to ship arms from Japan to the Republic of Korea.[12]

The United Nations Security Council, which was then being boycotted by the Soviet Union, asked for a cease-fire on June 25 and withdrawal of the North Korean troops from South Korea. Two days later the Security Council asked other United Nations countries to oust the invaders from the southern Republic.[13] President Truman immediately advised General MacArthur that "complete collapse" of the South Korean forces seemed imminent, and ordered him to furnish air and naval support.[14]

Even after the United States troops entered the battle, the North Koreans continued to make gains. There were weeks and months of uncertainty as the United States started a draft to fill out the Army ranks, took steps for civilian mobilization and rushed through appropriations for more military spending and bigger stockpiles of critical and strategic materials. Defense spending, only $13,018,000 in the fiscal year ending June 30, 1950, was nearly doubled to $22,-471,000 for fiscal 1951, soared to $44,037,000 in fiscal 1952 and $50,442,000 in fiscal 1953.[15]

General MacArthur's ability and his confidence were a strong factor in those first days when President Truman and his top advisers from the State and Defense Departments were trying to determine a wise course of action. Action was directed from Washington and through the United Nations, and General MacArthur took charge and followed his instructions. While there were many critics of President Truman, Defense Secretary Johnson and Secretary of State Acheson, there were only a few who blamed MacArthur for the initial reverses. Harold L. Ickes, former Secretary of Interior, was one of those early critics who denounced MacArthur for getting "caught flatfooted in Korea." [16] The impact of the Ickes criticism was lost in the general praise of the veteran general.

Differences that developed between General MacArthur and President Truman in the first weeks of the war concerned the issue of whether 33,000 Chinese Nationalist troops should be accepted for duty with the United Nations forces in Korea. Initially, General MacArthur wanted to use the troops offered by General Chiang Kai-shek, but Secretary of State Dean Acheson expressed his opposition and President Truman accepted the Acheson view. General MacArthur finally concurred with the decision to reject the Chinese Nationalist troops.[17]

Before the end of August, 1950, President Truman expressed resentment at a message General MacArthur sent to the Veterans of Foreign Wars, slashing out at "those who advocate appeasement and defeatism in the Pacific." The message was widely interpreted as criticism of the Truman Administration's policies, and it was at this point that President Truman first thought of relieving General MacArthur of his command.[18]

Within weeks after that telegram to the veterans, the United Nations forces under MacArthur were moving rapidly into North Korea and there were threats of possible intervention by the Chinese Communists. Warnings of caution came from Washington, and President Truman flew to Wake Island for an historic meeting with General MacArthur on October 15. Truman was accompanied by General Bradley, Army Secretary Pace, Assistant Secretary of State Dean Rusk, and Ambassador-at-large Philip C. Jessup. General MacArthur was accompanied by John Muccio, the United States Ambassador to Korea, and Admiral Arthur W. Radford, Commander of the Pacific Fleet.

President Truman awarded General MacArthur a fourth Oak Leaf Cluster to the Distinguished Service Medal for his Korean service, and when the meeting was over the President said it had ended in "complete unanimity."[19] However, there were strong differences of opinion that were not expressed publicly. The political current made it inevitable that all the differences would be exposed and emphasized in the most flamboyant manner.

Before President Truman returned, Harold E. Stassen, the perennial Republican candidate, charged the trip was a "sinful political escapade" to help the Democrats in the November election. And the twice-defeated Republican Presidential candidate Thomas E. Dewey removed himself from the political scene and commented that he "would recommend" General Dwight D. Eisenhower for the Republican nomination in 1952.[20]

The MacArthur push toward the Yalu River in North Korea collapsed on November 25 when 200,000 Chinese Communists moved down to meet the United Nations offensive. The blow was devastating, and unexpected. Intelligence reports had indicated that the Chinese Communist movement into North Korea had been no more than 50,000 to 100,000 men. MacArthur explained some of the reverses as attributable to "extraordinary inhibitions on the use of air power above the Yalu River," and this stirred new conflicts with the Truman Administration.

The United Nations forces stopped the Chinese Communist drive, and started a counteroffensive in mid-March, 1951, when President Truman indicated that he planned to try to initiate peace talks. General MacArthur took the play away by making his own offer to "confer in the field," after warning the opposition that if the United Nations expanded its operations it "would doom Red China to the risk of imminent military collapse."[21]

President Truman did not act immediately, although he said later that he had already decided to fire MacArthur. The final straw was a MacArthur telegram to House Minority Leader Joseph W. Martin, the Massachusetts Republican.

"Here we fight Europe's war with arms while the diplomats there still fight it with words," MacArthur wired. "There is no substitute for victory." [22]

President Truman consulted with his top civilian and military advisers and received what he said was a "unanimous" view that MacArthur should be fired. "By this act MacArthur left me no choice," Truman explained later. "I could no longer tolerate his insubordination."

On April 11, 1951, MacArthur was dismissed. The official explanation stated that he was "unable to give his wholehearted support to the policies of the U. S. Government and of the U. N. in matters pertaining to his official duties." [23]

The firing came in an atmosphere charged with politics, and MacArthur was brought back to Washington for a hero's welcome. His reception included an invitation to address a joint session of the Congress. MacArthur's speech and his confident and effective presentation of his position before the Senate made him more the victor than the vanquished.

The Korean War was a dominant issue throughout the 1952 political year, and the firing of MacArthur stood out in the public mind as the single most dramatic incident. It was an issue stressed by G.O.P. candidate Dwight D. Eisenhower in his campaign against Illinois Governor Adlai Stevenson. In the closing days of the campaign, General Eisenhower promised the American people, "I shall go to Korea" if it were required to bring an end to the Korean War.

A nation confused by a war that was frustrating in its developments and complicated and perplexing in its objectives, wanted to unload the responsibility on someone with an easy answer. General Eisenhower, a hero of World War II who seemed above the petty political bickering, appeared to most to be the right man.

13

THE CHAMBER OF HORRORS

IN the fall of 1951, a House Armed Services subcommittee started an investigation of procurement practices of the military services in the first two years of the Korean War. Representative F. Edward Hébert, a tough-minded Louisiana Democrat, chaired the Special Subcommittee on Procurement. Before being elected to Congress in 1940 Eddie Hébert had made a name for himself as a crusading city editor for the *New Orleans States.* His achievements in fighting the corruption of the successors of the Huey Long regime in Louisiana paved the way for his political triumph, and equipped him with a better than average know-how as an investigator.

From the time he entered Congress, Hébert had been concerned with the problem of waste, loose management and corruption in the military buying programs. He witnessed the scandals during World War II, and the promises of better management under the National Security Act of 1947 and the National Security Act Amendments of 1949. It had all been sold to Congress and the public as a "unification" that would eliminate wasteful duplication and provide the machinery that would make either bungling or corruption less likely.

That the Defense Department needed standardization of procurement of common items was glaringly apparent. There was no logical reason why the Army, Navy, Air Force or Marines should purchase different underwear, different soap, different towels, or different sheets, or the same items at different prices.

The problems in procurement that had become so obvious during the Korean conflict were not new. Representative Jack Anderson (Rep., Cal.), a member of the Hébert subcommittee, declared that the federal government had attempted since 1929 to establish a single catalog system, that being the year such a system was authorized by law. The catalog system was to provide common descriptions and order numbers for all items of military supply, regardless of the service for which they were purchased. This would have provided a concise method of inventory control, similar to that used by private industry.

But, as Anderson pointed out, "The twenty-three years since [the passage of the law] have been marked by frustration and failure." When the Hébert subcommittee began hearings, the military establishment still did not have a unified procurement catalog.[1]

Critics of the military foot-dragging felt the twenty-three-year delay in complying with the law was a disgrace and reminded the Defense Department and the public that it had never taken the armed forces so long to spend money appropriated by Congress.

The Pentagon excuses that a unified catalog system was an impossibility brought sharp rebuke from Representative Anderson, who reminded the military experts, "Actually, a single catalog system for communications items was developed and installed within a period of less than a year during World War II. This system was voluntarily adopted by all of the Armed Forces of the United States, Great Britain, Australia, and Canada [with the exception of] the United States Navy, so that a single system provided a useful management tool for the supply of those nations on a wider scope than that required of a United States Federal Catalog system."

Anderson further noted that the Interallied Cataloging Committee had recommended in 1945 that the system used on communications items be expanded, and that in 1949 a detailed plan was presented to a House Armed Services subcommittee that could have been installed in less than two years' time.

"No explanation has ever been given why this plan was not carried out," Anderson said. "Whether by design or because of ignorance, there is no single catalog system today."

The Hoover Commission, the California Republican pointed out, had been in unanimous agreement on the importance of a single catalog in its 1949 report.[2]

The first Defense Secretary, James Forrestal, strongly endorsed the idea of standardized purchases of common items, and the Munitions Board was given the job of doing a study of the supplies used by the various services and establishing a Defense Department supply catalog.

"We cannot afford to enter a future national emergency without having the military cataloging system so well completed, so well understood, and so well accepted, but that we will reap the full benefits which can be expected from it," Forrestal stated on May 12, 1948, in a memorandum to the Army, Navy and Air Force.

"It must be understood clearly that I consider the project to be of primary importance to the effective conduct of business in the Military Establishment; that I believe it will lead most positively to a simple and well understood approach of the three services to industry, and that I believe its proved results in segmental fields which have been explored demonstrate conclusively such great savings to the taxpayers in the process of procurement that we in the Military Establishment must not fail to prosecute the project with the utmost vigor."

Forrestal explained that the ultimate objective would be to name, describe, classify and number each unique item used, purchased, stocked or distributed by the military establishment. If done properly, he said, this would mean that one distinctive set of letters and numbers would identify any item for all of the services.

Glowing reports emerged from Forrestal's office on the prospects for completion of the cataloging task in three years. In 1949, when the House Armed Services Committee asked for a progress report, then incumbent Defense Secretary Louis Johnson assured Congress that great progress was being made and that no special legislation was needed. He listed the mechanical details necessary to produce the military purchasing catalog, and added: "All of these activities are well under way and there has been marked progress." [3]

Three years after the task was started under Forrestal, Chairman Hébert assigned the investigating job to Special Counsel John J. Courtney and his assistants, Richard W. Webb and Paul L. Monahan. Instead of finding the cataloging job completed or almost so, they found that virtually no progress had been made. Acting under instructions from Chairman Hébert, they began accumulating colorful examples of purchases by the military services to demonstrate to the public the waste of tax money that takes place when each of the military services goes off on its own to buy common items.

The investigators sent identical requests to each of the services for examples of specific items procured through the regular channels. Each item was to be marked clearly with the name, stock number, quantity in stock, average number issued per month and the unit cost. Each of the services responded wholeheartedly in its efforts to "cooperate" with the Hébert subcommittee. All the items and prices later considered by the subcommittee were provided solely by the branch of the services under fire.[4]

Hébert had been aware of reports in 1948 that the Marine Corps was paying $7.50 for the same weight canvas cot that the Navy bought for $3.20. He knew that at the same time the Marines and the Army used the same kind of blanket, one costing $2.50 and the other $1.77. Because there was no central cataloging system back in 1948, Hébert was not shocked to learn that the Navy was buying an ocean exposure suit for $25.91, but the Air Force was paying $47.31 for the same article. In that same period of time, the Air Force paid $121.78 for an electrically heated flying suit effective down to 65 degrees below zero while the Navy paid $122.47 for a suit effective only to 20 degrees below zero.

Startled when his committee lawyers told him that the picture had not changed, he was chagrined that they had found it quite easy to uncover even more absurd examples. The Navy, Air Force and Marines were all buying the same low-cut shoe from the same manufacturer, but there was a substantial difference in the prices paid in the same period of time. The Marines paid $5.31 a pair, the Navy $6.08 and the Air Force $7.29. Even more perplexing were the prices the Army and Marines had paid for heavy rubber-sole combat boots for use in Korea. Both bought the identical boot from the same manufacturer, but the Marines paid $16.80 a pair, while the Army paid $24.65 a pair.[5]

Although it was only a "spot check," enough items were involved to decide Chairman Hébert to set up a display in the House Armed Services hearing room 304, which he would call "The Chamber of Horrors." When the full display of information received from the services had been assembled for public viewing, the Louisiana Democrat declared that there should be a sign over the door stating: "Abandon Hope, All Ye Who Enter Here." [6]

As the open hearings began in February, 1952, Chairman Hébert explained the subcommittee's objectives and policies. "This committee wants to guarantee to the American taxpayer, an efficient and competent use of the dollar," he declared. "This committee is not on a fishing expedition. . . . The things which this committee seeks to accomplish are fundamental. I feel that I bespeak the sentiments of this committee when I say that all members individually and collectively refuse to supinely adopt the doctrine of frustration. A doctrine which decrees that nothing can be done about the situation and the only escape is to take the easy way out and float with the stream. . . . We are determined to do a constructive job and determined to discharge our responsibility to the full extent of our capabilities." [7]

Representative Anderson declared that despite the assurances of cooperation from the Pentagon, formal military policy was directed at goals in defiance of existing legislation. Anderson quoted an Army report as stating that "the Munitions Board cataloging program will never provide a useful management tool, as it will never produce a single name and a single number for each item."

The California Congressman charged that the Munitions Board, instead of working toward an effective catalog had been working on a system that was spurious.

"Over the years with this system it has been possible to show that great progress is being made in the development of a single catalog system because so many people are at work, producing so many millions of cards that are to be printed, distributed, and filed away —all at enormous expense," Anderson said. He declared that the process included the breaking up of functional parts of the cataloging process "so that duplicating, uncoordinated and often conflicting information is issued."

Representative Anderson also complained about the staffing of the cataloging organization with key personnel who did not understand the need for proper identification of all items: "A short time ago an officer was placed in charge of the Munitions Board cataloging program who in his first policy announcement made the statement that it was all right to assign more than one number to each item of supply—the direct opposite of a single catalog system."

Anderson maintained the Munitions Board had been destroying the possibility of obtaining a single catalog by constantly changing procedures, by scattering the authority and responsibility, by placing the responsibility for technical decisions in nontechnical hands, and by constantly changing administrators. "This may give the committee the impression that the development and installation of a single catalog system for the use of the Federal Government is of almost insurmountable difficulty," Anderson warned.

Anderson reminded the subcommittee of the success of the Interallied Catalog during the war, adding that this same system had been recommended as the basis for a Federal Supply Catalog. "Yet today there is no single catalog system; and the conclusion is inescapable that there exists either a colossal ignorance, a determined resistance, or almost criminal negligence," the Californian said. He cautioned that "there are two groups who will gain from the supply confusion resulting from the lack of a single catalog: unscrupulous manufacturers, and 'empire builders' in the Government."

According to Anderson, procurement was not the only problem resulting from the existing lack of organization within the military supply lines. "Inventory control of stock is impossible," Anderson commented. "Because of lack of inventory control, stocks in excess of 240 years' supply have been discovered and reported."

He declared that this lack meant that the Defense Department was paying millions of dollars for storage space and for employees to keep stock that was no longer needed. Also, the lack of accurate identification of goods in inventory meant that the "reports of emergency agencies and Defense Department Programs are meaningless.

"Facts showing that so much money is being spent on an emergency program is no criteria that the money is being spent wisely for it does not reflect the amount of money being spent for wasteful duplication of stocks, of facilities and of staff," Anderson said. "The maintenance and disposal of the $10 billion worth of unserviceable and uncataloged items clogging the supply systems are putting a strain on the individual economy and a tax burden on the individual citizen that is becoming unbearable." [8]

The Anderson indictment of the Munitions Board's activities was read to Deputy Secretary of Defense William C. Foster just before he took the stand as the first Defense Department witness on February 11, 1952.

"I came not to bury the Defense Department but to praise it," Deputy Secretary Foster stated, presenting his position to the subcommittee. "That may not accord with what Mr. Anderson has said, but I would like to make that clear at the beginning. I do not mean, Mr. Chairman, to suggest that we are not aware of some of the mistakes and errors that have been so well publicized. We are aware of them, sometimes painfully so. We are also conscious of other shortcomings that have not been publicized." He continued with the official Defense Department policy in regard to the hearings: "When I look back over the record of the last year—especially in the field in which you are interested—I cannot help but be impressed by what has been accomplished."

Foster did not argue with the facts as presented by Chairman Hébert or Representative Anderson, but he said he hoped to put the charges of waste and inefficiency "into proper focus, so that you and the public can judge our performance in the light of all the facts, both plus and minus."

The Deputy Defense Secretary said the hearings had made the

Department "more acutely aware" of shortcomings, "but at the same time I hope they will demonstrate that we have profited from mistakes of the past and that we are constantly improving our operations."

However, Foster registered the Defense Department objection to pending legislation that would have directed reorganization and completion of the single catalog. He declared that the Defense Secretary already had all the necessary power to complete the single catalog, and he objected to Congress passing laws that would cause a reorganization "which is a responsibility we believe belongs to the Secretary of Defense."

While agreeing that progress had been slow, Foster warned that "the catalog will not be a complete panacea in itself." It will not automatically eliminate all the endless avenues of possible waste and extravagance that exist in an undertaking as colossal and far-flung as our defense system," he declared. "This can be achieved only by watching every penny in every way, by constantly cultivating the ideal of thrift; by trying to make indifference to waste as immoral as indifference to duty at the front. This we must do, and this, in a growing measure, we have been doing."

Then Foster launched the Defense Department counterattack with claims of fantastic savings on better traffic management on both passenger service and freight hauling. The total savings, he claimed, was $71,611,109.

"The Munitions Board has requested the three armed services to recover every pound of iron and steel scrap available," Foster said. "The Army, Navy, Marines, and Air Force are all doing what I believe is an excellent job of economy, efficiency, and conservation. Cost-consciousness is being hammered into every member of the Armed Forces, from private to General."

The Deputy Defense Secretary claimed that the Army alone had saved "about $8 billion through its rehabilitation of old World War II equipment and its rebuilding of junk from the scrap heap.

"For a particular example, the Army has rebuilt 2.5-ton trucks for as little as $1,000, saving $6,000 on the cost of a new truck," Foster claimed. "In Korea, trucks which carry material up to the front come back loaded with scrap and salvage materials. All Army personnel have been repeatedly told that waste is a crime against our country that may affect our future freedom." [9]

Chairman Hébert expressed his skepticism over the claims of great cost-consciousness, and the millions and billions it was contended had been "saved." He commented on the "army of public relations officers" at the Pentagon who had been busy with press conferences and the distribution of "propaganda" to draw attention away from the obviously unjustified waste and inefficiency in "The Chamber of Horrors." [10]

Foster, who had been Deputy Secretary for only five months at the time he testified, insisted his view could be considered objective because he was not a responsible official during 1950 and early 1951 when the examples of waste, inefficiency and questionable decisions had taken place. To the members of Hébert's subcommittee, Foster was just another clever spokesman whose function it was to disregard the specific problems of waste and inefficiency and make claims of savings of billions of dollars in areas where it would be difficult to prove or disprove the validity of the "savings." [11]

Foster was not the only Defense Department official who had come into office since the problems of procurement had first come to light. Many other officials could not answer for the actions of their predecessors or were not responsible for the specific area the investigators were probing.

As Representative Hébert and his staff tried to place the responsibility for the specific "horrors" in purchasing practices, he ran into the usual problem that congressional investigators face: the man who was most responsible had either been transferred, retired or was otherwise unavailable.

Chiding military officials about the "Phantom of the Pentagon" as his hearings were getting started, Hébert said, "He's the little man who's responsible for military purchases, but always seems to be gone. Whenever I try to get him before the committee, he has either just retired or left on a trip to the Far East." [12]

When the Defense Department sent Vice Admiral Charles Fox to testify, in the hopes that he could succeed in taking the offensive from the subcommittee and directing the investigation into areas more favorable to the military, a scornful Hébert dubbed him "The Red Grange of the Pentagon." After the subcommittee had successfully established that Fox was the man responsible for the Navy's oversupply of flatware, the Admiral was referred to in the press as "Oyster Forks Fox." [13]

The Defense Department counteroffensive was not staged only before the Hébert subcommittee. Statements released by the service press offices attempted to explain away the misunderstandings created by the Hébert display and hearings. Different size lots, different purchase dates and "shoddy" materials in lower-priced items were a number of the reasons presented to the public to excuse the numerous discrepancies in prices. The subcommittee reminded the services that they had established the specifications for supplies and were therefore responsible if shoddy materials had been accepted for military use.

The military specifications came in for their share of criticism when Hébert pointed out that the bound volume of specifications for Army flyswatters weighed four pounds. The specifications for dog toenail-clippers comprised four single-spaced typewritten pages and two additional pages of photographs. In the four years preceding the Hébert hearings all the services had purchased only nineteen toenail-clippers for the canine corps of the military.[14]

When the Navy announced tremendous savings were to be realized by its discovery that a gasket it had been buying for 39¢ could be made by its own machinists for a penny, Hébert quipped, "That's fine, but did they tell the Army and the Air Force about it."[15]

The Defense Department released many such examples of savings as it tried to counter the impact of the public reaction to "The Chamber of Horrors." Chairman Hébert declared that he and his committee would not be stopped by the Potomac Pitchmen or the "army of alibi artists" the military unleashed against them.

In its final report, the Hébert subcommittee reported that the Munitions Board had spent $100 million from 1945 to 1952 in its ineffective effort to develop a single supply catalog, and an additional $87 million was spent on separate cataloging systems within the military departments in the same period.

That five-year effort had produced catalogs "so incomplete, [containing] so many duplications and [covering] so many imaginary and obsolete items that they are worthless."

Hébert's report stated that standardization and cataloging of all items used in the military department "will result in savings estimated at about $4 billion annually."

The report maintained that "The Chamber of Horrors" exhibit had "provided proof beyond a doubt of the failure of the Munitions Board's standards and cataloging." Identical common nails were brought together under a single identifying number, which is the principal objective of the catalog program. Some were described by the Army as "galvanized," and the Air Force described the same item as "zinc-coated." In other cases the Army gave the diameter in gauge size, an industry standard, while the Navy prescribed the diameter in decimals of an inch for the same item.

"Dress shoes displayed were procured under three different specifications [Army, Navy and Marine Corps]. Even the size designations varied so that a specific size is not the same for all of the services. Bed pillows were not standardized; and consequently, there were two sizes; one for the Army and one for the Navy. . . . Galvanized metal sheets were procured under two different specifications; and are issued by the pound in the Navy, by the square foot in the Air Force, and by the sheet in the Army. Similar variations in the quantitative measurement of a great many supplies were found in the present departmental catalogs now in use which block cross servicing." [16]

The many examples listed in the report of the Hébert subcommittee were only typical of the hundreds that could have been used to demonstrate the need for congressional action. It was a shocked and indignant Armed Services subcommittee that took the case for a single catalog system, against the Pentagon bureaucracy, to the House floor and won a 224 to 48 victory. The measure passed on a voice vote in the Senate, and became law in June, 1952.

Chairman Hébert and his subcommittee had pushed for the passage of the Defense Supply Standardization Act to force action to develop a "single catalog system and related supply standardization" over the objections of the Defense Department and the Truman Administration.[17] They had won a temporary victory over the "Phantom of the Pentagon," who constantly tries to avoid pinpointing the responsibility, and the "propagandists of the Pentagon," who adeptly compile great claims of savings to draw attention away from the clearest cases of waste and bungling.

Even as Hébert shepherded the legislation through Congress, the House was appropriating more than $50 billion for the Defense Department budget for fiscal 1953 to take care of the costs of the Korean War and to provide for a greater general military preparedness. As a result, Hébert and his staff acknowledged that the passage of the Defense Cataloging and Standardization Act was not a panacea for Pentagon purchasing practices dealing with $50 billion a year. They recognized that it would be a useful tool if there were constant vigilance on the part of Congress to make certain the Defense Secretary did not forget the importance of a single standard catalog.

Not only had the Hébert subcommittee uncovered the problems of interservice procurement, the investigators also brought out one glaring example of the difficulties of intraservice procurement.

Air Force experts had decided the increased emphasis on jet aircraft necessitated the purchase of 1,000 additional turret lathes used for building components in jet engines.[18] Until the fall of 1951 the Bullard Machine Tool Company of Bridgeport, Connecticut, had been providing all these Air Force lathes at a cost of $38,000 each. When Bullard advised the Air Force that it could deliver only eleven lathes per month, the service began searching for another company to augment the Bullard supply.

Bullard, in an effort to retain the full contract, requested $7 million in defense funds to expand its lathe-making facilities. The request was turned down on the grounds that it would better serve the interests of the Air Force if a portion of the order was subcontracted.

In September, 1951, the Fisher Body Company, a subsidiary of General Motors, was given a contract for 757 of the original 1,000 lathes at a price of $90,600 each—almost two and a half times the Bullard price. At that time Fisher was not equipped to produce any of the lathes, and had to undergo a complete conversion before it could begin production of this vital machinery.

In an effort to aid Fisher in its tooling-up, the government "loaned" the company all but 80 of the 507 machine tools it would need to begin production. (Later investigation proved that the "loan" had indeed been a gift.

In early February, 1952, the Fisher contract for turret lathes was suddenly canceled by the Air Force. The Hébert subcommittee wanted to know why. If the lathes had been so vital to our national defense that it had been necessary to pay well above the normal price for the machinery, why had the contract been canceled within six months? If the machinery was not vital to our defense posture, why had the contract been awarded originally? They also wanted to know who had made the decision to award the contract to Fisher at the expense of the Bullard Company, and on whose advice this decision was based.

Roswell L. Gilpatrick, Assistant Secretary of the Air Force, testified before the Hébert subcommittee, in executive session, on February 8, 1952, two days after the contract was canceled. Gilpatrick announced that the $69 million Fisher contract had been canceled because of recent cutbacks in jet aircraft procurement and the adoption of new engineering techniques for jet engines that reduced the need for the tools.

The Assistant Secretary admitted that it had been his decision to award the multimillion-dollar order to the General Motors subsidiary. Under questioning, Gilpatrick acknowledged that he had acted in part on the advice of Harold R. Boyer, chairman of the government's aircraft production board and a former General Motors executive. During this time Boyer had been on a leave of absence from his G.M. position.

Gilpatrick assured the subcommittee that Boyer had "personally recommended to me that the best way to get on with this job from a time standpoint" was to give it to the Fisher Body Company.

Another Air Force witness, Swan E. Bergstrom, told the subcommittee it was "perfectly normal" for Fisher to charge two and a half times as much as the original contractor for the lathes because they were "inexperienced" in making machine tools. When Bergstrom conceded that the $90,600 per lathe was prohibitive to private industrial customers, Representative Jack Dempsey (Dem., N. Mex.) remarked in disgust, "Nobody else would buy them except the Federal Government and its officials." [19]

The Air Force witnesses confessed that the government would lose close to $10 million on this contract with Fisher, but expressed the hope that perhaps $4 million could be recovered in the "insurance" the government would have against any future lack of companies prepared to turn out this vital machinery.

At the same time the Hébert subcommittee was hearing this explanation from the Air Force, an anonymous military mechanic discovered that the work of the turret lathes could be done more efficiently by an ordinary T-lathe, which cost the government only $28,000.

The turret lathes were probably too big to be brought to the House Office Building for display in Room 304, but, from a standpoint of price and general bungling, they deserved a prominent position in Eddie Hébert's "Chamber of Horrors."

14

EISENHOWER'S "NEW LOOK"

THE shadow of a New Look in the defense spending was cast over the Pentagon by the election of General Dwight D. Eisenhower as President on November 4, 1952. Candidate Eisenhower had promised the nation economy of operation, a more effective military posture and a personal inspection of conditions in Korea. The whopping 33,936,252 to 27,314,992 victory over Adlai Stevenson indicated a public belief that the pleasant-faced World War II hero could provide the needed miracle.

Within a month after he piled up the 442 to 89 [1] electoral vote margin, President-elect Eisenhower went to Korea to keep his campaign promise. He was accompanied by the key men he had chosen as his Cabinet officers—John Foster Dulles, New York lawyer, who was to be Secretary of State; George M. Humphrey, lawyer-industrialist and head of the Hanna Company, who was to be Secretary of Treasury; and Charles E. Wilson, president of General Motors Corporation, who had been designated the Secretary of Defense.

The defense policies of the Truman Administration were based upon "deterrence" and "containment" of the Communist world. After letting the United States defense posture sag from 1946 through early 1950, the Truman Administration had moved with a frenzied shift to major mobilization that boosted defense spending over the $40-billion-a-year mark. President Truman and his military advisers had concluded it would have to remain between $40 billion and $50 billion until about 1954 or 1955, when it would level off at about $35 billion to $40 billion.

The Truman plan in 1952 was keyed to a Strategic Air Command equipped with bombers and nuclear weapons sufficient to deter the Soviet Union from starting a general war. At the same time, there were plans for conventional land, sea and air forces to discourage and even put down any localized uprising, such as the Korean problem, around the fringe of the Communist world. The planning in 1951 and 1952 had been keyed to a year of "maximum peril" in 1954 or 1955. It was an expensive program, and regarded as too expensive for President-elect Eisenhower, who was pledged to "security with solvency."

The Eisenhower trip to Korea gave little reason for any real optimism over an end to that conflict, but the return trip aboard the *U.S.S. Helena* provided time to discuss a program for cutting defense spending. President Eisenhower, Dulles, Humphrey and Wilson were joined by Admiral Arthur W. Radford, who was later named by Eisenhower as the Chairman of the Joint Chiefs of Staff. Although it wasn't announced at the time, they started to formulate a shift in policy to what was later revealed as "massive retaliation." [2]

The New Look was to place more reliance upon the Strategic Air Command, with the massive threat of a nuclear attack as the major force. It was felt we were too far extended in Korea with our land and naval forces pinned down, and that the use of a flexible "mobile strategic reserve" would provide the only force we would need to supplement native forces.

The first budget-cutting efforts of the Eisenhower Administration ran into resistance from the holdover Joint Chiefs of Staff, who warned that the proposed $4 billion cut for fiscal 1954 and a $6.6 billion cut for fiscal 1955 would represent an undue risk to national security. In May, 1953, President Eisenhower made a drastic change in the Joint Chiefs of Staff, naming Admiral Radford to succeed General Omar Bradley as Chairman. General Matthew Ridgway was named to succeed General J. Lawton Collins as Army Chief of Staff; Admiral Robert B. Carney was named to succeed Admiral William M. Fechteler as Chief of Naval Operations, and General Nathan Twining succeeded General Hoyt Vandenberg as Air Force Chief of Staff.[3]

The civilian defense team under Defense Secretary Wilson was topped by Deputy Defense Secretary Roger M. Kyes, a vice president of General Motors, who gained a quick reputation as Wilson's hatchet man. Robert Stevens, chairman of the board of J. P. Stevens & Co., was Secretary of the Army; Texas financier Robert B. Anderson was Secretary of the Navy; and Harold E. Talbott, an industrialist and management consultant, was named Secretary of the Air Force.

The nomination of Wilson as Defense Secretary ran into a hornet's nest of opposition in the closely divided Senate Armed Services Committee when the sixty-three-year-old industrialist balked at selling his stock in General Motors, a major defense contractor. Wilson argued at a closed hearing that "what was good for our country was good for General Motors, and vice versa." His critics quoted him as saying "what is good for General Motors is good for the country," and in the ensuing political fury President Eisenhower nearly lost his Defense Secretary even before he was confirmed.

When Wilson agreed to sell his General Motors holdings, most of the opposition vanished and he was confirmed by the Senate by a 77 to 6 vote. Similar controversy erupted over Talbott, but the other civilian defense leaders were confirmed without contest.[4]

Although the controversy over Wilson's nomination dissolved, the memory of the "conflict of interest" problem was kept alive in Democratic jibes at Wilson and Treasury Secretary Humphrey as symbols of the big-business complex they contended dominated the Eisenhower Administration.

The difficult problem of doing anything about the Korean War was apparent to Eisenhower even as he went through the motions of his promised visit, and his press statement issued at the time held out little promise: "We have no panaceas, no trick ways of settling any problems." [5] The new President seemed resigned to the difficult task of a long struggle, but the death of Stalin on March 5, 1953, opened the way for a lessening of tensions and an end to the Korean War. Georgi Malenkov, the new Soviet Premier, seemed to be more conciliatory in his policies, and President Eisenhower asked the Soviet Union to demonstrate good faith by supporting an armistice in Korea as well as signing an Austrian peace treaty.

Unexpectedly, on March 28, only three weeks after the death of Stalin, the Chinese Communists took the initiative and agreed to an exchange of wounded and sick prisoners. A few days later, they came to agreement on one of the stickiest points of negotiation: transfer of healthy prisoners of war to a neutral agency. Negotiations were prolonged, but on July 27 there was formal signing of an armistice to end the three-year war that had never been an official war but only a United Nations "police action." It had cost the United States more than $22 billion, more than 25,000 dead and more than 115,000 other casualties.[6]

The end of fighting in Korea and the start of negotiation had permitted President Eisenhower to make his first public pitch for his New Look in defense posture. He explained that the Soviet Union had "hoped to force upon America and the free world an unbearable security burden leading to an economic disaster." He declared that the Pentagon defense budget "must first of all, be one which we can bear for a long—and indefinite—period of time."

The Truman Administration's plan for a 143-wing Air Force was among his first targets as he sought to justify spending cuts that must come from the Air Force if they were to be significant. He declared it to be "foolish and dangerous" for the nation to be hypnotized by magic numbers.

"There is no given number of ships, no given number of divisions, no given number of air wings in the Air Force, Navy and Marine Corps, no given number of billions of dollars that will automatically guarantee security," President Eisenhower said in a sweeping blow at those who opposed his budget cuts.

Regarded as an outstanding authority on military matters, the President was effective in lashing out at "the special pleaders both in and out of the military services." Eisenhower, the war hero, told the nation the budget cuts were a result of his "personal study and analysis [and] represents, in my judgment, what is best for our nation's permanent security." [7]

There were Democratic efforts to blame the civilian political appointees in the Pentagon for unwise decisions to refine the Air Force goal downward from 143 to 120 wings. "Civilians in the Pentagon with no military experience are thwarting the will of Congress," declared Representative George H. Mahon, the Texas Democrat. The Republicans quoted Eisenhower, the military hero, for their authority for making cuts, and Representative Errett P. Scrivner, the Kansas Republican, snapped that 120 "solid" wings were better than 143 "paper" wings.[8]

Senator Stuart Symington, the first Air Force Secretary and an air-power enthusiast, declared that President Eisenhower was no prophet in asking for great appropriations for planes, and other Democrats joined the chorus in demanding that the United States buy the planes necessary to deliver the nuclear bombs in our arsenal. It was all futile in the face of the Korean armistice and the assurances of President Eisenhower. Congress appropriated only $34.4 billion for fiscal 1954—nearly $10 billion less than the Truman Administration had suggested. The appropriation included $13 billion for the Army, $9.4 billion for the Navy, and $11.2 billion for the Air Force.[9]

President Eisenhower continued to speak in terms of getting more for the defense dollar, and the businessmen in his Administration were stressing the need for further reorganization to overcome the lack of "cost consciousness" on the part of the military. Certainly, the Korean War had spotlighted organizational weaknesses in the already twice-reorganized Defense Department. An impressive panel was named to make the recommendations for reorganization to provide for an "ever-prepared" Pentagon with "clear and unchallenged civilian responsibility" and "maximum effectiveness at minimum cost." Those were lofty goals for the panel members, Nelson Rockefeller, Arthur S. Flemming, Milton Eisenhower, former Defense Secretary Robert Lovett, General Omar Bradley and David Sarnoff, chairman of the board of Radio Corporation of America.

President Eisenhower said that the "clear and unchallenged civilian responsibility" could be best achieved by "decentralization of operations" of the Pentagon under what he described as "flexible machinery at the top." The recommended reorganization plan called for six additional Assistant Secretaries of Defense for decentralization. It also provided for abolition of the Munitions Board, Research and Development Board and the Supply Management Agency, which were regarded as being too cumbersome to be effective management tools.

The most controversial parts of the recommended reorganization plan involved steps that would centralize more authority over the Joint Staff and the Joint Chiefs in the Defense Secretary and the Chairman of the Joint Chiefs. Selection and tenure of the Director of the Joint Staff would be subject to the approval of the Defense Secretary. The tenure and selection of the members of the Joint Staff would require the approval of the Chairman of the Joint Chiefs. It also called for transferring responsibility for management for the Joint Staff from the Chiefs to the Chairman.

The proposal to concentrate more authority in the Chairman of the Joint Chiefs of Staff ran into instant opposition. Recurring fear of a single Chief of Staff brought forth a strong House move to block that aspect of the 1953 reorganization plan, but the opposition failed. In another noncontroversial reorganization in 1953, President Eisenhower transferred the authority for the stockpiling of critical and strategic materials to the Office of Defense Mobilization, headed by Director Arthur S. Flemming.[10]

With the reorganizations of 1953 out of the way, and with a new civilian and military defense team, the Eisenhower Administration financial advisers moved determinedly to try to cut the Defense Department budget to the $30 billion level for fiscal 1955. However, the economy force of Treasury Secretary Humphrey and Budget Director

Joseph Dodge ran into a sharp counterforce in the National Security Council, where the analysis of the Soviet military posture indicated that there should be no significant reduction of United States forces.

The new Joint Chiefs of Staff were in solid opposition to any reduction below the level of twenty Army divisions and the goal of a 114-wing Air Force by mid-1954 and a 120-wing force by mid-1955. It was a program requiring at least $42 billion in actual expenditures, and a minimum of $35 billion in new spending authority—a full $5 billion above the level the Eisenhower financial advisers wanted.

Months of jockeying and maneuvering passed before President Eisenhower could come up with a Defense Department budget in January, 1954, that called for $37.5 billion in expenditures for fiscal 1955, but provided for only $1 billion in new money. This meant the budget cutters had come up only $1 billion, and the Joint Chiefs had been persuaded to agree to a cut of $4 billion below the $41 billion they had initially insisted was a minimum. By a stretch-out on the programs, and by acceptance of a large number of qualifications, General Ridgway and Admiral Carney had given their approval with reservations.[11]

Although General Ridgway and Admiral Carney were persuaded to swallow their objections in 1954 when testifying on the budget for fiscal 1955, they were more outspoken in their dissent in early 1955 when the Democratic Senate started to consider President Eisenhower's budget request for fiscal 1956. Although the Democrats were back in a control position in Congress in 1955, they did not try to upset the New Look with its emphasis on air power and with its sharp cuts in Army manpower. The Democrats listened attentively, and with some sympathy, as General Ridgway spelled out his reservations about steady cuts in Army personnel and argued for a more balanced force. His plea had no impact on a Congress that seemed content to go along with $31.9 billion in new spending authority. The Air Force received the whopping $14.9 billion chunk of this, with the Navy receiving $9.1 billion and the Army only $7.3 billion.[12]

No protest attended General Ridgway's retirement in mid-1955, since he stepped outside the role of an Eisenhower-team man to give Congress his opposition to what he considered to be too much reliance on air power. It was to be several years before Democrats were to make "balanced forces" for "limited wars" their political battle cry.

15

THE ARMY-McCARTHY HEARINGS

IN the summer of 1953, Senator Joseph R. McCarthy began investigating possible Communist infiltration in the armed services in the New York and New Jersey area. Investigators for the Permanent Investigating Subcommittee ran into opposition from Army officers who refused to tell McCarthy's men the names of the officials who had given security clearance to several persons whom McCarthy suspected of Communist connections.

Army Secretary Robert T. Stevens promised to review the problem, and indicated that he wanted to be cooperative with the Senate subcommittee. However, before any solution, Senator McCarthy released a 75-page classified Army document that he characterized as "prize Communist propaganda." The document, distributed to Army intelligence officers and some others, was entitled "Psychological and Cultural Traits of Soviet Siberia."

The aggressive Wisconsin Senator had never been on friendly terms with President Dwight D. Eisenhower, and had no reluctance to try forcing the Republican Administration to cooperate in providing him with names he wanted. He produced testimony of two Russian refugees and a former Communist to try to establish his claim that the Army was distributing subversive material.

Chairman McCarthy, Committee Counsel Roy Cohn and Investigator G. David Schine took the initiative in broadening the investigation of alleged Communist infiltration of the Army in a manner that was certain to bring either a sharp clash or surrender from Army Secretary Stevens. Brief periods of cooperation from Stevens failed to relieve the tension built up in the last half of 1953 and 1954 as McCarthy developed the attitude that the Republican Administration was as difficult to work with as the Truman Administration.

The case of Dr. Irving Peress came to the attention of McCarthy and his investigators in late 1953, and it appeared to them to have all of the ingredients necessary to embarrass the Defense Department for questionable handling of a case with security implications. Dr. Peress, a dental officer, had been on active duty since January 1, 1953 at Camp Kilmer where he was inducted as an Army captain.

On October 23, 1953, Dr. Peress was promoted to the rank of major even though the Army "was aware of the fact that Peress was suspected of being a subversive and was under investigation by G-2." Senator McCarthy and his investigators wanted to know who was responsible for promotion of Dr. Peress, and they pushed for their own investigation into his background.[1]

On January 30, 1954, Major Peress was questioned by the McCarthy subcommittee. Was he then or had he ever been a member of the Communist Party? Peress took the Fifth Amendment. Had he attended leadership courses at the Inwood Victory Club of the Communist Party? Peress took the Fifth Amendment. Had he attempted to recruit military personnel at Camp Kilmer into the Communist Party? Had he acted under orders from Communist Party functionaries while at Camp Kilmer? Had Communists intervened to have his overseas orders canceled? Had Communists assisted him in securing a promotion to major?

Major Peress took the Fifth Amendment on all those questions, and members of the Senate Permanent Investigating Subcommittee voiced "grave concern" over the effectiveness of the Army's program for dealing with subversives as well as all the details in the background of this case.[2]

Chairman McCarthy didn't wait for a committee report, but fired off a letter on February 1, 1954, demanding a court-martial of Major Peress. Instead, the Army gave Peress an honorable discharge in what the subcommittee members concluded later was an "apparent disregard" of the letter from Chairman McCarthy.

An infuriated McCarthy demanded to know the identity of the Pentagon officials who had ordered the Peress discharge, and Army Counsel John Adams and Brigadier General Ralph W. Zwicker refused to reveal the names. A major, bitter controversy developed and McCarthy slashed out at General Zwicker as "not fit to wear that uniform."

The feud between McCarthy and Army Secretary Stevens was whipped to a fever pitch when the Army Secretary directed General Zwicker to refuse to appear for further questioning, and declared that he would be "unwilling to have so fine an officer [as Zwicker] run the risk of further abuse."

The Army Secretary said he would appear in Zwicker's place, but his lack of experience in political in-fighting showed, for he had moved himself into an impossible position in refusing to make records available on the Peress matter. A meeting was arranged by other Republican members of McCarthy's subcommittee to work out a compromise with the Army and the Eisenhower Administration. Present were Secretary Stevens, Senator Karl Mundt (Rep., S. Dak.), Senator Everett Dirksen (Rep., Ill.) and Senator Charles Potter (Rep., Mich.). Secretary Stevens agreed to give McCarthy the names of those involved in the Peress case, and all Army officers [including Zwicker] were to be made available for questioning.

The appearance of Stevens before the Senate subcommittee was canceled, and the problem appeared settled until news reports spoke of the Eisenhower Administration's "capitulation" to Senator McCarthy. It was embarrassing to Army Secretary Stevens to be publicly pictured in this manner, and he and some of his advisers decided to fight back.

The Army released a chronological report on the activities of Private David Schine, the former McCarthy investigator, in an effort to show that McCarthy's Counsel Cohn was trying to obtain "favored" treatment from the Army for his friend. McCarthy charged that the report on Schine was an effort to "blackmail" him to call off the investigation of Communists in the Defense Department, and the issue was drawn for one of the most moving and dramatic Senate hearings in history. It was to have repercussions much broader than the political careers of those who participated as major characters. Because McCarthy was involved, Senator Karl Mundt was named to serve as chairman during the special study.[3]

* * *

On the morning of May 17, 1954, the high-ceilinged Senate Caucus Room was jammed with spectators. At the end of the huge table at the front of the room Senator McCarthy leaned over a microphone and reviled the Eisenhower Administration, charging that high officials of the Administration were arbitrarily silencing witnesses from the executive branch, and in doing so were preventing him from defending himself and his staff.

The hearings had been in progress for eighteen days, and Senator McCarthy had done much to destroy his own case. An estimated twenty million television viewers had witnessed the heavy-handed humor and smirking disrespect that Senator McCarthy had used in his dealings with Army Secretary Stevens.

Many who agreed that McCarthy's subcommittee should have the right to question all Army witnesses had been antagonized by the crude manner in which McCarthy tried to make his points. He had created the worst possible climate in which to make any appeal to fair play or decency. And yet, the Wisconsin Republican on that day was making such an appeal and was to receive some sympathetic comments from Democratic as well as Republican Senators.

The point at issue was simple. Should Army Counsel John Adams be required to testify as to conversations at a meeting at the Justice Department on January 21, 1954? Adams had already testified to being present on that day with Attorney General Herbert Brownell, Jr., Deputy Attorney General William P. Rogers, Presidential Assistant Sherman Adams, White House Administrative Assistant Gerald D. Morgan, and United Nations Ambassador Henry Cabot Lodge. The January meeting had been called to try to find ways to curb Senator McCarthy's free-wheeling investigation of the loyalty-security program in the Defense Department.

A few days earlier Adams had balked at giving testimony about the meeting, saying that "instructions of the Executive Branch" barred him from telling of the conversations. Committee members were concerned. How could they obtain the evidence necessary to draw conclusions on the hearings if they were barred from all "high-level discussion of the Executive Branch"?

By this point the Army-McCarthy hearings had centered on charges and countercharges involving Army Secretary Stevens, John G. Adams, Defense Department General Counsel H. Struve Hensel, Senator McCarthy, Roy Cohn and Francis P. Carr, chief investigator for McCarthy's subcommittee.

The Army had formalized its charges that Senator McCarthy, Cohn and Carr had improperly used the power of the subcommittee to obtain preferential treatment for Cohn's pal, Private Schine. It was contended that the tough and aggressive little Cohn had tried to intimidate the Army and Defense officials to get Schine a commission or a special assignment as an assistant to the Secretary of the Army, or a post in the Central Intelligence Agency. It was claimed Cohn had suggested Private Schine might be given a special assignment to work with the McCarthy subcommittee. In fact, Schine, after a short time on regular Army duty following his induction, had been permitted to work with Cohn on the investigations.

On the other side, Army Secretary Stevens maintained that McCarthy and Cohn had launched a vindictive probe of the Army security programs in reprisal against those who had not cooperated to grant special treatment to Private Schine.

Senator McCarthy countercharged that the Army tried to blackmail his investigating subcommittee into dropping its probe of the Army loyalty-security setup by threatening to circulate an embarrassing report about Cohn and Schine. McCarthy reiterated that his investigation was justified, and he again pointed out that Major Irving Peress had been promoted despite his record as a "subversive."

It was easy to understand why the Eisenhower Administration held the January 21 meeting at the Justice Department to determine how to handle Senator McCarthy. However, it was not so easy to understand why, after testifying there had been such a meeting, Army Counsel Adams refused to disclose what was said.

Senator Stuart Symington, the Missouri Democrat, was amazed that there would be an effort to bar testimony on such a crucial meeting. He declared that testimony was essential to determine the responsibility for the Defense Department move to stop Senator McCarthy's investigation of the Peress case.

"This was a high-level discussion of the executive department, and this witness [Adams] has been instructed not to testify as to the interchange of views of people at the high-level meeting," explained Joseph N. Welch, the gentle-voiced Boston lawyer who served as special counsel for the Army.

"Does that mean we are going to get the information about low-level discussions but not about high-level discussions?" Senator Symington asked.

"That is only, sir, what I have been informed," Welch said and then carefully made it clear he was not passing on the right or wrong of the policy. "It isn't a point of what I like. It is a point of what the witness has been instructed."

Senator Henry M. Jackson, the Washington Democrat, was no McCarthy supporter, but he too was nettled by the instructions given Adams by Deputy Defense Secretary Robert B. Anderson. Jackson held that if the Defense Department had any right to refuse to testify on high-level conversations, then it had waived that right when Adams told of the January 21 meeting and the participants.

"I think that maybe this testimony may be embarrassing to the Administration, and I do not think that because it is embarrassing to the Administration and favorable to Senator McCarthy, that it ought to be deleted," he declared.

"I think this committee should find out now," Jackson continued, "whether it [the Administration policy] covers just this conversation or whether it covers all conversations that went on between the various officials within the Executive Branch of Government . . . [if] we are going to be foreclosed here immediately from asking any further questions relating to conversations between officials within the Executive Branch. Heretofore, those conversations have been coming in when they have been favorable. Now that they are unfavorable [to the Administration], are they to be excluded?"

The inequity in allowing testimony was apparent to many observers, even through the stream of feeling that surrounded the Army-McCarthy hearings. To justify such arbitrary secrecy, the Pentagon needed all the prestige it could summon.

It was decided that a letter should be forwarded from President Eisenhower to Defense Secretary Charles E. Wilson, a letter of lofty tone by which the well-liked President could convince the public some great principle was at stake. It had to be general enough to avoid saying just why John Adams couldn't testify, but specific enough to give the impression that the security of the nation and the foundations of the Constitution were in danger if John Adams were forced to talk. The letter, drafted between Friday, May 14, and Monday, May 17, carried the full impact of the influence of a highly popular President, but it obscured temporarily a sweeping assumption of executive power to withhold information arbitrarily.

On Monday morning, May 17, John Adams filed the Eisenhower letter with the Army-McCarthy subcommittee and a broad new doctrine of "executive privilege" was born. The glowing phrases about a "proper separation of powers between the Executive and Legislative Branches of the Government" misled the public and a good many newspaper editorial writers and columnists, even though it did not fool all the members of the Army-McCarthy subcommittee.

President Eisenhower's May 17, 1954, letter stated in part:

"Because it is essential to efficient and effective administration that employees of the Executive Branch be in a position to be completely candid in advising with each other on official matters, and because it is not in the public interest that any of their conversations or communications, or any documents or reproductions, concerning such advice be disclosed, you will instruct employees of your Department that in all of their appearances before the Subcommittee of the Senate Committee on Government Operations regarding the inquiry now before it they are not to testify to any such conversations or communications or to produce any such documents or reproductions. This principle must be maintained regardless of who would benefit by such disclosure.

"I direct this action so as to maintain the proper separation of powers between the Executive and Legislative Branches of the Government in accordance with my responsibilities under the Constitution. This separation is vital to preclude the exercise of arbitrary power by any branch of Government." [4]

The Eisenhower letter also stated that "throughout our history the President has withheld information whenever he found that what was sought was confidential or its disclosure would be incompatible with the public interest or jeopardize the safety of the Nation." The letter gave the impression that from George Washington down, a number of Presidents had taken action analogous to the silencing of John Adams.

How was the "public interest or the safety of the Nation" to be jeopardized by Army Counsel John Adams' telling of a meeting on strategy to curb Senator McCarthy's investigations? If this Eisenhower letter was "to preclude the exercise of arbitrary power by any branch of Government," then who was to stop the executive branch from such arbitrary silencing of witnesses? Were the Army-McCarthy investigating subcommittee and other committees of Congress to be barred from obtaining information on all "conversations or communications, or any documents or reproductions, concerning advice" within the executive branch?

These were the questions that immediately arose in the minds of Senator Jackson, Senator Symington, and Senator John L. McClellan, the Arkansas Democrat. Senator Everett Dirksen, the honey-voiced Illinois Republican, and Karl Mundt, the South Dakota Republican who was serving as chairman, also expressed some concern, although privately.

Stern-faced Senator McClellan was not awed by the popularity of President Eisenhower or by the fact that Senator McCarthy was a highly unpopular figure at that point. He decided that if the barrier to any testimony on the January 21 meeting prevailed, then it would be impossible to establish whether John Adams, Army Secretary Stevens, or some higher officials were responsible for directing actions complained of by Senator McCarthy, Roy Cohn, and Private Schine.

"If the committee is going to be left in a dilemma of not knowing whether the Secretary [Stevens] is responsible for the action taken after that date [January 21], or whether the responsibility is at a higher level, then we will never be able to completely discharge our responsibility in this proceeding," Senator McClellan said.

Senator Jackson expressed the view that the secrecy policy left the subcommittee "in a dilemma of passing on testimony that is incomplete. I think . . . that the Executive Branch is doing a great injustice to this committee and to all of the principals in this controversy by exercising the power which the President has, very late in the proceedings."

There was no question that President Eisenhower's letter had stalled the hearings at a crucial moment. If witnesses could not testify on an essential point, then there was little more that could be learned.

"I must admit that I am somewhat at a loss as to know what to do at this moment," Senator McCarthy said. "One of the subjects of this inquiry is to find out who was responsible for succeeding in calling off the hearing of Communist infiltration in Government. That the hearing was called off, no one can question."

McCarthy continued: "At this point, I find out there is no way of ever getting at the truth, because we do find that the charges were conceived, instigated, at a meeting [of January 21] which was testified to by Mr. Adams.

"I don't think the President is responsible for this," the Wisconsin Republican said in expressing his views that others had conceived the idea of silencing Adams and had merely obtained President Eisenhower's signature to accomplish their purpose. "I don't think his judgment is that bad.[5]

"There is no reason why anyone should be afraid of the facts, of the truth, that came out of that meeting," Senator McCarthy thundered. "It is a very important meeting. It doesn't have to do with security matters. It doesn't have to do with national security. It merely has to do with why these charges were filed.

"The question is . . . how far can the President go? Who all can he order not to testify? If he can order the Ambassador to the U.N. [Henry Cabot Lodge] not to testify about something having nothing to do with the U.N., but a deliberate smear against my staff . . . any

President can, by an executive order, keep the facts from the American people."

Senator McCarthy brought up the 1952 campaign in which government secrecy had been a key issue: "I do think that someone . . . should contact the President immediately and point out to him . . . that he and I and many of us campaigned and promised the American people that if they would remove our Democrat friends from control of the Government, then we would no longer engage in Government by secrecy, whitewash and cover-up."

It was a pathetic plea from a man who by now had completely destroyed his public image by his own brutal performance. His voice was raucous. His heavy beard gave him a rough, almost uncouth appearance despite his efforts to modify it by shaving during the noon recess.

Still, he hammered on. "I think that these facts should be brought to the President because the American people will not stand for such as this, Mr. Chairman. They will not stand for a cover-up halfway through a hearing."

Seldom had there been more right on the side of McCarthy, but seldom had there been fewer people on his side. Many people who at first had been inclined to approve Joe McCarthy as "doing some good against the Communists," had been antagonized by his television image. Many editorial pages of a press that was normally much more objective had developed an attitude that anything that is bad for Joe McCarthy is good for the country.

Public sentiment against him was so strong that it is doubtful if the public could have changed to his favor—even if the subcommittee had succeeded in eliciting testimony on the January 21, 1954, meeting and no matter how embarrassing it might have been to the Eisenhower Administration.

Greater danger, however, was possible if the Eisenhower letter could be used again. On the face of it, it seemed to extend the claim of "executive privilege" to prohibit Congress the access to *any* records or testimony that might involve communications within the executive branch. The letter was a directive with regard to excluding testimony in one hearing—the Army-McCarthy hearing. However, it was certainly broad enough that the Defense Department could use it to block any investigation.

Moreover, if an Administration could succesfully block any probe of high-level discussions in the defense establishment, why couldn't it use that same "executive privilege" to block any investigation in any other executive agency? The Teapot Dome scandals of the Harding Administration could have been buried if those officials had applied even the mildest interpretation of "executive privilege" set down by President Eisenhower in the May 17 letter.

Similarly the tax scandals of the Truman Administration could have been buried by claiming that all papers except those involving final decisions were "confidential executive communications." It had been vital to learn the nature of advice and recommendation of both high-level and low-level officials on settlements of huge tax cases. Attorney General J. Howard McGrath could have claimed that his conversations with T. Lamar Caudle, the Assistant Attorney General in charge of the Tax Division, were "confidential executive business."

Caudle and White House Aide Matthew Connelly could have claimed that their communications were "confidential executive business." As it was, the Caudle-Connelly communications were actually used as the basis of criminal charges on which Caudle and Connelly were convicted and sent to prison. A number of other officials of the Internal Revenue Service were convicted on charges arising out of revelation of the "advice and recommendation" they gave that were part of a huge tax "fix" operation.

The press had been misled by the memorandum that accompanied the Eisenhower letter saying, in effect, that President Eisenhower was doing no more than George Washington and many other Presidents had done. By invoking such names as George Washington and Thomas Jefferson, the memorandum made it possible to pass off the Eisenhower letter as a mere "clarification" of an old and settled principle. A close reading of "the precedents" disclosed in fact that President Washington actually *opposed* withholding information from Congress. He once refused to deliver treaty papers to the House, but only because the Senate, not the House, had jurisdiction to ratify treaties.

The Truman Administration did try to hide embarrassing facts from Congress. President Truman issued an executive order placing certain personnel files under a secrecy blanket, and on some occasions he ordered files delivered to his personal custody at the White House so they could not be reached by subpoena. His Administration stalled investigation of flagrant crimes for months. But President Truman never asserted any constitutional right by which all high-level officials could claim an "executive privilege" to avoid testifying or producing records.

What Truman would not do, however, the highly popular President Eisenhower did do. Ironically, his May 17 letter caused hardly a ripple of criticism. On the contrary, most editorial pages praised President Eisenhower for expressing some fine new theory on the United States Constitution or wrote off the letter as an historically unimportant, one-shot claim of secrecy.

Indeed, the whole story of the Army-McCarthy hearings had by this time taken second news billing to the United States Supreme Court ruling on school segregation. The unanimous segregation decision came out on May 17, 1954—the same date as the Eisenhower letter to Wilson. That segregation decision dominated discussions of constitutional law. And the few persons who did stop to think about the inherent threat in the broad use of secrecy could hardly get emotional about it—as long as the only victims appeared to be Senator McCarthy and his little knot of followers.

When the Eisenhower Administration took office in January, 1953, there were high hopes that arbitrary government secrecy would be ended. As a candidate, the President had talked much of his interest in open government and had pledged to make all but national security information available to the public. So had the Vice President, Richard M. Nixon.

As late as November 6, 1953, Attorney General Herbert Brownell, Jr., was continuing to stress the Republican party's interest in eliminating secrecy policies of the Truman Administration. In Chicago, before a convention of Associated Press Managing Editors, Brownell said he was "very much aware of the great importance of seeing to it that the obstacles to the free flow of information are kept to an absolute minimum.

"I would like to call attention to some of the procedures which we established," Brownell said. "At the very outset of the new Administration, we provided that any pardons or commutations of sentence shall be a matter of public record. Throughout the prior Administration, these executive actions were taken secretly, for political purposes and over the objection of the Office of the Pardon Attorney.

"We also started the policy of making a matter of public record matters which our predecessors buried in secrecy, such as settlements of all types of cases which we handle and involve monetary considerations, such as tax claims, damage suits and Alien Property settlements. We do not contend that we have achieved perfection in our efforts to provide a full flow of information. But we are working on it and each day find new ways to do our part."

At this same meeting, Attorney General Brownell announced that President Eisenhower was revoking a much-criticized executive order by President Truman dealing with defense information. He said President Eisenhower was issuing a new order which "attains the required balance between the need to protect certain types of defense information, and the need for keeping the citizens of a republic as fully informed as possible concerning what their government is doing.

"President Eisenhower considers the free flow of information from the government to the people to be basic to the good health of the Nation," Brownell told the editors. He declared that under the Truman Administration there "was a tendency to follow the dangerous policy heretofore used by dictator nations of authorizing government officials to use the term 'National Security' indiscriminately, and thereby throw a veil of secrecy over many items which historically have been open to the public of this country."

The Attorney General said he viewed the new Republican policy as an opportunity to "demonstrate to all the world the vivid contrast between our system of government, which believes in and practices freedom of the press, and the Communist system, which regards the concept of freedom of information as a threat to the continuance of its tyrannical rule."

Such attitudes in November, 1953, were difficult to reconcile with those of May, 1954, when the same Attorney General was helping fashion a policy that was more devastating to a free flow of information than simply refusing to give information to the press. The May 17, 1954, letter from President Eisenhower to the Defense Department said in essence that any high officials of the defense establishment might refuse to produce records or testify even when subpoenaed by a properly constituted congressional committee that was acting within its jurisdiction.

The Army-McCarthy hearings that had given rise to the famous letter ended on June 17, 1954. However, it was not necessary to wait for the official reports made public on October 30, 1954, to know that Senator McCarthy was finished as a political power—and that the Administration would use the "executive privilege" precedent again.

As an aftermath of the Army-McCarthy hearings, a charge was filed that Senator McCarthy had conducted himself in a manner "unbecoming a member of the United States Senate." And on August 2, 1954, the Senate decided by the overwhelming vote of 75 to 12 to investigate Senator McCarthy's conduct.

Senator Arthur V. Watkins, a Utah Republican, was named chairman of the select McCarthy Censure Committee to determine recommendations on Senator McCarthy's conduct. In barely more than a month Chairman Watkins ran smack into a roadblock of "executive privilege." [6]

The subject of inquiry was Senator McCarthy's severe tongue-lashing of Brigadier General Ralph Zwicker, of Camp Kilmer, New Jersey. Major General Kirke B. Lawton, a former commander general of Forth Monmouth, New Jersey, refused to testify about conversations with General Zwicker. He claimed "executive privilege" under the May 17, 1954, letter from President Eisenhower.

Edward Bennett Williams, who was serving as counsel for Senator McCarthy, questioned the applicability of the May 17 letter: "Don't you know, General, that order of May 17, 1954, referred only to the Government Operations Committee and the hearing then in session which was commonly known as the Army-McCarthy hearing?"

General Lawton replied that he had been advised that the May 17 letter "not only applied to the so-called Mundt committee [the Special Committee for the Army-McCarthy hearings] but it applies to this or any other."

Chairman Watkins excused General Lawton and wrote Defense Secretary Charles E. Wilson asking clarification. Wilson replied that Generals Lawton and Zwicker would be allowed to testify and produce documents unless their action would be "in violation of national security regulations or a violation of the President's order of May 17, 1954."

There could be little doubt now that the Defense Department intended to make the May 17, 1954, letter a part of its basic doctrine, with all the great blanket of secrecy this would provide. The new and expanded doctrine of "executive privilege" was just too convenient a cover for those who wished to hide their activities from Congress, the press, or the public. It could be used by the incompetent as well as the corrupt.

This doctrine of an "inherent right" of persons in the executive departments to refuse testimony or documents threatened our whole system of government. It was a naked claim of authority for unlimited secrecy, without regard for laws or the spirit of a democracy.

By claiming a right to withhold all information on opinions, conclusions, recommendations, or suggestions, this doctrine could allow the secrecy blanket to be dropped over virtually every document in most agencies, for there are few governmental documents that do not contain some opinions or suggestions.

The squabble was started by the Army effort to bar Congress from evidence dealing with administration of security programs at the Pentagon. It ended in a stalemate when the Pentagon pulled down the broader secrecy curtain of "executive privilege."

The Senate report was highly critical of the military reliance on secrecy and stated that the Secretary of the Army and his superiors in the Defense Department were to be severely criticized for "the delay of almost a year before the facts of the Peress case" were released to the public.

"Such unnecessary delay served to unduly arouse and increase suspicions of the public as to possible Communist influences and thereby was a disservice not only to Army personnel involved in the Peress case, but also to the Army as a whole, to this subcommittee, to the Congress and to the general public," the report continued.[7]

Any damage done by the mishandling of the Peress case was temporary, but serious consequences flowed from the Army-McCarthy affair.

The doctrine of executive privilege, accepted initially as a one-shot defense in the Army-McCarthy hearings, was to become a major barrier to full congressional investigations of the Pentagon.

16

REMEMBER HARRY (THE HAT) LEV

A REPORT of dishonesty in the handling of military clothing contracts was made to the Senate Permanent Investigating Subcommittee in the fall of 1954. The complaint involved the activities of Harry (The Hat) Lev, the millionaire owner of Mid City Uniform Cap Company of Chicago. It was contended that Lev, one of the largest hatmakers in the United States, was receiving favored treatment in the Armed Services Textile and Apparel Procurement Agency (ASTAPA) office in the New York area.

The first report was vague, but it was forwarded to the General Accounting Office. Supervisory Investigator Jack Balaban was assigned the case, and with Accountant Leslie C. Poole started the tedious task of trying to determine if there was substance to the allegation. Balaban, a graduate in accounting from Northwestern University and a law graduate from American University, needed all of his twenty years' experience as a government investigator as he began digging into the complicated affairs of the shrewd and evasive Harry Lev.[1]

Weeks of intense work produced only the outlines of an unhealthy pattern of activity, but there was little hard evidence until he talked with Leon M. Levy, a Brooklyn businessman who had been involved in some contracts with Lev. From the time Leon Levy talked to Balaban and Poole, the evidence started to fall in line on what appeared to be a pattern of bribery and corruption that extended from the awarding of contracts, through the inspection of goods, and even embracing the process for renegotiation of the military clothing contracts.

The General Accounting Office loaned Balaban and Poole to the Senate Permanent Investigating Subcommittee, where they teamed with the ace accountant-investigator Carmine Bellino to prepare the investigation for public hearings. It was not until May 18, 1955, that Chairman John L. McClellan (Dem., Ark.) was satisfied that the evidence was solid enough for public hearings.

"Each year millions of dollars are spent in the purchase and inspection of clothing and common-use articles for our Armed Forces," Chairman McClellan said in setting out the importance of the hearings. "One of the duties with which this subcommittee is charged is to examine into [*sic*] economic operations of the Government agencies, and to seek means to prevent waste and inefficiency.

"In the present hearing we are investigating more than mere waste and inefficiency. We are confronted with charges of graft and corruption in one of the procurement branches of the Defense Department occurring during the last three years. It is of the utmost importance not only that we have economic government, but that the public have confidence in the integrity and decency of its government and of its officials. The purpose of these hearings is not only to expose any such abuses that may prevail, but also to serve notice on others committing similar infractions that these practices will not be tolerated." [2]

Harry (The Hat) Lev, although illiterate, was extremely shrewd as a witness before the Senate subcommittee. The subcommittee characterized him as "a master of evasion and dissimulation," but his colorful Polish accent and his lavish entertainment caught the fancy of the press, resulting in full coverage of the hat contract scandals.

Harry Lev, born in Poland, had less than two years' schooling when he quit at eleven years of age to start work for his father making caps. When his father died two years later, Lev supported himself and younger members of the family until he emigrated to Palestine with his sewing machine. There it took him only two years to obtain the $12,000 needed to emigrate to the United States, where he settled in Chicago in 1923.

By the time Lev appeared before the McClellan subcommittee he was one of the largest military hatmakers in the country. Mid City Uniform Cap Company was his major firm, but his other enterprises included Isabelle Building Corporation of Chicago, Staywell Manufacturing Company, a firm that owned the patents on hat parts, the Illinois Outdoor Advertising Company, the Citation Hat Corporation, and the Spencer Manufacturing Company of Puerto Rico.

Testimony showed that Lev worked diligently to cultivate the good will of procurement officials, hired retired high-ranking officials of the Defense Department, and showered gifts of delicacies on anyone who might be helpful. He paid hotel bills of procurement officials, entertained them at his home and on his yacht, and bought dresses and other items of clothing for female procurement personnel.[3]

There was testimony that he entered into business arrangements with government officials who administered his government contracts, directly or indirectly. Further testimony revealed bribery, attempted bribery, and indications of easy access to inside information on multimillion-dollar contracts.

One of the most significant contracts examined by the McClellan subcommittee called for the production of 6,823,428 Navy white sailor hats for $2,040,204.97. Lev hired and retained Marvin Rubin, a so-called "manufacturers' representative," who gave him inside information on the contract. Although the Navy wanted the contract split among several suppliers, Captain Raymond Wool, the contracting officer, awarded the entire order to Harry Lev.

Financial dealings were difficult to establish since he often used cash. It was necessary to trace $1,403,745.25 that went through Lev's hands from 1952 through 1953 to pin down the fact that he couldn't account for $213,924 in cash. Lev could give no logical explanation for the large sums of cash, and the McClellan subcommittee called attention to the fact that "the dates when these cash withdrawals were made often showed a proximity to the date of the granting of favors to Lev by procurement officials.[4]

"Harry Lev through bribery, collusion and connivance with Government contracting officials and inspectors obtained improper favors, delivered defective materials to the Armed Forces, and made improper profits at the expense of the Government," the subcommittee found. "His testimony was evasive and in a large part obviously false and untrue. By his reprehensible, amoral conduct he corrupted and induced Government officials to betray their public trust. He has forfeited any right to engage in future business with the Government."

Marvin Rubin, a key witness in the investigation, was characterized by the McClellan subcommittee as "a fixer who had influence with Government procurement officials through friendship and bribery." Rubin was a persuasive salesman type who preferred to regard himself as a "getter of Government business." [5]

The suave New Yorker's operation differed from the so-called "five-percenters" in that he charged a considerably larger amount for his services in delivering Defense Department contracts. "He demanded an interest varying between 25 percent and 33 percent of the profits on Government contracts which the firm obtained," according to the subcommittee report. His major contacts were with the Army Quartermaster Corps and with the Armed Services Textile and Apparel Procurement Agency.[6]

In 1952, Rubin had started representing Leon Levy and Maurice Ades, owners of two clothing firms known as Bonita Originals, Inc., and Maurice Embroidery, Inc. A year later, he became associated with Harry Lev, and was a vice president of Lev's Spencer Manufacturing Company, which was organized for the purpose of handling the big contract for white sailor hats.

Bonita Originals was running in the red in 1952 when Melvin Carlin, an accountant for Leon Levy's firm, suggested he might make it a profitable business by hiring Marvin Rubin, who "had connections." Rubin demanded one third of the profits, but Levy agreed to the arrangement and delivered in short order on three contracts for manufacture of 1,050,000 Army garrison hats for a total price of $122,626.18. A day after the contract was let, Rubin asked for $1,000 to cover a pay-off to an Army major he contended had been instrumental in delivering the contract.

Levy testified that Rubin told him to enter the $1,000 pay-off on the books as an "entertainment expense." He said Rubin also instructed him to keep records of all pay-offs and explained that the pay-offs would be a continuing operation and that it would be necessary to keep some record to avoid any duplication of payments.[7] Levy said Rubin also told him the pay-offs would run about seven to ten percent of the contracts, and would be used to iron out problems in performance of the contracts and to arrange for authority to deviate from the standards established in the contract.

For purposes of secrecy, Levy said he kept notes on all of these transactions in Arabic. Later he expanded the Arabic diary notes and Arabic notes on telephone conversations he had heard between Rubin and Harry Lev and others.

Levy testified that his partner, Ades, questioned whether Rubin was actually making pay-offs. Levy said he questioned Rubin about this and Rubin agreed for Ades to be present when a pay-off was made to David Pollack, then a group chief of the Cost Price Analysis Section of the Armed Services Textile and Apparel Procurement Agency. Pollack's office evaluated bids and price adjustments to determine the low bidder. His group also had control over changes in contract specifications, price revisions and deviations from standards. Levy testified that Rubin gave Pollack $500 in cash in his presence in the office of Bonita Originals. A secretary testified that she had cashed a $500 check, obtaining $300 in $20 bills and $200 in $10 bills as the pay-off cash.[8]

Levy had other diary entries that involved pay-offs to Joseph G. Porreca, then Chief Inspector of the Textile Division of the Quartermaster Corps Inspection Service. The entry indicated that Rubin paid off Porreca with a deep freeze valued at $215, as well as with twenty-five or thirty pounds of meat for the deep freeze, and gift lingerie for Porreca's wife valued at $49.25. Porreca admitted that he committed perjury in an executive session of the McClellan subcommittee when he denied knowing the identity of the person who sent him the deep freeze. In the public hearings he admitted the deep freeze came from Rubin, insisting he had tried to pay for it but Rubin wouldn't accept the money. Porreca, who admitted receiving other substantial gifts from Rubin or Lev, was identified as the man who had ordered Michael Weintraub, a former Army Quartermaster Corps clothing inspector, to permit shipment of eighteen bales of hoods from one of Lev's plants without inspection for defects.[9]

The McClellan subcommittee found that the whole clothing procurement operation was shot through with corruption, but singled out Captain Raymond Wool for extensive questioning and comment. Wool, a contracting officer at ASTAPA, handled the contracts with Lev's Mid City Cap Company and Spencer Manufacturing Company. The investigation disclosed that Captain Wool had large amounts of cash at his disposal during 1951, 1952 and 1953. The greatest sum of money showed up at the time he was awarding the contracts to Harry Lev, when he made large cash outlays in buying a new home and in a contract to remodel the home.

Wool claimed that the $14,000 to $16,000 in cash traced to him in early 1953 was "savings" that he had accumulated in "a steel box" at his home. The first story of the accumulation of cash from savings seemed impossible to the committee investigators, and Wool then declared that much of it had come from some large loans. Pressed for the source of the loans and the amounts, Wool first stated it was a $9,000 loan from Patsy Luciano, a former landlord. Later he said he had received $5,000 from Luciano. Luciano was called to testify, and denied he had ever loaned either $9,000 or $5,000 to Captain Wool or his wife. He said they owed him money, but that this was the balance due on a store property they rented from him.

Wool was caught in a difficult position with the large amounts of cash, and the Senate subcommittee described his dilemma as "whether to admit (1) the crime of acceptance of bribery; if so (2) he perforce had to admit he committed another crime—falsification of his tax returns since he failed to show the receipt of this bribery on the returns.

"He [Wool] chose to admit one crime—that of filing a false tax return and thereupon sought to explain his possession of this large sum of cash by claiming that he had withdrawn cash profits out of the dress shop business operated by his wife over a period of two years," the subcommittee commented. Even that explanation fell through when two saleswomen at the dress shop testified that the shop had insufficient sales even to pay the $250 a month rent before it went broke and was closed out. It appeared to have been a subsidized business, and that meant Wool had obtained even more unexplained money than the earlier investigations disclosed.

Against that background of corroborative evidence, Leon Levy testified he had overheard a telephone conversation between Captain Wool and Rubin concerning the handling of government contracts. Also, Levy testified that Rubin had told him that Lev was paying Wool a total of $50,000 in installments for Wool's help in landing the contract for white Navy hats and for additional assistance during the performance of the contract.[10]

While there was testimony of irregular and questionable activity in connection with many clothing procurement contracts, these unusual aspects of the Navy contract for white hats were spotlighted:

1. Two unusually large requisitions for Navy white hats were merged in April 1953 and awarded to Lev's firm despite initial Navy insistence that they be split and awarded to several firms.

2. The pre-award survey of Lev's plant in Puerto Rico made by Inspector Louis Alperstein was questioned by the Navy, but Captain Wool defended the survey and maintained that Lev would perform the contract on time. In fact special arrangements were made so that Lev did not have to meet the delivery date requirements.

3. Pattern changes on the white sailor hats were demanded by Lev, but opposed by the Navy. Lev's request for permission to change the pattern was supported by Captain Wool. A Navy lieutenant testified that Captain Wool criticized him for opposing the pattern change. As a result of the change, over 250,000 defective hats were delivered to the Navy, with a resultant waste of government-furnished material. Under pressure, Lev finally reverted to the original pattern.

4. Wool granted Lev a deviation in the contract so that Lev could dispose of "scrap" material. This meant a profit of $49,406 to Lev.

5. Wool granted Lev a deviation in the contract that permitted a less expensive packaging arrangement over the objections of the contract administrative officer. This lowered Lev's costs by more than $37,000.

Those were only a few of the devices that permitted Lev to obtain the contract in the first place, deliver defective goods, avoid the standards of the initial contract, and in general clean up unreasonable profits.

In the face of a general court-martial, Captain Wool on June 6, 1955, tendered his resignation for the good of the service. He was granted a discharge on other than honorable condition, which barred him from veterans' benefits to the same extent as a dishonorable discharge. He was later convicted on a federal income-tax evasion charge and served a federal prison sentence.[11]

The report of the McClellan subcommittee identified dozens of officials—military officers, civilian contract administrators and inspectors—who were involved in either corruption or gross laxity in connection with the clothing procurement contracts through the New York Quartermaster Corps. The subcommittee found that a "major weakness in procurement practices" was the allowance of deviations from the contract terms.

"The practice of granting deviations to favored contractors but not to other contractors, on the same procurement order, constitutes flagrant favoritism, is contrary to good procurement practices and detrimental to the best interest of the Government," the subcommittee stated. "The low bid becomes meaningless if the contractor through collusion with the contractual officers of the Government can, by subsequent changes in the terms of performance and specifications, make large profits by apparent insignificant changes in the contracts." [12]

The report concluded that Harry Lev and his affiliated companies were enabled to make "large secret profits totaling hundreds of thousands of dollars through the modus operandi of various types of deviations." In addition to dealing with Rubin and his "contacts" in procurement, Lev was found to have "a strong penchant for the hiring of former highly placed Government procurement officials." They included a major general, three colonels and a major who had worked in the procurement offices.

Throughout his appearance on the witness stand, Lev continually made reference to the fact that he was "the low bidder." The Senate subcommittee stated that the Lev case demonstrates that it is often necessary to examine the activities of the so-called "low bidder" to discover any arrangements for deviation and lack of inspection of defective goods that may make the low bid meaningless.

The McClellan investigation indicated that the Defense Department had net claims of at least $454,000 against Lev and his affiliated companies for breach of contract through deviations from standards and delivery of defective goods.[13]

On April 26, 1957, Harry Lev, Captain Wool and three codefendants were convicted of conspiring with government officials to defraud the government on two Army and Navy hat contracts. Others convicted were Marvin Rubin, Maurice Ades, and Mella Hort, a secretary in the procurement office who accepted favors from Lev and Rubin and did favors for them. Lev was sentenced to a nine-month prison term and was fined $5,000. Wool was fined $1,000 and was sentenced to an eighteen-month prison term. Rubin was fined $1,000 and was sentenced to serve a fifteen-month prison term, to run concurrently with another fifteenth-month term for bribery. Mrs. Hort and Ades were fined $1,500 each, and received suspended sentences with a two-year probationary period. More than a dozen other officials were fired or forced to resign as a result of laxity or corruption disclosed by hearings on the activities of Harry Lev.[14]

The 1,150 pages of testimony on the investigation of textile procurement in the military services should have rocked the Defense Department for years. The forty-six-page report issued by the McClellan subcommittee on January 16, 1956, should have been made required reading for all high-level Pentagon officials. However, within a few months another Defense Department clothing contract problem was to result in the resignation of an Assistant Secretary of Defense.

* * *

Robert Tripp Ross, a Republican Congressman from New York, was defeated for reelection in 1952, but was named a Deputy Assistant Secretary of Defense for Legislative Affairs in March, 1954. He served in that capacity until March, 1956, when he was named Assistant Secretary of Defense for Legislative and Public Affairs.

In late 1956, the Military Operations Subcommittee of the House Government Operations Committee was informed that an $834,000 contract for the manufacture of Army cotton trousers had been awarded by the Quartermaster Corps to a firm that was headed by Claire Wynn Ross, wife of Assistant Secretary of Defense Robert Tripp Ross. The bid had been submitted by Mr. Herman D. Wynn, brother of Mrs. Ross, on behalf of the firm known as Wynn Enterprises, Inc. Just prior to the award of the contract, Wynn was succeeded in the presidency of the firm by his sister, Mrs. Ross.[15]

There were immediate press comments on the question of possible conflicts of interest, but within a few weeks the subcommittee concluded that this point was less important from a standpoint of procurement policy than was the whole complex of government procurement operations in which the Wynn companies had been involved.

While the Government Operations Committee found Ross free of any specific "wrongful acts" in connection with the Wynn Enterprises government contracts, a unanimous report charged that the award of a contract to a company headed by the wife of a high government official was "repugnant to public policy." That was also the opinion of the Comptroller General of the United States in his report.[16]

The committee found that Ross was at fault in his "failure to realize" that it was bad public policy for his wife to be engaged in dealings with the Defense Department while he held the office of an Assistant Secretary of Defense. Ross submitted his resignation in mid-February, 1957, and left the Defense Department in March.

Even as Wynn Enterprises was becoming involved in the transactions that resulted in the resignation of Ross as Assistant Secretary of Defense, another investigation forced the resignation of Secretary of the Air Force Harold Talbott.

17

HAROLD TALBOTT—A CONFLICT OF INTEREST?

THE problem of conflicts of interest was the subject of political discussion and speculation from the time the Eisenhower Administration took office. Initially the spotlight focused on the question of whether Charles E. Wilson would sell his stock in the General Motors Corporation before the Senate acted on his nomination as Secretary of Defense. Relatively little attention was paid to Harold E. Talbott, who had been nominated as Secretary of the Air Force.

When Talbott appeared before the Senate Armed Services Committee in January and early February, 1953, he was questioned about his holdings in various companies doing business with the Defense Department. He related that he held stock in such companies as Electric Auto-Lite, Baldwin-Lima-Hamilton Corporation, and Chrysler Corporation.

"Have you severed your relations with all of those companies?"

asked Chairman Leverett Saltonstall, the Massachusetts Republican.

"Yes, sir," Talbott replied respectfully and then volunteered: "I had one other interest. I have an engineering company in which I have dropped back as a special partner." [1]

"What is the name of that company?" Saltonstall asked.

"Mulligan & Co.," Talbott replied.

"What business does it do?" Saltonstall followed up, and Talbott explained:

"Industrial engineering, and they confine their work entirely to clerical companies, controls, clerical controls, or the study of clerks needed in an industry, and in their clerical work. And it is very successful in its analysis of how many clerks are needed in the operation of a business."

Talbott said that lawyers had drawn up an agreement for him and his partner, Paul B. Mulligan, "that no work was to be done while I am in Washington that had to do with defense work essentially.

"They may be doing some work for Ford, for example, but that is not essentially a war contract," Talbott said. "But where it is possible, they will stay away from any of the aircraft companies."

"In other words, you have divested yourself of every business interest, or will have divested yourself from every business interest when you are sworn in as Secretary of the Air?" Saltonstall asked a fuzzy question that missed the point of Talbott's continuing interest in the management consultant firm.

"Yes, sir," Talbott answered.[2]

In March, 1955, the Permanent Investigating Subcommittee staff received information indicating that Air Secretary Talbott had been active in promoting the business of Paul B. Mulligan & Co., in which he was "a special partner." The initial evidence indicated that Talbott had contacted some firms with defense contracts, and had used his official Air Force stationery for promoting the business of the management consultant firm.[3] Committee Counsel Robert F. Kennedy reported the evidence to Chairman John L. McClellan (Dem., Ark.), but there had been no public attention on the matter until news stories were written by Charles Bartlett, then a Washington correspondent for the *Chattanooga Times,* and later by William Lawrence, then a correspondent for *The New York Times.*

On July 18, 1955, Chairman McClellan asked Talbott to meet in a conference with his subcommittee members. The public furor over the stories dealing with Talbott's outside business activities caused the

Air Secretary to make a request for a public hearing on July 21, 1955, to explain why he felt there was nothing improper involved in his income from Paul B. Mulligan & Co.

Talbott denied any illegal or improper actions while serving as Secretary of the Air Force. He submitted a letter he had written to Paul B. Mulligan on January 8, 1953, to explain the change in his relationship with the firm during the period he was to be in public office.

"I have been designated Secretary of the Air Force in the new administration, and if confirmed by the Senate, will be in charge of procurement of aircraft and other materials, equipment, and services for that branch of the Armed Forces of the United States," Talbott wrote. "I have resigned all directorships and other positions of responsibility with all corporations with which I have been connected."

Then he commented that it was possible that Paul B. Mulligan & Co. "could logically acquire clients and receive compensation from business entities doing business with the Department.

"Because of possible criticism of such an eventuality and the fact that I will be fully occupied by my new duties, I wish to record now my view of how such accounts should be handled," Talbott wrote. "I do not believe our partnership should be discontinued, but believe some changes should be made in my participation in it."

Then Talbott suggested that "during my tenure of office, I be considered in the nature of a special or limited partner . . . with full complete authority in you alone to continue the business and to make all decisions without consultation or advice from me.[4]

"Should the firm secure clients whose business, in your opinion, is predominantly in the area of the procurement responsibilities of the Secretary of the Air Force, they shall be handled as special accounts and be segregated completely from the other business of the firm. Should you be in doubt with respect to the classification of any account, I authorize you to consult with my attorney Mr. Murray Smith, who will advise you concerning the same. With respect to such special accounts, I shall receive no income or compensation whatever."

The letter of agreement from Talbott to Mulligan indicated a considerable awareness of the problem of a possible conflict of interest, and it seemed to be an effort to insulate himself from the management engineering business.

However, when he testified, Talbott admitted that the so-called "special partnership" arrangement had never been used and he received a full share of the company profits throughout his term as Secretary of the Air Force, despite the fact that Paul B. Mulligan & Co. did business with a large number of firms having contracts with the Defense Department. The Air Secretary tried to justify this on grounds that these companies dealing with Paul B. Mulligan & Co. were not "predominantly" or "essentially" in the defense field.[5]

A statement on the operations of Paul B. Mulligan & Co. showed that the firm had flourished and had made a sizable contribution to Talbott's income—$42,163 in 1953, $65,379 in 1954 and $66,653 in 1955. The gross income of the business was $321,500 in 1952, dropped off to $285,000 in 1953, and then jumped to $405,300 in 1954 and $411,850 in 1955.[6]

Profitable business that it was, it contributed greatly to the financial position of the Air Secretary. Although he indicated initially that the firm's dealings with defense contractors were insignificant, he later acknowledged that approximately 50 percent of the business of Avco Manufacturing Company, one of the clients, was with the Defense Department. He drew a distinction because only six percent of the Avco business was directly with the Air Force.[7]

As letters were produced showing Talbott had written to some defense contractors on behalf of Paul B. Mulligan & Co., the Air Secretary said he did not believe there was anything improper in writing prospective clients, even if those clients happened to be defense contractors.

While some members of the McClellan subcommittee raised questions of propriety on a number of the Talbott letters, there was also emphasis on Talbott's personal contacts with officials of the Radio Corporation of America on behalf of Paul B. Mulligan & Co.

In his first session before the subcommittee, Talbott said he had learned that RCA officials had raised some question about the propriety of hiring Paul B. Mulligan & Co. in the light of Talbott's partnership in the firm. RCA had a number of contracts with the Defense Department and wanted to avoid any possible "conflict of interest" problem; the company had suggested that there be a letter from the Attorney General approving the transaction as proper. Committee Counsel Robert F. Kennedy asked Talbott what his reaction had been.

"I said, 'My goodness, if there is any such suspicion forget it. We won't do the contract or have anything to do with it.' " Talbott answered.

"That was the finish of it?" Kennedy asked.

"That was the finish as far as I knew," Talbott replied.

"Did Mr. Mulligan try to pursue it with the people from RCA?" Kennedy asked.

"Mulligan went back down there another time," Talbott said. "I don't know who he saw or what he did."

Talbott said he had no idea what had happened on the RCA matter, and he declared he did not press RCA to make the contract. He told the subcommittee under oath that he did not tell anyone in the Air Force that he was dissatisfied with RCA for not entering into the contract.

Kennedy pressed him to try to remember if he had talked to John A. Johnson, General Counsel for the Air Force, about the problem with RCA.

"I told Johnson about this but I didn't tell him to do anything, I don't think," Talbott replied.

"Did you tell Johnson to call Mr. Ewing at the Camden office of RCA?" Kennedy tightened his questions.

"I may have," Talbott answered.

"Did you?" Kennedy snapped back.

"I don't know," Talbott replied. "I really don't know."

"Did you get on the phone and talk to Mr. Ewing?" Kennedy followed.

"I don't know," Talbott replied. "If I did any such thing as that it skipped my mind because it was so unimportant."

"Does what I am telling you now refresh your recollection?" Kennedy asked.

"I remember talking to Mr. Johnson about it," Talbott started to remember.

"What did you say to Johnson?" Kennedy prodded him.

"I told Johnson that I was terribly disturbed about this thing that anybody would question about our doing business and would come about it the way they had through the lawyers and ask for this letter from the Attorney General," Talbott continued.

"What did Johnson say to you?" Kennedy pushed again.

"I don't remember," Talbott stalled.

"What was the reason for telling Johnson?" Kennedy goaded him.

"I think he was in the office or happened by," Talbott said. "He is one of my intimate contacts and intimate confidants in the Department. I don't believe that other than Johnson, I have spoken of Mulligan & Co. to anybody in the office."

"Do you remember you talked to Mr. Ewing [of RCA] on the phone?" Kennedy probed.

"No sir," Talbott replied.

"And you said you thought the position taken by RCA was foolish and wrong?" Kennedy asked.

"I don't know that I did," Talbott answered.

"Did you list the names of the companies that had contracts with Mulligan & Co. including defense contractors and say to Mr. Ewing that RCA should come down off their 'high horse'?" Kennedy shoved hard.

"No sir," Talbott replied.

"Did he [Ewing] then say to you that he had talked to your lawyer, Mr. Murray Smith, and Mr. Smith seemed to be handling the matter and you told him you had taken it out of the hands of Mr. Smith and turned it over to Mr. Johnson?" Kennedy tried to prompt him again.

"No sir," Talbott replied.

"All those are incorrect?" asked an exasperated Kennedy, who had information to back his questions.

"My memory is that I never made any such statements," Talbott insisted.

Kennedy observed that such conversations should have been important enough that Talbott would remember, but the Air Force Secretary persisted: "I am sorry. My memory is very hazy on anything of that kind." [8]

Secretary Talbott was in a tight position, and he knew it. The next morning, he wrote to Chairman McClellan to try to set the record straight: "This morning I talked with Mr. John Johnson. . . . He refreshed my memory regarding the conversation with a Mr. Ewing of RCA, Camden. Mr. Kennedy's statement yesterday that I had talked with Mr. Ewing is correct and my memory was at fault." [9]

Three days later, on July 25, 1955, Sam Ewing testified that a question of the legality and propriety of dealing with Paul B. Mulligan & Co. was raised by RCA officials in the light of Talbott's interest in the firm.

Ewing explained this came about after Talbott called David Sarnoff, chairman of the board of RCA, in November 1953, and informed him that his partner, Mulligan, was encountering obstacles in making a contract with the RCA company. As Air Force Secretary, Talbott suggested that Sarnoff might look into the matter to see if it could be expedited.[10]

After the RCA legal department questioned the legality of RCA dealing with Mulligan, Ewing said he informed Mulligan that no contract would be possible unless there was a letter or memorandum of approval from the Attorney General of the United States.

Ewing testified that he later received a call from Mulligan, who told him that Talbott was disturbed that this question of conflicts of interest had been raised by RCA.

"Later in the day, I received a telephone call from Washington from a man who identified himself as General Counsel of the Air Force, Mr. John A. Johnson," Ewing testified before the McClellan subcommittee. "He [Johnson] said he had understood that RCA was troubled about this proposed contract with Mulligan & Co. and that he was prepared to write a letter of opinion and give it to RCA stating that he saw no legal reason why the contract could not be entered into."

"What was your answer to that?" Counsel Kennedy asked.

"Well, we discussed or we got into somewhat of a legal discussion, as I was not clear that he understood all of the facts, and that he had really looked into the matter," Ewing testified.

"What happened then?" Kennedy asked.

"A new voice came on the wire, and the individual speaking identified himself as Secretary Talbott," Ewing replied. "He was talking quite rapidly and, among other things, he told me or listed over the phone the names of a number of other companies that he said were doing work for the Air Force that had contracts with the Mulligan Co."

"Did he say that these companies had contracts with the Air Force or with the Defense Department?" Kennedy asked.

"To the best of my recollection, he said the Air Force, but it might have been the Defense Department," Ewing replied.

Ewing testified that Talbott told him that Murray Smith was "just a lawyer out in Dayton" who "doesn't know what is going on around here." He quoted Talbott as saying: "Mr. Johnson is representing me in this matter."

"Do you recall some of the words he [Talbott] used?" Kennedy asked.

"I honestly don't," Ewing replied.

"Do you remember if I refresh your recollection of our first conversation, you stated that he said, 'Why is RCA acting so high and mighty?' " Kennedy prompted him.

"You are absolutely correct," Ewing replied. "He said that if all of these other companies could take contracts with Mulligan & Co., why was RCA acting so high and mighty?"

Ewing testified that Talbott spoke in an "annoyed" tone, and "was forceful and it seemed that he wanted some action." After reporting the conversation to his superiors in New York, Ewing said he received instructions from them to have no more contact with Johnson or anyone else in Washington on the contract. He said he called Johnson and told him that all future dealings should be with the RCA New York office.[11]

Johnson was called to testify, and he corroborated the Ewing testimony relative to the conversations with him, the conversation between Ewing and Talbott, and the Ewing notice that the matter was in the hands of RCA in New York. The Washington office of RCA contacted him later and said that nothing less than an opinion from the Attorney General would satisfy them. Johnson said he contacted Attorney General Herbert Brownell the next day, January 6, and showed him the memorandum he had prepared. The Attorney General expressed no disagreement with his legal conclusion, but had said he wanted to take it under consideration. Several days later Talbott told him to drop the matter, as there would be no contract between Paul B. Mulligan & Co. and RCA.

The Air Force Counsel declined to comment on the propriety of Talbott's action. He said he was meeting the duties of his office in giving Talbott a legal opinion as to whether there would be a violation of the conflict-of-interest laws.[12]

It was a much-chastened Air Secretary Talbott who appeared before the McClellan subcommittee on July 26, 1955, to admit that he was in error in his earlier testimony. He admitted that the testimony of Ewing and Johnson was correct, and that he was mistaken when he said he did not ask Johnson to take any action on the contract. He said he believed that the Attorney General had told him later that he could not give him the type of opinion that he wanted.

"In retrospect . . . I now see that I was mistaken in permitting myself to make phone calls or write letters about the Mulligan Co.," Talbott testified. "The few minutes I have given to the Mulligan Co. since I took office have been a trivial part of my time. I really doubt that I have given Mulligan & Co. and my other private affairs two and one-half days out of the two and one-half years I have been in Washington. My interest in the company has never influenced me in the slightest degree in the execution of my duties as Secretary of the Air Force, and I hope that that is the opinion of you all.

"I have asked that the hearings be public," Talbott said. "I have answered every question to the utmost of my ability, and if my memory has been faulty, under the pressure of work any Secretary has to do, I have come back and corrected it." [13]

In a last-minute effort to hold his job as Air Secretary, Talbott said he had written Paul B. Mulligan to divest himself of all interest in the firm, and he declared that the partnership would be dissolved as of July 31, 1955. His effort to correct the problem came too late, and after too many questionable acts.

President Eisenhower announced on July 27, 1955, that he would personally study the transcript of the testimony to determine if proper standards of ethics had been violated. Following this review, Secretary Talbott was asked to resign, and on August 1, 1955, he submitted his resignation to the President. President Eisenhower accepted it the same day as the "right" decision, but he praised Talbott's general performance in office.

In the official report, the McClellan subcommittee concluded that Talbott "made a mistake and acted indiscreetly in his position as Secretary of the Air Force.

"It [the subcommittee] agrees his resignation was quite proper under the circumstances," the report concluded.[14]

While Senator Karl E. Mundt, the South Dakota Republican, praised the forced resignation of Talbott as dramatizing "the new standard of ethics and propriety" of the Republican Administration, there was criticism from some Democrats.

Democratic National Chairman Paul M. Butler said that President Eisenhower's "friendly acceptance" of the resignation "makes a mockery of his pledges of uncompromising honesty in government."

On the day Talbott left office, he was awarded the Distinguished Public Service Award and the highest civilian award of the Defense Department, the Medal of Freedom.[15] Donald A. Quarles was sworn in as Talbott's successor as Secretary of the Air Force a few months before a major congressional investigation was begun to determine the status of United States air power compared with that of the Soviet Union.

The Talbott investigation provided the first national forum for Robert F. Kennedy, then an unknown counsel for the McClellan subcommittee. Also, it provided a dramatic lesson on how far the highest official in the mighty Air Force could fall when hazy testimony on outside business dealings was combined with the potential for a serious "conflict of interest." It was a lesson that should have been remembered all through the Defense Department, but it was not.

18

AIR POWER CONTROVERSY

THE 1955 May Day Air Show in Moscow was impressive and disturbing to many men in the Air Force and to members of the Senate Armed Services Committee. The Soviet Union unveiled a formation of its modern long-range bombers, the Bisons, which was equal to our entire production of the B-52, regarded as roughly comparable.

Senator Stuart Symington (Dem., Mo.), who had served as the first Secretary of the Air Force, was concerned over indications that the budget restrictions on United States production of B-52's endangered the national security and created the possibility that Russian air power could exceed ours by 1959.

"It is now clear that the United States . . . may have lost control of the air," Symington declared in a Senate speech on May 17. "In any case we should have an accounting, a balance sheet as to our strength against that of the Communists." The Missouri Democrat persisted in his criticism of proper expenditures for the buildup of our Air Force, and as the months went by more and more members of the Senate became concerned that there was a real danger the United States was losing effective control of the skies.

On February 24, 1956, Senator Richard B. Russell, chairman of the Senate Committee on Armed Services, appointed Senator Symington as chairman of a five-man subcommittee on the Air Force to delve deeply into a study of air power. Senator Henry M. Jackson of Washington and Senator Sam J. Ervin, Jr., of North Carolina were the other Democratic members. The Republican members were Senator Leverett Saltonstall of Massachusetts and Senator James H. Duff of Pennsylvania. In his formal letter establishing the subcommittee, Senator Russell said it had the duty "to examine into the condition and progress of the Department of the Air Force and ascertain if present policies, legislative authority, and appropriations are adequate to maintain a force capable of carrying out its assigned mission." [1]

Within a short time after the hearings opened on April 16, the scope of the inquiry was broadened to include a study of the air power of both the Navy and Army. In fact, it was necessary for the subcommittee to go into the whole picture of military spending, including the service requests to the Office of the Secretary of Defense, the specific requests for defense funds made by the President to Congress, and the amount provided by Congress.

From the outset, Chairman Symington and his Democratic colleagues leaned to the conclusion that our defense needs had been subordinated to a predetermined dollar limit and that "financial considerations have often been placed ahead of defense requirements, to the serious damage of . . . our national security." [2]

The Democrats used statistics showing President Eisenhower and Defense Secretary Charles Wilson had chopped substantial amounts from the sums requested by the Army, Navy and Air Force in the budgets under their control—fiscal 1954, 1955, 1956, and the budget for fiscal 1957, then under consideration. The services had requested $39,527,000,000 for fiscal 1954, but the Eisenhower Administration had cut it to $36,039,000,000—about 10 percent. In fiscal 1955, the military services requested $36,892,000,000, and the Eisenhower Administration cut it back to $30,942,000,000—a 16 percent cut. In fiscal 1956, the military services asked for $38,671,000,000, and the Eisenhower Administration reduced it to $33,685,000,000—a 13 percent cut.[3]

While Senator Symington was highly critical of the cuts in the defense budget by the Republican Administration, the Republican members of the subcommittee contended the cuts were justified and that the Defense Secretary and President Eisenhower had cut funds only to eliminate overlapping requirements of the services and to keep spending within the levels that could be wisely expended. The Republicans pointed out that the cutting of budget requests under the Eisenhower Administration had been less drastic than those under the Truman Administration through the Korean War period.[4]

The military services had requested only $14,629,000,000 for defense spending in fiscal 1950 in the era of the Truman Administration's economy wave directed by Defense Secretary Louis A. Johnson. The President and Defense Secretary had cut that request to $13,-627,000,000—about a 7 percent cut. That year Congress provided $13,166,000,000, which was very near what the Administration had asked for.

The requests of the military services went sky high with the Korean War, and even though President Truman permitted sharp increases in his budget requests, they were still from 26 to 39 percent lower than the military men wanted. The military services requested $79,074,-000,000 for fiscal 1951 when the probability of major military problems in Korea loomed ahead. President Truman's Administration cut the defense budget back to $48,271,000,000—a whopping cut of 39 percent.

The military services requested $96,161,000,000 for fiscal 1952 in a frantic effort to restore the fighting strength that had been dissipated by earlier economy moves. Although President Truman asked Congress for a $62,199,000,000 defense budget for fiscal 1952, this was still 35 percent lower than the military services had requested.

The budget requests of the military services for fiscal 1953 came to $72,085,000,000. The Truman Administration cut the defense spending request to $53,230,000,000, which was 26 percent lower than the military services wanted.

Senator Saltonstall and Senator Duff, as defenders of the Eisenhower Administration policies, outlined this whole pattern of activity on the military budget to demonstrate that the Republican Administration had been much less drastic in cutting the military men than had the preceding Democratic Administration. Also, in defending the Eisenhower Administration against charges of placing dollar considerations ahead of national defense, Senators Saltonstall and Duff pointed out that in each year from 1950 through 1956 Congress had made cuts in the defense spending requests of both President Truman and President Eisenhower. If dollar limitations had damaged the United States air-power picture, then Congress certainly had some responsibility for making deeper cuts than either President.[5]

In fiscal 1957, following the Soviet Union's display of air power, Congress increased the $35,974,000,000 budget submitted by President Eisenhower. However, even in that year, the $36,599,000,000 provided by Congress was nearly 13 percent less than the $41,129,-

000,000 that the military services had initially requested. The action of Congress came after the Symington subcommittee had dramatized the importance and difficulty of retaining air superiority. It was against this background that Congress added approximately a billion dollars to the Air Force funds for fiscal 1957 and 1958.

While the hearing reverberated with partisan politics as well as military politics, the 1,863-page published record compiled in a three-month period did shake some of the lethargy from the thinking about the nation's war machine. It provided the forum for leaders of World War II such as retired General Omar Bradley to warn: "I firmly believe that if a third world war should start, that it would start by an attack on the . . . installations within the United States very much like the . . . surprise attack on Pearl Harbor." [6]

The hearings brought forth testimony on the importance of having a "maximum force in being" because the advanced weapons of modern warfare allowed steadily decreasing time for any country to prepare its defenses against attack. Experts explained that the United States would no longer have a cushion of time after the start of hostilities in which to bolster its industrial capacity. No longer could the United States plan to mobilize its military strength after a war had begun.[7]

"I believe that in view of the sweeping scientific and technological developments in the past ten years, the military strength of any country at any given time rests largely on its force in being," testified retired General Walter Bedell Smith.[8]

General Bradley expanded the same theme: "In the past, oceans constituted a barrier to direct attack against our boundaries, and we were able to expand our giant industrial and armed potential even after our entry into War. Thus with the assistance of our allies, we won two conflicts: World War I and World War II. There is no assurance that time will work for us in the future. In fact, indications are just the opposite." [9]

Testimony brought forth information that the Russian long-range air force had, in operational units, more long-range jet bombers of the B-52 class with nuclear bombing capability than the United States had. General Nathan Twining, Chief of Staff of the Air Force, testified that Russia was then producing more bombers of the B-52 class than were being produced in the United States. He stated he had requested six additional wings of modern long-range jet bombers to provide the addition of about three hundred B-52's to the Strategic Air Command. At the time of the hearing his request was still tied up with more study in the Joint Chiefs of Staff and the Eisenhower Administration.[10]

There was disturbing testimony from General Curtis LeMay, then in charge of the Strategic Air Command, who indicated that if present plans and programs were not changed the Russian long-range air force would be stronger than the United States forces at some point between 1958 and 1960. He emphasized that the United States must not only have sufficient strength to match the Russians, but also strength to absorb a surprise attack and retaliate effectively.[11]

General Earle E. Partridge, Commander in Chief of the Air Defense Command and the Continental Defense Command, said our air-defense system was inadequate to discourage an enemy attack because most of our fighter planes in operation were not capable of attaining sufficient altitude to attack successfully a modern Russian bomber, and because of inadequacies in our radar warning network.

"We need additional radar and we need to improve the capability of the radar equipment which we already have," Partridge testified. "The aircraft presently in the inventory are subsonic and of insufficent altitude performance.

"We need to bring into the inventory as rapidly as possible better aircraft and new guided missiles with improved range, particularly Talos and Bomarc. Even in our present-day interceptor aircraft the unreliability of our fire-control equipment downgrades our capability to achieve operational effectiveness." [12]

The Symington subcommittee introduced into the record figures from the Bureau of the Budget showing that Defense Department expenditures were $43.7 billion in 1953, $40.3 billion in 1954, and then were cut to $35.5 billion in 1955, and were estimated to be on the $35 billion level for 1956 and 1957. In Symington's view, this just wasn't enough at a time when the military services insisted they needed about $48 billion, with the Air Force estimates at $23 billion.

In the light of all the testimony available, Symington's subcommittee concluded that the Soviet Union was producing more combat aircraft than the United States, and had outproduced the United States in modern aircraft in the prior three years.

The subcommittee also found at that time Russia had thousands more aircraft in combat units than the United States. The Soviet Union was then producing about ten times more fighter planes than the United States and had more jet fighters already in operational units than all types of jet aircraft combined in United States operational units.[13]

The subcommittee concluded that the Russians had more light jet bombers in operation than the United States, and that more heavy jet bombers were being produced at a faster rate. Only in the field of medium bombers did the report give the United States a superiority in numbers: "The United States has several times as many medium jet bombers as the Soviet."

The Symington subcommittee also spotlighted the amazing progress of the Soviet Union in research and development of scientific weapons. While the subcommittee members concluded the United States held superiority in this field, it warned that the Russians would attain superiority if the scientific work in the United States did not move at a faster rate.

Not only was Russia graduating twice as many trained scientists and engineers per year as the United States, the Soviet had developed high-energy physics research facilities superior to any others in the world, and "Soviet researchers are very capable."

While the subcommittee found the quality of our B-52 was much superior to the Soviet Bison, and that we had some quality edge in other fields, it pointed out that the Russians had operational aircraft jet engines "with substantially more thrust than any the United States has in operation."[14]

The Symington subcommittee could only speculate on the relative progress of ballistic missile programs, but declared that the Russians had started earlier in the development of ballistic missiles and were "believed to have made substantial progress in this field, to the extent of having exceeded the United States at least in some aspects of the ICBM and IRBM."

Trevor Gardner, the former Assistant Air Force Secretary for Research and Development, emphasized that the United States had to keep making advances constantly in these fields. He warned that the country could not pause and could not afford to lose its primary standing at any time.

Gardner expressed his own displeasure with the research money made available by the Eisenhower Administration: "The civilian and military management of research and development stated to the Secretary of the Air Force and the Secretary of Defense a need for $250 million more money than the current budget contains in it. . . . That was submitted January 16, 1956, to the Secretary of the Air Force, and we received a reply turning the project down on January 28, 1956. We resubmitted it February 10, and received a flat turndown for these funds."

"Now in your judgment and in the judgment of the people who signed the letter, was the $250 million needed for the research and development on the projects that are vital to the security of this country?" Senator Henry Jackson asked.

"That is correct," Gardner declared without equivocation.[15]

Admiral Arleigh Burke, Chief of Naval Operations, when questioned about cuts in the Navy's research and development funds in fiscal 1957, testified that the $86 million cut would slow up our research and development program proportionately.[16]

While there was much testimony about guided and ballistic missiles increasing in importance, at the time of the hearings in 1956 witnesses did not consider missiles as a replacement for manned aircraft in the foreseeable future. But they did agree that missiles were and would be an essential addition to total air power.

General LeMay repeated his previously stated views in support of giving the ICBM first priority: "I also stated that in my opinion the manned bomber will be used . . . as a primary means of long-range weapons delivery for several years to come." [17]

While military men agreed as to the importance of the whole range of guided and ballistic missiles, they also generally supported the LeMay view that the manned aircraft was going to be necessary for a long time to handle a wide range of missions for which it was best suited.

Although Secretary of Defense Charles E. Wilson and other Administration spokesmen constantly stressed that the United States had never been as strong militarily in peacetime, Senator Symington and his subcommittee declared that military strength relative to the Soviet Union should be the determining factor.

"Some seven years ago the United States had a monopoly on nuclear weapons," the subcommittee report stated. "Despite that fact the Communists attacked in Korea. Today that monopoly no longer exists.

"Likewise, but a few years ago, the United States had a bomb delivery capability which far exceeded that of all the rest of the world. That position of superiority has also disappeared." [18]

While concluding that the United States had a strong strategic striking force at that time, the Symington subcommittee majority credited this to contracts that had been let many years before.

The majority also found that defenses of the United States had been weakened through failure to act on national intelligence information and a tendency to either ignore or underestimate Soviet military progress.

One problem appeared to be the vast discrepancies between military needs and current and proposed inventories. The United States had an insufficient number of long-range modern jet bombers, and no program to produce the required number. The growing shortage of skilled manpower was resulting in inadequate aircraft maintenance and therefore unnecessary accidents and unnecessary deaths. Manpower shortages also blocked attempts to maintain a proper state of alert against possible attack.

The United States possessed the capacity to produce an adequate number of jet tankers yet completely failed to do so, the subcommittee charged. Nor was there any competent program to overcome this deficiency. This neglect, the subcommittee found, seriously decreased the effectiveness of American air power. The decline in strategic striking power of the Air Force, as compared to that of the Soviet Union, could not have been significantly overcome even by use of the Navy air capabilities.

The Symington subcommittee was critical of the lack of adequate air bases in the United States for best use of our striking force and for best dispersal of planes: "This deficiency in the continental United States is becoming increasingly dangerous because of the current deterioration in our overseas-base structure, along with the growing long-range capability of Soviet aircraft." [19]

The report accused the Eisenhower Administration of failing to develop an adequate defense warning system. The report declared that the Eisenhower Administration used the United States qualitative lead in aircraft as justification for having permitted the Soviet Union to acquire a quantitative superiority, even while lagging in the area of a quality Air Force.

"The duplicating approach characteristic of many research and development programs in the Department of Defense, along with the dollar limitations established for such programs, has retarded needed modernization of weapons systems," the Symington subcommittee majority charged.[20]

The most devastating charge made against the Eisenhower Administration was that defense requirements had often been subordinate to financial considerations. Symington alleged that this had resulted in serious damage to relative American-Soviet air-power strength and thus to American national security.

In general, Symington's group contended that Pentagon public relations had covered up the serious conditions that had resulted from cutting the funds available for the Air Force. "The public has failed to receive from official sources complete, accurate and timely information which it has the right to know," Symington said.[21]

Senator Leverett Saltonstall declined to join Senators Symington, Jackson and Ervin in signing the majority report. The Massachusetts Republican stoutly defended the Eisenhower Administration, and declared the Democrats took an "unduly pessimistic view of the state of our defense today and of our planning for the future."

Senator James Duff, the other Republican on the subcommittee, was no longer a member of the Senate when the report was released on February 20, 1957, but he authorized Senator Saltonstall to give his approval to the defense of the Eisenhower Administration.

Senator Saltonstall declared that the Democrats had emphasized the testimony of the career military officers, and did not give sufficient weight to the testimony of the civilian heads of the Defense Department. This ran counter to the principles of civilian control over the military forces that were inherent in the American form of government, the Senator said.[22]

"It confines its analysis almost exclusively to the four years since 1953," charged Senator Saltonstall, taking a slap at the lack of preparedness under the Democratic Administration just prior to the Korean War. "In my judgment, the present military effort cannot properly be evaluated without considering our position at the close of World War II, the speedy demobilization after that war, and the buildup for the Korean War, which determined the composition and capabilities of our defense forces in 1953."

In the opinion of the Massachusetts Senator our air power, our naval strength, together with our ground forces, made us superior to the Soviet Union. He credited those responsible for national defense with the firm determination to continue planning and to provide for adequate military strength, of which he deemed air power the most vital segment. He expressed his assurance that this conscientious diligence to American needs for years to come would be continued. The Senator declared that, in perspective, the defense establishment could never achieve a state of perfection because of the constant improvements in new military weapons and equipment that scientific progress constantly makes possible.

Senator Saltonstall placed emphasis on the testimony of Secretary of Defense Wilson, who attested the superiority of our eight-engine long-range B-52 over the Russian four-engine long-range jet bomber, the Bison.

"The B-52 without question is clearly a superior airplane to the Bison," Secretary Wilson had testified. "It is true that it is comparable because they are both heavy jet bombers. It is also true that they have four engines and we have eight. The horsepower of an engine in itself is no indication of superiority. I understand that they have followed the practice of putting the big engines in the wings which we think is a very poor one, which means that if they lose an engine they lose a bomber. There is no evidence that they have gained superiority by their type of design compared to ours. Our engineers happen to think that the distribution weight that they get with the eight engines is a favorable thing. It would seem that they are right because they have gotten the superior product." [23]

Senator Saltonstall took issue with Senator Symington's criticism of the Eisenhower Administration on the progress of the ballistic missile programs, where the United States seemed to be lagging behind the Soviet Union in some respects. The Senator directed attention to the testimony of General Bernard Schriever, who headed the ICBM project. General Schriever had stated that by action of President Eisenhower in September, 1955, the ICBM program received the highest national priority, and had testified that the program was going ahead about as fast as it could possibly go.

The Democratic charge of wasteful duplication in the missile programs was rejected by Senator Saltonstall. He quoted Admiral Radford, Chairman of the Joint Chiefs of Staff, as saying:

"I don't feel that there is too much duplication in the research effort of the departments. What there is is pretty well known and is probably desirable from the standpoint of having more than one approach to the problem. . . . Where duplication exists today, for the most part it is considered desirable duplication in obtaining a different approach to the same problem."

The Radford testimony tended to blame the Truman Administration's economy drive for any delays in research. He said: "Unfortunately . . . in the period 1945 to 1950, Defense Department appropriations were pared way down. We lost a lot of time that we could never make up moneywise on research." [24]

Undoubtedly there were many political factors that influenced the views of Senator Symington's Democratic majority and the views of Senator Saltonstall, the Republican who signed the minority report.

However, there were some things upon which there seemed to be agreement.

The Soviet Union was in the process of closing the gap on air power, and it had created new and expensive problems for the Pentagon. Bigger, more complicated and more expensive modern long-range bombers had to be built to keep pace, and there had to be a "balanced force" that provided for modernization of the Navy and the Army.

The ballistic missiles were on the scene, and it was obvious to all that the Soviet Union had made outstanding progress in this field and already demonstrated capability of firing ballistic missiles farther than the United States forces could fire them. As the Symington subcommittee report on air power was filed in February, 1957, there was a great deal of uncertainty as to what this long-range ballistic missile capability meant.

However, only a few months later the Soviet Union launched the first artificial earth satellite—the 184-pound ball of instruments known as Sputnik. That incident served to end the economy mood, for it dramatized to the world that the Russians had moved ahead of the United States in the large rocket boosters needed to place such an artificial satellite in orbit. It seemed to confirm their claim that they had developed "the ultimate weapon"—an intercontinental ballistic missile.

19

MANAGING THE MISSILES

BALLISTIC-MISSILE and space-program planning brought an era packed with new problems for the Pentagon. In some instances the Pentagon tried to keep the multimillion- and multibillion-dollar programs under rather firm control of the military and civilian technicians and accountants on the Defense Department payroll who were subject to the broad range of conflict-of-interest laws.

Ballistic-missile and space programs loomed too large and too complicated for the Defense Department to handle with "in house" capacity for the research and development and general systems engineering. It was impractical for the Department to develop and retain the "in house" capacity for the scientific development and efficient management of the huge programs, when the giants of private industry could provide a pool of scientific and industrial know-how. The big business concerns, not hampered with the salary restrictions that applied to military and civilian personnel in the Defense Department, seemed to be the logical place to turn with the whole problem. Neither were the big industries bound by the chain-of-command thinking and the tight bureaucratic bonds that so often crushed imagination and strangled new ideas at the Pentagon.

A most satisfactory arrangement was developed to farm out the big projects to private industry or to university-connected study teams, with excellent results in many individual cases. However, this arrangement brought with it new and perplexing problems in the area of conflicts of interest, endangering the whole concept.

Certainly, farming out an entire ballistic-missile or space-research program permitted the Defense Secretary, the Secretary of the Army, Secretary of the Navy and the Secretary of the Air Force to unload tremendous responsibility on a big industrial concern. However, it also created some awkward and embarrassing situations giving the appearance that those firms with the big research and development contracts had an inside track with the Air Force, Navy or Army on related matters. Even when there was no actual violation of conflict-of-interest laws or regulations, it often appeared that organizations or individuals had access to inside information on Pentagon thinking and planning and even to ideas submitted by competitors. The whole semblance was detrimental to Pentagon relations with other contractors, and to the image portrayed to the public.

As the Defense Department made the multimillion-dollar contracts that passed the responsibility of ballistic-missile and space programs to private industry, it became apparent that the necessarily loose contractual arrangement in the research and development field carried grave dangers. Thus the Defense Department was in fact handing over millions of dollars to private industry with the broadest discretion as to how the money should be spent to develop new ideas and new machinery, which could not be described in the contracts because they did not exist. The system contained some of the same dangers the War Department encountered in the Civil War when it handed a blank check to Captain Frémont for war preparation in the Western Division headquarters at St. Louis, and ended up with shoddy goods, overpriced guns and extravagant expenditures for lavish living quarters and ill-conceived and highly vulnerable forts.

Congress has recognized the potential for corruption and mismanagement when the Defense Department awards multimillion-dollar contracts permitting private industry such discretion in developing or building modern weapons or space systems. "The Government depends upon them not only for vital defense services and hardware but for the enforcement of public policies associated with the disbursement of Government contract dollars," the House Government Operations Committee capsuled the problem in its "Thirteenth Report" (H.R. 917) filed on November 22, 1963.

The House committee stated that the contractor's public policy responsibility included "allocating a fair share [of subcontracts] to small business, taking heed of depressed areas, [and] insuring nondiscrimination in employment.

"We may assume that the diligence and honesty of the contractor's employees are just as important to the Government, in terms of work well done and economies realized, as the proper conduct of Government personnel," the House committee said. "Yet the contractor's employees are not public employees; they are beyond the direct reach of the conflict-of-interest laws and regulations framed for Government personnel." [1]

The changing nature of government-contractor relationships raised questions as to whether and to what extent the contract agents of the Defense Department should be made to conform to the codes of conduct designed to minimize or prevent conflicts of interest. No single answer could be given, even after extensive study, but it was obvious that conflict-of-interest standards must apply where the continuing relationship between the firm and government makes the private industry a "relatively permanent adjunct of Government."

Congress recognized that huge firms operating for profit have an obligation to stockholders, and are involved in a fierce competitive drive for a bigger share of defense contracts and maximum profits. This does not promote high standards of objectivity in dealing with the government or with their competitors. "The facts of life in the business environment make defense contractors deeply suspicious of any among them who might gain undue competitive advantage by strategic placement in the inner councils of Government as a result of contract assignments," the House Government Operations Committee explained the problem.[2]

Undue competitive advantage not only causes resentment in industry, it also works against the Government's best interest in many ways. It provides advance knowledge of government plans and programs. It gives access to technical know-how and trade secrets of other government contractors. Most importantly, it provides the opportunity to develop design or system studies favoring the contractor's own hardware developments, which constitutes "organizational conflicts of interest."

In its attempt to remove the profit motive and the competitive advantage, the Defense Department had three basic alternatives. First, it could use existing in-house capacity to a greater extent or develop new in-house capacity to perform the needed technical services. This course was handicapped by salary ceilings and personnel ceilings within the military establishments, and the fact that they might be duplicating superior technical facilities already available in private industry.

Second, the Defense Department took steps to try to insulate the profit-making divisions of private industry from the research contracts by barring the contractor from bidding on hardware contracts when that contractor had served the government as a technical adviser and monitor of the production of other contractors.

Third, the Department favored the creation of nonprofit corporations in some instances to provide an organization with the flexibility of a private concern, but with the bothersome profit motive removed.

This did not constitute an attack on the profit motive, but was an effort "to insure that the best interests of the Government and industry both will be protected and served when the Government relies on contractors rather than its own personnel for such services as defense analysis, technical management, and systems engineering."

The RAND Corporation is the best-recognized early example of a not-for-profit organization used for defense analysis. RAND, organized in 1945 as a subsidiary division of Douglas Aircraft Corporation, was severed from Douglas in 1948 because it was recognized that sponsorship by Douglas would never permit RAND to acquire and sustain the needed reputation for complete objectivity on analytical defense studies. These studies by RAND would always be suspected of being used for the competitive advantage of Douglas Aircraft.[3]

The establishment of RAND as an independent nonprofit organization set a pattern that included Analytic Services, Inc. (ANSER), a nonprofit corporation under continuing contract to the Air Force Directorage of Development Planning for analysis and evaluation of Air Force weapons-system concepts and techniques; the Institute for Defense Analyses (IDA), a nonprofit corporation performing weapons-system evaluation and other technical studies for the Joint Chiefs of Staff; and Advanced Research Projects Agency (ARPA), which was created to do similar studies.

Shortly after ARPA came into being in 1958, it was under heavy criticism because it did not keep itself independent of industry, and "leaned heavily on industrial companies as a source of readily available high-caliber scientific and technical personnel." Roy W. Johnson, the first director of ARPA, went to that post from a vice presidency with General Electric Company. According to the House Government Operations Committee, he even encouraged industrial companies to contribute free services to ARPA by seeking no-cost research contracts. The House Government Operations Committee "was instrumental in stopping the appointment of a research scientist as Director of ARPA who intended to retain his company connections and a salary of $40,000 a year." [4] Such a salary arrangement would have completely destroyed insulation from private industry, the basic purpose of the not-for-profit organization.

While the necessity of relying on outside corporations touched the Defense Department, the Navy and the Army, it was the big missile programs of the Air Force that most clearly pointed up the conflict-of-interest problems.

In 1954, the Air Force contracted with the newly formed Ramo-Wooldridge Corporation to handle systems engineering and technical direction of the ballistic missile programs. The decision to deal with Ramo-Wooldridge was the alternative to depending on a single prime contractor, a Government-supported university laboratory, or establishing in-house technical know-how.

Ramo-Wooldridge was a profit organization. It performed well and grew rapidly through broad government contracts and loans from Thompson Products Company. In an effort to avoid conflicts of interest the Air Force imposed a restriction on Ramo-Wooldridge which prohibited that firm from obtaining any hardware contracts developing on the fringe of its work. The hardware exclusion clause stated:

"The contractor agrees that due to its unique position in the administration and supervision of the program contemplated hereunder, the Ramo-Wooldridge Corp. will not engage in the physical development or production of any components for use in the ICBM contemplated herein except with the express approval of the Assistant Secretary of the Air Force [Matériel] or his authorized representative." [5]

This hardware ban was intended to cover components for any big missile that came out of the program, but was not to restrict the right of Ramo-Wooldridge to fabricate and sell products unrelated to the missiles.

When Ramo-Wooldridge and Thompson Products merged in 1958, the hardware ban was continued for the new corporation, Thompson Ramo Wooldridge, and for its wholly owned subsidiary Space Technology Laboratories (STL). However, with the creation of Space Technology Laboratories to conduct specific systems engineering and technical direction, the hardware ban was modified so that Thompson Ramo Wooldridge could compete for any Air Force prime or subcontracts not originating in STL projects.

Although Thompson Ramo Wooldridge continued to have a strong interest in its subsidiary, STL, an effort was made to emphasize the corporate autonomy and independence of STL in its work for the Air Force. Thompson Ramo Wooldridge handed over some $20 million in assets to STL, and in its meetings and correspondence stressed the importance of STL and Thompson Ramo Wooldridge (TRW) operating as two entirely separate corporations.

On January 31, 1959, the executives of Thompson Ramo Wooldridge wrote to each member of the STL board of directors as follows:

"Apart from the financial data mentioned above, no information should be provided to any employee or official of TRW about the present or anticipated Air Force projects of STL unless it is specially authorized by the Air Force for release to TRW and other companies in accordance with normal need-to-know procedures. Similarly, in the unlikely event that STL ever assists the Air Force in judging proposals for a project in which TRW is one of the competitors, TRW must be treated no more favorably than any other company. We consider it essential that the directors and officers of STL establish and monitor whatever procedures they find necessary to insure that TRW receives absolutely no special advantages in competition for any Air Force project as a consequence of its financial investment in STL." [6]

This was a very proper instruction from the officers of Thompson Ramo Wooldridge, making an interesting paper record to indicate that every effort had been made to obtain the ultimate in autonomy for STL. However, even then, other contractors viewed the arrangement with suspicion and were reluctant to give STL the information necessary to amply exercise technical direction.

An investigation report by the Subcommittee on Military Operations of the House Committee on Government Operations recommended that the technical direction functions be assigned to a nonprofit corporation, and this approach was supported by an Air Force study group.

The study group and the House subcommittee concluded there would always be considerable suspicion among competitors if a profit-making subsidiary of one of the competitors was in control of technical direction of Air Force programs. Recommendations suggested the problem could be solved by making STL "a nonprofit organization exclusively devoted to governmental concerns." Officials of STL stated that they wished to continue in the profit-making role, and the Air Force was forced to create a new nonprofit organization, Aerospace Corporation.

In February, 1960, General Bernard A. Schriever, Commander, Air Force Systems Command, brought together an organizing committee to establish a new nonprofit corporation to take over the role of STL. The charter and the slate of trustees were approved by Air Secretary Dudley C. Sharp, and Roswell L. Gilpatric was named as chairman of the board of trustees.[7] Gilpatric had been Under Secretary of the Air Force from 1951 to 1953, and later became Deputy Secretary of Defense.

Aerospace was incorporated under the laws of California on June 3, 1960, and Gilpatric was among those who recruited Dr. Ivan A. Getting, a vice president of Raytheon, for the presidency. It was Gilpatric, as chairman of the board of trustees, who proposed on July 30, 1960, that Dr. Getting be paid an annual salary of $75,000 a year.

The minutes of the board stated that in proposing the $75,000 salary Gilpatric noted "the [Aerospace] corporation cannot give him a contract of employment, cannot assure him of tenure, and cannot offer him any stock options." There was the provision that "Dr. Getting would remain nominally an employee on technical leave of absence from Raytheon until August, 1961, for the sole purpose of completing ten years of service to secure vesting of pension rights in the Raytheon retirement system, but no mention was made of the fact that Dr. Getting's salary at Raytheon had been only $45,000 a year." [8]

Nonprofit Aerospace now moved into motion with an agreement that allowed for advance payments up to a total of $5,000,000 without interest, against amounts that would be later due under the Air Force contract dated June 22, 1960. Under general Air Force control, Aerospace was to be responsible for "advanced systems analysis and planning, research, experimentation, initial systems engineering, initial technical direction and general technical supervision in the complete field of Air Force ballistic missiles and space systems." [9]

In order to avoid disruption in the development program of Atlas, Titan, and Minuteman weapons systems, the Air Force continued these under contract to Space Technology Laboratories for systems engineering and technical direction. However, Space Technology Laboratories was to undertake no new programs, and was gradually to phase out of Air Force systems engineering and technical development work.

Within six months after the creation of Aerospace, 250 technical staff members of STL transferred to Aerospace. In addition to these scientists and engineers, more than 1,000 administrative and support personnel were also transferred from Space Technology Laboratories. At the time it was estimated that Aerospace would eventually grow to accommodate a technical staff of about 1,000.[10]

Recognizing the problems of the past, the Air Force prepared an extensive policy statement "on relations with Air Force-sponsored nonprofit corporations," which at that time included Aerospace, Analytical Services, MITRE, RAND, and Systems Development Corporation.

"These Air Force-sponsored nonprofit corporations have a close and continuing relationship with the Air Force that sets them apart from other organizations, profit or nonprofit," the Air Force policy stated.[11] "It is to this special status that our policies on relations with them must be shaped."

That policy statement seemed to demonstrate comprehension of nearly all the problems that had arisen in trying to obtain the expertise in science and management necessary to run the big space and missile programs.

"We look to these nonprofit corporations to focus the Nation's finest scientific and technical talents on selected and highly sophisticated tasks," the policy statement said, warning further:

"They must not become convenient catchalls for projects which could be performed by private industry; the elite nature of their technical staffs must be preserved. Any dilution of the select quality of these organizations can only have an adverse effect on their ability to carry out their vital Air Force work. Procedures must be developed to require them to coordinate with the Air Force before undertaking assignments from other Government agencies or commercial sources.

"It follows, moreover, that the business aspects of their affairs must be open to Air Force scrutiny, much as actual Air Force operation. Frills and other nonessentials cannot be tolerated, if public confidence is to be maintained in their unique role. Such accountability is not inconsistent with the freedom of thought and independence on technical matters that we seek from these corporations."

Possibilities of conflicts of interest drew this warning: "Standards of conduct likewise merit particular emphasis. There must be no conflict between the public interests with which these nonprofit corporations are impressed, and the private interests of their trustees, officers, members of technical staffs, and other employees. Each corporation will be expected to prescribe and enforce suitable regulations to this end. These should take advantage of the progress that certain companies have already made—as, for example, in the area of trustees. This includes disclosure by a trustee of any private interests which may be in conflict with his responsibilities, his disqualification in particular matters, and restrictions on his use of inside information."

The Air Force warned that the special position of these nonprofit corporations "exposes them to extensive technical information of other contractors.

"To prevent the possibility or appearance of private advantage to these corporations, our contracting officers should proceed in accordance with the recently revised policy of . . . the Armed Services Procurement Regulation. This policy provides guidance on the acquisition by the Government of title to inventions, in lieu of a comprehensive license of free use, where the services of the contractor are largely those of coordinating and directing the work of others."

The Air Force stated that the fees allowed these nonprofit corporations "must be tailored to their special status." The policy statement cautioned that while fees to be allowed would often be a matter of judgment, "it is clear that the traditional rules covering commercial companies do not fit these nonprofit corporations," which are not taxed and which often are assigned a contract on a "sole source" basis. As an example of a proper function for fees supplied by the Air Force, the policy statement cited those instances where it is to be "applied . . . toward the conduct of independent research programs."

"Such programs which foster a healthy scientific climate, are to be encouraged, provided they are carefully planned and held within reasonable bounds," the Air Force stated from a wealth of experience with programs that were not held within bounds. "The fee may also be reserved for some working capital requirements, but should not be regarded as a substitute for advance payment arrangements, the preferable source."

In general, the Air Force suggested that these nonprofit corporations should operate in buildings provided by the government. And the Air Force warned about wasteful purchases of unneeded facilities, the payment of "inordinate fees" and lease arrangements at unreasonable rental rates.

Even as Aerospace was being established, it was recognized in the Air Force policy statement that the most difficult problem posed would be determining the range within which salaries should fall.

"Charged with heavy and varied responsibilities, it is clear that these corporations must attract and retain talent of the highest order," the Air Force said. "Yet, their employment policies must be marked by good judgment and restraint. These companies have no license to outbid the market at every turn. If the compensation paid by these nonprofit corporations exceeds that paid by the Government, it should be because private industry—with whom these companies must compete—typically offers such higher compensations. The Air Force, on its part, must continue to review for reasonableness certain individual salaries as well as the overall compensation structure of these corporations."

It appeared that Aerospace was obligated to use its fees only in the general manner set out in the Air Force policy guidelines, and to avoid excessive salaries and the "frills and other nonessentials" that might grow up around the government-financed nonprofit corporation.

Above all, it appeared that the Air Force had its own obligation to see that the financial affairs of Aerospace were as carefully scrutinized as their own operations.

However, Dr. Getting, firmly settled in his job as president of Aerospace, had other ideas about salary levels, fringe benefits for top-level employees, the acquisition of real estate, and the general operations of Aerospace. Dr. Getting objected to the warning about "frills and nonessentials," and he disagreed with the sharp limitations the policy statement would have placed on the fees that Aerospace would receive from the Air Force.

He balked at making the financial records available to the Air Force or even to the General Accounting Office (GAO) auditors, and he insisted that the government must "be generous" to promote the "independence and objectivity" of Aerospace.

In the spirit of his generosity, Dr. Getting arranged for "incentive compensation" bonuses for the top-level officials at Aerospace that amounted to twenty percent of their annual salaries. For Dr. Getting this brought his total annual income to more than $90,000 a year—the highest income paid any chief executive of a government-sponsored nonprofit corporation. In addition, he was given a $350,000 life insurance policy that cost Aerospace $1,800 a year, and the corporation was kicking in another $9,000 a year to his retirement.[12]

Whether or not Aerospace was the answer to the Air Force problems, it certainly appeared to be the answer to the financial problems of Dr. Getting. He was living in a style comparable to that enjoyed by Frémont in St. Louis in the early Civil War days, and he was exhibiting just as much independence in his general spending policies. Also, like Frémont, his free-wheeling was to be the subject of a congressional investigation.

The House subcommittee was equally disturbed at the large public relations budget for Aerospace, and found this to be highly inappropriate in a firm that was organized solely under government direction to do work for a government agency. Aerospace spent more than a million dollars in four years for its own public information staff, and in addition paid $2,000 a month, plus expenses, for the services of a New York public relations firm.

"This public relations network appears to run counter to the provision in Aerospace's articles of incorporation to 'not engage in propaganda or otherwise attempt to influence legislation,'" stated the subcommittee headed by Representative Porter Hardy, a Virginia Democrat.

Equally unpalatable to the House subcommittee was the big advertising budget of $200,000 a year that Aerospace used for recruiting. "The result in large part was to recruit at increased salaries people who were already working on military programs of other organizations financed by Government contracts," the Hardy subcommittee said. "In effect, they moved from one Government contractor to another at a higher cost to the Government." [13]

The laxity apparent in the financial affairs of Aerospace also applied to their handling of security problems. Not only did Aerospace handle its personnel with "an extraordinary measure of forebearance," but the security office "was lax in following security regulations."

High-level security clearance was required to handle much of the work assigned to Aerospace, but the Hardy subcommittee was amazed to find that Aerospace officials had either ignored or were unaware that a $15,000-a-year member of the technical staff had a record of several morals arrests. The police record of this staff member came to light when he was in another city on business and was arrested on a charge involving a minor. The Hardy subcommittee commented critically:

"When notified by the out-of-town police, Aerospace bypassed its own security office and dispatched an assistant general counsel to recover documents in the employee's possession. The Air Force was subsequently notified orally about the arrest and told that no classified documents were in the employee's charge."

This arrest led to disclosure that this same individual, in the four years he had been employed at Aerospace, had been convicted on five other charges—drunkenness, prowling, hit and run resulting in injury to personal property, outrage to public decency (two counts of enticing young girls), and a violation of probation.[14]

The Hardy subcommittee found it incredible that Aerospace and the Air Force could be completely unaware of these arrests even though the employee was on probation.

When the facts became known, including the detail that the man had not made his arrest record known to Aerospace, Dr. Getting directed that the man be placed on temporary suspension, with pay, pending an analysis of the information. Later, he was granted a ninety-day medical leave of absence with pay, with the understanding that he would seek psychiatric help. At the end of the ninety-day period the psychiatrist said that the problem had been "totally eliminated from his behavior" and that "there is no security risk at this time." No objection was voiced by Aerospace security or by the Air Force and he was reinstated.[15]

It was not until late April, 1965, a few days before the Hardy subcommittee hearings started, that Dr. Getting, knowing the subcommittee would obtain information on the case, informed the Secretary of the Air Force of the employee's record and current security status.

This touched off a new Air Force investigation by the Office of Special Investigations that turned up two other undisclosed arrests—one when he was picked up for suspected drunken driving and dismissed with a warning, and the other an arrest on a charge of "following a female."

A military psychiatrist who examined the record was not so optimistic as the Aerospace psychiatrist. He concluded that "this individual has a history of an emotional condition in which recurrence is still a reasonable possibility, and that such a recurrence would have a potential effect on his reliability and judgment with respect to safeguarding classified information." [16]

Not until the day the Hardy subcommittee hearings began did Aerospace take action to deny the man access to classified material. The Air Force investigation had concluded that there was no evidence the man had compromised classified material, but the Hardy subcommittee was skeptical of the thoroughness of such a fast investigation: "Indeed, it would be surprising if an investigation so limited in time had found any such evidence."

It was only one of several cases with security implications that the Hardy subcommittee criticized, with the comment that there "was clearly a lack of awareness of potential security implications." [17]

The Hardy subcommittee did not try to assess the technical competence of Aerospace personnel or the achievements of the corporations in carrying out the mission for the Air Force. The report did state that "it appears that Aerospace's management wanted the benefits and prerogatives of private industry without any of the risks, plus the protection and security of the Government service without any of the restrictions.

"The Air Force must share in the responsibility for inadequate fiscal controls," the subcommittee said. "Up to the beginning of the subcommittee investigation, the Air Force failed to make a reasonable effort to keep the operation of Aerospace in line with established Government policy."

General Schriever had defended Aerospace during the hearings, and had commented: "The technical contributions of the Aerospace Corp. have far outweighed the dollars we have invested." This logic was rejected in the subcommittee report, which said it "does not consider this responsive.

"There is a question of moral responsibility for control of the people's money which is independent of the amount of money involved or the greatness of the achievement," the subcommittee stated. "No amount of technical perfection on one side of the ledger can balance waste and inefficiency on the other side. If it is wrong to spend millions of dollars of the people's money to buy facilities that are not needed, no amount of brilliant scientific achievement can make it right." [18]

Chairman Hardy declared that "public office is a public trust and the subcommittee believes that office in a nonprofit corporation wholly created and wholly supported by the Government is, in a sense, also a public trust." [19]

The Hardy subcommittee stated that it recognized the importance of providing a working environment that is both pleasant and challenging, as well as adequate salaries for men of the ability and rare talent that Aerospace was supposed to recruit. The subcommittee also stated it agreed with the importance of objectivity and intellectual independence in the kind of technical decision made at Aerospace.

Chairman Hardy and his subcommittee members could not believe that objectivity and intellectual independence were contingent upon Aerospace's holding title to the building in which the staff worked or on the legal arrangements through which the salaries were paid.

Without doubt the nonprofit corporations fill an important role, but in the federal employ there are many brilliant scientists, engineers and other personnel giving honest, courageous and efficient service. "The Navy has managed its nuclear-age research and development programs within the Department with such outstanding successes as the nuclear submarine and the Polaris missile," the Hardy subcommittee pointed out. "A reappraisal of the Air Force management concept should be undertaken to determine the feasibility of reducing the reliance on outside decision making."

Aerospace's contention that it was less costly in the long run than to use private industry was challenged by the Hardy subcommittee as not having been tested.[20]

The Hardy subcommittee indicated that the whole role of the nonprofit organization in the conduct of government business must be carefully watched. The proliferation of these organizations in recent years was noted with the caution:

"The establishment of a nonprofit corporation does not excuse the

Department of Defense or any other Government agency or the Congress from the moral responsibility for prudent control of public funds spent through the nonprofit organization."

A special warning note was sounded with regard to "where we are heading in terms of salaries" in the nonprofit corporations.

One of the reasons for setting up nonprofit organizations is to get around government salary restrictions, as pointed out by President Johnson's comments on May 12, 1965, on the need for boosting federal salaries to keep them in line with other salaries outside government.

"It appears that a ludicrous cycle could be set in motion," the Hardy subcommittee said. "Federal funds are to be used to set up nonprofit corporations so they can pay higher rates than Federal scales, then Federal salaries will be raised to make them competitive with nonprofits." [21]

The House Armed Services Committee unanimously agreed that Aerospace salaries were out of line, and it was recognized that there must be constant examination of the nonprofit organizations to see if they are functioning within the framework of good public policy.

20

MUZZLE FOR THE GAO WATCHDOG

EXPENDITURES for the Air Force ballistic-missiles work in fiscal year 1958 exceeded $1 billion, and Comptroller General Joseph Campbell decided it was time to audit the program. On June 13, 1958, Campbell wrote to Air Force Secretary James H. Douglas notifying him that the accountants for the General Accounting Office (GAO) were starting a review of the research and development programs to evaluate the effectiveness of Air Force policies, procedures and management.

"We have selected the ballistic missiles program for our initial review in the research and development field and our representatives are presently at the Ballistic and Missiles Division in Inglewood,

California," Campbell wrote the Air Force Secretary. "We understand that a report was recently prepared by the Inspector General [of the Air Force] covering a survey of management of the ballistic missiles program. In view of our current survey in the management aspects of the ballistic missiles program, we believe it would be mutually advantageous for our representatives to review this report and thereby minimize duplication of work performed by the Inspector General's staff." [1]

Comptroller General Campbell expected the request to be honored, for in his view the law made it mandatory that all agencies of the executive branch make all records available for periodic audits by the accountants and investigators of the GAO. He was surprised when the Air Force refused to permit the auditors to have access to the report of the Air Force Inspector General. The refusal made no sense under the agreements that the GAO had with the Defense Department. Although the law under which he operated authorized access to all papers and records of the executive branch, Campbell had agreed that he would not demand information dealing with confidential informants, certain criminal or personnel investigations or war plans.

The Air Force refusal was not based on national security grounds, for GAO auditors had security clearance. There was no claim that the names of confidential informants, criminal or personnel investigations or war plans were involved. It was a flat claim of the "executive privilege" that had been used increasingly to hide embarrassing records since the Army-McCarthy hearings.

The Air Force provided a two and one half-page summary of the sixty-one-page report of the Air Force Inspector General, but it was thoroughly inadequate for the GAO auditors' use.

"The survey of management of the ballistic missiles program was directed to determining the effectiveness and efficiency of various activities under the ballistic missiles program," Campbell wrote the Air Force. "It included appraisals of such activities as buying and contract administration, procedures for furnishing Government-owned facilities to contractors, administration of commercial leases, purchasing practices of Government contractors, and many other subjects of a general administrative nature as opposed to highly specialized scientific or technical matters." [2]

Campbell was not antagonistic to the Eisenhower Administration, and did not want to engage in a major dispute with the executive branch if he could avoid it. He had been treasurer and vice president of Columbia University when General Dwight D. Eisenhower was president of that institution. There had been a pleasant and friendly relationship between the two men, and it was General Eisenhower who had asked Campbell to come to Washington to be a member of the Atomic Energy Commission in 1953.

A year later President Eisenhower named Campbell Comptroller General of the United States—a job with a fifteen-year term and the responsibility of serving as financial watchdog for Congress on all executive departments. No single office in the government had a more vital task in forcing the sprawling federal agencies to administer the laws fairly and make expenditures according to the laws.

The GAO was established by the Budgeting and Accounting Act of 1921 as an arm of the legislative branch of government. Scandals and loose spending practices in World War I pointed up the necessity for an overseer for the vast sums expended. Once appointed by the President and confirmed by the Senate, the Comptroller General becomes an agent of Congress. To assure independence of the office, Congress established the long term and provided for removal of the incumbent only by impeachment or by a joint resolution of Congress.

The law establishing the General Accounting Office clearly and specifically gave the Comptroller General and his auditors power to examine all information and reports in order to determine whether money was being spent in a legal manner. The section on access to records states:

"All departments and establishments shall furnish to the Comptroller General such information regarding the powers, duties, activities, organization, financial transactions, and methods of business of their respective offices as he may from time to time require of them; and the Comptroller General, or any of his assistants or employees, when duly authorized by him, shall for the purpose of securing such information, have access to and the right to examine any books, documents, papers, or records of any such department or establishment."

The only exception to the Comptroller General's legal right to demand and obtain access to records of any such department or establishment was the one given to the Secretary of State to determine whether there should be a publication of expenditures of funds used in dealings or treaty-making with foreign nations.[3]

The law should have been clear to anyone. The GAO needed access to all records dealing with the expenditure of federal funds if it was to carry out its responsibility to conduct the careful examination necessary to determine if frauds, illegalities or improprieties were involved.

There were spotty problems between 1954 and 1958, but it wasn't until Campbell asked for the records on the multibillion-dollar Air Force ballistic-missiles program that he ran into such an obstinate refusal to make records available.

Representative F. Edward Hébert, the Louisiana Democrat, had been following the ballistic-missiles program as a result of his work as chairman of a House Armed Services subcommittee. He was gravely concerned when he learned that the Air Force was using the unjustified secrecy of "executive privilege" to bar the GAO from access to the Inspector General's report. From experience with dozens of investigations, Chairman Hébert knew the military services could not be relied upon to police their own spending. An adequate policing job on a Defense Department budget that totaled about $40 billion a year was vital. He recognized that it was essential for the various committees of Congress to be able to rely upon the staff of the GAO on complicated investigations.

The Air Force refusal to respond to Comptroller General Campbell's request for the Inspector General's report was a serious matter as far as Representative Hébert was concerned. When the periodic quiet protests by Campbell went unnoticed by the public, the usually mild-mannered Campbell fired off a letter to Defense Secretary Neil McElroy.

"These restrictions," Campbell wrote, "could seriously hamper the General Accounting Office in performing its statutory responsibility and will impede the performance of our work." [4]

He pointed out to McElroy that his GAO auditors could not do their job in the face of directives that prohibited them from examining the Inspector General's reports, and allowed them only a summary of reports as approved by the Secretaries of the various armed services.

Campbell also wrote to Hébert, spelling out his complaint: "Any information or factual data directly bearing on a program of activity subject to audit by the General Accounting Office should not be withheld or subjected to procedures designed to screen official documents, papers, or records, by the authority or activity being audited." [5]

With approval of Hébert, Campbell also wrote to Representative John Moss (Dem., Cal.), chairman of a House Government Operations subcommittee that was conducting a study on the availability of information from federal departments and agencies.

"It is essential that such reports be made available to the General Accounting Office in order that we can evaluate the effectiveness of the department's system of internal control and to preclude unwarranted and unnecessary duplication of effort in the internal audit and the independent reviews made by this office," Campbell contended.

"There is no basis why reports on the subject of the types pointed out above should not be made available to the General Accounting Office unless the purpose is to delay or hamper the efforts of the office to disclose all facts bearing upon the activity or area under audit.

"We believe that any departmental regulation denying to the General Accounting Office access to any report relating to 'internal audit and control' is contrary to the law." [6]

This was not a partisan political charge. It was Joseph Campbell, long-time friend of President Eisenhower, lodging a complaint that the Eisenhower Administration was acting contrary to the law in the claim of an "executive privilege" to withhold records.

Congressman John Moss declared that President Eisenhower was not discharging his duties under the Constitution when he permitted his subordinates to withhold records from the GAO. Under Article II, Section 3 of the Constitution, the President is obliged to "take care that the laws be faithfully executed. . . ." In this instance, President Eisenhower was not only disregarding the Budgeting and Accounting Act but also supporting those acting "contrary to the law," Moss said.[7]

Although the controversy started over GAO access to the Inspector General's report on the ballistic-missiles program, the issue was broader than that. It was apparent the real question was whether the Air Force, the Army, the Navy, or any other executive agency could arbitrarily refuse to give reports, papers, and financial records to the GAO. The logic of the Eisenhower Administration on this issue was difficult to follow. The President and many of his top Cabinet members were emphasizing that financial problems could be one of the nation's major worries. And one of the significant problems, they believed, was making certain the government was getting its money's worth from military spending. While talking in terms of more efficient and more honest handling of government, Eisenhower's actions supporting secrecy were a blow at the most important government watchdog organization, the GAO.

In times past, when GAO investigators were given maximum access to records, serious scandals had been unearthed. Most of them were not discovered by the military establishment but came to light only after the GAO or the congressional committees went to work. Chairman Hébert and Comptroller General Campbell were backed by a long record of fruitful hearings in questioning the wisdom as well as the legality of allowing our military spenders to erect more barriers against GAO auditors.

When President Eisenhower was questioned at his press conference about this arbitrary secrecy on Defense Department spending, he declared that he believed "that every investigating committee of the Congress, every auditing office, like the GAO, should always have the opportunity to see official records if the security of our country is not involved." [8]

However, when the specific question was raised in connection with the military inspectors of general reports, he backed the principle of arbitrary secrecy and the use of the claim of "executive privilege."

With this backing from President Eisenhower, the Army, Navy and Air Force officials continued to refuse to make the Inspector General's reports available. They provided sharply edited self-serving summaries to the GAO investigators. All law and logic seemed to have fallen by the wayside. No mechanism existed to force the Eisenhower Administration to abide by the provision of the Budgeting and Accounting Act requiring that records be made available on the request of the Comptroller General.

Almost immediately another big test arose, this time involving the Navy's refusal to make records available to the GAO. In February, 1959, Comptroller General Campbell wrote to the Moss subcommittee stating that the secrecy curtain made it impossible for him to fulfill his responsibility to audit Navy financial affairs.

"We consider it illogical, impractical and contrary to express provisions of the law for public officials to withhold, in their discretion, information concerning the discharge of their public trust," Campbell wrote.

"We are advising the Secretary of Defense and the Secretary of the Navy that we are unable to properly discharge our statutory responsibility if information needed in our work is denied to our representatives in the performance of our audits." [9]

Representative William L. Dawson (Dem., Ill.), chairman of the parent House Government Operations Committee, advised Moss to prepare for public hearings. He wrote Campbell:

"I am sure everything possible will be done to overcome the repeated arrogance of Federal executive officials whose denial of information to the General Accounting Office flouts the clear law of the land." [10]

Campbell said that the "executive privilege" claim was being made by the Secretary of the Navy on the ground that "he believes full disclosure of frank opinions, advice and recommendations from persons at lower levels . . . would not be in the public interest.

"This same reasoning is now being applied by the various bureaus and offices in the day-to-day work of their employees.

"We believe that sound management practices require that observations, opinions, recommendations by subordinates and any other matters considered in making a decision should be a matter of record.

"All of these [are] matters upon which judgments are founded and subsequent decision and actions are based. Such documentation serves as a protection to the individual making the decisions or taking the action as well as furnishing a sound basis for subsequent appraisal of their timeliness, effectiveness and honesty."

Campbell declared that under the procedure being used by the Navy "the individuals having custody of the materials are required to screen the material and remove from the official files any data they or their superiors feel we should not have.

"These actions provide a means by which the Department could conceal substantive evidence of waste, extravagance, improvident management, poor procurement practices, or other adverse conditions." [11]

By March of 1959, Campbell had full proof that he could not rely on the summary reports submitted to him by the Navy. He charged that the Navy had submitted two reports on one subject that were "incorrect representations" of the government's action. "The second version of the [Inspector General's] report, while containing twice as many pages, is also incomplete and inadequate because of the use of self-exercised censorship."

Campbell declared that the secrecy was not only illegal and the ultimate in bad government, but that it was also highly expensive. He explained that the secrecy deprived the GAO auditors of information already accumulated at the taxpayers' expense. The GAO was forced to send auditors out to duplicate work already done if they were to make any effort to fulfill their responsibility.[12]

The Comptroller General put no price tag on the extra cost for a

GAO audit to duplicate a Navy audit already in existence. However, the GAO did estimate that lack of access to the Air Force Inspector General's reports made the ballistic-missiles audit cost at least $125,000 more than necessary. Though the cost of the audit could have been avoided with the proper cooperation of the Air Force, the audit ultimately disclosed millions of dollars in bungling and waste in the Air Force missile program—all covered up for months in the name of "executive privilege."

The Moss subcommittee in its January 25, 1960, report on the "Navy Refusal to the General Accounting Office" had this to say: "The committee believes there is no foundation whatever for the alleged doctrine of 'executive privilege' to withhold information from the Congress or its agency, the General Accounting Office. Thus there is a clear violation of Section 313 of the Budget and Accounting Act of 1921."

Moss and his subcommittee sounded this broad warning: "Administrative officials far removed from the power of the electorate are exercising arbitrary censorship to hide the facts of government from the people and their representatives in Congress. They claim a power, above the duly enacted laws, which can be used to cover up waste, inefficiency—or worse. Unless this administrative arrogance is successfully challenged, democratic government must, in time, atrophy." [13]

The complaints of Congress and the newspapers went unheeded by President Eisenhower, who seemed unaware of how the Defense Department was being shielded from GAO and congressional investigations by the arbitrary secrecy of "executive privilege."

21

THE ARMY AND THE "LIMITED WAR"

GENERAL Maxwell D. Taylor was at odds with the "massive retaliation" concept of the Eisenhower Administration's defense policies almost from the time he was named Army Chief of Staff on

June 30, 1955. His predecessor, General Matthew B. Ridgway, had been a consistent dissenter against what he considered an overemphasis on a military posture that overlooked the possible threat of limited wars and prepared only for the all-out nuclear conflict.

General Ridgway had been a minority of one against the Eisenhower Administration's civilian political leaders and against the other members of the Joint Chiefs of Staff. His differing views were resented by Defense Secretary Charles E. Wilson, and efforts were made to keep General Ridgway from voicing his opinions where they would become public. While General Ridgway was usually discreet in his variance, because he was not a "team" player he fell into disfavor and retired in 1955.

If the Eisenhower Administration expected conformity from General Taylor, disappointment was in store, for the views of General Taylor were similar in many respects to those of General Ridgway. Although he fought for greater budgets, for a modernized Army and better preparedness for limited wars, he did not engage in the public dissent that would irritate Defense Secretary Wilson or his successor, Neil H. McElroy, who became Defense Secretary on November 9, 1957.

Sharp limitations on Army manpower and the lack of funds to modernize the Army and Navy for flexible response were regarded by General Taylor as unrealistic. The "massive retaliation" concept was more and more an irritant as the years went by. In 1958 and 1959, General Taylor believed a $50 billion defense budget was needed to meet the needs of national security properly. He found an ally in Admiral Arleigh A. Burke, the Chief of Naval Operations, who was concerned over the lack of spending to modernize the Navy and keep it up to proper force for the limited wars that seemed most likely.

The glamour of the ballistic missiles and the long-range jet bombers overwhelmed the complaints of General Taylor and Admiral Burke and their pleas for less spectacular tools to meet enemies in other Koreas. The Russian success with Sputnik did serve a purpose —it put a stop to further cutbacks in the Army and Navy budgets in 1958. But in 1959 military and political pressures for greater defense spending subsided quickly and the Eisenhower Administration reaffirmed its determination to keep the military budget below the $41 billion level.

The Joint Chiefs had made initial requests exceeding $50 billion, but later went through the process of giving formal approval to the

$41 billion program as "adequate." However, their testimony before committees of Congress made it apparent they believed there were possible dangers in the Eisenhower Administration's insistence upon an arbitrary ceiling for defense spending.

The full extent of General Taylor's dissent became more apparent after his retirement in the spring of 1959, when he expressed his full discontent with what he considered "declining military strength at a time of increasing political attention." In *The Uncertain Trumpet,* the retired former Army Chief of Staff charged "the defense of the United States is presently controlled by nonmilitary factors or by military factors which have become outmoded." [1]

He was highly critical of budget factors and concepts of military posture that had reduced the Army to authorized strength of 870,000 men. He called for a million-man Army, and defense spending of from $50 billion to $55 billion for five years to equip the Army and Navy properly with modern weapons in order to close the gap created by years of neglect.

"There is no living with Communism as an inferior," General Taylor said bluntly. He charged that the doctrine of massive retaliation had endangered our national security by saddling us with requirements for a general nuclear war but leaving us poorly prepared for brushfire wars.

Relieved of his responsibility as Army Chief of Staff, General Taylor freely discussed the efforts of the Eisenhower Administration to bar the public from knowledge of the conflicts by declining to give clearance to public statements that conflicted with approved Administration policy.[2]

In this atmosphere Senator Lyndon B. Johnson, the Texas Democrat, directed his Preparedness Investigating Subcommittee of the Senate Armed Services Committee to conduct an investigation of "Army Modernization."

"Many senior military officials have stated the threat of a limited war is more realistic than that of general war, involving an all-out nuclear conflict," Senator Johnson's subcommittee stated. "To be effective, it [the defense system] must contain military forces capable of defeating potential enemies in any type of conflict they might undertake ranging through the entire spectrum of warfare from limited wars in its many forms to global, all-out nuclear warfare. Each segment of the deterrent must maintain the required combat efficiency or the deterrent will be weakened as a chain is no stronger than its weakest link." [3]

The report directed attention to the fact that the Sino-Soviet bloc had demonstrated intercontinental ballistic missile capability, and had in being "large land forces possessing modern equipment that have added great stature to their avowed capability of surpassing the United States.

"It is reasonable to assume that they will not risk general war except as a last resort, for they realize they will reap devastation if they attempt to sow their thermonuclear warheads," the Johnson report concluded. "Hence, the United States must be ready to counter the other less distinctive forms of military power."

In a direct cut at the "massive retaliation" concept of the Eisenhower Administration, the Johnson report concluded: "This requires that our Nation, together with its allies, develop the necessary balanced, flexible forces, suitably deployed to meet the full range of the threat." While expressing the deepest concern over the so-called missile gap and the space race, Senator Johnson's subcommittee said these matters "sometimes tend to overshadow the fact that there is also a deadly serious contest afoot in many other elements and facets of military capability." [4]

The subcommittee found that while the Army had been reorganized under what was called "the Pentomic concept" to fight nuclear or nonnuclear wars, the Defense Department had not furnished the equipment necessary for this modern organization. The Johnson subcommittee found no fault with the "Pentomic" concept of organization, but was sharply critical of the lack of men and equipment to make it effective. The report explained that in World War II and Korea the Army had a standard of organization and maneuver that resulted in the roads being clogged and congested, men and equipment in concentrated areas, and with clearly defined battle lines.

"It is situations like these which the Army believes will be suicidal in a nuclear war," the Johnson subcommittee said.[5]

The Pentomic concept visualized a five-sided organizational structure under which the Army would be prepared to assemble quickly from dispersed areas, launch an attack, seize an objective, and again disperse to widely deployed formations. Defensively the Pentomic Army would be able to concentrate quickly and in sufficient strength to halt an enemy attack without becoming a likely nuclear target, and destroy the enemy with fire and counterattack.

The reorganization was guided by the requirement for "small, self-contained, highly mobile units with an organic nuclear capability, and units capable of semi-independent operations." This was to be met in part by increasing the infantry division maneuver elements from three to five. Battle groups within the maneuver elements were to be about 39 percent the size of the former infantry regiments to increase mobility and reduce the susceptibility to nuclear attack. Battalion headquarters would be eliminated in the chain of command to reduce the reaction time within the division.

However, the Johnson subcommittee found that although the Pentomic concept had been put into effect as early as 1956, the capabilities in 1960 were seriously undercut by a lack of weapons and equipment—"there is a 'gap' between the pentomic concept of organization and the present weapons and equipment to carry out the concept." [6]

The Johnson subcommittee found that as of 1960 Army troops in the field urgently needed modernization. "Their current weapons and equipment do not permit its combat units to enjoy the full benefits of the pentomic concept as they have not been substantially reequipped since World War II," the report said. "The weapons needed are in existence. They are not on the drawing boards nor are they 'dream' weapons. The need is for their production and issuance to the men in the field. Successfully proven prototypes and limited production models are not adequate substitutes for weapons in the hands of the troops."

This was in direct contrast with the Soviet Army, which has been completely modernized and reequipped since World War II.[7]

"Weapons and equipment of postwar design have been produced in quantity and are in the hands of the [Soviet] troops in most cases," the subcommittee said, and then spelled out the following status in the United States Army in a number of important areas:

(a) Only one sixth of its requirements for the new M-14 rifles were under contract through fiscal year 1960;

(b) Only one third of its needs for the new M-60 machine guns were in production;

(c) None of the new 90-mm. recoilless rifles were available to provide protection for small units in forward areas against enemy armor;

(d) Only one fifth of the new lightweight and greater-range armored personnel carriers were under contract;

(e) Only one tenth of its requirements for the new M-60 tanks were on order;

(f) Not a single piece of the new 105- or 155-mm. self-propelled howitzers was on order.[8]

With regard to missiles, which were fast becoming the core of firepower for a modern army, the Senate subcommittee had this assessment of six missile systems that had been developed and were regarded as essential:

1. Little John: "Substantial quantities are needed."
2. Sergeant: "Only one sixth of the active Army requirements are under contract."
3. Pershing: "Only two are on order at present."
4. Hawk: "Only one third of active Army requirements are in production."
5. Redeye: "None are in the hands of troops although an urgent need exists."
6. Davy Crockett: "Hundreds are on order when thousands are required."

The Senate Preparedness Subcommittee concluded that the Iroquois and Chinook helicopters were urgently needed to replace older, less effective machines. Also, the new Caribou Army transport planes and the Mohawk observation and aerial-surveillance aircraft were urgently needed, but were not being ordered at a fast enough rate. "At current production rates it will take several years for the Army to modernize its aircraft," the subcommittee said. There was also a great need for such "nonglamorous" but vital equipment as tractors, engineering equipment, the UL-102 rough-terrain forklift truck, and the LARC (lighter amphibious resupply cargo) five-ton amphibious lighter for unloading deep-draft ships where dock facilities were inadequate.[9]

Subcommittee investigators found that the Army had none of the LARC amphibious lighters on hand at the time of their survey, and that more than five hundred were needed to fill minimum active Army requirements and to replace the obsolescent World War II DUKW, which the Army reported should have been relegated to the scrap heap many years before.

The budget for fiscal 1961 then being prepared by the Eisenhower Administration contained a request for $1,524,000,000 in procurement moneys for the Army, but the Army had stressed to the subcommittee that "the vast bulk of these funds will be utilized to replace losses through consumption in training, wearout and obsolescence.

"It provides no quantitative increase in inventory," the subcommittee stated. "It will provide modernization of existing assets, but only to the extent it replaces obsolete equipment."

The Army emphasized that $2.5 billion of procurement funds would be needed in the fiscal 1961 budget to initiate a realistic modernization. The subcommittee asked the Eisenhower Administration seriously to consider adding another $928 million to the Army budget for more procurement of equipment and weapons.

It was pointed out that Congress in recent years had approved funds above the amount requested by the Eisenhower Administration in the area of Army modernization: "In fiscal year 1960, the Congress appropriated $383 million over and above the budget for Army procurement. The Army was not permitted to obligate $175 million. It is being carried over to fiscal year 1961."

Senator Johnson's subcommittee pointed out that $164 million was utilized to cover funding deficiencies, leaving only $43 million for Army modernization.[10]

The subcommittee gave an analysis of the Army of the Soviet Union in an effort to place the Pentagon's problem in perspective. At the time, it was estimated that the Soviet Union had more than 3,600,000 under arms, with about 2,500,000 of these in the Army ground forces. While it had been reported that this permitted the Russians to have about 175 organized combat divisions, the subcommittee said the best available information was that only about 60 percent of the divisions were sufficiently manned to operate effectively on short notice.

The figures on the strength of the United States Army as of June, 1961, included 14 divisions, 14 battle groups or armored cavalry regiments, five missile commands, and "numerous artillery, tanks, and other units of battalion size."

"If the ratio of 175 Russian divisions is repeatedly compared to our 14 divisions which has happened frequently in the past, then grave apprehension might well exist on the overwhelming disparity between U. S. and Soviet ground forces," the Senate subcommittee said, and added: "We believe a more accurate appraisal is to compare the 2,500,000 men in the Soviet Army ground forces with the 870,000 men in our Army. This comparison is more reasonable and more realistic. However, it does not permit any complacency when you are still outnumbered three to one."

Even when taking cognizance of the 175,000 men in the U. S. Marine Corps, which brings all U. S. ground forces to 1,045,000, the ratio is still two and one half to one, the subcommittee stressed.[11]

When it is apparent that the United States has less men, "it is essential that they be equipped with superior firepower, mobility, and strategic planning," the Johnson subcommittee said. It stressed that the minimum amounts of equipment necessary to do the job required more than simply adding up the number of tanks, guns or other weapons needed to supply the units. Replacements for tanks, guns and other equipment must be available, for studies on average combat losses indicate that it would take only five to six months in combat without replacement for a tank battalion to be reduced to 50 percent effectiveness.[12]

The subcommittee stated that the budget for fiscal 1961 did not provide equipment to bring the divisions up to initial strength on many important items, and certainly provided none of the necessary replacements. Only token quantities of many items had been ordered, and in some instances the quantity order "is almost microscopic when compared with the total required to equip even the Active Army, with no regard for the Reserve forces."

There was a lag in the supply of modern rifles—the basic arm of individual soldiers. Through fiscal 1960, the Defense Department budget had provided only about one sixth of the new M-14's required for the active Army and its combat support. While the Army stated a requirement for a minimum of 240,000 new M-14 rifles in the fiscal 1961 budget, the Eisenhower Administration had requested funds for only 120,000.

Although there were adequate quantities of the old M-1 rifle in the hands of the soldiers, the Senate subcommittee found that the M-1's "do not compare favorably with the current Soviet rifle." The M-14 is almost a pound lighter than the 9.6 pounds of the M-1, has an ammunition capacity of twenty rounds as opposed to eight for the M-1, and can be operated either fully or semiautomatically.

"The new rifle will utilize ammunition currently standard throughout the NATO countries and permit far greater interchangeability," the subcommittee found. "The M-1 rifle now in use does not permit this flexibility." The subcommittee report stated that the M-14 was also "more reliable under adverse conditions such as rain, mud, and dust, due in part to an improved gas operating system." [13]

The gap between the Pentomic concept and supply of M-14 rifles was only one of the more than a dozen specific cases spelled out by the Johnson Preparedness Subcommittee in its effort to prod the Eisenhower Administration into more expenditures to improve our ability to fight the limited wars.

While Senator Johnson assailed the gap on weapons and equipment to modernize the Army, he was upstaged by Stuart Symington, the

Missouri Senator who actively sought the Democratic nomination in 1960 with charges that the Eisenhower Administration had permitted a bomber gap and a missile gap. He repeated his charges that we were in danger of falling behind the Russians by a three-to-one margin on ICBMs.

The authority of the voice of General Maxwell Taylor, the former Army Chief of Staff, was added to the chorus of critics of American defense posture. "The trend of relative military strength is against us," he said. "Our manned bomber force is a dwindling military asset. Our long-range missile force is limited in size, uncertain in reliability, and immobile upon exposed bases. We have no anti-missile defense in being or in sight." [14]

Senator John F. Kennedy, who won the Democratic Presidential nomination in July, 1960, took up the chant about the missile gap as did his running mate, Senator Lyndon Johnson.

President Eisenhower stood on his laurels as a military hero, and talked down to the top military men who criticized our defense posture. He called them parochial in their thinking, and he charged them and their political associates with misleading the American people. Speaking on a subject that had to be obscured to a degree because of necessary military security, he pronounced our defenses "not only strong [but] . . . awesome, and respected elsewhere."

The subject of defense posture was an issue in the 1960 campaign, but probably not decisive—except as any issue might have been a decisive one when the margin is as narrow as the one Senator Kennedy posted over Vice President Richard M. Nixon, who ran on the Eisenhower Administration's record. It is doubtful that the election could have been a mandate for any particular change in specific programs, but one of the most significant immediate changes was the swing toward a bigger Defense Department budget and the flexible response theories of General Maxwell Taylor.

22

McNAMARA THE MAN

PRESIDENT Dwight D. Eisenhower rankled under heavy criticism in his last years in the Presidency. He caustically remarked that "political and financial considerations" were playing a part in causing his troubles, and added that "something besides the strict military needs" was involved in many military efforts to fight his decisions. The result was the so-called "munitions lobby" investigation by a House Armed Services subcommittee headed by Representative F. Edward Hébert.[1]

These investigations established that large numbers of retired senior military officers, including many admirals and generals, had taken high-paying jobs in defense industry; that manufacturers of rival Army and Air Force missiles spent large sums in advertising campaigns as a part of the service rivalry; and that high-ranking Air Force officers had been entertained lavishly at weekends in the Bahamas.

Months later in January, 1961, as he gave his farewell address, President Eisenhower was still irritated by the power of the forces behind what he believed was unwarranted criticism of his Administration.

"In the Councils of Government we must guard against the acquisition of unwarranted influence—whether sought or unsought—by the military-industrial complex," the retiring President warned. The sentence was to be repeated and interpreted by hundreds of students of the operations of the Pentagon.

The investigations of the Hébert subcommittee and the comments of President Eisenhower focused attention on the many dilemmas that arose in maintaining a modern defense establishment. The Department needed men skilled in management of big-business enterprises, and big defense contractors needed the skills and the backgrounds found in high-ranking military officers and civilians. The crosscurrent created problems of conflicts of interest, both active and potential, too complicated for Congress to handle solely with the law changes made in 1960 to deal with them.

It would be unfair to pass legislation flatly barring high military or civilian officials of the Pentagon from all positions with defense contractors for any extended period of time. Certainly, the Defense Department would have been barred from acquiring some of the best business brains if there existed a flat legal barrier to the appointment to top Pentagon posts of persons with close connections with big defense contractors.

Representative Hébert tried to pass legislation with criminal provisions and a $10,000 fine aimed at barring the "selling of information" to industry for two years after leaving the government payroll. The House Armed Services Committee stripped the Hébert bill of its most effective provisions only a few months before President John F. Kennedy took office.[2]

Although the law was loose, President Kennedy had been highly critical of the careless attitude on "conflicts of interest" in the Eisenhower Administration. He pledged a new comprehensive code of ethics and also vowed to use the best brains of the country to put efficiency into the operations of the Pentagon, to build the Air Force strength, close "the missile gap," and also strengthen the ground forces for the limited wars and crises such as Formosa, Hungary, Suez, Lebanon and Indo-China.

The man he selected for the job was Robert Strange McNamara, who had been named to succeed Henry Ford II as president of the Ford Motor Company on November 9, 1960—one day after John F. Kennedy was elected President of the United States. Only five days after McNamara met Kennedy on December 8, 1960, the forty-four-year-old executive agreed to accept the nomination. It is understandable why self-doubts kept McNamara from making a faster decision, for his one month as the president at Ford gave him limited experience as top man. The Defense Department, with a budget running in excess of $40 billion a year, made the Ford operation seem insignificant.

However, on January 21, 1961, the precise, bespectacled, former associate professor at Harvard became boss of an organization that included 2,500,000 members of the armed forces and 1,500,000 civilians.

The Ford Motor Company was a major defense contractor, but McNamara did not make the mistake Charles E. Wilson had made in first refusing to sell his stock in General Motors Corp. At the time of the announcement that he was to be Defense Secretary, he explained that he would sell his 24,250 shares of Ford stock and would relinquish an option on 30,000 additional shares. This represented a great financial sacrifice, and it was estimated his decision meant that he forfeited profits of about $3,000,000 for the next three or four years.

The studious young man who, as captain, major and lieutenant colonel, had been a management specialist for the Army Air Force in World War II, was hurled to the top of the most powerful military organization in the world. He went to work immediately, and within a matter of two weeks was informing the press of moves to streamline the Pentagon, cut out the fat, and create better efficiency by merging seven assistant secretaryships under five offices.

While announcing that he was speeding up such projects as the Skybolt, an air launched missile, he was also decreeing that seventy-three military installations were to be closed down in the United States and overseas. A carefully tailored picture of McNamara began to emerge: an executive with an IBM mind, a genius in cost effectiveness, and a man with the courage to say no to the wastrels, the politicians, and the scoundrels who would sap our defense strength. This was the man expected to frustrate the wastefulness of Congress, stamp out the interservice rivalry, and keep out the corruptive influence of conflicts of interest and political deals.

McNamara's lack of experience in Washington seemed his only weakness, and it demonstrated itself vividly in one of the so-called background conferences in which he talked frankly about a good many sensitive political matters, including the "missile gap." Apparently unaware of the bitterness evoked by Kennedy's charge of a "missile gap" in the Eisenhower defenses, McNamara made comments that were interpreted as his conclusion that there was no "missile gap." [3]

An immediate Republican demand arose that President Kennedy apologize for what the Republicans now called his irresponsible and phony election-campaign charges. Whether McNamara had said there was no "missile gap" or not, it created embarrassment for the Kennedy Administration. McNamara contended he had not said there was no "missile gap," but various reporters present disputed what actually was said.

President Kennedy, a veteran of the political wars of the House, Senate and the Presidential campaign of 1960, did not apologize. Although there was little more talk about whether the alleged missile gap did or did not exist, President Kennedy and McNamara did use every occasion possible to express the opinion, in a general way, that the Eisenhower Administration had permitted United States armed might to drop to a dangerous level.

In January, President Eisenhower had submitted a proposed Defense Department budget for fiscal 1962 of $41.8 billion. Within two months, President Kennedy and McNamara had added nearly $2 billion to the requests to provide more money for Polaris-armed submarines, increase research in nonnuclear weapons for limited wars and boost personnel in the Army. General Maxwell Taylor became the special military representative of the President, and took part in planning the defense budget, which soon jumped to $46.7 billion —nearly $5 billion over President Eisenhower's initial request for fiscal 1962.[4]

While much of the activity was aimed at budget boosting, some budget slicing was taking place. McNamara ended the nuclear plane program, and moved into a highly sensitive area by recommending that the development funds for the B-70 be cut from $358 million to $220 million.

The controversy this created with General Curtis E. LeMay, the Air Force Chief of Staff, was only a forerunner of the long and bitter dispute that was to surround the whole issue of whether the Air Force was to have a new manned bomber. In that first year of McNamara's reign as Defense chief, the House took the suggestion of General LeMay and boosted the B-70 funds from $220 million to $525 million. And when the whole defense appropriation was passed by Congress, it included $400 million for the B-70 program, and $515 million more for the B-58 and B-52 programs.

McNamara retaliated by declaring he would defy the wishes of Congress and not spend the additional funds;[5] it was his first real clash with the Air Force enthusiasts in Congress and with General LeMay.

If Robert S. McNamara was lacking in political know-how, the same could not have been said about the man President Kennedy named as Deputy Defense Secretary. The man was Roswell Leavitt Gilpatric, a suave New York lawyer with an Ivy League background and years of experience in dealing with the military-industrial complex. Like McNamara, he was graduated Phi Beta Kappa, but unlike

McNamara he was schooled in the operations of politics and government.

Following graduation from Yale College in 1928 and Yale Law School in 1931, Gilpatric became a partner in the eminent New York law firm of Cravath, de Gersdorff, Swaine & Wood. He left the firm briefly to serve, from 1951 to 1953, as Under Secretary of the Air Force. He returned to law practice in 1953, represented many big defense contractors, became active in Democratic politics, and served as chairman of the board of trustees of the Aerospace Corporation established by the Air Force during the Eisenhower Administration to conduct studies in connection with the major missile programs.

Gilpatric's Washington connections served him well. In 1958, one of his former Washington associates in the Truman Administration, Frank Pace, asked him to handle some rather extensive legal work for the General Dynamics Corporation, which Pace then headed. Pace had served as Secretary of the Army in the Truman Administration, and had moved out of high government office into a lucrative job with this large defense contractor. His experience as a lawyer for General Dynamics from 1958 to 1961 was only one segment of the background that made Gilpatric an important senior partner in the law firm that by 1961 had become Cravath, Swaine & Moore.

When Gilpatric became the number-two man in the Defense Department in January, 1961, he was regarded as the perfect type to team with McNamara. Smooth and knowledgeable in the ways of the big defense contractors, he knew the men in Congress who counted where Defense Department problems were concerned. The "Bob and Roz" team appeared to be one of the most effective combinations created by the Kennedy Administration. If McNamara dealt abrasively with the ordinary Senator or Congressman, Roz Gilpatric with his persuasive manner could smooth things over. He and his attractive wife gave wonderful parties to cultivate members of the Armed Services and Appropriations committees of the Senate and House. He also made an effort to keep a close relationship with his old friend Senator Stuart Symington, the Missourian who had been the first Air Force Secretary and who held an important post as a member of the Senate Armed Services Committee.

Other members of the top-level Pentagon team appointed by President Kennedy were Elvis J. Stahr, Jr., Secretary of the Army;

John B. Connally, Jr., Secretary of the Navy; Eugene M. Zuckert, Secretary of the Air Force; General Lyman Lemnitzer, Chairman of the Joint Chiefs of Staff; General Curtis LeMay, Air Force Chief of Staff; and Admiral George Anderson, Chief of Naval Operations. Probably the most significant appointment was that of General Maxwell D. Taylor as a special military representative of the President at the White House—a prelude to moving him to the Pentagon as Chairman of the Joint Chiefs of Staff. Taylor, strong dissenter from the massive-retaliation theories of the Eisenhower Administration, was to be a major figure in new shifts in defense posture.

Stahr, a Rhodes scholar and lawyer with a distinguished record in the infantry during World War II, seemed most in line with the Kennedy pattern. Although he rose to the rank of colonel in the Army, he also carried the credentials of the bright young men with whom Kennedy liked to be associated. Stahr had been named one of "America's Ten Outstanding Young Men of 1948" by the Junior Chamber of Commerce, had been a law school dean and president of West Virginia University.

The name of John Connally was associated closely with that of Vice President Lyndon B. Johnson, and there was no doubt the Fort Worth lawyer owed his appointment as Navy Secretary to his Texas political connection with Johnson. The handsome Texan had been linked with the Johnson political fortunes from the earliest days, and had even risked infuriating the Kennedys at the 1960 Democratic convention by enthusiastically pushing Johnson's nomination. He further roused their ire by questioning the physical condition of the then-candidate John Kennedy. Representing the big oil interests of Texas millionaire Sid Richardson had made Connally a wealthy man, but he possessed the flexibility to adapt to the pattern of the Ivy League or the Boston Irish.

From the start the McNamara Pentagon was stacked with Johnson men. Cyrus R. Vance, a long-time Johnson protégé, served as general counsel for the Department, later became Secretary of the Army and finally was named Deputy Defense Secretary. Solis Horwitz, another Johnson man, was director of organizational and management planning in the Defense Department general counsel's office and was later elevated to the job of Assistant Secretary of Defense for Administration. The Assistant Secretary of Navy was Kenneth E. BeLieu, who had been staff director of Johnson's Senate Preparedness Subcommittee a few years earlier.

When Connally resigned as Navy Secretary to run his successful campaign for Governor of Texas, another Johnson man moved into the Navy Secretary post—Fred Korth, a Fort Worth bank president who had been deputy counselor and Assistant Secretary of the Army during the last two years of the Truman Administration.

Air Force Secretary Zuckert, a graduate of the Yale Law School, had been an assistant professor and assistant dean of the Harvard Graduate School of Business Administration when McNamara served on the faculty. Zuckert had used his talents in law and business administration on a number of government jobs, including a term as Assistant Secretary of the Air Force from 1947 to 1952, and as a Truman appointee to the Atomic Energy Commission in a term that ran from 1952 to 1954.

General Lemnitzer, Chairman of the Joint Chiefs of Staff, was a holdover, as was General Decker, the Army Chief of Staff. The new men on the Joint Chiefs of Staff were General LeMay, who succeeded General Thomas D. White as Air Force Chief of Staff, and Admiral Anderson, who succeeded Admiral Arleigh Burke as Chief of Naval Operations. General LeMay and Admiral Anderson were expected to be McNamara team men, who would be placated by bigger Defense Department budgets planned by the Kennedy Administration.

Cuba, an increasingly difficult problem for the last few months of the Eisenhower Administration, became the first crisis for the Kennedy military machine within a few months after the young President took office. President Eisenhower severed diplomatic relations with Premier Fidel Castro's government on Januray 3, 1961—very shortly before Kennedy became President. The Central Intelligence Agency had been at work for months training a group of anti-Castro refugees for the highly controversial invasion of Cuba.

The disastrous effort to land 1,500 Cuban rebels at the Bay of Pigs on April 17, 1961, was not a direct test of United States military operations, for President Kennedy barred any direct involvement of American military forces in the invasion. Rather, it challenged the intelligence work of the CIA and the planning and judgment of the Pentagon and the White House. The military planning had included an air cover as an essential part of the invasion by the anti-Castro forces, but that air cover was withdrawn at the last moment. President Kennedy assumed full responsibility for the faulty judgment that had doomed the Bay of Pigs invasion, but even as he did so, various Administration spokesmen were blaming the CIA for having given the

President poor information and blaming the military leaders at the Pentagon for not having made their views clearer.

The Bay of Pigs fiasco was also an early warning to the Kennedy Administration of the bungling that can take place in the big bureaucracy of the Pentagon or the CIA. Suddenly the Administration became aware that the opinions and conclusions of the top intelligence officers, the top military advisers and the top civilian advisers can be wrong if those men are acting on only part of the material facts, have done insufficient work to give balanced judgment, or operate with blind faith in their own infallibility. Kennedy Administration officials, publicly and privately, tried to blame the entire mess on the sad state of military preparedness and planning under the Eisenhower Administration. The group asked by President Kennedy to make a thorough review of the operations of the CIA was comprised in part by McNamara, General Taylor and Attorney General Robert F. Kennedy, who included the whole question of military preparedness.[6]

No significant criticism of Secretary McNamara was possible in connection with the Bay of Pigs, for the Defense Secretary had barely taken office. Had there been any tendency to push some of the blame in his direction, it was stopped by President Kennedy's decision to accept full responsibility for the decisions that were made. In addition, McNamara was a Republican and was already starting to project the kind of an image of bright top management in government that Republicans liked to believe was symbolic of their party. McNamara did not know Kennedy during the 1960 election, but he later said he voted for him on a ticket-splitting ballot. Republican businessmen and other businessmen liked to think that the public relations view of McNamara as an efficient businessman in government would emerge as the true picture if sound men of management were permitted authority to overrule the liberals and the politicians. Even as McNamara was serving his first year as Defense Secretary, Republicans were suggesting privately that he was a man they would like to snatch from the Kennedy Cabinet for the Republican Presidential candidate in 1964.

But one phase of McNamara's operations of the Defense Department created minor irritation in Congress and in the press during his first months in office. Accustomed to the ways of the big business corporation, McNamara tended to treat Defense Department business as his business. If he performed in an efficient and economical fashion, he felt his word should be accepted and that politicians in Congress should not take his time with a lot of politically motivated questions.

The first disturbing aspects of McNamara's views came to light in testimony released in May, 1961, by the Senate Committee on Armed Services. McNamara had given the testimony in April, 1961, in a closed session of the committee dealing with the Nike-Zeus program for an antimissile missile, and it appeared that he favored giving less information to the public as well as outright misinformation if it served his purpose.

"Why should we tell Russia that the Zeus development may not be satisfactory?" McNamara expounded his philosophy. "What we ought to be saying is that we have the most perfect anti-ICBM system that the human mind will ever devise. Instead, the public domain is already full of statements that the Zeus may not be satisfactory, that it has deficiencies. I think it is absurd to release that kind of information." [7]

The Defense Secretary's interest in keeping American defense secrets away from the Russians, while laudable, hit a sour note among experienced men in Congress when it was suggested the Pentagon should be broadcasting to the Russians, and incidentally to the American people, much untrue propaganda indicating that the Nike-Zeus was a highly successful program when it was not.

Representative John E. Moss, chairman of the House Government Information Subcommittee, was quick to brand the McNamara comment as a "gross disservice" to the people of the United States and a contradiction of views expressed by President Kennedy. Representative Moss asked how the McNamara statement could be reconciled with President Kennedy's State of the Union pledge to "withhold from neither the Congress nor the people any fact or report, past, present or future, which is necessary for an informal judgment of our conduct and hazards."

The California Democrat declared, "Advocacy of a program of misinformation constitutes a grave disservice to a nation already confused and suffering from informational malnutrition. To claim perfection in a weapon system, thereby creating a false sense of security, only results in complacency complained about by the very officials who would further feed it."

While Moss was a liberal Democrat who wanted to support the Kennedy Administration, he did not hesitate to charge that McNamara "expressed an attitude which while not new is nevertheless most alarming." [8]

Faced with an avalanche of criticism, the Pentagon hurriedly issued a statement that McNamara did not intend to suggest he would mislead the American people but only the Russians.

At a quickly arranged press conference on May 26, 1961, the Defense Secretary proposed a four-point guide on information policy. "In a democratic society," his clarification began, "the public must be kept informed of the major issues in our national defense policy." While setting out the need to avoid disclosure of information that might aid our potential enemies, he declared that it "is equally important to avoid overclassification.

"I suggest that we follow this principle: When in doubt underclassify," McNamara said, a comment that seemed to endorse the best principles on information policy. The Defense Secretary also said public statements must reflect the policy of the Defense Department, and that Defense personnel should not discuss "foreign policy subjects, a field which is reserved for the President and the Secretary of State."

The McNamara statement won a carefully qualified bit of praise from Representative Moss for "recognition of the people's right to know." He singled out particularly the McNamara comment that "the public has at least as much right to bad news as good news." Moss reserved judgment on instructions restricting comments on policy matters, and asked to be advised on all directives or other instructions used in implementing the general information policy. He had learned through experience with the Eisenhower Administration that final policy statements often can mask the most intolerable withholding of information.

Representative Moss had reason to be cautious; within a few months there were loud complaints that McNamara was gradually tightening the curbs on speeches by military officers, and the press was finding it more and more difficult to gain free access to personnel at the Pentagon. Few complained about those actions of McNamara that he claimed were saving millions of dollars, but there were some misgivings about a trend toward arbitrary secrecy. The *Navy Times,* a private publication, commented: "There's an air of secrecy, of censorship, or arbitrary rulings."

As if to prove the magazine's point, the Defense Department tried to invoke the "executive privilege" claim to bar two committees, the Internal Security Subcommittee of the Senate and the House Select Committee on Export Control, from records in an investigation of shipments of strategic materials to various Iron Curtain countries.

The investigation of East-West trade controls was a repetition of an investigation that Attorney General Robert F. Kennedy had conducted five years earlier as counsel for the McClellan Permanent Investigating Subcommittee.

When the Defense Department appealed to the Justice Department for support in trying to claim "executive privilege" on this investigation, it ran into trouble; Robert Kennedy had gone on record against withholding such records from Congress. The Attorney General advised against use of "executive privilege" in this case, but that did not resolve the problem. McNamara's use of "executive privilege" and his efforts to find and squelch dissenters in the military services was to be an increasing point of bitter controversy.

23

MILITARY ARROGANCE AT FORT LEE

IT was easy for Secretary of Defense Robert S. McNamara to convince the press and the public that tough administration was needed to keep the "military brass" in line. The case of General Benny Meyers had demonstrated that there were instances in which high procurement officers were able to violate proper ethical standards in financial matters because of a tendency to overlook evidence of the misdoings of high officers. The five-percenter investigations involved military officers of the rank of general, and the Hébert investigations of the activities of the "munitions lobby" had demonstrated an unhealthy closeness in the relationship between some big defense contractors and high-ranking officers who accepted the lavish hospitality of weekends in the Bahamas.

When President Eisenhower spoke of the danger of the "industrial-military complex" in government, it was viewed in some quarters as a warning of the possibility of some military coup to take over the government, backed by the big industrial and political power in Congress. It was easy to mouth general criticism of the "military brass," for there were a few solid cases to make the point that some of our top military men had been negligent, wasteful, stupid or corrupt in a number of instances. Any overall indictment of the top military officers was invalid, but many had to carry the stigma because of the dishonesty, stupidity or outright arrogance of a few who had been promoted to high positions of responsibility and trust.

For years the public had heard much about the "squabbling brass" at the Pentagon, and the wasteful duplication caused by high officers who, it was argued, were more interested in increasing the budget appropriations for their individual service than they were in producing a well-balanced and effective fighting machine. Of course, occasionally the feuding of the military officers was indeed based on the desire for a greater part of the military budget, and there were organized public relations drives by the Army, Navy, Air Force and Marine Corps from time to time to put across the view that one type of warfare or weapons system was most important. There is no doubt that some of this "squabbling" among the top officers of the various military services was caused by an overemphasis of tradition that often blinded the high officers of one service to the needs of the other services or the needs of the nation. However, it would be difficult to draw the line between what was the proper amount of esprit de corps and what was simply destructive and blind service loyalty.

Regardless of the justification for the public image of arrogant, wasteful, squabbling "military brass," that image was a reality. It had been used as an argument to push the various Defense Department reorganizations in 1947, 1949, 1953 and 1958. While most high military officers are at least as competent, honest, dedicated and energetic as their counterparts in the business world, one factor in the military indoctrination tends to breed an arbitrary arrogance in officers failing to guard against it: the basic rule that a military man must instinctively obey commands from a superior officer. The tradition of obedience to superior officers is important, and vital, in a large military organization; without it the discipline would break down and anarchy would result. But the chain-of-command principle carries with it the danger of arbitrary action that will carry over into arrogant dishonesty and personal self-indulgence at the expense of the military establishment and subordinates.

If Secretary McNamara had wanted a case to demonstrate dangers of military arrogance, it would have been difficult to find a better incident than the one that came to light at Fort Lee, Virginia, within two years after he became Defense Secretary. It dramatized the worst aspects of the chain of command with senior military officers involved in willful disregard for the laws and regulations. But, worse than this, the Fort Lee case showed how junior military officers were instructed to destroy records of the law violations and to lie under oath to help cover up the illegal acts. It demonstrated that still higher officers in the Pentagon either misunderstood the record, or took part in decisions that had the effect of condoning the law violations, the destruction of records and perjury. The case showed that "the system" was well enough established at Fort Lee that junior officers believed it was futile to complain about law violations or even to refuse to carry out orders they knew violated the law.

The junior officers said they felt they had "to go along" to avoid bad fitness reports or reassignment to distasteful duties, which the law-flouting commanding officer could give them. It would be impossible to estimate how widespread such practices and attitudes are in the armed services, but when the record on the Fort Lee case was completed it was clear that in that instance the military arrogance of some top officers had reached a disgraceful stage.

The Fort Lee case involved the construction of an airplane landing strip. It was first uncovered by the auditors for the General Accounting Office (GAO), and it was later the subject of hearings by the Executive and Legislative Reorganization Subcommittee of the House Government Operations Committee. By the time it was uncovered, criminal prosecution was barred by the statute of limitations, so no one went to jail. However, the report of the House Committee called it a case of "falsification and deception . . . indeed a sorry record for the Army and for the nation."

The story began in 1956, during the Eisenhower Administration, and continued into the first year of the Kennedy Administration. Thus it is not a scandal to be blamed on Republicans or Democrats. Rather, it is symptomatic of what happens whenever a bureaucracy comes to regard the fulfillment of its whims as a standard larger than the law.

Fort Lee[1] is an Army Quartermaster Training Command near Petersburg, Virginia. The Petersburg Airport, twelve miles from Fort Lee, and Camp Pickett Blackstone Airport, forty-one miles away, were available for all necessary training purposes. High-ranking officers at Fort Lee twice requested permission to build a concrete airstrip to replace a grass landing field for aircraft. Twice the Department of the Army turned down the request, saying that the concrete strip was not necessary. But the Fort Lee officers, disregarding the laws and the regulations, decided they would have their airstrip regardless. Some of the junior officers complained that it was an "illegal project" that could send them to the penitentiary. They balked at signing their names to phony bills and reports. In the end, they took their orders, and the airstrip was built. It was not a large job, as U. S. military projects go, but more than half a million had been spent on this illegal strip when General Accounting Office auditors discovered the evidence of false bills and rigged files, and called a halt.

As early as February, 1956, officers at Fort Lee asked approval for construction of an airstrip that was to cost about $876,000. After the Pentagon twice rejected the project, the Fort Lee officers started looking for legal loopholes to avoid Pentagon approval. They found laws with less restrictive requirements for minor projects if "urgently needed." The law plainly said that these "urgently needed" projects should not include any that could have been reasonably included in the regular military construction program. And the law specifically limited spending on such projects to $25,000 over and above material and labor that a post already had on hand.

In September, 1957, Fort Lee made its third try on the airstrip. It attempted to get the Quartermaster General's approval for construction of a 1,500-foot flexible-pavement landing strip. The estimate for the whole project was $110,095, of which $73,086 represented the value of labor and supplies on hand; $37,009 would be required in new funds. The project was submitted by Lieutenant Colonel Louis H. Shirley, the deputy post commander. But this request, too, was rejected by Washington on several grounds: it exceeded the $25,000 maximum on supplemental money, the runway was too short, and the pavement was too thin.

Two months later, Colonel Shirley and Colonel William H. Jarrett, the post engineer, submitted revised project estimates. They lengthened the runway 2,500 feet and increased the thickness of the concrete to two inches. And they estimated the total project cost at $141,537, of which $116,589 now was figured to be labor and supplies on hand. By the sheerest of coincidences, this brought the amount of new funds needed down to $24,948—just under the $25,000 maximum, and low enough to start building.

Colonel Jarrett admitted later that the estimates "were arbitrary and were merely put down to meet the requirement of lowering the funds requested below $25,000." Colonel Shirley admitted that he made no effort to determine if the figures were realistic. Nor did he question the incongruity of enlarging the project while decreasing the cost for supplies.

The fact that the estimates were baseless was apparent as the project progressed. The basic cost of the project rose to $508,305, about $366,000 more than the authorized figure. Actually, the total cost was a great deal more. For one thing, $28,000 was spent on a building listed as "a warehouse." It really was a hangar, and came out of operation and maintenance funds for transportation and per diem pay for engineer troop labor from Fort Belvoir, Virginia.

When the officers at Fort Lee learned that the GAO planned to audit the construction work papers, hasty instructions went out to the assistant post engineer. He was ordered to get rid of any material in his files that might embarrass the command.

The GAO investigators began putting embarrassing questions to Army headquarters. After considerable prodding, the Army issued a report that carefully avoided mention of falsification of documents or removal and destruction of files.

Later it was revealed that Major General Alfred B. Denniston, the Quartermaster General, had taken light disciplinary action against subordinates who started the airstrip. He wrote a reprimand that, in effect, said they had been bad boys and were not to do it again. The Army's General Counsel in Washington, it was established, went along with this "disciplinary action."

The GAO persisted in its investigation, however, and work on the airstrip was halted.

Meanwhile the Government Operations Committee, under Chairman William L. Dawson (Dem., Ill.), began probing the case, and revealed the full sordidness of the "system." Most disturbing to the committee members was the evidence showing how officers were forced to lie and cover up for their superiors.

When they were called before the committee in March, 1962, the officers told conflicting stories relating to the destruction of records. Major Thomas S. Swartz, the former assistant post engineer at Fort Lee, had retired by the time he testified. He admitted that he removed documents from the files and destroyed them. He said he had objected when Colonel Jarrett ordered him to remove the papers from the files. But Jarrett, Swartz said, had told him that someone even superior to him wanted it done. Major Swartz told the committee that Colonel Jarrett later came down to his office to determine if he had followed instructions to destroy the papers. The materials removed and destroyed, Swartz testified, were copies of purchase requests and some project working estimates.

Colonel Jarrett testified that he, in turn, had been ordered by Colonel Shirley to have the files "cleansed." Subsequently, he said, Colonel Shirley asked him whether this had been done. He said he told Colonel Shirley that the files had been "cleansed" so the GAO auditors would find no evidence of false billing.

Colonel James W. Connor was subordinate to Colonel Shirley at the time the records were destroyed. He testified that he had understood Colonel Shirley's order to mean that embarrassing documents should be removed from the files. Colonel Connor stated that he had told Colonel Shirley a day or two after the orders were issued that he would not be a party to the removal and concealment of documents from the GAO.

Colonel Shirley, stern-faced and defiant, admitted calling Jarrett and Colonel Connor to his office. However, he denied that he had ordered files removed and destroyed. He insisted he had merely instructed Colonel Jarrett to put the files in order for the GAO auditors. Colonel Shirley also testified that he didn't remember Colonel Connor protesting to him about the removal and concealment of documents. "I don't recall that," Shirley said, "but he could have done that."

This was not the end of conflicting testimony and bad memory. Colonel James C. Pennington testified he had informed Colonel Shirley that the Pentagon had denied the request for waiving certain requirements on the airstrip construction. Shirley insisted that Pennington did not tell him the waivers had been denied.

Colonel Walter R. Ridlehuber, the project officer, and Colonel Shirley testified they had told General Denniston that both material and services for the airfield were being falsely billed to other projects. But General Denniston denied that either officer had informed him of the false billings.

Another direct conflict of testimony arose after Lieutenant Colonel Julian E. Pylant testified that Colonel Ridlehuber had told him to charge the airfield expenses to other projects. Colonel Pylant said that he had replied to Ridlehuber: "I'm not going to the pen for this." Later, Ridlehuber denied that Pylant had made this remark. In an effort to solve the conflict, Chairman Dawson recalled Pylant, who pointed to Ridlehuber and repeated the statement. In a direct confrontation with his accuser, Colonel Ridlehuber stated only that he did not recall the incident.

The House committee declared it was unable to determine "which officers were telling the truth in these instances and which were not." It added: "We do, however, regard the existence of these conflicts as a serious reflection on the standards of conduct of the officer corps of the Army."

William A. Newman, chief of the GAO's defense accounting division, testified that the highest officials at Fort Lee not only had spent $536,373 on the illegal airstrip but were ready to spend a million more at the time the accounting officer moved in and stopped the project.

Through two weeks of hearings, the House committee documented the subterfuge through which the Army officers at Fort Lee had concealed the costs of material going into the airfield. Obviously, the files had not been cleansed well enough.

One incriminating note from Major Swartz was found in the files. On a purchase order for 2,150 tons of stone, this notation appeared: "This order will be followed by additional orders and I will have to keep a record of them. Actually, although charged to road maintenance, this material will be used for the airfield."

Another false purchase request for stone for "maintenance of roads" was accompanied by a memorandum stating the material was actually to be used for "the construction of the airfield facilities by Company A, 87th Engineer Battalion."

A memorandum of a telephone conversation between Colonel Ridlehuber and Colonel Pennington explained how to buy an airplane hangar without calling it a hangar. Colonel Ridlehuber's memo stated:

"The immediate problem is the purchase of a metal hangar building for erection by troop labor at a later date. I asked Colonel Pennington to assure the Quartermaster General that we would not recommend anything that would put him in an embarrassing position. In the case of the hangar, it will be procured, if the purchase is approved and the . . . funds are available, for the aerial detachment and not directly associated with the airfield.

"In the case of a physical inspection by the Department of the Army representatives at some later date, it can be explained that this is a temporary building which will be moved to meet other storage requirements if and when no longer required at the airfield site."

The most revealing insight into the system came from Colonel Jarrett. In explaining his failure to make stronger objections to the illegal actions, he told the Congressmen:

"Of course, I feel that an officer does not have to blindly follow orders, but I think that my following these orders was predicated only on personal feeling in the matter, having been in it from the beginning, that this whole operation was known within the command."

Colonel Jarrett said there had been conversations with the Chief of Engineers, visits by the Deputy Chief of Staff of Logistics, and continuous discussion of an airstrip at Fort Lee.

"In other words, even though it was illegal . . . everybody was doing it," Representative John Anderson (Rep., Ill.) commented.

"That is right, sir," Jarrett replied.

"Regulations notwithstanding," Anderson noted.

"I think," Jarrett replied, "that if the committee were to check with my associates overseas and other post camping stations I have been in, you would find I have been a stickler for regulations and had a reputation for it. However, I was burned in Austria when I made reports too factual and was given a verbal reprimand and told I would be relieved immediately if I ever wrote such a letter.

"The letter happened to be truthful, but it did not please the post commander," Colonel Jarrett went on. "He [the area commander] rewrote the letter and got the other letter back. He was the area commander in Salzburg, Austria."

"What suggestions would you have to make in view of your experiences there in Salzburg, Austria, where you were threatened with removal from command if you complained about something?" Representative Anderson asked. "What do you think the Congress can do, and should do, to make sure that things like this do not happen?"

"There is too much flexibility allowed at station level, in my opinion, for interpretation of what the regulation means," Colonel Jarrett replied.

"I do not care how flexible these regulations were," Representative Anderson said, "they did not bend them, they broke them."

"That is right, sir," Colonel Jarrett answered. "Certainly after we got the bear by the tail we knew what we were doing, at least I knew what I was doing. We were evading the regulations as they were written."

When General Denniston, a much-decorated veteran, was called to testify on the airstrip project, he fumbled for answers and quibbled.

Finally, he broke into tears. The General admitted he had "failed in leadership."

In answer to questions by Representative Neal Smith (Dem., Iowa), General Denniston said he did not know the cost of the project would exceed $25,000. He said he had delegated most of the responsibility to subordinates.

"And . . . among these persons then was Colonel Shirley?" Representative Smith asked.

"That is correct," General Denniston replied. "He was my deputy, and I had known him longer and better than any of the rest."

Representative Smith, through his next questions to Denniston, recalled the fact that the General's trusted deputy, Colonel Shirley, had been the subject of a critical report by the Senate Permanent Investigating Subcommittee a few years earlier. At that time, the subcommittee was investigating procurement scandals involving Harry Lev and others in New York. The investigation resulted in the indictment and conviction of several officials. Colonel Shirley had been a witness before the Senate group and, in his testimony, had suffered a lack of memory on many points.

"You were his superior officer at another time when procurement scandals were investigated by a committee of Congress, were you not?" Smith asked.

"I knew it after the fact," Denniston replied. "I followed the hearings. I was completely out of the Quartermaster procurement at that time."

"In view of these previous procurement problems involving Colonel Shirley, should you not have been . . . a little bit hesitant about delegating all of these or some of these financial matters here?" Smith asked.

"Colonel Shirley, in turn, delegated almost as much as I did in this particular case," General Denniston replied.

Admitting that he was "lacking in leadership," the General told his questioners he had failed to notice the $25,000 limit on spending was being violated. He also acknowledged that false statements were filed to circumvent the law.

Under intensive questioning by Chairman Dawson and Representative Clarence Brown (Rep., Ohio), General Denniston admitted that even after he found the conspiracy to destroy "embarrassing" records, he did no more than issue letters of reprimand.

"This has been a terribly distressing investigation," Representative

Brown said. "There is something wrong with our military system when . . . men who have . . . served their country in war ably . . . will come in here and . . . admit they had advised superior officers that they did not want to sign certain papers . . . to do something that was a direct violation of the law.

"They had advised these superior officers they did not want to go to the penitentiary by signing such a thing, and yet they said they signed . . . because they were afraid of the system.

"It is a pretty sorry mess," Representative Brown added, then asked:

"Now, the only thing that worries me, General, and it rather hurts me to ask this question—did you know all of those things were going on?"

"No, sir, I did not," General Denniston answered. "I should have."

Reminding the General that an enlisted man would have been court-martialed for a petty theft, Brown demanded to know:

"How can we, as members of Congress, go out and tell the country that we do have a fair system . . . that we have the same law and the same demand for a respect of morality, honesty, and decency for officers as we do for enlisted men?"

"It was not my final decision," General Denniston answered. He said he left the way open for the Army Department in Washington or the Justice Department to take criminal action, but none was taken.

Representative Anderson said he was sure that the prime interest of the committee was to see "that there is no repetition of the tawdry and sordid series of events.

"Our concern," Anderson commented, "is whether or not a reprimand . . . is anything more than just a slap on the wrist, or whether it is of sufficient import to drive home to the Army and to the people involved that this kind of thing is not going to be countenanced."

"I can promise you that it hurt me," General Denniston replied. "It hurt me more than going to jail, that after thirty-nine years of service with nothing but commendations on my record, I don't like that reprimand. I deserve it and that is what hurts."

Denniston added another example of how it hurt. "I cannot run into a general that I have not seen for a while that does not make some remark . . . needling me. . . . Behind it, there is a consciousness . . . [that] he sure is glad he is not in my shoes.

"I went through a receiving line, and the Vice Chief looked at me and said: 'My God, Danny, I thought you were in jail.' And I said: 'No, I don't go until day after tomorrow.'

"Now there, right at the top, is an indication that when he sees me, the first thing he thinks about is the Fort Lee airfield and why I am not already in jail for it. Now I am not being facetious, Mr. Anderson."

When the hearing was concluded, the House Government Operations Committee wrote a scathing official report. Published as a House document on June 20, 1962, the report said:

"This particular incident . . . furnishes an almost unbelievable example of the workings of the military and bureaucratic mind. A change in nomenclature, clever gimmick and an easy acceptance of a subterfuge cannot change a fact, no matter how much the military mind wants them [*sic*] to do so. There can be no doubt that despite the testimony of the officers and other personnel involved, the building at the Fort Lee airstrip is a hangar, was a hangar when it was built, and had always been planned and intended to be a hangar.

"The amazing thing to the committee is not only that the laws were evaded and violated, but also that, having failed in their scheme to disguise the nature of the building and to deceive any future inspectors of the installation, the personnel involved still persist in the attempted deception. . . . It was conceived in violation of the law and applicable Army regulation. Falsification and deception accompanied every step of this construction; and in the end when all attempts to cover up the record and destroy relevant papers had failed, the actions of the officers responsible were condoned and excused by their superiors. This is indeed a sorry record for the Army and the nation.

"When confronted with illegality . . . subordinate officers either did not protest or made weak protest which they soon swallowed," the report continued. "These officers indicated by their testimony that they were only too conscious of the traditional techniques for indirect reprisal against a subordinate officer who stands on principle against the desire of his superiors—such techniques as unfavorable fitness reports, delayed promotion, undesirable assignments, early retirement and social ostracism. . . . The committee knows that the officers at Fort Lee, who protested the illegal actions which they felt required to take, were not without courage and conviction. Nevertheless, none, obviously, thought he could have survived an attempt to expose the illegal actions in which he later participated."

The report went on: "The operation of the 'system' was further demonstrated by the failure of responsible officers to bring court-martial proceedings against those guilty of the offenses, by their failure to investigate the matter except under extreme pressure, by their general reluctance to take disciplinary action, and by their attempts to cover up and excuse the offense rather than to get to the bottom of the whole affair."

By the time the investigations were concluded and the reports made, the three-year statute of limitations had barred prosecution on what the subcommittee concluded was violation of eighteen different criminal laws. The only action taken by the Defense Department was to place simple reprimands in the files of the officers. Some in government would heed the warning. Some would not.

The importance of the Fort Lee affair is that it could happen in any military service or civilian agency where fear of displeasing superior officials is so deep that it permeates every major decision. In the official report of the Government Operations Committee, the story is permanently recorded as a warning of the police-state attitudes that can grow up in a large organization when men abuse the "chain-of-command" philosophy.

High-ranking officers lied, contradicted each other and contradicted their own records. After the GAO first uncovered the illegal act, the responsible military officers destroyed records and made every effort to play down the seriousness of the offenses and to avoid enforcing the laws. A colonel told the Congressional investigators that he believed violation of the law was justified if an Army man was obeying a superior officer, and when he was finally caught and trapped in his own evasions, the commanding general wept in the witness chair.

This shabby little mess had powerful support. It was actually aided by the Quartermaster General's office and the office of the General Counsel of the Army. The Quartermaster General did eventually reprimand the post commander, Major General Denniston. But the subcommittee found that the Quartermaster General disregarded flagrant illegal spending and false statements. The Army attributed the unlawful actions to mere "overzealousness" and sought to excuse the officers involved.

The Fort Lee case showed the need for congressional checks on bureaucracy as well as a constant examination of the military bureaucracy by the civilian political appointees at the Pentagon. However, its basic lesson, on the danger of arrogant administration to stifle dissent, was equally applicable to the civilian bureaucracy.

24

MUZZLING THE MILITARY MEN?

IT had long been the policy of the Defense Department to review the speeches of top military officers to make certain that those speeches were not in conflict with the government policy. Under any circumstances this represented a difficult job, but for the most part there were few public complaints about this policy until the summer of 1961. At the time there were approximately 1,250 generals and admirals on active duty in all branches of the service, which indicated something of the scope of the problem. It was generally accepted that the executive branch of the government, acting through the civilian political appointees of the Defense Department and State Department, had this as an inherent power.[1] Obviously, irreparable harm could result if any and all the highest military officers were free to express publicly their own personal views in conflict with or dissent from the policies laid down by the President in his role as Commander-in-Chief.

There existed, however, a minority opinion that high-ranking military officers and civilian officials should be exempt from what was regarded as the "humiliating" experience of having speeches reviewed. In the summer of 1961, irritation arose over irresponsible and unreasonable censorship of public speeches. High-ranking military officers expressed concern over changes made by the censors that did not seem to make sense, and for which they received no explanation.

During the same period of time, members of the House and Senate became concerned to learn that statements prepared by military officers for presentation to the committees of Congress in executive sessions had been subject to review and clearance by censors. This review included a censorship by both the Department of Defense and the Department of State.

While most members of the House and Senate were willing to accept the principle of policy censorship of public speeches by top military officers, they regarded the censorship of testimony for Congress as highly objectionable. Many members of the Senate Armed Services

Committee felt this censorship of military testimony before committees of Congress was an "improper practice and can only be calculated to obstruct unduly the free flow of information to which the Congress is entitled." [2]

It was accepted that military officers testifying before committees of Congress had the obligation to state the official Defense Department or national policy on the issue under consideration. However, there was a strong belief in Congress that these military officers should also be free after setting out the Department position to give their own personal judgments, opinions and convictions as long as they identified them as such. If high-ranking military officers were not free to do this, Congress would be restricted to hearing one-sided presentations merely parrotting the views of the Defense Secretary and the President.

Congress almost uniformly believed that "arbitrary and unjustified restriction upon the free flow of information to the Congress can only have the effect of hampering the legislative branch of the Government in the discharge of its constitutional duties and functions." [3]

A number of steps had been taken by Defense Secretary McNamara to stifle the dissent by military leaders, and by the fall of 1961 Senator Strom Thurmond, the Democrat from South Carolina, demanded an investigation of efforts to "muzzle" military officers.

Early in 1961, the Defense Department had reprimanded Major General Edwin A. Walker for allegedly indoctrinating his troops with biased right-wing political propaganda. Military commanders had been encouraged to provide training programs for troops that would instill and develop belief in the American principles of democracy and freedom and an awareness of the threat of Communism. However, even with large amounts of training material developed and distributed by the Defense Department in Washington, the actual handling and balancing of the training program had to be left to the local commander. Considerable variation in the programs developed in different areas, which opened the way for laxity as well as abuse in the program. There were few trained and experienced instructors, and no effective measures to appraise and assess the value or the balance of a troop training program.

The John Birch Society, with its extreme conservative views, came into prominence in 1961, and cries of outrage arose from a number of liberal groups that General Walker was indoctrinating his troops with John Birch propaganda.

Reacting to liberal warnings that the military political education programs might be misused by many right-wing military men, Senator William Fulbright sent a long memorandum to Defense Secretary Robert S. McNamara urging that military leaders be stopped from conducting political education programs. The Arkansas Democrat asked that McNamara revoke a 1958 directive that encouraged high military officers "to arouse the public to the menace of the Cold War." In the memorandum, Senator Fulbright expressed the opinion that these Cold War seminars by military officers probably had the "net effect of condemning foreign and domestic policies of the Administration in the public mind." [4]

Even before all the details of the Fulbright memorandum had been released, Senator Thurmond and Senator Barry Goldwater sharply assailed it as "an insidious attack upon our military leaders." Thurmond and Goldwater, both major generals in the reserves, were bitterly resentful of what they called an effort to "muzzle" our top military men.

Senator Richard Russell (Dem., Ga.), Chairman of the Senate Armed Services Committee, turned the investigation over to the Senate Preparedness Subcommittee headed by Senator John Stennis (Dem., Miss.). Thurmond, a member of the Senate Armed Services Committee but not the Preparedness Subcommittee, was made a member of the subcommittee for the probe of "Military Cold War Education and Speech Review Policies." [5]

The investigation was broken down into three major phases:

(1) A study of the practices and procedures relating to the policy review or censorship of public speeches of military personnel for the purpose of determining whether they are established and administered properly and whether there have been abuses or improper practices in the administration of the program.

(2) An examination of the military troop information and education program to determine the effectiveness of the existing program, the scope of the desired program, and the question of what can and should be done to strengthen the program and make it more effective.

(3) A study of the proper role of military personnel in informing, educating, and alerting the civilian population to the menace of the Cold War, including participation by the military in Cold War or anti-Communist seminars and the external information program in general.[6]

It was obvious from the start that it would be necessary for the probe to encompass a study of the nature of the Communist threat and the broad field of civilian-military relations in modern government.

Defense Secretary McNamara was just beginning his second year as boss of the Pentagon when the hearings opened on January 23, 1962. Hundreds of witnesses were interviewed and sixty-seven witnesses actually appeared before the Senate Preparedness Subcommittee in the thirty-six days of hearings.

The Stennis subcommittee worked with no major internal controversy through most of the hearings. It was a properly authorized committee, operating within its jurisdiction and headed by a responsible chairman. Members of the subcommittee were orderly in their conduct, and there was no abuse of witnesses.

General Walker, relieved of his division command in Germany eleven months earlier, was a bitter witness. He charged that "with this nation's survival at stake, our armed forces are paralyzed by our national policy of 'no win' and retreat from victory." He blamed Secretary of State Dean Rusk and others in the State Department for the "no win" policy he said existed. Other military men did not go that far.

However, other high officers expressed dissatisfaction with inconsistent and unexplained censorship that cut such words as "victory" from their speeches. But none of the testimony represented a challenge to the civilian authority to conduct a proper censorship of the speeches of top military men. The generals and admirals whose speeches had been censored exhibited more concern over inconsistent and meaningless actions of the censors than over the existence of the reviewing system.[7]

Lieutenant General Arthur G. Trudeau was highly critical of the "substantial" amendments in his speeches that made little sense. However, General Trudeau declared that the amendments "have not prevented me from getting across my basic message" on the nature of the threat of Communism. He also testified that there had been little noticeable difference between the operations of the review system under the Eisenhower Administration and under the Kennedy Administration.

"It appears apparent to me that there has been little difference in policy review procedures between this administration and the last, despite a change in the very top level officials," General Trudeau said. He indicated that he did not believe the difficulties with speech review constituted a political problem. Testimony to the same effect was given by General Lyman L. Lemnitzer, General Thomas D. White, General David M. Shoup and General George H. Decker.[8]

Typical of the changes was that made in a speech prepared for delivery by Brigadier General John W. White to the National Security Forum, Columbus, Ohio, on March 3, 1961. A State Department review substituted the phrase "defeat of Communist aggression" for the word "victory." When the Senate Preparedness Subcommittee asked for an explanation, the State Department replied:

"The word 'victory' has a militaristic and aggressive ring less suited than the substituted phrase for describing our national objectives. It also implies an 'all or nothing' approach leaving no room for accommodation."

When Under Secretary of State George W. Ball was called to testify, he rejected the original State Department explanation as "perfectly fatuous." Ball said the recommended change did not reflect any reluctance to speak of "victory" but was based on a desire to make it clear that the Communist bloc was responsible for "aggression" in the Cold War, and that victory was possible only by defeat of Communist aggression.[9]

The Senate subcommittee stated officially that it was "not impressed with either explanation.

"The change appears to be completely unjustified and incomprehensible," the subcommittee stated. "There is no valid or logical reason why official spokesmen of the Government, whether military or civilian, should not be permitted to speak of 'victory' for our side or of our desire to 'win' and 'emerge victorious.' These terms are commonplace in debates on the floor of the Senate. Arbitrary and unrealistic restrictions of this nature are not helpful to our cause in any manner."

The Preparedness Subcommittee explained that it was not engaging in blanket condemnation of all changes and deletions that would make speeches conform to national policy. The criticism was aimed at censorship by the Defense Department and State Department "characterized by ineptness, inconsistency, caprice, arbitrary personal judgment, and even irresponsibility.

"Many of the changes [in speeches] simply defy logical explanation," the Senate subcommittee found.[10]

In trying to examine the problem of senseless administration of the whole speech-review problem, the Stennis subcommittee obtained copies of the original speeches, had the record of the censored pages, and made an effort to try to question the censors themselves to determine why many questionable deletions were made.

Defense Secretary McNamara refused to allow the censors to

testify. President Kennedy gave him a letter authorizing him to use the highly controversial "executive privilege" claim as a reason for barring the testimony of the censors.

The redoubtable Mr. McNamara told the members of the Senate subcommittee that he was responsible for running his department, and that he would make any explanations he thought necessary. McNamara's position indicated the subcommittee members would have to content themselves with what he chose to tell them, and that they could not go behind his statements in exploring why deletions were made.[11]

He made no claim that national security was involved in the "muzzling" investigations or that he was protecting classified defense secrets. Instead, the Defense Secretary presented the letter from President Kennedy, dated February 8, 1962, which set forth a vague claim that the national interest was at stake.

The letter from the President read: "I have concluded it would be contrary to the public interest to make available any information which would enable the subcommittee to identify and hold accountable any individual with respect to any particular speech that he has reviewed. I therefore direct you, and all personnel under jurisdiction of your department, not to give any testimony or produce any documents which would disclose such information; I am issuing parallel instructions to the Secretary of State.

"The principle which is at stake here cannot be automatically applied to every request for information. Each case must be judged on its own merits. But I do not intend to permit subordinate officials of our career service to bear the brunt of congressional inquiry into policies which are the responsibilities of their superiors."[12]

The letter seemed to claim an absolute right for the executive branch to bar testimony before Congress by any subordinate career officials. This concept was attacked by various Senators as a "dangerous" precedent that would have barred Congress from investigating the Pearl Harbor disaster or the war scandals of the Civil War, World War I or World War II. If the principle of that letter prevailed, any Administration could limit Congress to the evidence and the explanations the Defense Secretary wished to give.

President Eisenhower's earlier letter on "executive privilege" written on May 17, 1954, had claimed the right to bar testimony or records of communications or actions of "high level" officials of the government. In his letter to McNamara, Kennedy was extending it to cover the activities of lower-ranking officials of the government. If Congress could be denied access to testimony by both high- and low-level officials, it would be powerless to get any information, except what the executive branch sanctioned.

Representative John Moss, the California Democrat, declared that he believed the Senate subcommittee had the legal right to ask questions to determine which censors had blue-penciled which speeches. In a letter to President Kennedy, Moss expressed his great concern over the possibility of wide use of the precedent set out in his letter of February 8.

On March 7, 1962, President Kennedy assured the California Democrat that "executive privilege . . . will not be used without specific Presidential approval." However, the use of the executive-privilege claim in the muzzling hearings was a bad omen for the future. McNamara, highly popular, had a reputation that most of the Democratic members of the Senate Preparedness Subcommittee did not wish to challenge. Chairman Stennis permitted the claim of "executive privilege" to stand, and members of the subcommittee failed to appeal the decision.[13]

While the Democrat-controlled subcommittee was permitting a precedent for total arbitrary secrecy to be established in the "executive privilege" claim, it was expressing grave concern over what it considered to be a direct curb on the information Congress could receive from high military officers.

"The subcommittee was both surprised and disturbed to learn that statements prepared by military officers for presentation to congressional committees in executive sessions have been subject to prior review and clearance, not only by the Department of Defense, but also by the Department of State," the subcommittee said.

"Congressional committees are entitled to receive in executive session, the personal and individual views, opinions, and concepts of our military leaders without the discoloring effect of the prior policy review.

"It is to be remembered that very often grave and serious questions and issues are involved in these presentations to the Congress. It is not inconceivable that direct and specific questions on matters of vital importance may be overlooked if the military witness is not free to give his opinion without direct interrogation. Members of

Congress cannot be expected to know every detailed aspect of all matters presented to them. Therefore, without a full and free presentation by the knowledgeable military people, the Congress cannot obtain the full benefit of their specialized and expert views and thoughts. It is unthinkable that in our deliberations we should be restricted to the views and opinions of the Secretary of Defense." [14]

Because of the widespread publicity surrounding disciplinary action taken against former Major General Walker, the subcommittee felt compelled to make a brief statement on disciplinary action against him that eventually led to his resignation to run for political office in Texas. The general impression was that General Walker had been disciplined because of his troop indoctrination through the "pro-Blue" program, characterized by some liberal writers as including the teachings of the John Birch Society.

In attempting to straighten out this "popular misconception" the Senate Preparedness Subcommittee stated: "The Army investigating officer specifically found that the division information and education program conducted by General Walker under the name of 'pro-Blue' was 'basically sound' and he consequently recommended that 'it continue to be implemented in the 24th Infantry Division.' " [15]

Any effort to go over the whole case of General Walker would have been meaningless at the time of the "muzzling" hearing, for he was out of the Army and involved in a highly controversial as well as unsuccessful political career.

While the training programs of General Walker were a factor in initiating the whole investigation of military Cold-War education, it had faded to a minor position by the time the investigation was concluded. The general policies dealing with censoring of speeches and testimony to be given before Congress had become the major focal point.

Even with the investigation sharply restricted because of McNamara's use of "executive privilege," it was apparent that the whole censorship operation was confused. Actual censorship was done by relatively low-ranking officers with no specialized training; no effective guidelines on policy had been established.

"We were not able to determine clearly during the hearings exactly how those persons writing, delivering and reviewing speeches are kept advised of policy and the constant changes in it," the subcommittee concluded.

"More than the usual confusion about the true review policy developed and existed during the first months of responsibility. This confusion was magnified and compounded by Secretary McNamara's directive of May 31, 1961, stating that Defense officials should 'avoid discussion of foreign policy matters' and his prior public statements to the same effect." [16]

That McNamara position contrasted with the previous rule prohibiting a public statement "as to foreign policy which is in conflict with our established foreign policy."

"The May 31, 1961, directive was far too broad and literally precluded all discussion of foreign policy," the Senate subcommittee critically commented. "It was not definite or specific. While it has not been formally modified, in actual practice its application seems to have been clarified. It is now recognized that discussions of foreign policy matters are permissible provided they do not conflict with established foreign policy and provided they are cleared with, and approved by, the Department of State."

The confusion of the new McNamara policy was compounded by the fact that Defense Department censors "seemed to have no clear and consistent understanding of what does and does not constitute foreign policy.

"Individual judgment, differing from reviewer to reviewer, controlled," the subcommittee said. "As a result many speeches were sent to the State Department for review which should not have been so sent. More adequate guidelines in this area are clearly necessary." [17]

The subcommittee found no evidence that the foolish and capricious censorship practices were a result of any lack of devotion to American principles or any tendency to sacrifice our national interest by appeasement of the potential enemy. The evidence did indicate administrative chaos caused by lack of training and guidelines for censors, with the confusion increased by McNamara's ill-advised directive that Defense officials "avoid discussion of foreign policy matters."

While a McNamara directive helped create the chaos, he managed to emerge from the hearings stronger than ever.

The report of the Senate Preparedness Subcommittee squelched the controversy over charges of political "muzzling." But it set the stage for greater conflict between the Secretary of Defense and the Congress on the right of Congress to frank testimony of military officers. Defense Secretary McNamara pulled down the curtain of "executive privilege" in the muzzling hearings and he got by with it. His triumph over the Senate Preparedness Subcommittee bolstered his confidence in his ability to handle the dissenters in the Pentagon and in Congress.

25

A PYRAMID OF PROFITS

IN May, 1961, the Permanent Investigating Subcommittee of the Senate Government Operations Committee received information indicating that excessive profits were being made in the missile program. Chairman John McClellan, the Arkansas Democrat, assigned the investigation to Chief Counsel Jerome Adlerman, Assistant Counsel Robert E. Dunne and Accountant Investigator Thomas Nunnally.

The large missile programs were being farmed out by the Army and the Air Force, and there were indications that some of the prime contractors were not being properly supervised. In fact, the indications were that the Army and Air Force had lost control of some of the missile programs and the military officers were for the most part dependent upon the firms they were supposed to police.

Adlerman, Dunne and Nunnally had been accustomed to investigations of incompetence, waste and mismanagement in government programs, but the extent of the bungling and graft revealed by a precursory survey shocked them. These problems were complicated by the necessity of studying the financial affairs of the contractor, the subcontractor and even sub-subcontractors and sub-sub-subcontractors.

After some preliminary investigation three major missile procurment programs were selected for more detailed studies: the Army's Nike missile and the Air Force's Bomarc missile, both of which were ground-to-air defensive weapons, and to some extent the Air Force's Atlas, an intercontinental ballistic missile.[1]

As the weapons of war became increasingly complex, the Pentagon was moving more and more to private industry to supply munitions. Prior to World War I, the Army arsenals and Navy shipyards had supplied most of the armaments, but the trend toward private industry had increased in World War I and again sharply in World War II through the Korean War and in the tense Cold War period of the 1950's.

McClellan's investigators soon learned that the Defense Department tended to negotiate contracts for major weapons systems with one firm—a weapons system manager. The Pentagon believed this was the most economical method of acquiring the complex missile systems. Committee Counsel Adlerman and his staff listened to the arguments that such negotiation of a contract resulted in "a significant savings," but they also noted that once the weapons system manager was selected the competition ended and the Pentagon continued with that one weapons system manager regardless of whether costs were excessive or not.

Quick judgments as to what constituted a fair price were difficult if not impossible to determine for these large and unusual munitions requirements. The investigators noted that the tools necessary to produce the large missile systems are so expensive that even after the research and development phase was concluded, the Pentagon would find it impossible to buy the item under competitive circumstances because of the prohibitive cost for tooling a new producer.

They found that once a so-called "marriage" had been established between the Defense Department and a defense contractor on a major weapons system, it was usually binding until the program was completed. Committee Counsel Adlerman and Dunne recognized the advantages of this arrangement, but also noted that it had the effect of permitting the contractor to take arbitrary and unreasonable positions on costs and performance.

The more they dug into the big missile projects, the more concerned the McClellan subcommittee members became over the high costs and the high margin of profit for the prime contractor, the subcontractor and sub-subcontractors ad infinitum. The history of the Nike program and Western Electric Company became a classic case in the investigation.

German scientists with their advanced knowledge of rocketry fell into the hands of the United States Army as World War II was drawing to a close. Their research revealed the likelihood of replacing the antiaircraft shell with a missile that could be guided from the ground.[2] Western Electric Company officials reluctantly undertook a study on the feasibility of the guided missile when first requested to do so by the Army. The firm executives were more interested in concentrating all available plant facilities and manpower in expanding as a supplier of telephone equipment to the parent firm, the American Telephone & Telegraph Co.

The project moved slowly in the first years from 1945 to 1949, with limited funding and no real sense of urgency as the Truman Administration cut its Defense Department budgets to the bone. In 1949, the Nike-Ajax was successfully test-fired at White Sands Proving Ground in New Mexico. Armed with a dummy warhead, the missile closed in on a drone B-29 bomber, crashed through the windshield and tore out through the tail.[3]

The Korean War brought a sharp increase in the Pentagon budget and a sense of urgency that resulted in more funds being made available for the Nike-Ajax, and then for a Nike-Hercules—the second generation of the Nike, modified to provide more range and altitude to meet the threat of new supersonic Russian bombers. Even as the Nike-Ajax and the Nike-Hercules were in production from the early 1950's, there arose a need for the development of a third generation of Nike missiles to demonstrate the weaponry to meet the threat of Russia's intercontinental ballistic missiles. In 1957, Western Electric was awarded a contract for the research and development of the Nike-Zeus as America's first antimissile-missile.[4]

As the McClellan investigators started their probe in 1961, the Nike-Zeus was still in a research and development stage although Congress had authorized funds to start limited production. For reasons not made public, the Defense Secretary had not moved forward with production at the time the investigation began. Chairman McClellan was not going to try to make any decisions for the Pentagon on what weapons were needed or when or where they should be bought. He was interested in exploring evidence that, his investigators said, indicated excessive profits accruing to Western Electric as well as some of the firm's subcontractors.

As the systems manager, the Western Electric Company had decided in 1945 that it would concentrate its work on the electronics aspects of the Nike system and would subcontract the three other major subsystems to other firms. Western Electric was to produce the electronics loops, the three radar systems, the computer, and the guidance section of the missile.

Douglas Aircraft Company, of Santa Monica, California, was selected by Western Electric as the subcontractor to provide the aerodynamic, mechanical and automotive portions of the contract, which included the missile body itself.

Since Douglas Aircraft was primarily in the aircraft manufacturing business, it awarded a substantial third-tier subcontract to Consolidated Western Steel Division of United States Steel Company for the production of steel mechanical rails and launcher loaders, which position the missile and elevate it into firing position.

Douglas awarded another third-tier subcontract to the Fruehauf Trailer Company to produce the trailers and vans to house the personnel, radars, and computers that comprise the automotive subsystem.

Since it was impossible for the Army and Western Electric to arrive at a cost figure because of the nature of the Nike program, the Army agreed to guarantee to reimburse the Western Electric for whatever it actually cost plus a ten-percent profit on its work and a six-percent markup on the costs of its major subcontractor, the Douglas Aircraft Company.[5]

Western Electric had permitted Douglas to do its own work and subcontracting with only the essential coordination. As McClellan's investigators looked into the contract they found there was no privity of contract between the Army and Douglas, and consequently the Army had little to say about what Douglas did. The Army had to rely upon Western Electric for performance and the subcontract arrangements with the two sub-subcontractors, Consolidated Western Steel and Fruehauf Trailer Company.

The Senate investigators recognized that in the research and development stages of the contracts the cost patterns and the profit patterns might be unusual, so when they did an analysis of the Nike program they did not include approximately $1 billion paid to Western Electric in connection with research and development projects over the period of years. Adlerman, Dunne and Nunnally concentrated their investigation on the production contract costs of $1,545,-100,000. It included Western Electric's profit of $112,500,000 plus reimbursement of $1,432,600,000 for Western Electric's costs.[6]

This $112,500,000 seemed to the investigators to be a reasonable 7.9 percent profit for Western Electric if it was stacked beside a total of $1.4 billion in "costs." However, they noted that of the $1.4 billion so-called "costs" for Western Electric, Douglas Aircraft had received $644,540,000 for production contracts for the Nike-Ajax and the Nike-Hercules. Also, other Western Electric suppliers were paid $428,760,000 for a wide range of component parts. The investigators made no effort to examine the details of the miscellaneous contractors and suppliers, but they felt obliged to look a bit deeper into the Douglas Aircraft costs. Of the $644,540,000 for which Douglas had billed Western Electric, $598,960,000 comprised Douglas' total costs and $45,580,000 was the Douglas profit figure.[7]

Closer examination by the investigators showed that the total "in house" effort by Douglas, including all overhead and general and administrative expenses, was only $102,990,000—about 17.2 percent of the total. Other firms had furnished 82.8 percent of the work to Douglas in the third tier of subcontracts, and those farmed-out contracts totaled $495,970,000.

As the McClellan investigators figured it, Douglas' apparent profit was only 7.6 percent if it was based on the overall cost figure it submitted to Western Electric. However, if the profit was compared to the actual "in house" costs for Douglas, it constituted a whopping 44.3 percent profit. The firm had $45,500,000 profit on "in house" work that totaled less than $103,000,000.[8]

At this stage the investigators felt they had uncovered a wasteful and uneconomical practice that was costing the taxpayers dearly. Douglas was taking a profit on all material furnished by the third-tier subcontractors, and was passing the whole profit and cost bundle up to Western Electric, where that firm was basing its profit on the overall cost figure that had come up through the three tiers of subcontractors through Douglas Aircraft.

Then the investigators for the McClellan subcommittee dug down one layer more to examine the details of the costs of Douglas' two principal suppliers—Fruehauf Trailer and Consolidated Western Division of United States Steel Corporation. Fruehauf had tacked on profits of $4,500,000 to total costs of $49,300,000 and had billed Douglas for $53,800,000. Consolidated Western had produced $146,223,000 in mechanical parts, had added a $9,285,000 profit figure and had billed Douglas for $155,508,000.[9]

By the time Chairman McClellan opened hearings in April, 1962, the staff investigators had been able to develop figures showing that the government paid $182,182,070 for the Nike launcher loaders produced by Consolidated Western for costs of $146,223,000. Even after Consolidated Western included a 6.3 percent profit, the billing cost to Douglas was only $155,508,000. Douglas had taken that $155,508,000 billing from Consolidated Western, had slapped on a

6.7 percent profit totaling $10,354,659 and had billed Western Electric for $165,862,659.

In its turn, Western Electric took the billing of $165,862,659 and added administrative costs of $6,478,936 plus a 5.7 profit of $9,840,-475 and billed the Pentagon for $182,182,070. The way Accountant Investigator Tom Nunnally figured it, the total profits on the $182,-000,000 contract were $29,480,134. This was $26,674,070 more than the Defense Department would have had to pay if it had bought the Nike launcher loaders directly from Consolidated Western and had not gone through the "profit pyramiding" of buying through Western Electric and through Douglas.[10] It was far from the most economical way of buying.

What had taken place on the Nike launcher loaders was not an isolated case. Essentially the same pattern was disclosed in examining the costs for the Nike trailers produced by Fruehauf Trailer Company for $49,330,255 but bought by the Pentagon for $62,970,846. The total profits were $11,469,457, or more than 23 percent.

The pyramiding of profits on the Nike trailers happened in this way. It cost Fruehauf $46,889,345 for producing the Nike trailers, and the firm had added on $2,440,910 in general and administrative costs and 9.2 percent profit that totaled $4,519,072. Fruehauf billed Douglas Aircraft for $53,849,327.[11]

Douglas Aircraft had taken the $53,000,000 bill, added on 6.8 percent profit of $3,674,543 and had billed Western Electric for $57,523,870. Western Electric took that $57,000,000 billing, added $2,171,134 in general and administrative costs, tacked on 5.9 percent profit of $3,275,842 and billed the Pentagon for the grand total of $62,970,846.

The total amount the government paid was $9,121,519 more than the price would have been if the Army had purchased directly from Fruehauf. Such buying practices didn't make sense to Chairman McClellan and most of the other members of his subcommittee.

He was even more distressed when he heard testimony that a government auditor at the Douglas Aircraft plant had been severely critical of the profits taken by Douglas on the Nike launcher loaders but had been ignored by his superiors. The auditor had termed the profits "unreasonable," but the Army contracting officer, Colonel John Graham, failed to take action to cut the pyramided profits. In fact, Colonel Graham questioned the authority of the Defense Department auditor to criticize the profits.[12]

Under interrogation by the McClellan subcommittee, Assistant Secretary of the Army Paul R. Ignatius was critical of conditions in which the Pentagon found itself forced to deal with one systems manager and unable to ask for bids or buy directly on such component parts of a contract as the Nike launcher loaders or the Nike trailers.

"When companies are actively seeking the business you have to offer, there is bound to be a sharpening of pencils and a downward pressure on the price," Ignatius testified. "A price established competitively is usually one that requires a company to exert careful management control in order to avoid a loss contract, with resulting benefits to the Army. Competition is the animating force in the American economy, and we should put it to work to the maximum extent possible in our Army procurement." [13]

The McClellan investigators found some of the same problem of cost pyramiding in the contract for the Bomarc, another air defense system similar to the Nike in that it was designed to intercept and destroy enemy bombers or aircraft. The Air Force had awarded the initial research and development contract on Bomarc to the Boeing Company of Seattle in 1951. Between 1951 and 1960 the Air Force entered into thirteen principal prime contracts with Boeing in connection with the Bomarc-A and the improved longer-range Bomarc-B. The total cost was approximately $1.6 billion. This total cost figure included the $1.5 billion in costs to Boeing and its subcontractors and a total Boeing profit before taxes of $124 million—approximately 8.2 percent of the total contract cost.[14]

Digging into this contract, the McClellan Permanent Investigating Subcommittee examined cost figures of three of Boeing's subcontractors—Lear Inc., Westinghouse Electric Corporation, and Aerojet General Corporation.

Lear, Inc. had subcontracted for the development and production of the Bomarc-A coordinate converter, which was a part of the guidance system. Lear was responsible for the design, research and development within performance specifications established by Boeing. Lear billed Boeing for $17.3 million, which included Lear's profit of $1.2 million. The McClellan subcommittee accountants figured that Boeing was charging the Air Force $18.7 million, which meant "Boeing will receive a profit of $1.4 million on the Lear effort." [15]

Westinghouse Electric Corporation was awarded the subcontract for the design, research and development of a subsystem known as the target seeker and ground-control equipment for both Bomarc-A and Bomarc-B. The subcommittee found that "the total price to Boeing for the Westinghouse effort was $155.6 million, including a Westinghouse profit of $12.2 million.

"On this [Westinghouse] effort it is calculated that Boeing will receive a profit of $12.6 million," the subcommittee concluded.[16]

Aerojet General was awarded the subcontract for the design, development, testing and production of the rocket booster of the Bomarc-A. The way the investigators figured this one, the total price to Boeing for the Aerojet General work was $26.9 million, which included a profit of $2.9 million for Aerojet. Boeing tacked on another $1.9 million before submitting the final bill to the Pentagon.[17]

The subcommittee investigators established that the total profits earned by the twelve major subcontractors on the Bomarc program were $36.8 million, while Boeing's profits allocated to these subcontractor costs were $41.6 million. "Thus, Boeing's profits as related to the effort of the subcontractors who actually designed, developed and produced the subsystems or components, are greater than those of the subcontractors themselves," the subcommittee commented critically.[18]

Under questioning the Air Force officials admitted that it would have been more economical to have had "a breakout" of the various subsystems from the Bomarc contract so the Pentagon could have bought directly and not paid profits on top of profits to Boeing in the profit pyramid.

Major General W. A. Davis, Commander, Aeronautical Systems Division, Wright-Patterson Air Force Base, stressed that at the time the Air Force first entered into the production contracts, the Bomarc was still in a research and development status with major problems yet to be worked out. He declared that the Air Force simply did not have the "in-house engineering and management capability" required to go out and buy the subsystems and component parts. Boeing did have the capability, developed over years of Bomarc research and development at heavy cost to the government.

In the Bomarc program, the only exception to the purchases through Boeing was the ram jet engine produced by the Marquardt Corporation. The total cost to the government for the Marquardt contract was $177 million, and the subcommittee concluded: "There can be little doubt that had Marquardt continued in category I [as a Boeing subcontractor] Boeing's profit would have been increased by more than $10 million. . . .

"The record shows that although the Air Force procured the

ram jet engine directly from Marquardt, Boeing continued to be responsible for the proper integration of the ram jet with the entire weapon system," the McClellan subcommittee stated. "As a matter of fact, considerable difficulties were experienced with the ram jet after breakout. The fact that Marquardt was no longer a subcontractor did not preclude Boeing from rendering effective assistance. Boeing was reimbursed by the Air Force for additional costs of $527,000 incurred for this aid." [19] That $527,000 was much less than the $10 million Boeing would otherwise have received.

The McClellan subcommittee investigation of the Atlas missile program involved a variation in Pentagon procurement known as "the associate contractor method." The subcommittee was interested in determining whether this "associate contractor" system permitted the tiers of subcontractors and the pyramiding of profits as had been disclosed in the Nike and Bomarc programs.

Under the "associate contractor" method, the Pentagon did not select one business firm as a systems manager but placed contracts for various subsystems with different individual companies who were merely joined together in association. In the case of the Atlas program, Major General Thomas P. Gerrity, Commander, Ballistic Systems Division, Air Force Systems Command, said it was decided that no one company had the competence to do the entire job.[20]

"So therefore we gathered together a group of scientists and engineers under the Ramo-Wooldridge Corporation, now identified as Space Technology Laboratories, to do the detailed systems engineering and technical direction of such a large management effort," General Gerrity explained.

"We portioned out to individual companies in industry specific subsystem tasks to be performed. For example, we contracted with General Dynamics to do the missile frame effort. We contracted with Rocketdyne to develop and manufacture rocket engines. . . . We contracted with General Electric and others to do the tough guidance job." [21]

As the McClellan investigators probed the Atlas contract they found that the problem of several tiers of subcontractors and the profit pyramid was again present.

General Dynamics/Astronautics, as associate contractor for the major component, the missile frame, also had the contract for the launch-control system. With the approval of the Air Force, General Dynamics subcontracted the launch-control system work to Radio

Corporation of America. Then Radio Corporation of America in turn engaged in a sub-subcontract for the cable manufacturing and installation at the bases to three electrical contractors.[22]

The third-tier contractors—the three electrical firms—had costs totaling $16,924,261. They tacked on 4.6 percent profits totaling $751,306.93 and billed Radio Corporation of America for $17,675,-568. In turn, Radio Corporation of America took the bill for $17,-675,568 and tacked on costs of $1,150,333 and 5.9 percent profits of $1,111,807 and billed General Dynamics for $19,937,708.37.

General Dynamics then took the billings from Radio Corporation of America totaling $19,937,708.37, and added 5.4 percent profits totaling $1,084,800 and billed the Air Force for the total.

The total profits allocated to the work of the third-tier electrical contractors were $2,947,914 on work that initially had cost the third-tier contractors only $16,924,261.[23] Although the "associate contractor" method appeared a means of getting away from profit pyramiding, the investigation disclosed that the wasteful practice and the "excessive profits" existed.

When the hearings were ended, the subcommittee concluded that there had been a clear demonstration "that much of the defense dollar is being improvidently spent, and that great savings could ensue to the taxpayers by careful contract procedures, by proper auditing methods, and by more attention of Government personnel, from the contracting officers to the secretarial level, to prevent excessive profits."

The McClellan subcommittee was sympathetic with the problem of contracting for complex major weapons systems, but was caustic in declaring that "the Government has abdicated its responsibilities for program management, and delegated these responsibilities, in many cases, to the contractors.

"Even the most reputable and ethical contractor is placed in the conflicting position of managing a program where the feasibility, technical, and economical decisions which should be made by the customer-Government are made by the producer-contractor," the Senate subcommittee stated. "The absence of competition, coupled with the urgency to get the program underway, removes normal safeguards against large profits and weakens the Government's negotiating position."

The subcommittee stated that while these weapons systems programs are relatively few in number, "they account for a substantial portion of our defense appropriation.

"Better safeguards need to be provided for this portion," the subcommittee stated. "The Nike program is an example of advantages accruing to the contractor in both unreasonably high profits and unwarranted control over the program. . . . During these years the Government had paid tens of millions of dollars in profit to this company [Western Electric] on the cost of work done independently by its subcontractors and their subcontractors." [24]

The Senate subcommittee said that "inadequacy of Army technical and administrative forces and its admitted inability to manage missile systems procurement" was responsible for inability of the Army to cope with a threat of a pullout by Western Electric.

Western Electric's profits of $112.5 million were only 7.9 percent when viewed in relation to the total costs of the Nike-Zeus contract. However, the Senate subcommittee pointed out that when viewed against the $359 million in costs Western Electric generated as in-house costs, the rate of profit became 31.3 percent.

In general the McClellan subcommittee found there was "no justification for paying both nonproducing upper tiers in the pyramid more profit than the actual manufacturer.

"The payment of these profits becomes more difficult to understand when it is found that Western Electric's actual assistance to Consolidated Western Steel amounted to a few inspectors and one technical visitation in all the years the launcher was being produced," the report stated.[25] There were equally critical comments about Pentagon officials responsible for the profit-pyramiding in the Bomarc and the Atlas programs.

There were two dissenters from the majority of the members of the Senate Permanent Investigating Subcommittee. They were Senator Sam Ervin, the North Carolina Democrat, and Senator Carl Curtis, the Nebraska Republican. Both disagreed with the contention that the profits of the systems managers were "unreasonable." Senator Ervin said that he viewed the defense contractors as different from most contractors, and believed that they were entitled to better profits because they "are constantly exposed to the economic hazards incident to changes in programs and cancellation of programs.

"Economic hazards of this nature are largely alien to those engaged in nongovernmental production," Senator Ervin stated.[26]

Senator Curtis also questioned the severity of the report in its criticism of the profits of the systems managers, and he expressed the view that the systems managers opposed the "breakout" of the contracts because of "sincere judgment that, in a rapidly moving technology, premature breakout would jeopardize the success of the undertaking." [27]

Both Senator Ervin and Senator Curtis agreed with the majority report in concluding that the investigations did show that the weapons systems programs needed closer surveillance, better personnel, and improvements in administration.[28]

As weapons systems continued to grow more complicated it was apparent that it was going to be more and more difficult to find ways of providing expertise capable of difficult jobs, incentives for successfully completing difficult jobs, and the administrative safeguards to avoid scandals and wasteful practices.

26

AEROSPACE— A NONPROFIT FRANKENSTEIN

IT was the job of Milton A. Fogelman to administer the Air Force contracts with the Aerospace Corporation. As Administrative Contracting Officer from 1960 until November, 1964, Fogelman was to see that Aerospace made a proper accounting of the millions of dollars in government funds, to see that fees paid to Aerospace were within the Air Force policy, to guard against excessive salaries, to see that proper security measures were in force and to make sure the American taxpayers were not paying for "frills and nonessentials."

Almost from the outset, Fogelman ran into trouble in obtaining needed information from Aerospace under the tight "independent" policies enforced by Dr. Ivan A. Getting, president of Aerospace. As early as March 19, 1962, Fogelman notified Aerospace that certain aspects of the negotiations for a contract for fiscal 1963 had not been in full compliance with the Air Force policy directives. Fogelman took the position that the fees to Aerospace should be paid only on a "need" basis, in which case the Air Force auditors would have the responsibility to examine each project and the costs and to determine Aerospace's actual financial "need."

Aerospace rejected this concept, and insisted on what they called a "worth of task" basis for determining the amount of fees. Under this procedure, Aerospace would not make its records available on the actual costs but would claim a fee on the basis of what it felt the project was worth to the Air Force. Thus, Aerospace would not have to reveal any fee expenditures to the Air Force.

While Fogelman insisted on fees meeting the "need" standard in line with the Air Force policy, Dr. Getting and other Aerospace officials simply refused to change their position or to make records available. Fogelman was not backed by his superiors, who went ahead with a new contract for Aerospace, and as administrator he was left in what was later described as "the incredible position of trying to determine fee needs without being given any information regarding their use." [1]

Fogelman continued to protest that Aerospace was not meeting Air Force policy standards, and two hundred times at meetings with Aerospace officials he asked them to reveal how they were spending the millions of dollars in fees. In each case his request was rejected by Aerospace.

When Representative Porter Hardy (Dem., Va.) started an investigation of the "fiscal and management policy control" of the Aerospace contract, the problem Fogelman had in obtaining information was one of many things investigated by the Subcommittee for Special Investigations of the House Armed Services Committee.

Representative Otis G. Pike (Dem., N.Y.) asked Fogelman: "Two hundred times you went to the well to find out how Aerospace was spending their fees—two hundred times they rejected it and you never got the information. Did you ever complain about this to your superiors?"

"I did not complain to my superiors," Fogelman answered. "My superiors were aware of my actions."

"Did you say to your superiors at any time that something ought to be done about this?" Pike asked.

"In the memorandum of negotiation for the 1962 contract, I made very detailed comment on the subject, stating that the total amount of fees that had been paid to the contractor up until that time were now beginning to add up to a substantial amount of money," Fogelman replied.

As Pike pointed out that "several million dollars" were involved, Fogelman continued: "I had felt during the first two negotiations that the precise detail was not too vital because they were going to need a certain amount of money in their operation, but we were reaching a point [later] where I felt somebody should satisfy themselves that we were not going beyond that amount."

Fogelman related in answer to questions from Chairman Hardy that up until the time of the investigations in 1964 and 1965, Aerospace continued to consider certain financial information as "privileged from the Government."

"How were you going to determine a fee?" Hardy asked.

"It was a sporty course," Fogelman quipped.[2]

The Aerospace Corporation had been organized and totally financed by the Air Force, and yet its officials were adamant in their refusal to make an accounting on the fee matters. "To every question put to the contractor on these subjects the answer was that the Aerospace board of trustees alone were responsible for corporate financial management and would make all determinations on these matters without reference to or the knowledge or acquiescence of the Government," the Hardy subcommittee stated in a report.[3]

The subcommittee commented critically that "there is no evidence that Mr. Fogelman got the additional guidance and assistance requested from higher authority."

It was pointed out that Fogelman did not criticize his superiors, but said he thought the Air Force's failure to take any action was a show of confidence in him and in his ability to work out the problem at the contracting level.

The Hardy subcommittee expressed this view: "Denied the cooperation of Aerospace and adequate support of his superiors, Mr. Fogelman attempted to determine the fee policy by the best judgments he could make. This incredible position was further illustrated when he stated during the hearings that money was provided for fee to pay for the needs of building facilities. He was asked how he was informed that it was proper Air Force policy to provide fee money for Aerospace for buildings."

"You know, I don't know that I was ever formally informed of it, except there across the street rose up the building," Fogelman said.

Representative Charles S. Gubser (Rep., Cal.) asked the follow-up question: "You assume that it is Air Force policy because no one objected to what was happening?"

"That is probably a good statement," Fogelman replied.[4]

The justification for the fee system for Aerospace is most often given as the need for independent research funds. However, the investigation led the Hardy subcommittee to "question the validity of this claim."

In the negotiations for fiscal 1963, Aerospace officials had included a $900,000 item for "independent general research," and Fogelman approved $500,000 of the request on the theory that this was to be used for "independent general research" as was proper under Air Force policy.

"In effect, Aerospace knowingly led the contracting officer to believe it was going to spend a high level of fees for independent research," the Hardy subcommittee stated. "As a matter of fact, up through June 30, 1964, Aerospace had spent only $82,548 for research out of total fees of more than $12 million. . . . A breakdown of expenditures from fees through June 30, 1965, shows fees have totaled nearly $16 million and the total fee expenditures for independent research have been only about $411,000." [5]

The Hardy subcommittee found the whole financial arrangement with Aerospace to be unsatisfactory in the light of the refusal to make any information available on the so-called "fee" expenditures.

"The fee arrangement is a self-defeating process for the Air Force, not only in preventing unjustified expenditures through fee, but in controlling reimbursable expenses," Hardy's subcommittee stated. "The contracting personnel are only too aware that if an expenditure is disallowed as reimbursable, it well may be paid for anyhow out of Government funds allotted as fee." [6]

The subcommittee cited the example of what transpired when costs were questioned by Mr. Raoul Cristin, the Air Force resident auditor. Cristin's report for 1961 had questioned the propriety of a total of $1,623,925. The items questioned included such things as salaries, overtime, meal expenses, sick leave, executive life insurance, food service, entertainment, employee amusement, Washington office expenses, moving expenses, trustee expenses, advertising materials, airmail subscriptions to financial publications, consulting fees, and the credit union manager's salary.

It took more than a year of negotiations before Aerospace agreed to withdraw $46,950 of the $1,623,925 in expenses the auditor questioned. But even then Aerospace officials indicated that since they could not obtain approval of the $46,950 as "reimbursable" items, they would simply charge it off to an overhead account that would be paid through the "fee" arrangement on which Aerospace refused to produce records.

"It is apparent that with the contracting arrangements prevailing there is no incentive for the contractor to be prudent in expenditures," the subcommittee concluded. "The conclusion is inescapable that it is impossible to administer such contracts in line with Government policy unless the contracting officer knows the details of fee expenditures." [7]

The House investigators concluded that Fogelman "was forced to operate with blinders" up to the time he was replaced in 1964 by Colonel Jesse Hamby.

It took Committee Counsel John T. M. Reddan and Investigators Walton Woods and John J. Ford to pry loose the information that between $6,000 and $7,000 in Aerospace "fee" money was used to purchase memberships in country clubs for high-salaried Aerospace officers.

When Fogelman was asked if it was Air Force policy to pay country-club memberships for Aerospace officials, Fogelman replied: "I was unaware of the fact until I heard it mentioned [at the hearings] yesterday." [8]

Colonel Hamby, who took over on November 1, 1964, told the House subcommittee in mid-1965 that there "has not been any improvement" in the accounting by Aerospace.

He said he tried to get answers to questions from two Aerospace officials—Bruce Garoutte, assistant treasurer, and Don Price, director of contracts—and received only "the idiot treatment."

"They remained mute, both of these gentlemen," the Colonel told the subcommittee, in the face of questions dealing with a broad range of questionable expenses and excess salary items. "I got no reply."

He said that there was the briefest acknowledgment relative to a $15,000 item for the Detroit office that did confirm "the Government is paying twice—once in fee and once in overhead . . . for the same thing." Colonel Hamby explained that this was only a sample of "the resistance" that he had received from Aerospace. "I think something needs to be done. I am not sure we need any more rules or regulations . . . but I think maybe the man [on the job] should exercise his authority," Colonel Hamby said. "There is not a human being in a department of Government that can make me give a man money for the same thing twice." [9]

The Hardy subcommittee commented, "In an inquiry so filled with coverup, where so many refused to be candid with the Congress, Colonel Hamby's performance was like a breath of fresh air." [10]

However, the vigorous activities by Colonel Hamby to bring Aerospace into line did not last long. On July 1, 1965, the Air Force relieved Colonel Hamby of his position as contracting officer at Aerospace and assigned him as Deputy for Contract Administration, Air Force Contract Management Division, Air Force Systems Command, Los Angeles, California.

Although the Air Force pictured the move of Colonel Hamby as a "promotion," the Hardy subcommittee was more than a little skeptical. "The conclusion is inescapable that Colonel Hamby was removed from his job because he refused to bend before the willful pressures of Aerospace management. This 'promotion' of Colonel Hamby calls into question the sincerity of the Air Force in its dealings with Congress and its ability to cope with the day-to-day management problems attending our military space programs." [11]

Chairman Hardy served notice that his subcommittee staff intended to keep a close watch to determine whether Aerospace and the Air Force followed through with an agreement that was to provide for "full disclosure of information" in the future.

The members of the House Armed Services Subcommittee stated that they would expect any nonprofit corporation to be willing "to operate in a goldfish bowl" and that this would seem even more likely in "a nonprofit corporation created and financed by the Government."

Subcommittee members were infuriated with the attitude of Dr. Getting and Aerospace that the use of government "fee" money was not the public's business, and "was none of the business of the Government offices for whom they function and who paid their bills, and incredibly, none of the business of the Congress of the United States." [12]

The Hardy subcommittee was particularly irritated with the comments of Dr. Getting linking the "independence" and "objectivity" of the organization with its failure to make a financial accounting. "Leaving aside the question of whether an independent organizational structure is necessary to get objective, honest opinions from talented scientists and engineers, the subcommittee notes that this craving for independence became almost an obsession with Aerospace officials and led them to some remarkable attitudes toward the Government which created their corporation." [13]

The pattern of noncooperation by Aerospace continued in its dealings with the Hardy subcommittee. Aerospace also took the position that it did not have to make its books available to the General Accounting Office (GAO) auditors.

Dr. Getting even objected to the Air Force policy statement and the necessity for eliminating "frills and nonessentials." He called the phrase "obviously vague" and subject to all types of interpretation. "What is a 'frill' or 'nonessential' to one person or under one set of circumstances may very well be considered a fundamental unquestionable necessity to another person or under another set of circumstances," Dr. Getting said.[14]

"Our only customer is the Government," Getting said. "But nonetheless, we are a private company, operating in a free enterprise environment." This was his justification for refusing to make a full financial accounting, and at the same time the Air Force policy to force him to demonstrate "need" for the fees was labeled as "suggestive of the familiar Marxian doctrine." Thus the president of Aerospace quoted the Marxian doctrine—"from each according to his ability, to each according to his need"—as justifying his firm's refusal to produce the record to show his "need" for government funds.[15]

* * *

The problem of questionable use of "fees" extended over into the purchases of real estate by Aerospace under circumstances that seemed to violate the policy requiring Aerospace to use government property where available.

The investigation disclosed that "Aerospace spent a total of some $22 million to purchase land and construct facilities at El Segundo and San Bernardino, California, with the construction financed from fees and borrowed capital.

"All of the costs, including more than $2 million in interest on the borrowed capital, will ultimately be borne by the Government," the Hardy subcommittee found. "However, at both El Segundo and San Bernardino, Government facilities were available which could have been modernized and made suitable for Aerospace's use at a saving of millions of dollars."[16]

The report also called attention to the Aerospace purchase of land at Cocoa Beach, Florida, for $261,304 "without Air Force approval." Aerospace said the purchase was for the intention of building a facility to support its operations at Patrick Air Force Base, but "the Air

Force Commander at Patrick had stated it would not be feasible to have Aerospace personnel located off base.

"This land, which has appreciated in value to more than double the price Aerospace paid for it, has never been used," the report said. The subcommittee noted that as the Aerospace charter and contracts were drawn there was no guarantee that the Government would ever gain title to the land or the proceeds of the land when it was sold. It could be sold and divided up by the officials of Aerospace as additional compensation.

The subcommittee recommended that the Air Force take steps to obtain title to the land purchased by Aerospace, and suggested: "Government ownership of facilities used by Government created nonprofit corporations should be standard policy." [17]

The personnel practices at Aerospace were found to be "uneconomical, unnecessary, unreasonable, or unjustified." [18]

As of September 1, 1964, Aerospace had a total of 4,306 employees, with thirty percent of that number earning basic annual salaries of $15,000 to $75,000. Another nineteen percent earned from $10,000 to $15,000, which meant that a total of forty-nine percent of the employees were earning over $10,000 a year.[19]

The subcommittee questioned the salary increases given to employees who joined Aerospace, the salary boosts given within a short time after joining Aerospace, and the "incentive compensation" bonuses of up to twenty percent of the annual salary given to most of the higher-paid employees.

In some cases the starting salaries offered at Aerospace were thirty to forty percent higher than the employees had been receiving. "A sample of forty-eight employees made by the General Accounting Office showed average increases of eighteen percent, with increases ranging as high as one hundred percent over previous salaries," the subcommittee found.

The examples of large increases included a physics professor earning $14,055 a year who was employed by Aerospace at a starting salary of $28,000. An employee of the National Aeronautics and Space Administration earning $17,500 a year was hired by Aerospace at $24,000 a year. An employee of Space Technology Laboratories earning $22,500 a year was hired by Aerospace at a starting salary of $30,000 a year. In addition to the salary boost, all three of these employees also received the "incentive compensation" bonus of twenty percent of annual salary each year.[20]

It was Dr. Getting who instituted the "incentive compensation" arrangement in the fall of 1960—before Aerospace was really off the ground. To qualify for the twenty percent annual bonus, the employees had to meet two criteria:

(1) Occupy a responsible position and be associated with the successful performance of a major function or project.

(2) Demonstrate potential for growth and development by performance under exacting and difficult conditions.

"It is difficult to understand how employees could have met these criteria in October of 1960, barely four months after the corporation was formed," the subcommittee commented with skepticism. "Investigation also revealed some participants were offered incentive compensation at the time they were hired. It is impossible to understand how a person could meet the criteria set for the incentive plan before he was even working." [21]

In the first four years of the program, Aerospace paid out a total of $816,816 in incentive compensation. Since Air Force officers refused to allow it as a reimbursable item, it was paid out of the "fee" arrangement under which there was no precise accounting. Either way, the taxpayers picked up the tab. The "incentive compensation" plan covered only twelve high officials in 1960, but it has grown to include fifty-five. All the employees making more than $30,000 a year receive it, and fifty-six percent of those with salaries over $24,000 a year.[22]

The investigation disclosed that Dr. Getting was a major beneficiary of the relaxed and "generous" financial operations at Aerospace. In 1964, Dr. Getting received a salary of $76,442.31 and incentive compensation of $15,288.46, to bring his total direct pay to $91,730.77—more than double the salary of the Cabinet officers or the Supreme Court Justices.

The "incentive compensation" was justified as taking the place of stock options and higher salaries in private industry. However, Dr. Getting had a salary of only $45,000 a year at Raytheon Corporation, where he was a vice president just prior to joining Aerospace. The subcommittee revealed that Dr. Getting had exercised his options on only about half of the stock options he acquired at Raytheon.[23]

The investigation also moved into some other "fringe benefits" that Dr. Getting received, including a $350,000 life insurance policy and $9,000 in annual contributions toward his retirement. One item the Hardy subcommittee noted "with interest" was the $3,133.02 that

Aerospace paid to truck Dr. Getting's forty-foot boat from Gloucester, Massachusetts, to San Pedro, California. This was part of a $7,840.14 relocation cost to move Dr. Getting and his family.[24]

Neither the investigations of the House Committee nor the stinging report caused Dr. Getting to lower salaries or abandon the much criticized "incentive bonus" arrangement.

The investigation of the Aerospace Corporation demonstrated that the establishment of a nonprofit corporation to handle research and management jobs for the Pentagon could result in some of the same abuses that had been found to exist when big business corporations were given too free a hand with the tax money.

While Aerospace was regarded by some Air Force officials as highly successful from a standpoint of its work in those first years in operation, the investigation by the House Armed Services Subcommittee demonstrated that even the so-called nonprofit corporations needed rather close scrutiny. The very independence that the corporation was given to keep it out from under the bureaucratic Pentagon control on programs was the same independence that made it possible for the lavish salary and bonus arrangements and the arrogant refusal even to make an accounting to the General Accounting Office auditors.

27

THE MANNED BOMBER FUSS

GENERAL Curtis LeMay and other top Air Force generals accepted the fact that the ballistic missiles with nuclear warheads would eventually replace the manned bomber as the major deterrent to Communist aggression. But in the early 1960's, the Air Force Chief of Staff and his supporters in the Pentagon and in Congress were not willing to accept the view that the missiles could be accepted as the ultimate weapons system, and that it was safe to start to phase out the manned bombers. Major controversy was to rage for years over the cuts that Defense Secretary Robert S. McNamara insisted in making in the manned-bomber program.

Defense Secretary McNamara's dispute with General LeMay and Congress centered on two major areas. First, he wanted to cut back the budget for new B-52 and B-58 manned bombers as much as $500,-000,000 a year on the theory that the Strategic Air Command was strong enough to serve as a deterrent force until the missiles could take their place. Second, he was highly skeptical of the need for proceeding with plans for the expensive 2,000-mile-an-hour B-70, which was planned as the follow-on bomber to take the place of the B-52 and the B-58. He saw no sense in proceeding with the B-70, and in his first year proposed cutting the B-70 funds from $358 million to $220 million.[1]

While Defense Secretary McNamara was sharply boosting the total budget for the Pentagon, he was using much of the money to expand and modernize the Army along the lines of General Maxwell Taylor's plans to be better prepared to meet the threat of limited wars. The Defense Secretary was willing to abandon the B-70 as "too expensive," and to take the first steps on the phaseout of the B-52 and B-58 on the theory that the Pentagon's potential arsenal of missiles could be depended upon to serve as our major deterrent to the Soviet Union, Red China or any other potential aggressor. McNamara also terminated the program to develop a nuclear-powered aircraft. He held up production of the Nike-Zeus antimissile system pending further experiments because he was not convinced that it would be successful.

General LeMay, as the Air Force Chief of Staff, was the leading opponent of McNamara's plans to phase out manned bombers and he had the prestige with Congress to make his views count. General LeMay conceded that the missiles would be the major deterrent of the future, but he challenged the idea that the manned bomber should be phased out. A bomber could perform many missions a guided missile could never perform, LeMay argued. Also, the outspoken Air Force General declared that even if the missile was the ultimate weapon of the future, it was still far from fully developed. He declared it was just plain foolhardy to base national defense plans on a system that had not been fully tested.

The Congress went along with General LeMay in 1961 and, in approving a $46.7 billion defense budget for fiscal year 1962, appropriated $515,000,000 for more B-52 and B-58 bombers and $400,000,-000 for the B-70 program. In all, the Congress provided $780,000,-000 more than Defense Secretary McNamara and President Kennedy had requested.

In its report, the House Armed Services Committee expressed the concern of Congress:

"Our recent history in the field of weapons development has placed heavy stress upon the intercontinental ballistic missile. The committee considers it reasonable to believe that the principal offensive capability of this country, and of the enemy, will in the future rest with ICBM's. During the committee's extended hearings, both on posture and procurement, there slowly developed among the members of the committee a perceptible hesitancy in placing sole reliance and dependence in the ICBM for now or the near future.

"Like all new weapons systems, and like all new things in very many fields, indeed, there tends to be sudden upsurge, and perhaps unthinking reliance, placed upon the latest entrant upon the scene. What in reality is a variation and extension of what has existed before tends to become, by its very newness, an ultimate." [2]

While the House committee stated that it did not in any way intend "to minimize the importance of the intercontinental ballistic missile," it posed the question to itself and to Congress: "Are we proceeding too rapidly in the area of what is essentially an unknown weapon at the cost of weapons whose capabilities are tried and known?

"The current plans of the Department of Defense are headed toward the ultimate elimination of bomber aircraft," the House Armed Services Committee said. "Even within the next few years there will be a substantial decline in the number of bombers. The bomber is a vehicle of known capability for the carrying of weapons of many kinds. In one way or another, every weapon in the inventory of the world today has been carried, has been used, and has worked when carried by bomber aircraft."

The committee stressed the flexibility of the bomber: "The intercontinental ballistic missile has two modes: Go and not go. The bomber aircraft has an almost infinite variety of modes. It can go, it cannot go, it can go part way and wait, it can go part way and turn around; it can proceed or not proceed in any fashion whatsoever since it is at all times under the intelligent control of a human being." [3]

The committee also questioned: "Who knows whether an intercontinental ballistic missile with a nuclear warhead will actually work? Each of the constituent elements has been tested, it is true. Each of them, however, has not been tested under circumstances which would be attendant upon the firing of such a missile in anger. . . . The scientists may say that all of these things are determinable by extrapolation. Perhaps this is so. To the committee, however, it seems that our only knowledge of the actual workability of an ICBM fired in anger is in textbooks and in laboratories. The committee is unwilling to place the safety of this country in a purely academic attitude, and for this reason has added to the bill authorization for bombers." [4]

In the face of the warnings of the House Armed Services Committee and in flat defiance of the wishes of Congress, Defense Secretary McNamara announced that he would not spend the extra funds for the B-70 program or for the additional B-52 and B-58 bombers that General LeMay said were needed.

McNamara's refusal infuriated many important members of Congress, including Representative Carl Vinson, the Georgia Democrat who served as chairman of the House Armed Services Committee. It appeared likely that there would be a showdown between the House Armed Services Committee and the Pentagon Chief when the B-70 program was brought before Congress in 1962 as part of the proposed budget for fiscal 1963.

General LeMay still wanted the B-70 developed as a follow-on bomber, and he still wanted more B-52 and B-58 bombers to keep the Strategic Air Command up to strength. The B-70 was redesignated as the RS-70 in the Air Force proposals and would need from $400,000,000 to $500,000,000, according to LeMay. Instead, McNamara included only $171,000,000 for the RS-70 to develop it only as a prototype.

Again the House Armed Services Committee sided with General LeMay, but went further than it had in the past by including terminology that "directed" the Defense Department to "utilize authorization in an amount not less than $491,000,000 during Fiscal Year 1963 to proceed with production planning and long leadtime procurement for an RS-70 weapon system." [5]

"The manned bomber, the one strategic weapon which has been tried and which works, appears to be destined to become the forgotten weapon in our arsenal," Vinson and his committee declared.[6]

In hearings before the House Armed Services Committee, Defense Secretary McNamara defended his actions. "I believe my reasons for not using the additional B-52 funds are well known to this committee, but it may be useful to restate them briefly once more," the Pentagon boss said. "Procurement of another wing of B-52's would increase the operational inventory of that aircraft by only seven percent. Furthermore, manned bombers present soft and concentrated targets and they depend upon warning and quick response for their survival under nuclear attack. This is a less reliable means of protection than hardening, dispersal, and mobility. Moreover, reliance on warning and quick response means that the bombers must be committed to the attack very early in the war and cannot be held in reserve to be used in a controlled and deliberate way.

"Finally, bombers are expensive," McNamara emphasized. "It costs well over $1 billion to buy a wing of B-52's, together with its tankers and Skybolt missiles, and to operate it for five years. For the same cost, we can buy and operate for the same period of time 250 hardened and dispersed Minuteman missiles or six Polaris submarines."

The committee said it was willing to concede that Defense Secretary McNamara's argument was "at least reasonable" even though the committee members continued to disagree with his conclusion.

"Perhaps, indeed, we should not proceed with the procurement of additional bombers of the type now in the inventory," the committee report said. "But the committee leaves that question in precisely that position—perhaps." [7]

While conceding that McNamara "perhaps" might be right, the House Armed Services Committee was not willing to take the risk with his judgment. It considered the Defense Secretary's refusal to move forward with the funds provided for the RS-70 to be "still another rebuff of congressional will."

The House Armed Services Committee reviewed the record of the executive branch's disregard for the action of Congress, including the cancellation of the Forrestal carrier in 1950 and the impoundment of $615 million for the purchase of airplanes in 1949.

"Since that time, and in only the very recent past, we see these congressional actions failing through nonobservance by the executive," the House committee stated.[8]

It was pointed out that under Article I, section 8, of the United States Constitution, Congress was given these specific authorities:

"To raise and support Armies, but no Appropriation of Money to that Use shall be for a longer Term than two Years;

"To provide and maintain a Navy;

"To make Rules for the Government and Regulation of the land and naval forces."

The committee reasoned that the Constitutional authority did not intend to limit Congress "to the passive role of supine acquiescence in programs handed to it by the Department of Defense." [9]

But while asserting its right to more than a passive role, the committee conceded that "it is eminently clear that role of the Congress in determining national policy, defense or otherwise, has deteriorated over the years.

"More and more the role of the Congress has come to be that of a sometimes querulous but essentially kindly uncle who complains while furiously puffing on his pipe but who finally, as everyone expects, gives in and hands over the allowance, grants the permission, or raises his hand in blessing, and then returns to his rocking chair for another year of somnolence broken only by an occasional anxious glance down the avenue and a muttered doubt as to whether he had done the right thing," the committee said. "Perhaps this is the time, and the RS-70 the occasion, to reverse this trend. Perhaps this is the time to reexamine the role and function of Congress and discover whether it is playing the part that the Founding Fathers ordained that it should."

The House committee declared that there would be voices raised in protest against congressional interference, and arguments would be made that our society has become so complex that we must "leave the determination to experts—with the clear implication that the experts are all in the executive branch.

"Expertise is not infallibility," the House committee said in an obvious jab at the much-heralded Pentagon expert, Defense Secretary McNamara.[10]

The members of the Armed Services Committee, men with from as much as ten, fifteen, twenty and twenty-five years' experience on defense matters, believed themselves "reasonably competent to form a judgment which warrants consideration." That judgment told them that Congress should have the authority to require that the RS-70 weapon system proceed at all possible speed.

"This Nation's changing strategic posture has many implications which are not often recognized," the committee said. "With the development of advanced weapons of great firepower and the increasing capability of Communist nations, the requirement for human judgment and action will be at its greatest premium in history. However, our planned strategic force is approaching an inflexible state with a much reduced capability for exercising trained human judgment and control.

"This committee is gravely concerned that we are abandoning to the enemy the development and production of the flexible weapon system which has kept the peace for many years. Although there is a clear need for a manned strategic reconnaissance-strike aircraft, no manned strategic aircraft system is planned for development or production in the entire free world. The United States is the only Western nation with the capability to meet the challenge."

The Armed Services Committee declared that the RS-70, when properly equipped with missiles, communications and reconnaissance sensors, "is ideally suited for operation in the missile era.

"Unlike ballistic missiles, the RS-70 will not have to rely primarily on high speed, high altitude and low radar cross section for penetration," the committee pointed out. "It will have other important advantages—it is maneuverable, it can carry large quantities of countermeasures, it can employ tactics, it does not have to fly over or into the target, it has its own defense suppression weapons and finally, it has men aboard to exercise judgment to adjust to a changing environment." [11]

The House Armed Services Committee was unanimous in arguing that the RS-70 "would complement the future ballistic missile force.

"It would fill a serious void by adding vision, strength, flexibility, and human judgment which is so essential to our strategic posture," the committee pleaded. "Failure to provide this capability may result in an inflexible force which cannot cope with the unexpected."

The House committee declared that the purpose of the extensive report was to make it clear exactly what it meant authorizing $491 million for the RS-70 system.

"The Secretary of the Air Force, as an official of the executive branch, is directed, ordered, mandated, and required to utilize the full amount of the $491 million," the House members declared. "If this language constitutes a test as to whether Congress has the power to so mandate, let the test be made and let this important weapon system be the field of trial." [12]

The brave position of the House Armed Services Committee did not last for long. President Kennedy asked Chairman Vinson to come to the White House, and prevailed upon the aging committee chairman to drop the word "direct" and to substitute "authorize." In exchange, President Kennedy promised that the Defense Department would "restudy" the whole problem of the RS-70. This amounted to promise of no value, for Defense Secretary McNamara had been studying the RS-70 from the time he had taken office, and his only conclusion had been that the whole program should be cut back and probably killed.

In a letter to Chairman Vinson, President Kennedy rejected the claim the House Armed Services Committee made to a right to "direct" a Defense Secretary to proceed with any specific program. However, in a tone of conciliation, President Kennedy thanked Chairman Vinson for his cooperation and commented on the need for a spirit "of comity" between the two branches of government.[13]

Although Chairman Vinson tried to save face by asserting that Congress "has made its point," it was not much of a point. Although Congress earmarked $363 million for the RS-70 program, McNamara continued to downgrade the project, spending only a small part of the money to keep the program alive and diverting substantial amounts of the money to other projects.

General LeMay, still a champion of the RS-70 as the successor to the subsonic B-52 bombers, had the same support in the House and Senate Armed Services Committees in 1963, as he appeared to testify on the budget for fiscal 1964. The Senate Armed Services Committee took the same line the House Armed Services Committee had taken and expressed "profound misgivings about abandoning manned aircraft and concentrating our retaliatory power in missiles." The Armed Services Committees authorized $363 million for the RS-70 that the Defense Department had not requested for fiscal 1964, but this victory for the manned bomber enthusiasts was not to last long. Because of Kennedy Administration opposition, the additional RS-70 money was not included in the appropriations bill.[14]

Secretary of Defense McNamara, by persistent rejection of the RS-70 program, managed to downgrade it and kill it off in the face of the most stubborn opposition from General LeMay. General LeMay tried to arouse interest in another bomber program to follow the B-52, and he warned that the attrition rate in the B-52 force would cause a "bomber gap" unless immediate steps were taken to replace the aging bombers.

Although the controversy over a possible "bomber gap" became an issue in the political campaign in 1964, it was never a serious issue in a campaign that saw President Lyndon B. Johnson pile up a landslide victory over Senator Barry Goldwater, the Arizona Republican. Goldwater, a pilot and a major general in the Reserve, made several attempts to focus attention on the warnings of General LeMay and other Air Force officers of comparable stature.

Defense Secretary McNamara simply characterized Goldwater's

comments as "completely misleading" and "politically irresponsible." [15]

President Johnson extended General LeMay's term as Air Force Chief of Staff for another year, which prevented the blunt-talking champion of the manned bomber from becoming involved in the 1964 political campaign. When LeMay retired as Air Force Chief of Staff in January, 1965, he had been unable to change McNamara's plans to phase out the manned bomber. Despite continued warnings from Congress and from members of the Joint Chiefs of Staff, Defense Secretary McNamara gave no indications of plans for a follow-on bomber until the nation was deeply involved in the war in Vietnam and the voices in Congress took on such a note of urgency that it was impossible to ignore them. Even when he moved into a follow-on bomber program, the Defense Secretary chose a highly controversial version of a fighter plane that had never been intended to be a bomber. The Defense Secretary gave the military men no choice; they accepted his FB-111 bomber as better than no follow-on bomber at all.

The FB-111, a bomber version of the controversial TFX fighter, had never been intended to be used as a long-range bomber. It lacked range, load carrying capacity and general performance characteristics needed in any follow-on replacement for the B-58 supersonic bombers and the later models (G and H) of the B-52 bombers. It had the range to hit no more than seventy percent of the targets of the Strategic Air Command (SAC), and was accepted by the Air Force as an interim bomber simply because McNamara left no alternative. This was to be the subject of more controversy later.

28

THE CONTROVERSIAL TFX

THE multibillion-dollar TFX warplane contract was the most coveted prize the Pentagon ever dangled before bidders. Government spending, it was estimated, would exceed $6.5 billion—the largest contract for military planes in the nation's history.[1] The program was planned to include more than 1,700 planes for the Navy and the Air Force. Such a contract could mean prosperity for an entire state, and the competition was intense.

Early in 1962, the rivalry for the TFX contract narrowed down to two major firms. The Boeing Company with headquarters in Seattle, Washington, proposed to build the plane at its plant in Wichita, Kansas. The General Dynamics Corporation's Convair Division, in Fort Worth, Texas, cooperating with the Grumman Engineering Company of Bethpage, New York, planned to build the Air Force version in Texas and the Navy version in New York.

Inevitably, political figures from the states of Washington, Kansas, Texas and New York became interested in the TFX award. One who followed the progress of the contract from the beginning was Senator Henry M. (Scoop) Jackson. His interest was threefold: he was a Senator from Washington, one of the states involved; he was a member of the Senate Armed Services Committee; and he was a member of both the Senate Government Operations Committee and its important Permanent Subcommittee on Investigations.

One of the original Kennedy supporters, Senator Jackson had good personal and political relations with the President. However, from a practical standpoint he had good reasons to avoid a political tug-of-war over the TFX contract. Politically, the Texas-New York combination backing General Dynamics and Grumman had a distinct advantage. Texas electoral votes (24) and New York electoral votes (45) went to Kennedy in 1960, while Washington's nine electoral votes and the eight Kansas votes had gone to the Republican candidate, Richard M. Nixon.

Late in the summer of 1962, persistent rumors of Texas political pressure on the TFX contract came to Senator Jackson. Calling Deputy Defense Secretary Roswell Gilpatric, he told him he had heard General Dynamics was certain to receive the contract. Gilpatric assured him there was nothing to it and that the decision would be made "strictly on the merits."

Senator Jackson dismissed the rumors as untrue and trusted budget-minded McNamara to buy the best plane at the lowest cost, even if politically potent Texans were trying to lasso the contract for the home-state firm. There seemed to be no point in taking his fears to the President.

On November 24, 1962, the blow fell with the Pentagon's announcement that the TFX contract would be awarded to General Dynamics. Senator Jackson at first accepted Boeing's loss as part of the game, but a few days later he was told that four separate evaluation studies by the services involved stated the Boeing version promised "superior performance." Also, he learned that Boeing's bid was "substantially lower" than its competitor's. Reports indicated Boeing's bid was $100 million lower on an initial development contract and that the cost difference might run as high as $400 million on the total $6.5 billion procurement.

Scoop Jackson rejected the report that cost-conscious McNamara would take the second-best plane and pay more for it. He asked Senator John L. McClellan, chairman of the Permanent Subcommittee on Investigations, to examine the TFX contract.

The McClellan subcommittee investigators questioned witnesses, examined basic documents and established:

(1) The four service evaluations *did* favor Boeing.

(2) The Boeing price *was* $100 million lower on the first phase of the contract, and it might be $415 million lower on the total job.

(3) The Pentagon Source Selection Board, composed of top generals and admirals, was unanimous in its finding that the Boeing plane would be cheaper and better.

(4) The only document at the Pentagon that supported the General Dynamics plane was a five-page memorandum of justification, dated November 21, 1962. It was signed by McNamara; Eugene Zuckert, Secretary of the Air Force; and Fred Korth, Secretary of the Navy. (Gilpatric also agreed with the award, but his signature was not necessary because McNamara had signed.)

This document was loaded with errors, according to the investigators from the McClellan subcommittee. Thomas Nunnally, a veteran accountant for McClellan's subcommittee, found errors in arithmetic amounting to $32 million and $22 million.

In addition to these factual errors, the memorandum contained other statements that were highly questionable when viewed against the comments of technical experts. The performance claims for the General Dynamics plane were inflated and contrary to military evaluations. McNamara and the civilian secretaries did not approve the "thrust reverser" braking device called for in the Boeing design. They termed it a risky development and preferred the conventional dive brake in the General Dynamics plane. However, military engineers maintained the thrust reverser had been proved a highly desirable feature of the Boeing plane and that the element of risk had been eliminated.

The Secretary also contended that the use of titanium in the Boeing plane was risky and might interfere with Boeing's ability to meet the specified delivery dates. According to the McClellan subcommittee investigators, McNamara was disregarding the expert opinion of the engineers and metallurgists to the contrary. These experts told the investigators that Boeing's use of titanium in the wing structure was a "conventional use" of the metal. It made possible a lighter plane, which the Navy had requested for use on carriers, and Boeing's use of it entailed no unusual risk.

McClellan and his Chief Counsel, Jerome Adlerman, wished to spare the Kennedy Administration any possible embarrassment if it could be avoided. They considered themselves friends of both the President and the Attorney General dating from close association with them during the labor-racket investigations of 1957 through 1960. Chairman McClellan preferred to give the Kennedy Administration every opportunity to reverse an apparently wrong decision. Curt answers and sharp comments from former friends in the Administration plainly demonstrated to McClellan and Adlerman that McNamara had the backing of the White House in this matter.

Many of McNamara's decisions infuriated members of Congress and Pentagon officials. Over the recommendations of Air Force Chief LeMay he dealt the death blow to the RS-70 program. He abandoned the Skybolt missile over the objections of many Pentagon officials as well as the British, who wanted it for part of their defensive armaments. McNamara then offered Polaris missiles to the British without informing his own Joint Chiefs of Staff until the deal was completed.

Nevertheless, from each controversy McNamara emerged stronger than ever. If military officials disagreed with him, McNamara was hailed as putting the brass in its place. He rode roughshod over Congress and sallied forth as a man of lofty principle intent on minimizing the influence of politicians. While the Defense Department budget soared from $42 billion to $52 billion, McNamara shone as a true economizer whose savings would be apparent in the budget three to five years in the future.

Even when McNamara awarded the TFX contract to General Dynamics—a sprawling giant that personifies military-industrial magnitude—many seized on this as a telling blow at the military-industrial complex mainly because he overrode a decision by top military men.

McNamara now boasted that the contract would "save" the American taxpayers approximately a billion dollars at the same time that McClellan investigators were compiling figures showing that the General Dynamics TFX award could waste $415 million in tax money.

Nervous men in top spots—both civilian and military—were asked to testify as the hearings began on February 26, 1963. Their testimony was in opposition to an important decision by Defense Secretary McNamara, a man with a marked distaste for dissenters.

Some remained firm in their positions, but others vacillated and tried to compromise. A few frankly admitted they were fearful their careers would suffer if they maintained a strong position against McNamara's decision. Fortunately, most of the key witnesses had made written records of their opinions on the $6.5 billion airplane program.

Classified data involved in the TFX performance ratings required the hearings to be held behind closed doors. After scrutiny by Pentagon and committee personnel, a "security cleared" transcript was made available to the press. Some of the drama was lost, but the public nevertheless was jolted by the cold facts. It was appalling to learn that McNamara's decision to award the contract to General Dynamics could result in wasting $100 million to $415 million on a second-best plane.

Republicans derisively dubbed the plane the "LBJ" since it appeared to have been peremptorily awarded to Texas. Senator Clifford Case (Rep., N.J.) on the Senate floor called attention to the possibility of political influence in the awarding of multibillion-dollar defense contracts.[2]

Case warned Congress that "national interest" must be the sole base for awarding government contracts. "The scale of space and defense commitments calls for unusual measures to safeguard the integrity of the contract award system, to make sure that awards are made on the basis of merit—and that politics, influence or any other extraneous interests are ruled out."

The New Jersey Republican said that the TFX award, and statements by top officials, including President Kennedy, "raise doubts as to whether what actually goes on . . . conforms with official policy" of awarding contracts on merit. He further emphasized his remarks by recalling the questionable circumstances of the granting of the Mohole Project—a scientific research effort to drill a hole in the bottom of the ocean. Senator Case said that the five-year Mohole contract had been awarded to Brown & Root, Inc., of Houston, Texas, "despite the fact that one National Science Foundation panel rated this firm third best in a field of three.

"Initial progress reports on this project indicate an eventual cost of $70 to $85 million—almost double the original [$43,600,000] estimates—and the contractors are behind schedule," the Senator declared. That Brown & Root was owned by some of Vice President Lyndon Johnson's strongest political supporters was well known to most of the Senators who heard Case attack the contract award.

Hanson W. Baldwin, military writer for *The New York Times,* wrote a scathing attack on "McNamara's Monarchy" at the Pentagon. Dean of newspaper military analysts and an Annapolis graduate, Baldwin focused attention on the TFX award as the hearings before the McClellan subcommittee began.[3]

"Objections or dissent, even to Congress, are discouraged, muted or, when possible, stifled," Mr. Baldwin wrote. "Mr. McNamara has pressured the Joint Chiefs of Staff to sign written statements testifying to Congress that the Administration's defense budget is adequate. He has censored, deleted and altered statements to Congress by the chiefs of the services and their secretaries. He has downgraded, ignored, bypassed or overruled the advice of the Joint Chiefs of Staff."

He wrote that McNamara had not yet forced the military services to speak with one voice "but he has come much closer to it than anyone before him."

Mr. Baldwin warned of the threat of the concentration of politico-military power in one department, and explained:

"It places more and more power over the military-industrial complex in the hands of a few men in the executive branch of the government. The dollar volumes of military contracts amount to more than $20 billion annually, with billions more in backlog orders outstanding. The individual services no longer have the final power to contract." The awarding or cancellation of contracts "is now ultimately controlled by a very few men in the top echelons of the Defense Department," Baldwin said.

The TFX warplane contract had become a pressing aggravation for the Kennedy Administration by late March, 1963. At his press conference on March 21, President Kennedy was asked:

"Mr. President, the TFX contract is causing a lot of controversy on

Capitol Hill. Senator Symington told the Senate today that the investigation was affecting military morale and ought to be wound up quickly. How do you feel about it?"

"I see nothing wrong with the Congress looking at these matters," President Kennedy replied. "Mr. McNamara chose the [General Dynamics] plane . . . because he thought it would save the government hundreds of millions of dollars. . . . I think the Secretary did the right thing. . . . I think this investigation will bring that out and I have no objection to anyone looking at the contract as long as they feel that a useful function is served."

"Do you think the hearing that has been held has been fair and objective?" the President was asked.

"I am confident that we all know a lot more about the TFX than we did before and that is a good thing," the President temporized. "My judgment is that the more this hearing goes on, the more convinced people are finally that Secretary McNamara is a very effective Secretary of Defense and that we are lucky to have him."

The next questioner recalled Senator Case's criticism a few days earlier of Democrats who campaigned for office promising that, if elected, they could bring more government defense contracts to their home states. Obviously, it was in reference to the President's youngest brother, Edward Kennedy, who campaigned in 1962 for a United States Senate seat with the brazen promise that he could do more for Massachusetts.

"Do you feel that this . . . builds confidence that these big defense contracts are being let fairly?" President Kennedy was asked.

"I think the contracts are being let fairly," the President replied, dodging the question. "Of course, there is great competition and it is no wonder because of thousands of . . . jobs [that] are involved. . . . The fact of the matter is that we have a Secretary of Defense who is making very honest judgments in these matters."

"Mr. President, in regard to the TFX contract, would you describe your personal role?" Kennedy was asked. "Specifically, did you make any suggestion as to who should get the contract?"

"No, I did not," was the reply. "This was completely the Defense Department."

McNamara's reputation was challenged by the thorough research McClellan's staff had done, and at the hearings the mass of devastating testimony from senior Air Force and Navy officers accumulated.

Admiral Frederick L. Ashworth, senior naval representative on the Source Selection Board, testified that "Secretary McNamara compromised the requirements" by insisting on a single plane for the Air Force and the Navy. Then McNamara had injected an additional compromise by awarding the contract to General Dynamics, the Admiral said.

The Navy cast its vote for Boeing on the basis of performance and price, Admiral Ashworth stated. Strong reasons were given by the Admiral as the basis for the Navy's preference for Boeing: lower gross weight, better subsonic flight characteristics vital to a carrier operation, better performance rating on Navy combat missions, and a substantially lower price. The Navy further recognized that the Boeing plane possessed significant operational advantages for the Air Force, the Admiral said.

"It would be an economic catastrophe if we end up producing an aircraft for either the Navy or the Air Force that would not do the job," Admiral Ashworth declared.

Major General Robert G. Ruegg, chairman of the Source Selection Board, said the board had carefully considered the "commonality" factor. McNamara leaned heavily on the fact that the General Dynamics plane had more parts that could be used in both the Navy and the Air Force versions and insisted this was a vital reason for his decision.

Commonality or identical parts of the General Dynamics plane literally "outweighed" the Boeing plane, but Ruegg felt this was a liability, not an asset. He conceded General Dynamics had more identical parts, but this "commonality" was achieved at the cost of 1,450 pounds of weight added to an already overweight Navy plane, which, incidentally, was far heavier than was desirable for aircraft operation as far as the Navy was concerned. In other words, because of "commonality" the Navy was going to get an overweight plane that would create other problems. As General Ruegg further explained, the particular parts that had "commonality" in the General Dynamics version were "parts that we do not normally stock and buy as spares."

"In other words, those were parts that are seldom replaced because if they got broken, the plane was destroyed, is that right?" McClellan asked.

"Generally, that is right," Ruegg replied.

"You think you would be getting more for your money if you got the Boeing plane, I mean in weaponry and meeting the requirements?" McClellan asked.

"Yes, sir, I think my statements [on that] are plain enough," the Source Selection Board chairman said.

General William F. McKee, the Air Force Vice Chief of Staff, testified:

"It is my view that the operational factors [favoring Boeing] should be the overriding consideration."

The Air Force gave Boeing a "clear and substantial" recommendation over the General Dynamics plane, he said.

General McKee differed with McNamara's opinion on the Boeing "thrust reverser" braking device and insisted it had special merit because it "provides better deceleration, whether it is for air-to-air maneuvering, diving or landing roll."

General Walter C. Sweeney, Commander of the Tactical Air Command (T.A.C.), testified he recommended the Boeing TFX because of "superiority in all major aspects of operational capability.

"The Boeing plane is a much better aircraft . . . far superior for the T.A.C. role," General Sweeney testified.

George Spangenberg, the Navy's top civilian aeronautical engineer and holder of the Defense Department's Distinguished Service Medal, also refuted the Defense Secretary's "commonality" argument. Spangenberg, an engineer for twenty-five years, had earlier told the subcommittee investigators that the weight of the General Dynamics TFX constituted a serious problem. The General Dynamics plane had been rejected on three previous evaluations, and even on the fourth the weight was far in excess of what the Navy considered acceptable and safe for carrier use. Now, addressing himself to McNamara's "commonality" factor, Spangenberg said:

"It's all poppycock. We think that Boeing gave us a better proposal at a better price. You certainly don't want to pay more money to get an inferior product just because it meets some word—commonality—better."

General Curtis E. LeMay, the Air Force Chief of Staff, testified that he was not consulted prior to McNamara's decision to overrule the Source Selection Board.

"I thought we had such a clear cut and unanimous opinion all up and down the line that I was completely surprised at the decision," the Air Force Chief declared.

"Did any group, any authority at any level from you on down to the evaluation group ever recommend the General Dynamics plane?" McClellan asked.

"No, sir," LeMay answered. In all his experience he was unable to recall a single instance where the decision of the service selection board had been rejected by a civilian secretary.

"Would you have expected . . . that you would have been consulted and the matter would be discussed with you?" McClellan pressed.

"Yes, sir," LeMay replied. "I was surprised that the decision was made without consultation."

For nearly a year more than two hundred experts had spent 275,000 man-hours appraising the Boeing and General Dynamics designs, and General LeMay added: "The Boeing team had a much better knowledge of what was required in this sort of an airplane."

The crusty airman finished his testimony by stating flatly that McNamara had made a "wrong" decision when he awarded the contract to General Dynamics.

Admiral George W. Anderson, then the Chief of Naval Operations, was concerned over what McNamara's decision could mean to the United States and warned of possible loss of "the edge" to Russia in air power.

Anderson did not stress price though he was aware of Boeing's lower bid. Superiority of one plane over the other was his prime concern and he stated unequivocally the Boeing plane had it. Admiral Anderson said it was vital for the United States military services to obtain the best possible performance from new weapons if the country were to keep the lead over the Communists.

Russian capability for developing superior aircraft is well demonstrated, according to Anderson. He cited the MIG-15, which surpassed performance of all American planes except the Navy F-4H Phantom. He recalled for the subcommittee the marked superiority in maneuverability displayed by the Japanese Zero at the start of World War II and how long it had required to overtake their accomplishment, without trying to calculate the cost in lost pilots, planes and ships.

Phantom Fighters had been mustered from all parts of the country to the southeastern area the preceding October to provide protection against possible aggression from Russian MIGs during the Cuban crisis, the Admiral related. Any discernible "edge" in performance is vital to success in a crucial period.

"We put our best [plane] there," Admiral Anderson said. "In the military profession as in every other, an edge of advantage is of greatest importance. . . . If a potential enemy either believes or knows his prospective adversary possesses such an edge, he thinks twice before committing himself to armed conflict. If other considerations compel him to act, this edge can make the all-important difference between being able to defeat the aggressor . . . or lacking the edge, losing quickly."

Admiral Anderson then dropped his bombshell: If the General Dynamics plane were selected, he warned, *the Navy could be saddled with a plane too heavy to operate from the majority of the aircraft carriers.*

"Now we will have an aircraft 13,500 pounds heavier than our original specification and 8,500 over the revised Navy requirement," the Chief of Naval Operations said.

"Did you have anything to suggest to you . . . that the unanimous verdict and recommendation, all the way up from the military, would be doubted or rejected?" McClellan asked Anderson.

"No, sir, I did not, and it came as quite a surprise to me that the recommendation was reversed," Admiral Anderson said.

More damaging contradictions of McNamara's stand were yet to come. At this point Chairman McClellan felt compelled to probe McNamara's claim of a billion-dollar saving. All available cost studies at the Pentagon were again scrutinized by the investigators. New evidence weakened all grounds for McNamara's decision—including the claim of a billion-dollar savings.

Accountant Nunnally unearthed conclusive evidence that the only cost studies available to McNamara contained substantial errors—errors of the magnitude of $290 million and $340 million. Any decision resulting from those cost figures could not have been a correct one.

Information of McNamara's feverish attempts in April to reconstruct a paper record to establish justification for his decision six months earlier came to the attention of McClellan's investigators. Testimony already on file showed efforts by the political secretaries at the Pentagon to pressure career military men into changing their position and supporting McNamara.

While an avalanche of freshly contrived documents and statistics flowed from the Pentagon, the McClellan subcommittee was thwarted in its attempts to obtain the one bona fide document it really needed.

This was a file memorandum, dated March 1, 1963, from Albert W. Blackburn, the key TFX technician in McNamara's own office.[4]

To many persons Blackburn was "Mr. TFX." A Naval Academy graduate, he was an aerodynamics engineer and a test pilot. His background made him eminently suited for the job: an impressive combat record, a master's degree in aeronautical engineering from the Massachusetts Institute of Technology, and considerable experience with the North American Aviation Company, an airplane manufacturer. In 1959, he became a special assistant in the Office of the Director of Defense Research and Engineering, in the Office of the Secretary of Defense.

He was probably the best-informed man on TFX in America. For two years he kept pace with the day-to-day developments in the TFX program. Blackburn was the man who provided the information to McNamara's office.

His surprise and bewilderment when the Defense Secretary awarded the contract to General Dynamics is evidenced in his memorandum of March 1, 1963, which stated:

"There is no real, supportable case to be made for his [McNamara's] choice of . . . [General Dynamics] on the grounds of operations, technical, management, or cost considerations."

Blackburn concluded: "The Secretary [McNamara] chose to make a decision on the basis of information different from that evaluated under the established ground rules."

When Blackburn appeared before the subcommittee as a witness in May, 1963, he testified that lawyers in McNamara's office had asked him for historical and technical background for use in building McNamara's case. In response, he prepared the March 1st memorandum, which struck at the heart of every argument that McNamara had put forward.

Never before had contract consideration required four evaluations, and Blackburn's memorandum revealed that Boeing had eclipsed General Dynamics on each. He praised Boeing and contrasted it with the difficulties General Dynamics was undergoing.

"At this point in time, there was no doubt in anyone's mind as to the relative competence of the two competing companies," Blackburn stated. Secretary McNamara "made it known he would not permit the continuation of the program with a single contractor and elected to continue . . . giving each contractor an additional $2.5 million to further refine their design proposals and validate their data.

"During the ninety days following the three submissions by the contractors, two very different types of activity were taking place at Fort Worth [General Dynamics] and Seattle [Boeing]," Blackburn related. "The General Dynamics engineers were desperately seeking to evolve a satisfactory configuration, whereas the Boeing engineers were carrying their design into detailed wind-tunnel analysis for both subsonic and supersonic performance. . . ."

General Dynamics lagged far behind when the competition ended with the fourth design, Blackburn said. "The General Dynamics engineers were still in the early stages of their configuration evolution . . . whereas the Boeing designers . . . were clearly much further down the line in coming to terms with the total design problem.

"When the announcement was made that General Dynamics would be given the development program, it was clear to all those involved that this decision could be justified only on the basis of a broad, high-level policy of the administration, and could not in any way be associated with the merits of the two proposals on either an operational, technical, management or cost basis."

Blackburn praised the "depth of technical development of the Boeing design . . . and its imaginative innovations such as thrust reversers" and other factors in Boeing's favor. He compared it with the "notoriously poor management exercised by General Dynamics" in its jet-transport program, which resulted in a $400 million loss to the company.

Blackburn testified that McNamara's estimate of a $1 billion saving was only a "rough ball park figure" and that it applied to possible savings if one plane were used for both the Navy and the Air Force. McNamara could not properly claim the $1 billion figure once he had selected the higher-priced General Dynamics plane, Blackburn said.

However, the challenge to McNamara's claim to frugality was not based on Blackburn's testimony alone. Senator McClellan had initiated other studies of the billion-dollar saving, as well as other cost estimates used by the Secretary. On April 2, 1963, he requested Comptroller General Joseph Campbell, of the General Accounting Office, to send him "an independent review of the cost standards prepared by the Air Force and used by the Department of Defense in making its decision on the award of the contract." McClellan urged the GAO to make "careful distinction" between figures available prior to the TFX award to General Dynamics and the after-the-fact studies.

On April 26th, Campbell replied to McClellan: "We have found no independent or additional cost estimates covering the TFX program as a whole, and the Secretaries advise us that none exist. . . . Both Secretary McNamara and Secretary Zuckert have stated to us that the conclusions reached by them were on the basis of their judgment, rather than on independent [cost] studies." [5]

McClellan regarded this as incredible. McNamara, who boasted of deep cost documentation for every decision, had no cost studies to support him on a multibillion-dollar program.

William A. Newman, Director of the Defense Accounting and Auditing Division of GAO, testified of the meeting with McNamara: "We requested any information that was prepared at his level concerning the cost estimates. . . . When it came time to examine the records . . . he stated that he had the figures in his head, indicating that he did not have them on paper."

After revelation of this complete lack of documentation McClellan asked Comptroller General Campbell what standard figures would normally be available for an audit of this sort. The Comptroller General replied that he "would expect the fullest kind of documentation" because of the "enormous expenditures" involved and the need for supporting documents for later audits.

Boeing's president, William M. Allen, and his top specialists ridiculed the Defense Secretary's use of a "rough estimate" on cost realism and testified his firm had cost studies in great depth available to back their TFX bid.

"It has been stated that our cost estimates were unrealistic, demonstrating that we did not appreciate the complexities of developing the TFX," Allen said, paraphrasing McNamara. "According to the testimony, the government has contracted [with General Dynamics] for a 23-airplane test program at an adjusted contract ceiling price of approximately $630,000,000. Our contract ceiling price . . . similarly adjusted for 23 airplanes, would be approximately $482,000,000 or $148,000,000 less than our competitor. . . . Yet, we were definitely downgraded by reason of our lower price. In fact, our low price is one of the principal reasons given for awarding the contract to our competitor."

Boeing, according to Allen, had based its bid on careful calculations, not on a "rough judgment," and could support the figures fully. Those figures were never challenged by the Defense Department, Allen said. Designation of his company to produce the TFX would save $148,000,000 for the government on the test program alone, and he asserted Boeing was fully prepared to carry out its commitment at the quoted price.

Allen told the subcommittee it was "discouraging and disillusioning" to be judged to have the superior plane and the lowest price and still to lose the contract. It was particularly bitter to lose on the basis of rough estimates and, as Senator McClellan put it, "the arbitrary judgment" of Defense Secretary McNamara.

Though McNamara disclaimed any political motive in giving the contract to the Texas-New York combine, the big question remained: Why would McNamara award a multibillion-dollar contract on the basis of an apparent arbitrary estimate and with no independent cost studies? Senator McClellan and his subcommittee turned their scrutiny to two of McNamara's principal advisers—Roswell Gilpatric and Fred Korth.

29

ROZ GILPATRIC AND FRED KORTH

DEMOCRATS had been sharply critical of the "conflict of interest" of Air Force Secretary Harold Talbott in the Eisenhower Administration, and some Democrats had harped constantly on the "conflict of interest" by a Bureau of the Budget consultant that had forced President Eisenhower to cancel the so-called Dixon-Yates power project.

The problem of the potential "conflicts of interest" at the Pentagon had been brought to public attention again as Representative F. Edward Hébert investigated the "munitions lobby" and put the spotlight on the large number of high-ranking military officers who had gone to work for big defense contractors. In a report on the "Employment of Retired Commissioned Officers by Defense Department Contractors" Chairman Hébert's committee had compiled a list of 726 retired military officers above the rank of colonel in the Army and Air Force and captain in the Navy who were then employed by the one hundred largest defense contractors.[1]

Chairman Hébert did not contend that it was improper for retired military officers to go to work for the major defense contractors, but he did point out that there was an ever-present danger that retired admirals and generals might use Defense Department knowledge and connections to gain favored treatment for the defense contractors who employed them.

"The 'coincidence' of contracts and personal contacts with firms represented by retired officers and retired civilian officials sometimes raise [*sic*] serious doubts as to the complete objectivity of some of these decisions," the Hébert subcommittee commented.[2]

The subcommittee declared that the problem of "conflicts of interest" was not confined to retired military officers but included civilian employees of the Defense Department, political appointees and the whole range of difficulties created when men are one day representing a large defense contractor and a few days later may be holding a high political office.

In the report, the Hébert subcommittee quoted from comments of Senator Augustus Bacon, the Georgia Democrat, at the time one of the early conflicts-of-interest laws was being passed in 1896. Senator Bacon observed that "the most honest and upright man who ever lived is not allowed to sit on the bench in a case in which he has an interest, not because he is dishonest, not because he is unpatriotic, but because his relationship warps his judgment and prevents him from being an impartial and upright judge." [3]

That was the spirit behind the actions of President Kennedy in early 1961 when he announced his Administration would institute a tough, comprehensive code of ethics designed to eliminate any circumstances that might give rise even to suspicions of a "conflict of interest."

In the Pentagon, Deputy Secretary of Defense Roswell Gilpatric was given the job of implementing the new, tough code of ethics. Gilpatric signed the order warning all military and civilian employees of what was heralded as a most strict directive to bar even the appearance of a "conflict." This directive was to serve notice on "the munitions lobby" and the "military-industrial complex" and every political appointee and career government employee. The Kennedy Administration would not tolerate even the appearance of "conflicts of interest."

Ironically, Deputy Defense Secretary Gilpatric was the first high-ranking Administration official to come under sharp congressional criticism in connection with the new code of ethics. The TFX warplane contract investigation raised questions of the "conflicts of interest" problem against Gilpatric and also against Navy Secretary Fred Korth.

Gilpatric had been in and out of the Defense Department in the period from 1951 to 1953 when he served as Under Secretary of the Air Force. In 1953 Gilpatric returned to law practice, and combined legal representation of big defense industries with an active role in Democratic politics. Even under the Eisenhower Administration, the Air Force had given him a leading role in establishing the Aerospace Corporation.

From 1958 to January, 1961, Gilpatric was a lawyer for the General Dynamics Corporation, that huge industrial-defense complex that included 186 high-ranking retired military officers among its 91,700 employees. The Hébert subcommittee reports had listed General Dynamics as the number-two firm in the nation with regard to total volume of defense contracts.

The number-one defense contractor was Boeing, which included 61 high ranking retired military officers among its 89,981 employees. However, Boeing's stress on retired high-ranking military officers was small compared with the General Dynamics operation. Not only did General Dynamics employ three times as many retired military officers, but General Dynamics had more than five times as many generals and admirals on the payroll as Boeing. The ratio was 27 to 5 in the general and admiral category.[4]

Even as a major defense contractor, headed by former Army Secretary Frank Pace, General Dynamics was in serious financial difficulty in 1958 following a disastrous loss by the Convair Division estimated at about $400,000,000. New money was needed to keep General Dynamics moving, and Roswell Gilpatric[5] had a major role in a merger between General Dynamics and Material Services Corporation, a Chicago construction firm controlled by Colonel Henry Crown, an influential Democratic political figure. Frank Pace and other high officials of General Dynamics were Gilpatric's personal friends, and the New York lawyer had an office in the General Dynamics headquarters. Gilpatric's law firm was not "the counsel" for General

Dynamics, but the work was substantial and the legal fees paid for Gilpatric's services came to more than $100,000.

When Gilpatric became Deputy Defense Secretary in January, 1961, he left the law firm of Cravath, Swaine & Moore with a financial arrangement that was to pay him $20,000 a year for several years, which he explained as a sort of severance pay.[6] Of course, Gilpatric bowed out as lawyer for General Dynamics but the law firm continued to represent General Dynamics. It was Gilpatric who "arranged" for M. T. (Tex) Moore to take over the General Dynamics account.

General Dynamics, deeply in debt, had a vital interest in the multi-billion-dollar TFX warplane contract. With that TFX contract, General Dynamics could recover from the shattering financial loss by the Convair airplane division. If General Dynamics failed to win the award of the TFX contract, the huge defense complex faced the possibility of more serious trouble.

Some lawyers felt that the Kennedy Administration's new code of ethics would bar a former attorney for a big defense contractor from having any participation in negotiating a contract with that client. Gilpatric did not view it in that light. He reasoned that he had resigned from his law firm, and he contended that he was not the type of man who would be influenced by his former close associations in the law firm or in General Dynamics.

Gilpatric took part in the Defense Department's negotiations with General Dynamics and the Boeing company, engaging in discussion on the huge contract and writing letters of instructions on the TFX matter.

When the last of the unprecedented four evaluations by the Pentagon Source Selection Board was completed, the unanimous verdict was for the Boeing Company. Gilpatric, as the number-two man in the Defense Department, concurred in McNamara's decision to disregard Boeing's low bid and the "superior" performance rating and award the contract to General Dynamics.

If there was any lingering doubt in Gilpatric's mind about a possible "conflict of interest" he had cleared that away by telling Defense Secretary McNamara all about his prior representation of General Dynamics. On the basis of the facts Gilpatric revealed to him, McNamara gave full approval to Gilpatric's continued participation in the TFX contract negotiations.

McNamara announced the award of the contract on November 24,

1962, and less than a month later it was Gilpatric who signed a letter to Senator John L. McClellan rejecting the committee chairman's request that formal signing of the TFX contract be delayed pending completion of a preliminary investigation. The contract was signed the same day the Defense Department received McClellan's request, and Gilpatric wrote McClellan stating that he considered it in the "national interest" that the contract be signed immediately.

That was the same week that General Dynamics officers had a meeting and named Tex Moore, of the Cravath, Swaine & Moore law firm, as a director of General Dynamics. Also, the status of the law firm was changed. Instead of being "a counsel" for General Dynamics, the law firm became "the counsel" for General Dynamics.

While some members of the Senate and House raised questions of "conflicts of interest" and general impropriety in Gilpatric's role, the suave New York lawyer explained that his law firm had represented so many firms that were part of the defense industry that it would be thoroughly impossible and impractical for him to try to disqualify himself from participation in all contracts involving clients of the Cravath, Swaine & Moore law firm. He would have been unable to carry out his responsibilities as Deputy Defense Secretary, he argued. Consequently, he saw no reason for disqualifying himself in the TFX contract simply because he had represented General Dynamics.

Representative H. R. Gross (Rep., Ia.) and Senator Milward Simpson (Rep., Wyo.) questioned both the propriety and the legality of Gilpatric's participation in the contract negotiations. However, President Kennedy and Attorney General Robert F. Kennedy expressed no concern over the role Gilpatric played in the TFX award, even when Chairman McClellan, Senator Karl Mundt (Rep., S. Dak.), Senator Carl Curtis (Rep., Nebr.) and Senator Henry M. Jackson (Dem., Wash.) questioned whether it would be possible for Gilpatric to approach the TFX competition with complete objectivity.

The difficulty of Gilpatric's personal role in the TFX affair certainly made it unlikely that he would be enforcing the new code of ethics on such others as Navy Secretary Korth, who had a similar problem.

Korth,[7] a Fort Worth lawyer and bank president, became Navy Secretary in January, 1962. He succeeded John Connally, another Fort Worth lawyer who resigned to seek the Democratic gubernatorial nomination in Texas. Fred Korth was an enthusiastic booster of his home town and of the General Dynamics firm, which had the huge

Convair plant in Fort Worth. Fred Korth numbered two top officials of the Forth Worth plant among his close personal friends, and the General Dynamics Corporation was one of the best customers of Korth's Continental National Bank of Fort Worth.

Only three months before Korth became Navy Secretary, he had given his personal approval to a $400,000 loan from the Continental National Bank to the General Dynamics Corporation. It was a small loan in the overall borrowing by General Dynamics in those desperate days, but it was substantial to the small bank Korth headed, a bank that had a loan limit of $600,000.

When Korth appeared before the Senate Armed Services Committee in January, 1962, he stated that he was resigning as president of Continental National Bank. However, he did retain $160,000 in stock in the Fort Worth bank and he told the committee members he intended to return to a position in the bank when he had finished his tour of duty in the Pentagon.[8]

Korth had been in and out of the Defense Department before. He had served as Assistant Secretary of the Army in the last years of the Truman Administration, and had successfully combined law, banking and Democratic politics in the period when the Eisenhower Administration was in office. His continued ownership of $160,000 worth of stock in the Fort Worth bank was considered by Korth to be too small and unrelated to the bank's loan to General Dynamics to be important in the TFX contract award. He was a self-proclaimed "man of integrity" and declared that his judgment would never be swayed by such an interest.

High officials from the General Dynamics plant in Fort Worth were shuttling in and out of Korth's office in the Pentagon throughout 1962 when the TFX was up for decision, but Korth insisted all these calls from his old Fort Worth friends could not influence his objectivity. He believed his declaration that he was a "man of integrity" should end it. He insisted he had no continuing interest in the bank's loan to General Dynamics or any other firm, and no interest in the deposits General Dynamics had in the bank.

When it came time for Korth to make a decision on the TFX contract, the Navy Secretary overruled the recommendations of the top Navy admirals and suggested that the Defense Secretary award the contract to General Dynamics. It meant disregarding the Pentagon Source Selection Board's unanimous recommendation for Boeing. Korth said he did not understand the recommendations to be so strong for Boeing, and explained that he had been under the impression that after the fourth evaluation "both designs [are] now considered acceptable." Regardless of his reasons for his decision, Korth ended by approving award of the contract to General Dynamics and signing the five-page memorandum of justification with Defense Secretary McNamara and Air Force Secretary Eugene Zuckert.

Chairman McClellan brought up the question of possible conflicts of interest, but it was raised more directly and with more force by Senator John J. Williams, the Delaware Republican, Senator Simpson and Representative Gross.[9] Senator Williams wrote to the Justice Department and set out the admitted facts on the interests and the roles of both Gilpatric and Korth and raised questions of both legality and propriety.

It was Norbert A. Schlei, Assistant Attorney General in the Office of Legal Counsel, who wrote Senator Williams stating that in his opinion there was no law violation in Gilpatric's role or Korth's role in the TFX matter. He did so without consulting with the McClellan subcommittee staff to determine if there was any further information that might be relevant to the question of "conflicts of interest." The Justice Department did not try to make a determination of propriety, for that was up to the Defense Department, where Gilpatric continued to rule as the number-two man. The Justice Department stated that since Gilpatric had "resigned" from his law firm and had no binding arrangement to return to the law firm, the severance of his ties with General Dynamics was sufficient to avoid a "conflict of interest" within the meaning of the law.

In the case of Korth, the Justice Department went along with the reasoning that Korth used before the Senate Permanent Investigating Subcommittee. Justice characterized Korth's $160,000 stock interest in the bank as insignificant when viewed in the context of the total bank business, and likewise found the $400,000 loan from the bank to General Dynamics as an insignificant part of the $20,000,000 borrowed by General Dynamics. In addition, the Justice Department reasoned that Korth had resigned as president of the bank and at that point severed his interest in the deposits the bank had from General Dynamics or the loans the bank had made to General Dynamics.

The McClellan investigators, acting on a tip supplied by Senator Karl Mundt, obtained access to the records and correspondence of the Continental National Bank of Fort Worth. Korth had testified that he paid no attention to the details of the bank's business with General

Dynamics, and had stated clearly: "I do not know now, as I have testified before, nor have I kept abreast of, nor am I interested in, whether General Dynamics Corporation continued to maintain an account at that bank of which I was president, of which I am a stockholder, or whether they presently owe any indebtedness to that bank."

It sounded as if Korth had severed his interest in the bank, but the correspondence obtained by Counsel Adlerman, Dunne and Nunnally indicated otherwise. Letters between Korth and operating officials of the Continental National Bank showed that Korth, while serving as Navy Secretary, had received glowing letters of praise from officers of the bank for bringing them $20,000 and $30,000 accounts—much smaller amounts than the $500,000 account the General Dynamics firm kept in the bank. The correspondence disclosed that Korth was kept posted on bank matters and that his associates at the bank wrote to him regarding their eagerness to see the TFX award go to General Dynamics.

In a letter to Leigh Thornton, senior vice president of Continental National, Robert R. C. Pape, vice president of the Chase Manhattan Bank in New York, commented: "I hope that the enlarged payrolls resulting from the TFX find their way into your deposit picture."

In another letter, Leon Jordan, vice president and comptroller of the Continental National Bank, thanked Navy Secretary Korth for having helped obtain two new accounts. In the letter to Korth dated September 14, 1962—nine months after Korth became Navy Secretary—Jordan commented:

"I note on today's new account list that you have secured a [$]25,000 account from Neiman-Marcus for us and only a few days ago another [$]25,000 savings account the name of which I don't recall at the moment *but suffice it to say that this is probably more business than the people who are primarily responsible for new business have gotten in the past two or three months*. So may I add my thanks to you—just hurry up and get back here."

Some of the letters written by Korth to promote the bank's business were written on his official Navy stationery, and included Korth's invitation to some of the bank's "very best customers" for a pleasure ride on the Navy yacht *Sequoia*. When the investigators brought the correspondence and other evidence to Chairman McClellan, he concluded that the Kennedy Administration simply did not know all the facts on Korth's continued activity for Continental National Bank of Forth Worth.

Chairman McClellan called Attorney General Kennedy and confronted him with the fact that Korth had been promoting the bank's business on Navy stationery, and he wondered if the Justice Department had known these facts when the letter was written stating that Korth had no conflict of interest. Robert Kennedy had taken a strong and decisive position against such activity on the part of Air Secretary Talbott; if he wished to exhibit any consistent pattern, he had no choice on the Korth matter. He expressed the opinion that Korth should resign, and within a few days the Navy Secretary submitted a letter stating that he was leaving government "so that I may return to private business and attend to my pressing business affairs."

At his press conference on October 31, 1963, President Kennedy was asked about the legality and propriety of Korth's activity in the TFX matter. The President reiterated the thesis that Korth had only a small interest in the bank and that the bank loan to General Dynamics was "a small amount of money, as bank loans go.

"So I have no evidence that Mr. Korth acted improperly in the TFX matter," the President said. "It has nothing to do with any opinion I may have about whether Mr. Korth might have written more letters and been busier than he should have been in one way or another." [10]

The McClellan subcommittee investigators obtained more interesting correspondence in the files of Gilpatric's old law firm. Gilpatric had insisted he had "resigned" from the law firm in 1961, and had no commitment to return to the law firm. However, letters in the law-firm files stated that Gilpatric and his secretary were simply on "a leave of absence" for two years. Letters dealing with the group life insurance of Gilpatric and his secretary, Anne Hatfield, were written by an official of Post & Kurtz, a New York insurance broker, to Percy A. Hartwell, of the Cravath, Swaine & Moore law firm on January 30, 1961. This correspondence stated that the insurance firms were willing to continue the coverage while Gilpatric and Miss Hatfield were at the Pentagon.

Each of three insurance firms dealing with the group coverage agreed to extend the coverage to Gilpatric and Miss Hatfield "during their leaves of absence to serve in the Defense Department.

"If either Mr. Gilpatric or Miss Hatfield should leave the Defense Department and not return to the service of Cravath, Swaine & Moore, their insurance will, of course, be cancelled," the Aetna Insurance Company warned. "Furthermore, if their leaves should continue beyond two years the matter of further continuation should be referred to us."

The letters made it appear that Gilpatric was simply on a temporary "leave of absence" that would extend no more than two years. However, he insisted that the correspondence represented some misunderstanding or mistake by subordinate clerical help in the Cravath, Swaine & Moore law firm. Gilpatric maintained he had "resigned," and that there was no doubt of this in his oral agreements with other senior partners of the law firm.

The evidence challenging Gilpatric's contention he had "resigned" came into the hearing on November 19 and 20, 1963—two days before the assassination of President Kennedy. The tragic death of President Kennedy shocked the country and made it impossible to continue the TFX hearings.

The Justice Department lawyers by their letters, and later by their lack of interest, cleared Gilpatric and Korth of any law violations, but the activities of the two men certainly appeared to many in Congress to violate the new code of ethics that President Kennedy had so proudly set forth in 1961.

Defense Secretary McNamara said he knew all the facts on both the Gilpatric and Korth cases, and he insisted that he saw no conflict of interest or other impropriety. What McNamara said was the law of the Pentagon, and Gilpatric remained as Deputy Secretary of Defense until January 9, 1964, when he returned to the law firm of Cravath, Swaine & Moore as a senior partner. His continued high standing with McNamara and President Johnson was attested by his appointment by the President in September, 1964, to a high-level Committee on Nuclear Proliferation, a Presidential task force established to study means of preventing the spread of nuclear weapons.

In the face of the decisions on Gilpatric and Korth, McNamara went ahead with his plans to build the TFX at the Texas-based General Dynamics plant. He stayed with the decision even as the costs soared nearly a billion dollars beyond the high bid that General Dynamics had submitted. There were dozens of development problems, including increases in weight that Admiral Anderson and others had warned might make the plane too heavy for use on the carriers. There was also Air Force dissatisfaction because the speed and maneuverability of the plane did not represent the substantial improvement over the F-4H plane then in use. However, Defense Secretary McNamara had made his decision on the General Dynamics version of the TFX, and the renamed F-111A (Air Force version) and the F-111B (Navy version) were going into production regardless of the opposition in the Pentagon and in Congress. And, in addition, when he finally agreed to a follow-on plane to replace the B-52 bomber, McNamara rammed through a revamped TFX—the FB-111—as his candidate for the new bomber fleet. Congress and the Pentagon grumbled, but finally accepted and funded the FB-111, for McNamara had made it clear that they would have the FB-111 or nothing.

McNamara did it in the face of military testimony and a House Armed Services Committee report that stated the FB-111 did not have the range, the bomb-carrying capacity or the general performance to carry out properly the missions of the B-58 or late model B-52 bombers.

Reports of scandalously high costs of the TFX project leaked out in the fall of 1966, and they renewed Chairman John L. McClellan's interest in complete exposure of McNamara's multibillion-dollar blunder. In awarding the contract, McNamara had indicated that the cost for each plane would be a whopping $2.8 million. In fact, the costs had skyrocketed to more than $6 million for each plane by the summer of 1966, and there were indications that the much-bungled Navy version might run as high as $9 or $10 million each.

In a Senate speech on August 16, 1966, Chairman McClellan announced a new intensified investigation and asked the General Accounting Office for help in breaking the secrecy that McNamara had used to bar Congress from the full facts on the TFX fiasco.

"We seek nothing except to get the truth," McClellan told the Senate. "Congress and the people of this country are entitled to know the truth." [11]

By this time McClellan had the support of many others in Congress who were questioning the credibility of Secretary McNamara on many things and who doubted his judgment as well.

Pentagon secrecy had covered the details of costs, progress and performance on the F-111 warplanes, and frustrated the efforts of the McClellan Permanent Investigating Subcommittee. Defense Secretary McNamara exhibited the same reluctance to make detailed information on the F-111 costs and performance available to the Senate and House Armed Services Committees. Although there were periodic complaints and almost constant grumbling about McNamara's refusal to provide information for Congress, he rode through more than five years without a serious challenge to his exercise of the broadest arbitrary authority. The showdown was likely in early 1967.

30

KILLING THE NUCLEAR CARRIER

CONGRESS had taken the initiative in the early 1950's and had prodded the Defense Department into development of a nuclear-powered submarine. The program was begun in 1951 under the direction of Vice Admiral Hyman Rickover, and the highly successful start resulted in the launching of the *Nautilus* submarine on January 21, 1954, the first to be powered by nuclear energy.

In the period from 1954 to 1959, the Navy moved forward with construction of three nuclear surface warships, the aircraft carrier *U.S.S. Enterprise,* the cruiser *U.S.S. Long Beach* and the destroyer *U.S.S. Bainbridge.* The success of the nuclear-powered surface warships made the Navy eager to build more surface ships, including a carrier: the then unnamed CVA-67.

Defense Secretary Robert S. McNamara had rejected all starts on new construction of surface warships in his first two years in office, and he was cool to a nuclear-powered carrier on the grounds of cost.

In April, 1962, members of the Joint Committee on Atomic Energy boarded the newly commissioned *Enterprise* for a demonstration of the operations of the first nuclear-powered carrier. Highly enthusiastic following that experience, a few months later they had an even more solid base for their enthusiasm. The *Enterprise* took part in the blockade of Cuba during the Cuban crisis in October, 1962, and the reports on the nuclear carrier's performance were better than anticipated.

Rear Admiral J. T. Hayward, Commander, Carrier Division Two of the Atlantic Fleet, was fully convinced of the great military advantage of a nuclear fleet. In a letter[1] to the then Navy Secretary Fred Korth, Admiral Hayward declared:

"My experience in *Enterprise* to date has convinced me more than ever that the military advantage of nuclear propulsion in surface combatant ships more than outweighs their extra cost.

"I wish that others who so easily dismiss the admitted advantages of nuclear power as not being worth the cost could have shared our experience during the past two months on the Cuban blockade," Admiral Hayward wrote. "*Enterprise* outperforms every carrier in the fleet. Her planes are easier and cheaper to maintain and are combat-ready more of the time because they are not subject to the corrosive attack of stack gases. They can fly more missions because much of the space normally used for fuel oil tankage is available for ammunition and jet fuel. The rugged reliability designed and built into her propulsion plant gives her a sustained high-speed and ever-ready maneuvering rate that greatly enhances air operations The absence of boiler uptakes has allowed the arrangement of communication and radar systems superior to those on any other carrier. In Washington these often cited advantages of nuclear propulsion seem to get lost in a shuffle of paper—off Cuba they were real.

"I think the Cuban crisis made all of us do a lot more thinking about how we will fare in war," Admiral Hayward continued. "On blockade duty our conventional escorts were usually refueled every other day. Protecting that oil supply train under air and submarine attack would have been tough enough right here in our own backyard—in advanced areas the problem will be magnified manifold."

He stated that the advantages of a nuclear carrier "will be even greater when we have learned how to fully exploit nuclear power and have nuclear-powered escorts that can keep up with the tremendous capability of this ship."

Admiral Hayward related that over the years he had seen many programs pushed with what seemed "endless documentation . . . cost comparisons, promises, and often sheer propaganda.

"Many times we have spent large sums only to achieve illusory gains that weren't really there. More than once a whole program has slipped into nothing after vast expenditures.

"I have learned, often through bitter experience, that real improvements in our hardware are only made through building and evaluating in service," he said, adding that the nuclear carrier had been through the test and that nuclear surface warships should be pushed "in order to continue making improvements.

"To maintain fleets at sea against the hostile forces that are sure to oppose us will require every technological advantage we can possibly muster," Admiral Hayward said. "I am deeply disturbed that we are not exploiting to the fullest the technological advantage we hold in the nuclear propulsion that has been gained through such great effort."

Admiral Rickover declared that the way to reduce costs on the nuclear propulsion plants was to start building more nuclear surface ships. He cited the improvements that had been made in nuclear submarines through the multiple production, and said he believed comparable advances would be made as more nuclear surface ships were constructed.

Admiral Rickover pointed out that the *Enterprise,* the first nuclear-propelled carrier, was put in service faster than two conventional carriers. One of those carriers had been started a year before the *Enterprise* and the other two years earlier.[2]

Senator John Pastore, the Rhode Island Democrat who headed the Joint Committee on Atomic Energy, was in favor of an immediate decision to make the CVA-67 a nuclear carrier. The members of his committee unanimously favored nuclear propulsion as providing "significant military advantages for surface warships." [3]

Dr. Glenn T. Seaborg, Chairman of the Atomic Energy Commission, had written Defense Secretary McNamara in January, 1963, summarizing the progress made since the *Enterprise* was completed in the area of increased performance and cost reduction in nuclear propulsion plants. He urged that McNamara expand the use of nuclear propulsion in future surface warships.[4] There were equally glowing reports on the performance of the nuclear surface ships from dozens of persons in the Defense Department and from experts in the field of nuclear power. Pastore and other members of his committee were concerned over the long delays in a decision by McNamara on the recommendations that the CVA-67 be nuclear-powered, and they were shocked to read newspaper reports in the first week of October, 1963, indicating that McNamara had already decided against nuclear propulsion in the new carrier.

On October 9, 1963, Chairman Pastore wrote to McNamara calling his attention to the published reports and reiterating the committee's concern over the lack of information on plans for utilizing nuclear power, and informing him that he planned hearings on the subject.

On that same day, Defense Secretary McNamara sent a memorandum to Navy Secretary Korth directing him to proceed with construction of a conventionally powered carrier.

The next day, Navy Secretary Korth requested that the decision against a nuclear carrier be reconsidered.

On October 11, 1963, Deputy Defense Secretary Gilpatric wrote to Chairman Pastore and informed him that, contrary to press reports, a final decision with respect to the type of propulsion to be installed in the new carrier had not yet been made, and that the Department would be happy to cooperate in the committee hearings.[5]

Only a few days before the hearings started the Defense Secretary made available the copies of correspondence and memorandums that revealed that he had actually directed that a conventional carrier be started on October 9.

There was some irritation about what was considered a deceptive, or at least misleading, reply indicating that no decision had been made to scuttle the nuclear carrier. As the Joint Committee on Atomic Energy opened its hearings on October 30, 1963, Representative Chet Holifield (Dem., Cal.), vice chairman of the committee, reminded members that they had gone through the same problem eight or nine years earlier in forcing the Defense Department to proceed with the nuclear submarine program.

Chairman Pastore commented that it appeared to him that McNamara's October 9 decision "was deliberately done to foreclose this committee from carrying out its responsibilities.

"Now the only way you can cure this is by reversal, which is always much harder to do," Pastore told Korth and added: "You might never have had the *Nautilus* if it hadn't been for this committee—and I think Admiral Rickover will substantiate that statement."

"It was this committee that forced the construction of the *Nautilus,* sir," Admiral Rickover said. "Even after our success with the *Nautilus,* the Navy did not want to build additional nuclear-powered submarines. It was the Joint Committee that forced more nuclear submarines." [6]

The testimony was solidly in favor of a nuclear carrier, from Admiral David L. McDonald, Chief of Naval Operations, through Navy Secretary Korth, and on down. Admiral McDonald declared that the operational experiences with the *Enterprise, Long Beach* and *Bainbridge* "combine to offer promises of improved military capabilities beyond our most optimistic expectations.

"The military advantages demonstrated thus far, together with those which we confidently expect in the future, make it most desirable for us to proceed with the introduction of nuclear power into naval surface ships as rapidly as our budget will permit," Admiral McDonald said. "In this connection, the long-range fiscal implications promise savings in the eventual reduction of oil storage, fleet oilers, and related logistic economies."

However, Admiral McDonald knew the rules of the game. He had been named Chief of Naval Operations to replace Admiral George Anderson, who was dropped after he gave testimony that sharply challenged Secretary of Defense McNamara's decision on the TFX contract. While stating his personal preference for a nuclear carrier, he added: "We accept the Secretary of Defense's decision that it shall be conventionally propelled and concur in his belief that we must get on with the construction of this ship with minimum delay." [7]

Representative Melvin Price (Dem., Ill.) fired the next question at Secretary Korth and Admiral McDonald: "Mr. Secretary and Admiral McDonald, both of you in your statement referred to accepting the decision of the Secretary of Defense in order to avoid delay."

"Yes, sir," Korth acknowledged.

"What would be the cause of delay in the event the Secretary had determined this would be a nuclear-powered carrier?" Price asked.

"If he had determined, Congressman Price, that this was to be a nuclear carrier, we could proceed with dispatch," Korth replied. "We were unwilling to delay for further study of six months or any indeterminable time into the future a decision on whether it was to be nuclear or conventional."

"Then what would cause the delay?" Representative Price pressed to pin the responsibility.

"Only in presenting further facts to the Secretary of Defense to convince him that nuclear propulsion is a more appropriate means of propulsion than conventional," Navy Secretary Korth answered.[8]

Admiral Rickover testified that the Atomic Energy Commission had been working on the development of the four-reactor propulsion plant for more than three years, and declared it was definitely ready to be used in the new aircraft carrier. He stated the Navy should insist on the best propulsion system available in each major warship constructed, for the ships themselves would last twenty to thirty years and would serve as "a platform" for many new types of weapons systems in that period.

"In my opinion it is foolhardy to put in a propulsion plant which you have today when you know something else is better," Rickover said. "If you are thinking twenty or thirty years from now, you cannot afford to put in obsolete equipment." [9]

When McNamara was called as witness, he conceded the effectiveness of a nuclear-powered carrier, but contended that such a choice would not strengthen us in relation to the Russians. "I say this because with the total force we have available we are, in our opinion, completely protected against Soviet military and political pressure and we don't need additional forces." [10]

Would our potential enemies discontinue their attempts to improve their capabilities over, under and on the sea? The Joint Committee members did not believe so. They reasoned that it is foolhardy to rely on conventional power in a carrier that is supposed to be in use for years, and members concluded that construction of a conventionally powered carrier would "create an intolerable peril to our national security."

Committee members charged that the Defense Secretary was misinformed as to the performance advantages and the cost of a nuclear-powered carrier. McNamara gave the committee cost figures indicating that nuclear warships would cost about two and a half times as much as conventional ships. The comparison was based on the costs of the first nuclear ships, the carrier *Enterprise,* the cruiser *Long Beach,* and the frigate *Bainbridge.*

In its report, the committee challenged McNamara: "The fact is that on a comparable basis these nuclear-powered ships cost less than fifty percent more than they would have cost had they been conventionally powered." Although precise figures were difficult to pry from McNamara, finally he was pinned down to a price of $440.4 million for the nuclear-powered ship as against $277.2 million for the conventional carrier.

The nuclear carrier figure was padded with costs not included in the conventional carrier, the Joint Committee pointed out: "The Department of Defense overestimated the cost of nuclear propulsion for the surface ships. . . . For example, it was claimed that a nuclear-propelled carrier would be capable of carrying an additional squadron of aircraft. The purchase and operation costs [$37,400,000] of the additional aircraft squadron were charged to the nuclear-propelled ship and used as a cost argument against nuclear propulsion. This nearly tripled the extra cost attributed to the nuclear carrier over its lifetime. Obviously, the additional costs are not related to nuclear propulsion and can be eliminated by not supplying the additional squadron of aircraft."

In fact, the Navy witnesses had testified that their plans included the same number of aircraft for both the conventional and the nuclear carrier. The extra capacity on the nuclear carrier was simply there if it was needed.

The Joint Committee pointed out: "Also, in the construction of cost comparison, the initial reactor cores [$32,000,000] which provide fuel for at least seven years, were charged against the cost of the nuclear carrier while no comparable fuel costs were attributed to the conventional carrier." [11]

Some of Mr. McNamara's famous "cost effectiveness" studies were used by the Defense Department to support a contention that nuclear propulsion in surface warships had no significant advantage. The Joint Committee on Atomic Energy charged that these comparisons contained a "fundamental weakness" that destroyed their validity:

"The comparisons cited [by McNamara] were based on the assumption that in wartime, logistic support forces will be able to operate unhampered and without losses as they do in peacetime. The defect in this analysis is immediately apparent."

The Joint Committee spelled out the problem of maintaining fuel lines in wartime for conventional ships, while nuclear ships do not have to return to a base or meet an oiler for a continuing fuel supply.

"We must plan for time of crisis," the Joint Committee warned. "It is precisely in such situations that the superior mobility, maneuverability and reliability of nuclear warships will give the United States an unequaled striking force. It is fundamentally illogical and wasteful to fit our new first line warships with power plants that are perhaps, already, obsolete." [12]

The committee stated that if proper comparable costs were employed, the lifetime cost of the nuclear carrier, with all its aircraft, was only about three percent more than the lifetime cost of the conventional carrier and its aircraft.

"It is apparent that the increased cost of nuclear power is not significant in relation to its demonstrated military advantages," the Joint Committee declared in a unanimous report.[13]

When McNamara was asked why he did not buy the best and most advanced aircraft carrier, he replied: "We don't buy the best there is in terms of technology in one of our weapons systems.

"We would be fools," he continued. "No one does. . . . We would be foolish if we bought the best . . . in terms of speed and range and firepower, when we don't need it. . . . We should buy only what we need and what we need is usable effective combat power." [14]

In the sharpest disagreement with McNamara, the committee warned that "our first line of naval striking force [major warships] should be the best that our technology will allow and should, therefore, have nuclear propulsion, even if a somewhat higher cost is incurred to pay for the increase in military capability."

In an obvious personal thrust at McNamara, the Joint Committee warned: "Our potential enemies may not use the same cost effective criteria and thus will oppose us with the best weapons technology can provide."

What authorities, technical or military, backed McNamara and advised him to decide against nuclear propulsion in the new carrier? The Defense Secretary testified he had talked with Navy Secretary Fred Korth; Admiral David McDonald, Chief of Naval Operations; Captain Vincent P. dePoix, former commanding officer of the *U.S.S. Enterprise*; Dr. Glenn T. Seaborg, Chairman of the Atomic Energy Commission; and Vice Admiral Hyman G. Rickover, manager, Naval Reactors, Division of Reactor Development.

"All of the above mentioned persons testified to the committee that they had recommended that the new aircraft carrier be equipped with nuclear propulsion," the Joint Committee recounted in its report.

Even Dr. Harold Brown, Director of Defense Research and Engineering and usually a McNamara supporter, conceded that all the military and technical men he knew of "have taken an unequivocal position that there is no question at all about it that nuclear-propelled surface ships are much superior and have tremendous military advantages over conventional" ships.[15]

Then Dr. Brown tried to straddle the dispute by stating that there was a "cost effectiveness" factor that had to be taken into account by the Defense Secretary. "A Cadillac is better than a Chevrolet," Dr. Brown noted. "It costs more, too. And nuclear power costs more than nonnuclear power."

While declaring that he personally thought immediate construction of a nuclear carrier is "the right way to go," he tried to avoid a break with McNamara by adding, "I haven't seen any proof."[16]

"What better proof can we have than Captain [Eugene] Wilkinson [of the *Long Beach*], Captain [Raymond E.] Peet [of the *Bainbridge*], Captain [Vincent P.] dePoix [of the *Enterprise*]," declared Chairman Pastore. "They were there."

Senator Bourke B. Hickenlooper, the highest-ranking Republican on the Joint Committee, injected that under the "cost" arguments used by McNamara, "it would not cost as much to build the old wooden frigates, sailing vessels.

"The purpose of a carrier is to be used in time of emergency in war," Senator Hickenlooper said. "It is not a yacht for pleasure purposes in peacetime. . . . It seems to me that in this ship construction we are not building ships merely for pleasurable peacetime operations, with a microscope on costs exactly. We are building it against the time when we might need it in a war emergency and then we had better have the best one we can get."

With regard to the ability to build a nuclear carrier, Senator Hickenlooper commented that "we have had a vast amount of knowledge, far more knowledge than we ever had when we built the *Nautilus* and the first atomic-powered ships.

"I am not impressed with these continuing studies," the Iowa Republican said, expressing the unanimous view of the Joint Committee that it was time McNamara started building another nuclear carrier.[17]

McNamara "cited two authorities supporting his view," but the Joint Committee discredited both these so-called experts.

"The first was a flag officer from another service who had recommended that we not build any aircraft carrier," the Joint Committee said. "When it was suggested that perhaps this officer, being of another service, was not fully qualified to speak on this matter, the Secretary defended the officer as having broad military experience and judgment in other matters. The advice of this officer, however, was apparently rejected since the Secretary stated that he personally thought we should build more aircraft carriers and that plans are being made to build a new aircraft carrier."[18]

The Joint Committee noted parenthetically: "The Secretary of Defense did not indicate whether the . . . officer concerned had expressed any opinion on whether the new carrier should have nuclear or conventional propulsion, once it had been decided a carrier of some type would be built." This was hardly the support McNamara had indicated it was.

The other authority cited by McNamara was a report by the Center for Naval Analyses. McNamara said that the Naval Analyses study indicated there was nothing "to show that the nuclear power forces are superior to conventional forces of equal cost."

The Joint Committee said that this report by the Center for Naval Analyses was rejected by the Navy as being based on "erroneous assumption." The report, the Navy said, "clearly does not represent Navy views, opinion and findings on nuclear propulsion."

Putting it bluntly, the only analysis McNamara relied upon in questioning the value of nuclear-powered forces was regarded by the Navy as without substance. But there was an even more interesting aspect of McNamara's method of operating.

Under questioning by the Joint Committee, McNamara admitted he had not read the erroneous report before making the decision against the nuclear-powered carrier. He had come across it while making preparation for the hearings in which he was to try to defend his decision. Even as the Defense Secretary quoted the Center for Naval Analyses study as his authority, he admitted he "had not made any thorough study of it all."

"What is the conclusion?" Chairman Pastore asked, trying to pin McNamara down on his reasoning on the discredited study.

"I haven't read it all because I just got it," McNamara admitted.

"You had it when you made your decision?" Pastore asked.

"No," McNamara replied. "I didn't. . . . I glanced through it very quickly last Saturday when I first received this." [19]

In its report, the Joint Committee drove home the point on McNamara's lack of any real support: "In summary, the committee still does not know of any qualified technical person or group who recommended to the Defense Department that nuclear propulsion not be installed in the new aircraft carrier." [20]

Again it appeared to be McNamara's rough judgment against the technical experts and the military men. With all the opinions and facts against him, Robert S. McNamara made the decision that the United States should not go ahead with a nuclear carrier.

A McNamara decision, in McNamara's view, needed no competent studies to support it. Nor did he think it necessary to have technical advice or military expertise. The Defense Secretary made his own decisions and his own declaration on whether his decisions were sound. His claims of possible savings sounded good at the White House and seemed sound enough to many magazine writers and editorial writers who were uncritical members of the McNamara fan club.

A few writers of stature, such as Hanson Baldwin, Pulitzer-Prize military analyst for *The New York Times,* wrote of their grave misgivings about McNamara's claims of great savings and great efficiency. Baldwin cited the McNamara decision against the nuclear carrier, and pointed to testimony by Admiral Rickover that criticized the Defense Secretary's office for asking for "more studies, [and] more analyses; to the point that we don't build ships." [21] One of the cost studies that McNamara wasn't talking about was to demonstrate how seriously he had blundered in deciding against the nuclear carrier.

On May 5, 1965, Representative William H. Bates (Rep., Mass.) told the House that according to Department of Defense cost studies, a conventional carrier is more expensive than a nuclear carrier when the cost of oilers and protection for oilers are figured into the analysis. "This is borne out," he told his colleagues, "in a detailed classified analysis submitted to the Joint Committee on Atomic Energy on January 13, 1965 by the Assistant Secretary of Defense, Mr. Charles J. Hitch."

This study shot holes in the cost argument—the only argument McNamara had made in defense of killing nuclear power for the new carrier. By mid-1965, however, it was too late to correct McNamara's multimillion-dollar blunder. The construction of the carrier, now named the *U.S.S. John F. Kennedy,* had progressed so far as a conventional carrier that it would have been pointless to try to convert it to nuclear power. Figures submitted to the House Armed Services Committee by the Defense Department indicated that conversion of the *U.S.S. John F. Kennedy* in 1965 would cost an additional $157,-800,000 and would delay the completion of the carrier at least a year.

Representative Mendel Rivers (Dem., S.C.), chairman of the House Armed Services Committee, called McNamara's decision for a conventional carrier "an error in judgment." With regret he reported that Admiral Rickover, though an early and leading supporter of nuclear propulsion, "now feels that the progress on the *U.S.S. John F. Kennedy* now makes conversion to nuclear power too expensive."

Representative Chet Holifield, vice chairman of the Joint Committee on Atomic Energy, in an exchange of letters with Rivers pointed out that "the only new surface warship authorized for our naval striking force in the 1963, 1964, 1965 and 1966 programs is the aircraft carrier . . . the *U.S.S. John F. Kennedy*." The California Democrat, usually an Administration supporter, termed it "a costly mistake for this great ship to be built with conventional propulsion." But the damage had been done, and the *U.S.S. John F. Kennedy* was destined to travel the seas in the nuclear age dependent upon fuel from a fleet of oilers—an "obsolete" monument to the McNamara reign at the Pentagon.

In the fall of 1964, the world's first nuclear-powered task force—the aircraft carrier *Enterprise,* the guided-missile cruiser *Long Beach,* and the guided-missile frigate *Bainbridge*—made an historic 30,000-mile cruise around the world without logistic support of any kind.

Chairman Mendel Rivers[22] declared that this cruise, named Operation Sea Orbit, proved conclusively "the feasibility of operating nuclear surface ships throughout the oceans of the world on a self-sustaining basis." He declared that this operation independent of support ships is "a feat out of the question for conventionally powered ships."

In a speech at Mare Island, California, on October 23, 1965, the House Armed Services Committee Chairman spoke of the "logjam of disinterest" that the Congress had found in seeking wider use of nuclear power for a surface fleet.

Recalling that Congress had forced action to build the two first nuclear submarines, the *U.S.S. Nautilus* and *U.S.S. Seawolf,* the South Carolina Democrat declared:

"Today history is repeating itself—Congress has had to take the initiative to overcome the reluctance of the Department of Defense to use nuclear propulsion in new surface warships. . . . Congress this year authorized construction of the fifth nuclear powered surface warship—a guided missile frigate [the *Truxton*]. This nuclear powered ship was added to this year's Defense Department authorization even though the Secretary of Defense had overruled a Navy proposal to build such a ship.

"We reject the idea that we must not build nuclear powered surface warships because we could build more conventional ships with the same money," Rivers said. "There is a real danger in continuing to produce ineffectual cost effectiveness studies to justify decisions affecting our national security," Rivers warned. He emphasized that we must be prepared at the outset of any modern war, and emphasized:

"When a war starts, we must fight with what we have—not with equipment still on the drawing boards or in the minds of men. You will recall that the aircraft used throughout World War II had been designed prior to the war. Remember that it takes years to produce military equipment from the drawing board. For example, it takes four or five years to build an aircraft carrier. We may not be fortunate enough to have such time available in the future."

Under the prodding of the Joint Committee on Atomic Energy and the Senate and House Armed Services Committees, Defense Secretary McNamara had indicated that it was highly probable he would request funds for another new carrier in 1966 and that it would be a nuclear carrier.

"A nuclear powered carrier will appear in next year's bill when presented on the floor regardless of any foreseeable circumstances, technical, fiscal, or otherwise," Rivers declared. "We may even go further and direct that it be constructed."

Rivers said it was "startling to reflect that the Department of Defense has procured only one surface warship of destroyer size or larger for the fleet during the past four years, and this is the conventional aircraft carrier, the *John F. Kennedy,* now under construction."

Chairman Rivers and other key committee chairmen in Congress were in favor of immediate action to begin converting the entire fleet to nuclear power, but McNamara still indicated reluctance to go beyond the one new nuclear carrier; in early 1966 he showed no great enthusiasm for paying for that progress. The problem of progress on the construction of a nuclear fleet was certain to bring more tests between Congress and the Defense Secretary over a period of several years.

31

BASE CLOSINGS—MAYOR RYAN AND THE PENTAGON

BASE closings were among the most dramatic and widely publicized results of the so-called "cost effectiveness" studies of Defense Secretary Robert S. McNamara. Over a period of five years, the Pentagon press office reported closed or curtailed operations at 862 bases. McNamara claimed that his frugality in closing unneeded facilities would save the American taxpayers a minimum of $1.5 billion a year.

The first announcement of base closings was on March 30, 1961—only two months after McNamara became Defense Secretary. He claimed that the 73 actions announced in that one press release would result in savings of $220,000,000 a year. Complaints came from areas in which bases were being closed, and there was grumbling from Senators and Congressmen who either were irritated about the base closings or felt they had to go through the motions of protests for the benefit of voters in the home district. But overall, the public reaction was good. Continuing to operate old bases or unneeded bases for reasons of sentimentality or to please some local chamber of commerce made no sense.

While a few charged that the Pentagon actions were not based on sound studies, the complaints were largely lost in the chorus of cheers for a Defense Secretary who courageously insisted upon closing the bases in the face of opposition from local political pressures.

Four major announcements on base closings were made in the next five years. On December 12, 1963, McNamara announced that he was taking 33 actions to curtail military bases that would save taxpayers $100,000,000 a year. On April 24, 1964, the Defense Secretary announced another 63 actions, which he claimed would save more than $68,000,000 a year. On November 19, 1964, he announced curtailment of activities or closing of 95 bases and claimed this would save $477,000,000 a year. On December 8, 1965, McNamara's press office reported the biggest bundle of all—a total of 149 actions that he claimed would save another $410,000,000. By early 1966 a scattering of similar small announcements over the years totaled 862 base closings with savings of more than $1.5 billion a year.

Complaints grew louder and fewer cheers followed each new announcement. McNamara's claims of saving millions of dollars continued to dominate the headlines, but in many communities there were allegations that the cost figures used by the Defense Department were in error. There were charges that the estimates of savings were inflated by the Pentagon to make a more dramatic showing in the Pentagon press releases. More and more states were being hit by base closings, and there was less automatic acceptance of McNamara's claims of multimillion-dollar savings.

McNamara remained firm in the face of complaints. He refused to reverse himself, insisted his decisions were right, and protests seemed futile. In December, 1964, the Defense Secretary went right ahead with a shutdown at the Brooklyn Navy Yard in the face of protests by his old friend, Senator-elect Robert F. Kennedy, who had become a New York Democrat. It was not clear whether Senator Robert Kennedy's protest was a tough effort to prove McNamara was wrong in closing the Brooklyn Navy Yard, or merely a formality to convince his new constituents of his sincere interest in local economic conditions.

Also caught in the November, 1964, base closings was an important installation in Massachusetts, where Edward F. Kennedy served as a United States Senator. McNamara contended that he could save more than $4.6 million a year by closing out the Springfield Armory in western Massachusetts. His plan was to shut down the small-arms production lines at the old historic Springfield Armory[1] and transfer some of the small-arms research and engineering functions to Rock Island Arsenal, near Rock Island, Illinois. Closing the Army would cut more than 2,400 jobs in Springfield, a community of about 175,000 already suffering from heavy unemployment that placed it in the Labor Department's "Class E" area of "substantial unemployment." Rock Island was a "Class B" area of "low unemployment."

Mayor Charles Ryan, Jr., a thirty-seven-year-old lawyer, was concerned about the impact of the Armory closing on the community, but his initial reaction was tempered by his great admiration for the late President John F. Kennedy and Defense Secretary Robert S. McNamara. Mayor Ryan, an Irish Catholic and a Democrat, jumped into politics because of his admiration for the image of the Kennedy Administration and he had believed that McNamara represented the best of the Kennedy appointees. If real economy and the national interest dictated closing or curtailing the operations at the Springfield Armory, then Mayor Ryan wanted to live the spirit of the man who had said, "Ask not what your country can do for you. Ask what you can do for your country."

Even when men from the Springfield Armory brought information indicating that the base closing would not save the estimated $4.6 million, Mayor Ryan raised only the mildest protest. If it could be proven there was something wrong with the cost studies, then Mayor Ryan was confident that such a man as Defense Secretary McNamara would be quick to see the error and quicker to correct it. Also, he counted on the fact that Senator Edward Kennedy, who had vowed to "do more" for Massachusetts, would make certain the full facts were presented to Defense Secretary McNamara.

Within a few days, Mayor Ryan became concerned over the lack of aggressive action by Senator Kennedy, Senator Leverett Saltonstall (Rep., Mass.) and Representative Edward Boland, the Democrat who represented the Springfield district in Congress. With a group of experts from the Springfield Armory and help from a local lawyer-accountant, Henry Downey, Mayor Ryan went to work to try to prove McNamara's claim of a $4.6 million-a-year savings was wrong.

Within a few days, the young mayor was thoroughly convinced the Pentagon decision was wrong for many reasons. The Pentagon figures on cost for transferring the research and engineering personnel and facilities to Rock Island were low to the point of being absurd, according to Downey. Those estimates indicated the cost would be only about $8,000,000 while Henry Downey and the experts had figures showing that it would cost $73,000,000.

While the Pentagon had indicated a $4,600,000 savings each year, the Committee to Save the Springfield Armory came up with figures indicating maximum savings would be about $640,000 a year.

The reports McNamara had used in making the decision to close Springfield indicated that the costs for moving the research and engineering facilities to Rock Island would be absorbed in about two and one-half to three years. The figures Mayor Ryan's committee developed indicated that it would be forty-five years before the Pentagon would start to break even on the closing of the Springfield Armory.

The Springfield mayor had a great respect for McNamara's reputation as a cost expert, and he wanted no errors in the figures he hoped to present to the Defense Secretary. He and Henry Downey read the ten volumes of hearings on the TFX investigation to study the techniques the McClellan Permanent Investigating Subcommittee had used to make a clear presentation of a highly complicated subject. Downey had the cost figures examined by six other accountants.

As they dug deeper into the facts involving the decision to close the Springfield Armory, Mayor Ryan and the committee members became unalterably convinced that there was more at stake than just the economy of Springfield. As they studied the background of the decision, they arrived at the conclusion that closing such facilities and disbanding the corps of experts was indeed taking a great risk with the future security of the nation.

At some point, it appeared Defense Secretary McNamara or someone else was making a radical change in policy that could eliminate important in-house research and development and production capability in the small-arms field and in other areas as well. Past history had demonstrated that to fill the needs for ordnance matériel during an emergency, it was necessary to have an adequate system in existence at the time the emergency occurred. Private industry was perfectly willing to move in on the production of small arms and other war matériel when it was highly profitable. However, in the past private industry had refused to retain the research personnel and the production capacity on a standby basis during times of peace.

Mayor Ryan and Downey found support for their point of view in a September, 1960, report on operations of various arsenals. The then Assistant Secretary of the Army for Logistics, Courtney Johnson, made a survey[2] in which he set out his strong conviction for the necessity of preserving the Army Arsenal System.

"I am convinced that the in-house capabilities that we have are essential to the Army's role in the defense of the country," he stated in his memorandum. "It is historically obvious that we retain, by this method, capabilities during peacetime which would not and could not be maintained by industry. Industry cannot hold its own properties in standby, producing no income, and cannot pay and preserve the hard core of knowledgeable engineers, scientists, technicians, and teachers who deal specifically with military problems and products in which industry is not interested unless money is continuously available for production, thus affording the opportunity to make a profit."

Johnson pointed out that arsenal facilities, including Springfield, were operating at a low level of capacity. "Overheads, which are incurred in order to preserve for future mobilization purposes, facilities and knowledge, are charged against the small current production for the installation, thus raising materially the selling price of the items produced."

He suggested solutions through allocation of larger amounts of research and development funds to arsenal programs so that high standby costs would not be reflected in production costs. He declared that any revamping of the arsenal financing should "establish the operation of these in-house facilities on the basis that meets essential military requirements for special research, production engineering methods, pilot line operations, education and retention of scientific personnel, military production specialists, inspectors and teachers."

Johnson's program of studies on the arsenal system were lost in the confusion of 1960 election results and change of administration that brought McNamara into office as Defense Secretary. Nothing much was done until March, 1963, when the Army initiated a review of the arsenal complex that ended in a study entitled "The Future of the AMC (Army Matériel Command) Arsenal System." The Board making the study concluded that five of the ten arsenal facilities performing substantial manufacturing functions must be retained because of the clear need for research and development functions as well as manufacturing capacity.

That study suggested two of the remaining arsenals be closed with one of these to be maintained on a standby basis in case of mobilization and two receive further study before any conclusion. Retention of Springfield Armory, one of those slated for further study, in an active status was "suspect" because of what was called a general availability of comparable development and production capacity in private industry.

The Board's recommendation for further study of Springfield was followed up in February, 1964, by direction to the Army Weapons Command to find alternate methods for doing the job that Springfield Armory had been doing.[3] To Mayor Ryan and his committee members it appeared the decision to close Springfield was made prior to the study, and the directive to the Army Weapons Command was to find a way to relieve Springfield of its job so it could be closed.

At this time, there had been some buildup of forces in Vietnam and new contracts had resulted in much of the small-arms production being handled by private industry. However, Mayor Ryan and his committee noted that private industry had been able to move into small-arms manufacture quickly because of the pilot plans at Springfield and the guidance of technical experts at Springfield in establishing quality production.

Looking only at the great amount of production of small arms by private industry, the Army Weapons Command concluded that private industry could do the job of producing small arms, that Springfield could be closed, and the research and engineering functions could be transferred to Rock Island.

Mayor Ryan and his committee regarded this as a shortsighted view, for if at some future time private industry found itself unwilling to keep small-arms production on a standby basis it could mean the United States was left without an essential facility. They were enraged when they obtained a copy of a memorandum of guidelines to be used by the Army Weapons Command in its study.[4] The memorandum directed that the Army Weapons Command "establish the fact that Springfield is excess to requirement.

"This determination having been made and properly supported by facts, we will move into the next section," the memorandum continued. "Based on the foregoing alternate plans, conclusions should be drawn terminating with the conclusion that it is in the best interests of the Government to close Springfield Armory and transfer the R & E [research and engineering] functions to Rock Island."

Under such instructions there had not been much chance for Springfield to be judged on an objective basis, Mayor Ryan and his committee decided. The conclusion was stated and then the study was directed to support the preconceived conclusion. This was hardly the type of thorough, IBM-like precision that the Springfield men expected.

These circumstances would have made Mayor Ryan and others in the Springfield community suspicious of Defense Department claims of great savings even if they had not already come up with facts that clearly established that McNamara had made his decision on the basis of fallacious cost figures.

Mayor Ryan and Downey cautioned the members of the Committee to Save the Springfield Armory to take great care to avoid any slips that might be embarrassing in their presentation of the case to Senator Edward Kennedy or later to McNamara. Ryan wanted them to make certain there was solid proof behind every claim they made on the costs for moving the research and engineering from Springfield to Rock Island. He wanted the same care on all figures used to demonstrate that the Springfield Armory was an economical plant for the development and production of small arms. He directed they should "lean over backwards" to keep any questionable figures out of the studies.

The Springfield Armory—with an annual payroll of $17,000,000 and purchases of another $17,000,000 within a radius of one hundred miles—was vital to the western Massachusetts community. They couldn't afford to be wrong.

Initially, Senator Kennedy was cool to a serious challenge to McNamara's decision, but the detailed study presented by Ryan and Downey was impressive. In addition to the new cost figures, even Pentagon reports used to justify closing the Armory were filled with comments on "other considerations" that raised doubts about the wisdom of closing the facility.

At a time when the Administration was talking about a War on Poverty, the report stated that the closing of Springfield "will have a significantly adverse impact on the economy of the community." Men losing their jobs would have rights at other Defense Department installations in the Boston civil service region, but it was regarded as "very doubtful" that there would be jobs for the semi-skilled workers in the metal trades who made up the bulk of the employees soon to be thrown out of work.

In addition to the serious economic impact on Springfield, one of the principal disadvantages expected from closing the Armory was the destruction of a highly skilled small-arms development team.

"An estimated 75 percent of the skilled R & E personnel currently employed [at Springfield] would be lost through failure to transfer with their functions," the Pentagon report said. "This would hamper [small-arms] mission accomplishment for an undetermined period of time which could well exceed three years."

Other disadvantages in moving to Rock Island were set out:

"The distance of Rock Island Arsenal from the majority of commercial small arms producers [New England area] presents some rather considerable problems in monitoring commercial production particularly for pilot lot runs where close coordination between the producer and government engineering personnel is always important and sometimes critical.

"The local labor market in Rock Island, Illinois area is not particularly good for recruiting professional personnel of any type and such personnel with small arms experience is even more limited.

"Providing adequate R & E facilities comparable to those available to Springfield would be quite expensive and time consuming. Particularly, the problem of locating outdoor test facilities as free from firing restrictions as those at Camp Edwards [near Springfield] is a problem which has not yet been completely solved."

The information obtained by Mayor Ryan and Downey indicated that it would take more than five years to recruit, train, and coordinate a comparable small-arms team at Rock Island.

In the face of the facts developed by the Springfield group, Senator Kennedy arranged for a special meeting with Defense Secretary McNamara to permit his constituents to make a full explanation of the facts as revealed by their investigation and analysis.

On February 27, 1965,[5] an impressive Massachusetts delegation went to the Pentagon to brief Secretary McNamara on the reasons they believed he should reverse the decision to close the Armory. Secretary McNamara was accompanied by Deputy Secretary of Defense Cyrus Vance and Assistant Secretary of Defense Paul Ignatius. Representative Boland served as a sort of chairman for the Massachusetts group, which included Senator Kennedy, Senator Leverett Saltonstall, Massachusetts Governor John Volpe, Representative Silvio Conte, Mayor Ryan, Henry Downey and a dozen of the technical experts.

Representative Boland introduced Edmond J. Massa, Chief of the Support and Engineering Branch at Springfield, and chairman of the Springfield Armory Technical Committee. Other specialists on the committee present were Richard W. Colburn, of the Development Unit of the Production and Engineering Branch; Warren Mason, head of the Quality Assurance Division; Harry F. Lynch, Assistant Chief in Industrial Activities in Research and Engineering; Theodore J. Trudeau, of the Programs and Budget Branch in the Civilian Personnel Office; Paul E. Sullivan, Chief of the Processing Section of the Engineering Branch; Robert J. Hassett, Army Matériel Manager; Joseph M. O'Brien, Chief of the General Accounting Section; Raymond F. Kennedy, the Assistant Chief, Installations Facilities Office; and Richard Colby, Small Arms Research Engineer.

The Defense Department had only one argument for closing Springfield—it was an old facility in existence since 1794, and it was no longer economical to develop and produce small arms there.

"No one will quarrel with the policy of the Department of Defense and your responsibility to produce all the defense that our Nation needs and to procure it at the lowest possible cost," Representative Boland started the discussion. He reviewed the 170 years of performance of the Springfield Armory through World War I when the Armory was producing 1,500 rifles a day, through World War II when more than 4,000,000 of the M-1 Garands were produced, and up to the M-14 fully automatic rifle and the special weapons systems for helicopters in Vietnam.

He explained how in recent years, it was the teams of technicians from Springfield who "bailed out" private industry when trouble developed in the production of precision weapons. He castigated the Army Matériel Command and the Army Weapons Command. He declared that the Small Arms Mission Study "used the wrong computer, and came up with inaccurate figures and facts.

"They [the cost figures] will not stand up in the light of the painstaking, laborious study that we have completed," Representative Boland said. "It isn't the Springfield Armory that is suspect; it's the Small Arms Mission Study of the Springfield Armory."

Downey, a lawyer-accountant, dug into cost figures in detail; his major assault was on the $8,000,000 that the Small Arms Mission Study had estimated to be the cost of moving the research and engineering facilities from Springfield to Rock Island.

"We submit that the implementation is more like $73,000,000 for this complete close-out and move," Downey declared.

It was estimated that only about one hundred of the 2,385 employees would transfer to Rock Island with 39 percent of those left eligible for retirement after December 31, 1966.

"The cost of these forced retirements, to put these people on a side track from the time they're 54 to 65, . . . is going to be $17,-800,000 plus," Downey said, producing a statement from an actuary expert. This was one figure not taken into account on the initial determination of "cost" for moving to Rock Island.

In addition the cost of recruiting new men for the skilled jobs in Rock Island, an area where there was a known shortage of skilled labor, had not been considered. To recruit 660 technicians and engineers at a minimum of $2,000 each would represent an additional cost of $1,320,000.

Downey declared the study recommending closing of Springfield had not included any cost for training personnel at Rock Island; with specific figures for minimum training for each class of employees, he stated these training costs would exceed $9,000,000.

The cost of new machinery for establishing the research and engineering at Rock Island was set at $25,000,000, while the machinery and equipment to be disposed of in Springfield would bring no more than $2,500,000—a loss on disposal of equipment of $22,500,000, Downey explained. There would be another $10,000,000 loss sustained in the sale of the land and buildings at Springfield.

When Downey completed a most detailed explanation of these and other cost figures, Representative Boland asked Defense Secretary McNamara if he had any questions about the validity of any of the cost figures presented.

"There are some figures here which I think you would want to question, one of them being the forced-retirement cost," Boland said. "You're one of those who is going to advise the Government in respect to our problem, and the Civil Service Retirement Fund is now $40 billion in the red. Mr. Charles Brown, who is Chief Actuary for the Civil Service Retirement System, indicates that this is an item that ought to be considered in every single activity or in every single instance where any Department has closed out an activity. This is an item that should be considered and was not considered at all by the Small Arms Mission Study."

"I don't want to give you a hasty opinion on what is really a complex technical problem," Secretary McNamara replied, avoiding the opportunity to challenge the figures. He never challenged them later.

Governor Volpe, a building contractor, directed most of his comments to the "quality of the structures" at Springfield. Although the original Armory was constructed in 1794, 12 percent of the buildings had been built since 1950 and 44 percent of the structures at Springfield had been built in the last twenty-five years. He compared this with the fact that only 2 percent of the buildings at Rock Island had been constructed since 1950, and only 16 percent had been built in the last twenty-five years.

The Massachusetts Governor declared that when 84 percent of the buildings at Rock Island are more than twenty-five years old and only 56 percent of the buildings at Springfield are more than twenty-five years old, one of the reasons for wanting to move from Springfield to Rock Island—the antiquity of the buildings at Springfield—was demolished.

For the same reason he compared the 12-year-old test-firing facility at Springfield with the 88-year-old test-firing structure at Rock Island.

Governor Volpe declared that the loss of jobs would be "a catastrophe" for Massachusetts in an area where unemployment was high and the state was "trying desperately to keep the industry we have." He pointed out that billions were being appropriated for the anti-poverty program, while the Springfield closing seems "to make some poverty here."

Mayor Ryan touched the other points, but he stressed the service the Springfield Armory provided to small business firms in starting small-arms production. He pointed out specific examples of the "quality control" function of the Springfield Armory technical teams in checking production of private industry to make certain that weapons delivered to fighting men were not defective.

The Springfield mayor also stressed that 7 percent of the families in Springfield had annual incomes of less than $2,000 a year, and additional 15 percent had annual incomes of between $2,000 and $4,000 a year and 10,000 individuals were receiving some form of public assistance.

Senator Saltonstall declared that the purpose of the Defense Department study in 1964 appeared to be "to present facts to your Department which could support the contention that it was to be closed." The soft-spoken Massachusetts Senator said it was like "sentencing the accused before he's brought to trial."

By this time Senator Edward Kennedy said he believed the issue had been "decided wrongly" and that "it would actually be in the interest of the Defense Department as well as the State of Massachusetts and the City of Springfield to keep the Arsenal operating." He was strongly critical of "the errors we believe the Army made" in the cost figures, and put his emphasis on the economy involved in keeping the Armory with its small-arms experts in New England near the areas where small-arms industries are located.

"What you intend to do is try to accomplish this function from the Middle West," Kennedy said. "This will involve far greater travel expense for personnel . . . and we're just not going to provide the kind of services that the Springfield Armory provides today."

The young Massachusetts Democrat pointed out that "Springfield is now doing the research and development job on ten [weapons] subsystems for helicopters to be used in Vietnam.

"This team is doing very important work," Kennedy said. "The only way to keep this team going is to keep the team at Springfield."

Senator Kennedy declared that Springfield had an expert team in being and said "the trend in recent years has been to locate the Government facilities where the contractors are and where the skilled workers are.

"This decision goes the other way," Kennedy said. He declared that "times are too perilous" for cutting back the Armory and asked that McNamara make a personal visit to Springfield.

When the technical experts had concluded, McNamara praised the presentation as "magnificent" and added that "because it was so thorough and so extensive it deserves far more than the superficial opinion that I could give it at the present time."

He said he would personally review Army cost figures that the Springfield team challenged, and promised a personal visit to Springfield before arriving at a final decision.

The Defense Department conducted some review of the cost figures and on March 17, 1965, McNamara made a visit to Springfield. Mayor Ryan and the local committee expected McNamara would then either challenge the cost figures they had presented or would reverse the decision to close the Armory. He did neither. He made no mention of the original Defense Department study that had been the basis for the November, 1964, decision to close the Armory. Instead, he made a hurried survey of the Springfield Armory facilities and then told Mayor Ryan and the committee that he would like to keep the Armory open but just couldn't do it in the light of excessive costs for production. The Defense Secretary indicated that he had studies showing that arms produced at Springfield cost one hundred to two hundred percent more than those purchased from private industry. He would be willing to pay up to a 25 percent difference because of the research and engineering facilities at Springfield, but could not justify paying one hundred to two hundred percent above private industry.

Immediately he was challenged by Mayor Ryan and Downey. They admitted they did not have precise studies on this subject, but said that they did not believe Springfield was that much more expensive than private industry. They asked if he would leave the facility open if it could be proved that arms could be produced for about the same price as private industry, and McNamara indicated that such proof would induce him to change his mind.

In this instance it took only a few days for Mayor Ryan, Downey and their committee to produce figures showing that arms cost at Springfield were comparable to private industry and in some cases were lower if bonuses paid to some private manufacturers were taken into account.

By the time the Springfield committee had relayed the results of their study to McNamara, he had declared that the entire armory matter was so complicated that he would hire a private management firm to do a study for him. The firm he selected was Booz, Allen & Hamilton,[6] a consulting firm that was to a large extent dependent upon the Defense Department and defense contractors for business. It was also actively engaged in trying to obtain more small-arms business from the Defense Department for one of its subsidiary organizations.

Initially, Mayor Ryan and his committee members liked the idea of a management consultant firm. Later they became suspicious and informed Senator Kennedy, Senator Saltonstall and Representative Boland that they believed that this constituted a "conflict of interest." How could Booz, Allen & Hamilton be objective if the firm was actively interested in obtaining more small-arms business?

However, as they were bemoaning the selection of Booz, Allen & Hamilton, the escalation of the Vietnam war made it appear that the

Springfield Armory would be sorely needed. The Armory was flooded with orders for small arms and helicopter weapons systems needed in Vietnam, and some of them were top-priority requirements. It was hoped the crisis created by the escalation in Vietnam might jolt the Defense Department into reversing its decision to close the Armory, but such was not the case.

On November 16, 1965, the Springfield community received what McNamara said was to be his final word on the subject. The Armory was to be closed. McNamara directed that all activities at Springfield be "phased out over the next two and a half years."

"Reaffirming a decision announced on November 19, 1964, the Secretary has ordered the facility to be closed and reported to the General Services Administration [for disposition] by April 1968," the press release said.[7]

McNamara cited three paragraphs from the study by Booz, Allen & Hamilton. He said the company concluded:

"The long-range retention of the Springfield Armory for the acquisition of small arms weapons and weapons systems is neither necessary nor desirable."

McNamara said the consultants had recommended: "The Springfield Armory not be retained as an active installation in the Defense Establishment."

There was nothing about errors in the first Defense Department cost figures. There was nothing about what was regarded as a McNamara promise to keep the Armory open if it could prove it could produce at about the same price as private industry. In fact, the text of the Booz, Allen & Hamilton report was initially kept confidential by the Defense Department.

When Mayor Ryan's committee finally obtained access to a copy, they were amazed to find that it stated that the actual costs of manufacture for the Armory and for small-arms industrial contractors are about the same for all practical purposes. That major point supported their case, Mayor Ryan and Downey said.

Looking further they found that the study revealed that the proposed move on nonmanufacturing functions from Springfield to Rock Island "is distinctly marginal from a savings-cost standpoint," and that the transfer involved some risk in destroying the ability to perform the research and engineering functions necessary to the Armory small-arms mission.

As Representative Boland examined the case he concluded that the Defense Department had given the Booz, Allen & Hamilton firm such guidelines that it would have been impossible to come to any conclusion except to close Springfield. The Defense Secretary had asked the management consultant firm if private industry could do the complete job in small arms so that Springfield would not be needed.

In a memorandum to Representative Mendel Rivers (Dem., S.C.) Representative Boland asked that the House Armed Services Committee conduct an investigation of the entire decision to close down the Springfield Armory. He outlined the whole case from the first "fallacious" cost studies used by the Defense Department through the whole "incongruous affair."

At the same time, Senator Saltonstall asked that the Senate Preparedness Subcommittee conduct a thorough investigation of those aspects of the Springfield Armory decision that might be related to shortages in Vietnam or in our Army combat divisions in other parts of the world.

On March 22, 1966, Chairman Stennis[8] opened hearings on the Springfield Armory closing as part of the overall investigation of Army readiness.

"That [Springfield] installation has long had an important and substantial role in small arms development and production," Chairman Stennis said. "We need to know what impact the loss of its capability will have upon our future national defense programs in the small arms field and whether the resources and capabilities which it now represents can adequately be provided by private industry or other sources."

Senator Kennedy[9] criticized the "completely new concept" of military preparedness by which "total reliance should be placed on private industry to develop and produce" all small arms in the future.

It was with reluctance that he criticized McNamara's "lack of wisdom" in instituting a new policy that he said "presents a possible threat to our national security."

The young Massachusetts Democrat declared that the original Defense Department contentions of a large savings in closing Springfield had been met with "a thorough rebuttal." Also, he pointed up that even the Booz, Allen & Hamilton report "showed that manufacturing costs at the Armory were identical with the costs of private industry.

"Furthermore, it showed that relocation of the Armory's non-manufacturing functions would result in distinctly marginal cost savings," Senator Kennedy said.

He charged that the Defense Department had "decided to scuttle our arsenal system and hope that private industry's initiative and sense of responsibility will insure that continued development and production of weapons."

Senator Kennedy declared that the new policy "seems founded upon ignorance of the past and false hopes for the future.

"It is unwise to evaluate the capacity of private industry on the basis of its current efforts because Springfield Armory personnel helped these industries set up their production lines," Senator Kennedy explained. "Weapons like the M-79 grenade launcher, M-6 helicopter system and the M-60 machine gun are crucial in our Vietnam effort, but without the assistance of the Springfield Armory private industry could not be producing them.

"Ironically, the Springfield Armory is also currently producing weapons for which no private industrial capacity exists and for which no private industry has shown interest. Examples of these weapons are the M-75 grenade launcher and the M-73 and M-85 machine guns. These weapons are needed in Vietnam."

Senator Kennedy's theme was hit time after time with new examples and with new force by Senator Saltonstall, Representative Boland and Representative Silvio Conte,[10] a Massachusetts Republican.

"To proceed with this action [to close Springfield], if there is the remotest possibility that in so doing we will short change the men who are fighting . . . in Vietnam, . . . will be to commit the grossest kind of betrayal," Representative Conte said. "Guesswork lies at the heart of the Defense Department's plan to phase-out the Springfield Armory. But there is no guesswork in the evidence we will present on behalf of retaining the Armory."

In well-coordinated order the witnesses testified. Mayor Ryan and Downey were first, followed by Edmond and Massa and the other technical experts.

They used the figures from the Defense Department's own audits of Springfield to demonstrate that in many instances the Armory was producing weapons at much lower costs than private industry. With colored slides and graphs they were able to demonstrate that private industry had failed to respond to the call for production the first months of the Vietnam war, and that the Springfield Armory was laboring on a heavy sixty-hour week to catch up with back orders that industry could not or would not produce.

Financial experts and technicians produced the figures from actual costs at Springfield to show that some firms in private industry took advantage of the Vietnam escalation and tried to charge as much as two or three times the price it cost for weapons at the Springfield Armory.

Defense Secretary McNamara was unavailable for this eyeball-to-eyeball confrontation with the men from the Springfield Armory Technical Committee. Deputy Defense Secretary Cyrus R. Vance[11] appeared in his place to answer the questions and try to justify phasing out the small-arms facility during a war. Vance assured the Preparedness Subcommittee that it was not McNamara's intention actually to close Springfield until they had found some source in private industry for production of the high-priority items needed in Vietnam.

Chairman Stennis was troubled by the appearance that there was too much reliance upon private industry to continue on production and development of small arms even in periods where no large purchases were being made. Vance said he expected private industry to remain interested and the purchases to be substantial for some time.

Deputy Defense Secretary Vance told the Preparedness Subcommittee that he and McNamara had personally reviewed the decision to close the Armory and that it is "in accord with sound and efficient management of the defense establishment, and is consistent with and serves the public interest."

He challenged some of the general cost figures presented by Downey as "grossly inflated" and in this line contended that the cost of early retirement would be only $4,990,000 according to Booz, Allen & Hamilton as compared with the $17,800,000 figure Downey had used.

Downey and Mayor Ryan snapped back with comments that figures that Vance used were not soundly based, and declared that if Vance and McNamara were relying upon Booz, Allen & Hamilton they should have noted the finding that Springfield could produce arms at about the same price as private industry.

While Mayor Ryan and the technical experts enumerated dozens of instances where the Armory costs for weapons and weapons systems were lower than private industry, Vance was able to reply with only one instance of higher cost. He said that at one point the Springfield Armory costs for the M-14 rifle were $155, while the Thompson Ramo Wooldridge firm sold it to the Army for $82.

Mayor Ryan countered that the one instance Vance cited involved a period when the Springfield Armory was required to divert its work force from other projects "to bail out" some other private industry firms that had "miserable" production records. In doing the work on the other projects, Springfield had been required to use expensive pilot-line tooling and expensive overtime to build the M-14 rifles.

For a brief period of time Springfield costs were far above those of Thompson Ramo Wooldridge, Ryan conceded. However, he and others pointed out that this was an exception. He said that in measuring the costs of the private industry it should be kept in mind that the Springfield Armory had produced the research and the production package that cut the costs for all private firms.

Defense Secretary McNamara was adamant in his view that his November, 1964, decision to close the Springfield Armory was a right decision and that no amount of argument from a team of small-city accountants, lawyers, and government armory technical employees was going to reverse his edict.

The Defense Secretary's normal reluctance to admit error and reverse himself was intensified in this instance by a side issue in the case. At the same time the Defense Department was moving to close out Springfield, negotiations were underway to make purchase of between $50,000,000 and $75,000,000 worth of .20-caliber machine guns from West Germany. Resentment raged in Springfield, where the unemployment level was high, against the decision to go abroad to purchase weapons they felt might better be bought in Springfield.

The Defense Department contended that the comparable gun being developed at Springfield was not far enough advanced to be of practical use, but the Springfield Armory Technical members shot back that the Springfield gun was stalled because McNamara had "starved [it] to death" by not providing proper funding.

Those conflicts were sharp enough to irritate the touchy Defense Secretary, but the accusation that enraged him was the announcement that the purchase of the guns was being negotiated from the Rheinmetall-Borsig A.G., in Germany, one of the largest munitions industries during World War II. Several Jewish groups protested any purchases from Rheinmetall-Borsig on grounds that the firm had been a slave-labor industry under the Hitler regime, and had refused to make any reparations to persons who had been victims of the slave-labor operations. Also, it was contended that two high Rheinmetall-Borsig officials were former Nazis.

McNamara was infuriated when Mayor Ryan wired President Johnson questioning the wisdom of doing business with this German firm while closing Springfield. Later, at a House Appropriations Committee hearing, McNamara was questioned about the wisdom of dealing with Rheinmetall-Borsig; this sent him into a rage that ended in a defiant declaration that his decision to close Springfield was final.

Senator Stennis wrote to the Defense Department stating that his Preparedness Subcommittee felt the Springfield witnesses had made a good case, and asking that McNamara reconsider the closing of the Armory at least until the developments in the Vietnam war were clear. It was useless. McNamara had made his decision, and he refused to change.

For the members of the Springfield Armory Technical Committee, the hearings before Congress meant the end of a long and disillusioning eighteen months of work. Initially, they had believed that hard work and accurate studies showing the value of the Springfield Armory would bring them the decision they wanted. Initially they had believed in the Defense Secretary, but in the spring of 1966 they regarded him as the leader of men "with deaf ears and closed minds across the [Potomac] river." They had been thoroughly initiated into the difficult and frustrating business of trying to do business at the Pentagon. Only the passage of many months would reveal whether their work achieved any lasting results for their home community.

Although the Defense Department had been able to squelch most of the controversial base closings with less noise and less embarrassment, there were dozens of other problems pressing down on Defense Secretary McNamara as the Vietnam war was escalating rapidly throughout 1965 and 1966.

32

COUNTING THE CONFIDENTIAL CASH

IT would be difficult to estimate how many millions of dollars the Pentagon has available each year for espionage, sabotage and other types of secret expenditures. The money is buried in many places in the huge $50 billion annual appropriation, and only a few key members of the House and Senate Appropriations Committees have even a general idea about the details of this type of spending. Since the purpose of the big bundles of confidential cash is for the secret pay-off, the method of disbursing it must be carefully concealed through a series of "fronts" so no concrete way exists to trace the money back to the high officials who authorized its expenditure for the more sordid types of international intrigue.

As long as nations are forced to compete in shady games of international espionage and bribery, large sums of cash for playing the games will be necessary, and the huge Defense Department budget will be one of the most convenient places to hide it. Since the source of the money must be hidden, it is inevitable that there will be considerable relaxation of the normal accounting practices with regard to millions of dollars in cash each year. This loose manner of accounting for large sums of cash creates an ever-present danger of large-scale thievery and misuse of the money. It is conceivable that it might be channeled into political slush funds or advertising campaigns of a wide variety within the United States.

Because of the danger of misuse of these funds, the disbursal must be limited to a few men with accountability directly to the Office of the Secretary of Defense or similar high office. This envisions the type of close personal supervision from the top as the only reasonably safe way of preventing all of this confidential cash from becoming a personal, private slush fund.

Under one of the systems established in the Pentagon, the confidential cash has been drawn in cash or in checks by top officers known as "Class A Agents." These agents may obtain money for rather routine uses, but they may also be used to pass the money to various other officials to carry out assignments with the highest national security classifications.

Class A Agents, usually high-ranking military officers, are regarded as ambulatory fiscal officers. They draw funds from the Army Finance Office in amounts designated by their supervisory appointing officer and then advance the money to third parties, who in turn may make the expenditures through a wide variety of "fronts" to achieve the objectives of the Defense Department or some other department of government.

The total system of accounting for funds by many Class A Agents consists of a statement of funds received from the Army Finance Office, the amount of cash and checks in the Agent's safe and what are called "hand receipts" from the government employee or others to whom advances have been made. Even a casual look at the system makes it apparent that a dishonest person or group of persons might milk it for thousands of dollars, and cover this dishonesty with checks or fictitious handwritten receipts purported to represent disbursal of funds.

Often no running account on the disbursals and refunds in the handling of confidential funds was available. Even the hand receipts that might be a valuable way of making a partial reconstruction of financial activities of any single individual were returned to the signator when the advances were refunded or otherwise accounted for, rather than being canceled and retained by Class A Agents as a part of a permanent record. Individual agents, on their own initiative, did occasionally endeavor to keep some permanent records, but it was not usual.

James Robert Loftis, fifty-two-year-old administrative assistant to Defense Secretary Robert S. McNamara, had direct responsibility over the Budget and Finance Branch of the Office of the Defense Secretary. John Archibald Wylie served as Director of Budget and Finance in the Office of Secretary of Defense with authority to name Class A Agents and responsibility to set up the rules and regulations for proper control of these cash funds.

William Hermann Godel, Deputy Director of the Advanced Research Projects Agency (ARPA), made many trips to Vietnam and other areas with substantial amounts of cash provided by Wylie through one of the Class A Agents. The large amounts of cash Godel carried with him on his trips was reported to be for highly sensitive missions to help the armed forces of South Vietnam.

It was inevitable that there would be periodic rumors of misuse of large amounts of cash, for there was awareness of the laxity in accounting for these funds by many experienced military and civilian officials who handled the money. The auditors of the General Accounting Office were barred from making inquiry into the use of some of these funds. Who would be able to check to determine if all the money was actually delivered to a confidential agent in Saigon, Berlin or Hong Kong? Even if the money was clearly misused, how difficult would it be to make a criminal prosecution when the system had so many possible loopholes? How many Pentagon auditors, most of them in the middle ranks, would challenge the word or the loose documentation of spending of confidential cash funds?

If the top career officials and the political appointees were both honest and aggressive, then it was probable that most of these confidential funds would be used as they were intended. However, any laxity or dishonesty at the top opened the door to serious trouble.

In the fall of 1963, some disturbing circumstances arose in connection with the records on some of the Class A Agents' accounts. A shortage of about $2,000 came to light in one account, and the money was quickly supplied by John Wylie. At this, Joseph P. Welch, director of audit operations in the Office of the Secretary of Defense, became concerned. Why would the Director of the Budget and Finance Branch dig down in his pocket to square the account of a Class A Agent?

Only a few months earlier, Welch had directed what he believed was a thorough investigation of the Class A Agents' accounts. He had found irregularities that appeared to be of a minor nature, and had attributed most of it to carelessness even as he served notice that he intended to enforce a tighter accounting in the future.

The manner in which the $2,000 shortage was covered by Wylie was as disturbing as the shortage itself, and there were other suspicious incidents that made the young audit director decide to conduct a surprise simultaneous cash count on all Class A Agents within the Office of the Secretary of Defense.[1]

During that October 29 cash count, auditors discovered that several thousand dollars were outstanding against receipts signed by John Wylie. Wylie was not at his Pentagon office that day, but early the following morning, Welch and Eugene Vadeboncoeur, one of his auditors, went to the office of the Director of Budget and Finance. In a routine manner they requested access to all of the Class A Agent accounts in Wylie's possession.[2]

It was a difficult ordeal for Wylie, a free-wheeling and confident operator who had appeared to be above questioning by the Defense Department auditors. It was an equally difficult time for Welch, a young audit director five Civil Service grades below Wylie's supergrade GS-18. If Wylie resented the demand for an accounting it could have meant a serious setback for Welch's career.

Wylie's response was slow when Welch asked for access to records of his Class A funds and the receipts, and he told the auditor it would take him a little time to put his account in order. Wylie suggested that Welch and Vadeboncoeur leave him alone to straighten out the records and come back "about noon" when he would have the accounts ready.

It seemed a reasonable request, but Welch said that his duty as an auditor required that he remain in the office while Wylie did whatever was necessary to prepare for the audit. A long uneasy silence followed as Wylie continued to sit in his chair staring at Welch and making no attempt to provide any of the information the auditors wanted.

John Wylie and Godel had worked with high political figures at the Pentagon for years. Godel had the confidence of such men as Struve Hensel, an Assistant Secretary of Defense and General Counsel for the department in the Eisenhower years,[3] former Assistant Defense Secretary Fred Seaton and former Deputy Defense Secretary Robert G. Anderson. Wylie, a close friend of Godel, also was close to top political figures, but now he lost his confidence, and had no answers for the young auditor.

As he saw he was getting no satisfaction from Wylie, Welch left the office to explain that matter to Wylie's supervisor, Loftis. Vadeboncoeur remained in Wylie's office to keep it under surveillance. As soon as Welch left, Wylie got up and went to his files in the reception room, looked through several of the folders, and then strode into the office of his budget officer, Carl Fisher. Although Vadeboncoeur walked close behind him, he did not hear what Wylie whispered in the ear of Fisher.

Wylie returned to his office, and a short time later Fisher entered and gave Wylie a brown envelope. Wylie opened it, inserted a check he had in his pocket and shoved the envelope into an inside coat pocket.[4]

A short time later, Welch returned and Wylie continued to decline to make an accounting of the funds to the auditors but asked to speak to Loftis. All three filed into Loftis' office, where they met with Loftis and Morris Landman, Assistant General Counsel for Financial Management, and Landman asked for a general description of the funds the auditors wanted. Wylie volunteered that he was accountable for approximately $9,800. He removed the envelope from his inside coat pocket, placed it on the table, took a $100 bill out of his billfold and placed it beside the envelope and said that this was the money for which he was accountable.

It was Vadeboncoeur's job to take the money from the envelope. The envelope contained $5,600 in cash and a check for $4,000 made payable to Wylie and his wife, Harriett W. Wylie.

Welch and Vadeboncoeur were surprised when Wylie mentioned the sum of $9,800, for they had believed that he was accountable for only $7,400. Even the fact that Wylie appeared to have more money than was required raised further suspicions, particularly when it was totally inappropriate to account for funds borrowed from Class A Agents with a check and personal money. Welch pointed out these irregularities and turned the case over to Loftis and Landman with the suggestion that the Inspector General should perform a full investigation to determine all the facts surrounding the irregular accounting.[5]

On the morning of November 1, 1963, Wylie, Godel and a Marine major, William Corson, met for breakfast at a motel near the Pentagon. Godel, who served as a Marine in World War I and II, had been a civilian employee of the Defense Department from 1951 and was a Grade 18 Civil Service employee. He and Wylie had worked together for several years, and it was Wylie who arranged with the Class A Agents for him to receive large amounts of confidential cash prior to his visits to the Far East, where he had been active in establishing certain combat development and test centers in South Vietnam. Major Corson, a Class A Agent assigned by Godel, had arranged for drawing some of the money that had been given to Godel for the alleged purpose of carrying out some highly secret government project.

Wylie had called them the night before to arrange the breakfast meeting and made it clear to Godel and Major Corson that he did not wish to hold this discussion at the Pentagon. Wylie asked Major Corson if his Class A account had been audited, and the Marine officer replied: "You know it has. It was just last month." Major Corson was unaware at the time that his account had been inadvertently missed in the surprise audit that Welch conducted just two days earlier.

With no indication that he had any serious trouble, Wylie explained the visit by the auditors the previous morning. "They came to me and they wanted to count my money and they gave me a hard time about my using Harriett's [his wife's] check," he said. Wylie wanted to know the specific details on his and Godel's outstanding Class A account balances with Major Corson.

Godel, sensing some trouble, volunteered: "If there is a problem you have sort of got three kinds of choices: You can seek to make restitution if there is a shortage, or if it is a serious matter I suggest you go see your superiors and explain it to them, or if it is worse then I suggest that you find yourself a competent attorney." [6]

During the ride back to the Pentagon with Godel, Major Corson agreed to bring his accounts up to date and provide both Godel and Wylie with a statement of their outstanding indebtedness to his account. However, Welch and his auditors learned of the existence of

Major Corson's Class A account within the next day, and what they found was to raise more questions and broaden the investigation to include both Godel and Loftis in its sweep.

On the next Monday morning, November 4, Welch made a recheck on the Class A Agent accounts and found receipts from Wylie for $550 and $1,000, and a $3,031 receipt from Godel in the records of Major Corson's account.

Also in Major Corson's account they found two government checks, one for $2,055 and the other for $5,800, that did not appear to be normal transactions. They found that the $2,055 check was a disbursement made from a special contingency fund for Mr. Loftis' use, and the $5,800 check came from Army funds. Welch found it "very unusual for an OSD [Office of the Secretary of Defense] Class A Agent to have received money from the Army Official Representation Fund moneys." [7]

By this time, there was no doubt in Welch's mind that the entire matter needed the most thorough probe possible, and he turned it over to the Defense Department investigating agency to follow through.

By November 5, it was apparent the irregularities in the Class A Agent accounts were serious, and on directions from the Secretary of Defense all Class A Agents were instructed to close out their accounts and turn in the cash to designated members of the budget office. When Major Corson arrived the next morning to turn in his records and funds, Welch met him and with Loftis present directed that he obtain the cash from Godel and Wylie to redeem the receipts he had in his possession. Welch said the money was due immediately, and set a general deadline of 2:30 P.M.

Corson left to find Wylie and met him in a corridor on the E Ring of the Pentagon. Wylie's good humor faded when Major Corson told him he had to repay $1,550 by 2:30 that afternoon. Corson went with him to his office where Wylie "in some state of agitation . . . made a telephone call." He told Major Corson: "I will be back at 1:30 or thereabouts with the money." At 1:30 P.M. Wylie strode back in his office, counted out $1,550 in cash to Major Corson, asked for the receipts that had been in the Class A file and shredded them.[9]

Godel had a harder time obtaining the $3,031 he needed on such short notice. He told Major Corson he would have it when he returned from lunch. During a luncheon meeting at a Maryland motel, Godel sold his car to Robert Phelps, a business associate, for $2,195.[10] Unfortunately, he arrived back at the Pentagon after the 2:00 P.M. bank closing hour and was unable to convert the check to the cash he needed for Major Corson. He explained his problem, and with Corson tagging along went to the David Mann Jewelry Company in the Pentagon concourse.

The vice president and manager of the jewelry company was a friend of Godel's and he agreed to get his check cashed for him. Richard Mackedon, the jewelry store manager, wrote and cashed his own $2,000 check at the side door of the bank when the bank would not accept Godel's check. Mackedon accepted Godel's check for $2,000 in return, and Godel returned to his office where he took $1,031 in cash from his office safe to complete the payment to Major Corson.[11]

Though Wylie and Godel cleared up their indebtedness to the Class A accounts, their troubles were just starting—the investigation into their use of these funds was barely beginning. Every new day seemed to bring new evidence that raised more and more questions about how the confidential cash had been handled.

Although Wylie had authority to appoint Class A Agents, there was no reason why he should have been given any of the funds. The agents were named to provide funds for Godel. Although Godel was authorized to receive large cash sums from the Class A Agents, the instructions to Major Corson had been loose and there had been no proper procedure outlined at any stage.

Wylie was recognized as a high-living fellow. Bank records disclosed much of the picture of how he progressed from rowboats to a $12,600 cabin cruiser on a government salary. The records showed that on March 15, 1963, Wylie opened a personal checking account in the Fairfax County National Bank with a deposit of $7,257—a loan on his new $12,600 boat. On March 26, his secretary, at his request, deposited $6,000 in money advanced from a Class A Agent's account into Wiley's personal bank account. The bank ledgers on March 30 disclosed payments of an $8,000 check drawn on March 22 as part payment on Wylie's boat.[12]

Records from a bank account maintained by a former Class A Agent, Marine Colonel Thomas Brundage, showed that in March, 1962, Wylie had presented his personal check for $1,500 in lieu of the regular hand receipt when drawing advance funds. Unfortunately, Colonel Brundage did not hold the check quite long enough before presenting it for payment. When it was deposited on April 10 to the Colonel's Class A account it was returned because Wylie's bank account had "insufficient funds." On Wylie's advice, Colonel Brundage held it for two weeks, put it through again and it was paid. On another occasion Wylie had used his personal check as a receipt for Class A funds.[13]

As the investigation progressed and as more Class A Agents were questioned in detail, it was revealed that Wylie had used his position as Director of Budget and Finance to obtain information on coming audits. This made it possible for him to warn Class A Agents when their accounts might be audited, and made it possible for him to arrange to obtain cash to give to the Class A Agent who was being audited so there would be none of the objectionable personal checks or handwritten receipts in the accounts at the time of an auditor's visit.

Colonel Brundage explained how Wylie had redeemed his outstanding receipts just prior to an audit of Brundage's Class A account, and then came around shortly after the audit to withdraw the cash and place the personal checks or handwritten receipts in the account again. This type of manipulation could go on forever if Wylie could have notice of the audits, and as long as there was no simultaneous audit of all Class A Agents such as Welch had initiated.

Brundage said that Godel had cleared his account in the same manner and at the same time, and Godel was equally prompt in accepting a new advance of cash in the same amount as soon as the audit was completed.[14]

Like Wylie, Godel was not averse to running large amounts of government money through his personal checking account. The most questionable of these deposits concerned part of a $10,000 advance he received for special combat training work in Vietnam. The funds were turned over to Godel in the early part of June, 1961. On June 30, after his return from Vietnam, Godel endorsed $3,000 of the funds to Wylie and Wylie cashed the check the same day. Another cashier's check for $5,000 advanced to Godel in early June, 1961, was later converted into $2,500 in traveler's checks and a $2,500 cashier's check, payable to Godel. The cashier's check was deposited to Godel's personal checking account a few months later.[15]

Investigators centered considerable attention on the $10,000 in cash that Godel drew for a trip to Vietnam in June, 1961. When Godel returned he submitted a voucher for expenses of $10,000 with no itemization. This expense memorandum submitted to account for $10,000 contained the notation that "the documents necessary to support this transaction are on file in the Office of the Secretary of Defense, Budget and Finance Division." Investigators were unable to locate the receipts, or anyone who had seen the receipts.[16]

In the initial days of the investigation some Class A Agents and other subordinates were reluctant to cooperate, and only grudgingly told what they were asked about the loose handling of the funds. There were two reasons. In bowing to the demands of their superiors, some of them had permitted gross laxity in the handling of the confidential cash. Also, as one explained to a Justice Department lawyer later: "I just didn't believe anything would come of the investigation. I figured that if I yelled 'cop' they would have taken care of me later."

Audit Director Welch was one of the few who moved ahead in a straight line with no equivocating, and with an insistence that top officials dealing with thousands of dollars in confidential cash be held to the line in the same way that lower-level government employees would have been held responsible under the same circumstances.

While the existence of such corruption and laxity at a high level was embarrassing to the Office of the Secretary of Defense, Welch was backed and further investigations were directed by Frank A. Bartimo, Assistant General Counsel in the Office of the Secretary of Defense.

On January 7, 1964, Wylie was notified that Defense Secretary Robert S. McNamara intended to remove him from his position as head of the Budget and Finance Branch, and a week later the case was forwarded to the Justice Department for further investigation by the F.B.I.

Although Wylie was given notice that he would be suspended from his job, on February 4 he was permitted to apply for disability retirement and remain on the Defense Department payroll. The Civil Service Commission granted the disability retirement in April, with the provision that it not become effective until June 12—the day after Wylie's annual leave and sick leave ceased. On that date, Wylie started drawing his total disability retirement benefits of $516 a month despite the fact that the evidence continued to pile up more firmly establishing his involvement in a conspiracy to defraud the Defense Department.[17]

In January, 1964, a week after Wylie was initially informed he would be suspended, Defense Secretary McNamara ordered a reorganization of the financial functions in the office that transferred all functions of the Budget and Financial Branch of his office to the office of the Comptroller of the Defense Department. The remaining duties that had been handled by Loftis as head of that office were transferred to the Assistant Secretary of Defense for Manpower.

In early February, Loftis was notified that his position was being abolished and that he no longer would have a job because of a technical "reduction in force." Although Loftis was only fifty-two years old at the time, this made him eligible for an optional retirement at a more beneficial pension than he could have received if ouster action had been sought. Loftis went on a government retirement pension of $735 a month on March 28, 1964.[18] Later, this action was to be the subject of sharp criticism in the Senate.

Although the Defense Department did not move against Godel until July 16, 1964, that action turned out to be the most severe. He was notified of suspension and was relieved of all duties, and on August 24 he was fired. Because he was fired, Godel was ineligible for retirement benefits such as those that continued for Loftis and Wylie. He was entitled to a refund of the $13,199.40 he had paid into his retirement fund through payroll deductions, but his application for this money was denied pending a final decision on his possible indebtedness to the government in connection with the loose handling of the confidential cash.[19]

On December 16, 1964, Wylie, Godel and Loftis were indicted by a grand jury in the United States District Court in Alexandria, Virginia, and Herbert J. (Jack) Miller, then Assistant Attorney General in charge of the Criminal Division, assigned two bright and able young lawyers—Plato Cacheris and Abraham Dash—to handle the prosecution.

The indictment, containing more than forty counts, charged that Wylie and Godel were involved in a conspiracy to milk the confidential cash funds through a falsification of documents and a diverting of Defense Department money to their personal accounts from the accounts of Class A Agents. It was charged that more than $60,000 in government funds was embezzled through the conspiracy. Six counts of the indictment named Loftis as the defendant on charges of false statements and embezzlement of $3,873.

(Wylie and Godel were convicted on charges of conspiracy, false statements and embezzlement of government funds and were sentenced to five-year prison terms. Godel's conviction is on appeal. Wylie dropped his appeal, went to prison, and served as a government witness in the Loftis trial. Loftis was acquitted on all counts in the indictment.)

While the prosecution was proceeding in an aggressive manner, aspects of the handling of Wylie and Godel troubled Senator John J. Williams, the crusading Delaware Republican. Always an active investigator of either laxity or corruption in government, the Delaware Senator wrote the Civil Service Commission for a full explanation of the circumstances under which Wylie and Loftis had been permitted to take their pensions.

On August 10—just two weeks before Godel was fired—Senator Williams had written to Secretary of Defense McNamara stating that he had received reports of still-unpublicized irregularities in the funds of the Budget and Finance Branch. He wanted all the details concerning the persons involved, the nature of the financial irregularities, the actions taken against those involved and "the method in which they were separated: that is by abolishment of jobs to provide early retirement, etc." [20]

On August 31, a week after Godel was fired, David E. McGiffert, Assistant to the Secretary for Legislative Affairs, replied stating that Wylie had "exercised his right to take leave in lieu of suspension" under Civil Service regulations, that Loftis had taken his optional retirement after his job was abolished and that Godel had been "removed from his position on 24 August 1964." McGiffert referred Senator Williams to the Civil Service Commission for further details, while assuring him that an intensive investigation by the F.B.I. was continuing.[21]

From the Civil Service Commission, Senator Williams received a report on the size of the pensions Loftis and Wylie would receive, together with a complete breakdown on the extra benefits they received as a result of the higher pensions they were permitted to take. He did not receive the reply until the spring of 1965—a few weeks before Wylie and Godel were to go on trial. Loftis was granted a severance and was to stand trial later.

Because he did not wish to create undue adverse publicity just prior to the trial, Senator Williams withheld his criticism until after the trial was concluded with conviction of the two men in late May, 1965.

On June 2, 1965, Senator Williams rose on the Senate floor to criticize Defense Secretary McNamara sharply for permitting Wylie and Loftis to retire under particularly beneficial pensions. He declared that while the Pentagon was releasing information indicating that the whole matter was being "efficiently handled," still "a rather strange set of arrangements . . . were followed whereby it was made possible for two of the employees, rather than being fired, [to be] placed in a position where they could claim immediate retirement benefits far beyond what they would have been eligible to receive had they been routinely separated."

Senator Williams declared that "two of the men [Wylie and Loftis], assuming they will reach the age of seventy-seven [the normal life span], together will collect additional retirement benefits of around $120,000 over and above what they would have received under normal circumstances." [22]

Going through all the details, Senator Williams showed how Wylie, then a convicted embezzler of government funds, "will collect an additional $39,204 as a result of being carried on the payroll after the embezzlement was discovered until he could be classified as disabled.[23]

"Mr. Loftis was the second employee to get kid-glove treatment after being suspected of embezzlement," Senator Williams said. The Senator stated that Loftis had not yet gone to trial, but that he was certainly not entitled to special pension benefits under any circumstances. He declared that after the laxity and crime was discovered in Loftis' office, the "special arrangement" was made under which Loftis "will be able to collect an additional $77,400" over what he would have received under a normal pension.[24]

"Apparently Mr. Godel did not have any friends in court," Senator Williams said. "He was fired." Even his retirement fund was held by the Defense Department, Williams said, contrasting the action that took place on Godel's case.

"It is hard to understand why this was allowed to happen," Senator Williams told his colleagues. "Particularly, is this difficult to understand when we consider that during the same interval in which all of this was taking place in the Office of the Secretary of Defense, the Air Force Academy, a division of the same Defense Department, was expelling some students for cheating in school and severely disciplining, if not expelling, other students not because they had cheated but because they knew of boys who were cheating and had not told on them.

"How can the Defense Department justify this dual standard of ethics?" Senator Williams asked.[25]

Loftis went to trial in September. Wylie, a key prosecution witness, testified that Loftis knew of the irregular handling of the Class A Agents' funds. Wylie testified that on occasion he had loaned money from these funds to Loftis, and that they were not repaid. Wylie also testified that he had purchased gifts, including cases of scotch whisky, for Loftis out of these funds.

Wylie testified that a $475 check he gave to Loftis came from government funds. Two Army colonels testified about delivering confidential cash to Loftis in the amounts of $2,000 and $1,000.

Loftis did not take the stand as a witness in his own defense, but relied upon character witnesses who said he was a man of good reputation. The defense centered its fire on efforts to discredit Wylie as a convicted conspirator, embezzler and falsifier of government documents.

In the arguments to the jury, E. Waller Dudley, Loftis' lawyer, admitted that there had been laxity in the handling of the Class A Agent's accounts, but contended there was no substantial evidence linking Loftis to these matters except the word of Wylie, the convicted embezzler. He charged that Wylie had made a deal with government attorneys to receive promises of a lighter sentence. He wound up with the plea that Loftis might be guilty of being a sloppy administrator of Defense Department funds, but that the government had not produced believable evidence to link Loftis to the frauds of Wylie and Godel. The jury was out for two hours before returning with acquittals on the four counts of embezzlement and one count of false statements with which Loftis was charged.[28]

Despite his indictment and trial, Loftis did not fall from favor with some of his friends at the Pentagon. One high Pentagon official was even helpful in clearing the way for Loftis to be hired for a $25,000-a-year job with the Communications Satellite Corporation.

Deputy Defense Secretary Cyrus Vance told James McCormack, chairman and chief executive officer of the Communications Satellite Corporation, that there would be no Defense Department objection if Loftis was hired as director of organization and manpower planning. It was only a few months after the acquittal of Loftis that McCormack called Vance to see if the hiring of Loftis would adversely affect relations between the Defense Department and the Communications Satellite Corporation, a government-created corporation.

"Not in the least," Vance had replied. He said he regarded the acquittal as wiping the slate clean for Loftis. The Deputy Defense Secretary said he had not examined the Loftis trial record on testimony relative to the loose handling of confidential cash and had not consulted the files of the Defense Department or the Justice Department before giving Loftis a letter to use in seeking employment.

"I don't think he [Loftis] was a very good manager," Vance said in explaining that this was a primary reason for abolishing the job Loftis had held as administrative assistant to McNamara.

Senator John Williams called attention to the fact that in the midst of his troubles over the government's confidential cash, Loftis had improved his income considerably.

"The same man is now drawing an income of $33,820 per year, which includes a $25,000 salary from Communications Satellite Corporation and an $8,820 Government pension," Senator Williams told the Senate on July 18, 1966. "Here we have a man who under charges of embezzlement two years ago left a Government position and a $20,000 salary and is now drawing a total of $33,820. . . . Who said the Great Society is not generous—especially when spending the taxpayer's money?" [26]

On the House floor, Representative H. R. Gross scolded Vance for being "perfectly willing to help send Loftis to his reward of a substantially higher paid job."

"It is almost impossible to believe that the No. 2 official in the Department of Defense, Deputy Secretary Cyrus Vance, would help clear the way for the appointment of J. Robert Loftis to a $25,000 a year job with the Communications Satellite Corporation," Gross said.

"If he is not a good manager in the Pentagon at $20,000 a year what reason would there be to think he would be a good manager on the payroll of Comsat at $25,000, plus a Government pension of $8,820 a year, compliments of Defense Secretary McNamara?" Gross asked.[27]

While the investigations and the trial were limited to an exploration of the activities of three men during the period from May 29, 1961 through November 6, 1963, it gave a rather deep insight into the problems of policing the conduct of the men who handle the responsibility for millions of dollars in confidential cash. Even if the problem of criminal activity was ignored, the Pentagon stood convicted of guilt of the sloppiest loose handling of large amounts of money at a very high level.

33

THE ARMY'S COMBAT READINESS

ARMY combat readiness was not regarded as one of the controversial issues in early 1965 as the Vietnam war escalated rapidly. Disputes raged over the phase-out of manned bombers, the failure to build more nuclear surface ships, the base closings and the plans to merge the Reserves and the National Guard, but it was assumed that Defense Secretary Robert S. McNamara had a sound and solid posture on the question of the combat readiness of the Army.

Democratic Administrations had made much of a program to strengthen the Army for the "limited wars" and to swing away from the posture of the Eisenhower Administration with its emphasis on reliance upon the deterrent force of "massive retaliation." Defense Secretary McNamara had followed the lead of General Maxwell Taylor, spending had soared over $50 billion a year, and more funds had been available for modernization of the Army.

During the Berlin crisis and the buildup in 1961, it became apparent that the system then in operation for evaluating Army readiness was not adequate. Reports on Army readiness were made only once every six months, and they certainly did not present a clear picture of the combat condition of any individual units. They made it possible to forecast only the most general, optimistic reports, which seemed to have been based more upon willingness to perform a combat mission rather than on any precise determination of whether all the workable equipment and trained personnel were available for a successful military mission.

In 1963, Defense Secretary McNamara established a new system for division evaluation, which it was hoped would be a more objective method for judging combat readiness. Each commanding officer was to be required every three months to file detailed reports on personnel, training, and logistics, which would then be forwarded up through the chain of command for review and corrective action.

Under this system, the Army set up a grading pattern with four levels of combat readiness—C-1 down to C-4. If the reporting was accurate with a reasonable follow-through for corrective action, the Defense Department was in a much better position to evaluate its Army divisions.

In the last months of 1964 and the first weeks of 1965, the investigators for the Senate Preparedness Subcommittee came across indications that the readiness of divisions was not always what it appeared on the paper reports. The laxity did not seem serious, but it was worth further examination. On January 25, 1965, Chairman John Stennis, the Mississippi Democrat, asked his Preparedness Subcommittee for authority to launch a broad investigation of Army readiness. Unanimous approval was given this noncontroversial study, which it was believed would be a routine and time-consuming task. Committee Counsel James Kendall and Staff Investigators Ben Gilleas, Sam Shaw and Stuart French started immediately on the study of the Army's twenty-two-division authorized force—sixteen active divisions and six National Guard divisions in high-priority status. There were five active Army divisions in the Seventh Army in Europe, two divisions in Korea, one division in Hawaii and eight divisions within the continental United States.[1]

The first examination covered the eight divisions in the United States, and Gilleas and French made personal inspections of four—the 101st Airborne Division at Fort Campbell, Kentucky; the 82d Airborne Division, Fort Bragg, North Carolina; the 4th Infantry Division, Fort Lewis, Washington; and the 2d Armored Division, Fort Hood, Texas.

Between the time the investigation started and the hearings in mid-May, 1965, the number of United States troops sent to Vietnam increased significantly and other United States troops had been used in the effort to restore order in the Dominican Republic.

As they made their investigation, Gilleas and French were surprised to find what they considered to be significant shortages of equipment and spare parts in the four U.S.-based divisions they visited. The shortages and the number of inoperable machines made a difference between some units being combat-ready or not.

As Chairman Stennis opened the hearings on May 13, he declared it was vital "that the Congress be fully informed of the quality and quantity of the Army's inventory of arms and equipment and its ability to carry out its assigned mission.

"We must be certain that we have the men, equipment and material to fill our commitments in Vietnam, the Dominican Republic, and elsewhere as contingencies may arise," Stennis said. "We must be equally certain that the requirements of these activities do not result in an unacceptable impairment of the combat readiness and effectiveness of other high-priority combat units in the United States and elsewhere." [2]

There had been friendly cooperation as Gilleas and French had interviewed approximately two hundred individuals from commanding generals down to sergeants in individual squads and platoons, and Chairman Stennis assured the witnesses that it was "a friendly inquiry even though it could become adverse later."

Initial testimony by Gilleas was enough to irritate the Secretary of Defense, who was extremely sensitive about criticism even when no effort was made to put personal blame at his feet. Gilleas said there were "shortages of equipment" and "shortages of repair parts" and he made reference to a third problem as "the serviceability of equipment." [3]

Much of the details of the specific shortages could not be made a part of the public record for security reasons, but in general terms Gilleas explained that the Army term "Redcat" designated the "level of readiness required for a unit to accomplish assigned operational missions.

"By July of 1964 the Army found that it was impossible for many of its divisions and units to achieve its Redcat, and the reason for this was that they did not have the equipment and the resources to bring them up to their requirement," Gilleas testified. "So they established an intermediate requirement level called Redcape which stands for readiness capability." [4]

Under either the Redcat or Redcape assignments, the divisions were graded on the basis of the C-1 through C-4 conditions. Gilleas explained the meaning of these conditions:

C-1—Fully prepared for and capable of undertaking sustained combat operations within twenty-four hours.

C-2—Capable of initiating combat operations but requires fill of shortages to perform for sustained periods. Can attain C-1 in fifteen days.

C-3—Limited capability to perform combat operations and only for a short period. Can attain C-1 in thirty days.

C-4—Not capable of conducting combat operations. Requires more than thirty days to attain C-1.[5]

Serious shortages of equipment prevented some of the divisions from attaining anything above a C-4 readiness conditions, Gilleas testified. He and French asked, at the Pentagon, about the shortages of equipment and personnel that placed certain divisions in the lower categories of readiness.

The Pentagon moved quickly to improve the conditions of readiness, but it was hardly the move that Gilleas and French had expected. The so-called "Table of Organization and Equipment" was simply revamped to reduce the strength of the division and to cut back the amount of equipment required to meet the readiness standard.

"The Army came out with a new table of organization which cut back further the equipment that these two divisions will have," Gilleas explained. "As a matter of fact, sir, it reduces the strength of the division 1,000 people from 13,500 approximately down to 12,500, so they are reducing the strength and equipment," Gilleas said. "This is one way that some of the shortages have been resolved." [6]

Gilleas said he was not being critical of the way the Army was meeting the shortage problem, but was merely stating the facts for the consideration of the Preparedness Subcommittee. He gave a specific example of how the Army whipped the shortage that had existed in the 7.62 machine guns in the continental United States.

"There is no current shortage under the new TOE [Table of Organization and Equipment] for this item which, in effect, means they reduced the quantity of machine guns authorized the division by more than twenty-two so there is now no shortage," Gilleas testified.[7]

Gilleas also demonstrated how the 101st Airborne Division had met its shortages of observation aircraft and utility helicopters by again using a change in the number authorized under the Table of Organization and Equipment and the simple declaration "no shortage under the table of organization."

The statement of the commanding general on the change in the table of organization was placed before the subcommittee by Gilleas and was read by Chairman Stennis and Senator Leverett Saltonstall, the Massachusetts Republican. It was not left in the record by the Pentagon censors for security reasons, but Senator Saltonstall made its import clear: "I think the significant sentence in the report is the last one. . . . That implies certainly that the commanding officer of that division feels that if anything went wrong in some undertaking that he was required to undertake, he would not be responsible." [8]

In this instance, Committee Counsel Kendall pointed out that the commanding general of the division was not concerned so much about reduction in certain equipment under the table of organization as he was about another type of equipment that had not been increased in sufficient quantity to meet what he believed to be the minimum needs for his division.[9]

National security classification by the Defense Department prohibited the Preparedness Subcommittee from pinpointing the extent of the shortages, but it was possible to state that there were shortages of helicopters, shortages of 3.5-inch Rocket Launchers, shortages of radio sets, shortages of two and one-half-ton trucks.

Gilleas testified that in some instances the active units were obtaining sufficient radio sets by redistributing rehabilitated radio sets that were being withdrawn from the reinforcing Reserves. The investigator told the Preparedness Subcommittee that this was only one of the examples of the "rob Peter to pay Paul" activity that was masking real shortages.

"For example, when we were at Fort Bragg with the 82d Airborne Division, they told us they took [deleted for security] trucks from the Reserves which were given to other units at Fort Bragg so that the 82d could acquire a more recent model," Gilleas testified. "This is not the most satisfactory way to make up shortages." [10]

The committee investigator detailed the cuts that had been made in Army requests for funds by the Office of the Secretary of Defense. The cuts of $632,000,000 in the budget for fiscal year 1966 had cut the Army spending for equipment from $2,600,000 to about $2,000,000.

"This shows the reductions and shows it by aircraft, aircraft spares, missiles, missile spares, and repair parts, weapons and combat vehicles, tactical and support vehicles, communications, ammunition, and so forth," Gilleas explained with charts. "The Army reclamaed—which meant they took an appeal on this amount of money—and got $13,100,000 restored." He pointed out that the Army was cut $179,000,000 in aircraft alone.[11]

Chairman Stennis and the members of his staff did not believe that Defense Secretary McNamara was obliged to give the Army, Navy or Air Force all the money they requested. Nor did they expect to find all the active divisions operating with one hundred percent efficiency and supplied with all the latest in equipment. However, after boosting spending to about $50 billion a year for five years, they had expected to find all the divisions fully equipped on such standard items as the M-14 rifle, the two and one-half-ton truck and radio communications equipment.

They were sympathetic with the tremendous job of running the

Pentagon, but they had expected to find the Army in a better condition or they had expected that Defense Secretary McNamara would keep them informed of any problems so that additional money could be supplied by Congress. The picture that Gilleas and French painted was not one to create panic—there was equipment and properly trained manpower to meet most emergency matters—but it was disturbing to Stennis and other committee members to find shortages in standard items and to find that as the Vietnam effort was escalating, equipment and trained manpower was being stripped out of divisions in the United States and in Europe.

The testimony of the committee investigators was corroborated by that of Richard W. Gutmann, Associate Director, Defense Accounting and Auditing Division, General Accounting Office; by John Flynn, the Assistant Director; and by Chester S. Daniels, a Supervisory Accountant for GAO.

"Our reviews disclosed generally that equipment was not being maintained up to the standard that it could have been with a more effective application of available resources," Gutmann testified. "For example, in a report of November 1964 on 19 high priority units in the United States we disclosed that [deleted for security] of the combat units and about [deleted for security] of the combat-support vehicles inspected by Army inspectors, under our observation, had uncorrected defects which were serious enough to limit combat effectiveness, constitute a hazard to vehicle crews or operators, or cause further damage to the vehicles."

Gutmann told the Preparedness Subcommittee that "another unit experienced delays in deployment during the Cuban crisis because 73 of its 89 aircraft required extensive maintenance.

"In a report of February 1965, we showed that the [deleted for security] capability of the [deleted for security] was significantly reduced below designed capability because major items of the [deleted for security] were frequently deadlined," Gutmann said.

When Senator Stennis asked what "deadlined" meant, Gutmann replied: "Inoperable, just could not be used." [12]

Gutmann said his investigating unit had examined divisions in Europe, in Korea and in the United States and found little action was being taken to improve the condition of equipment although the equipment condition records "showed serviceability and readiness conditions far below those permitted by Army standards.

"Furthermore, formal periodic reports to higher headquarters contained inaccurate, incomplete, and misleading information, portraying a much better serviceability and readiness condition than that shown by the records or actually existing and the full extent and seriousness of these conditions was not known," Gutmann testified.[13]

Senator Stennis declared that the classified reports and details on shortages gave him "a very bad impression of the situation."

Gutmann told the subcommittee that most of the reports on matériel readiness had been classified by the Army, and that this made it impossible for the GAO to issue reports on the specific problem areas they found. Gutmann was dealing with figures that involved December 31, 1964; he explained that the GAO auditors were having trouble obtaining current information, which often left the Defense Department in a position to state publicly that there had been "changes" of significance since any critical report was written. In answer to questions from Senator Margaret Chase Smith, the Maine Republican, Gutmann explained his reason for believing the unsatisfactory conditions existed up through the hearings in May, 1965.

"In this particular instance," Gutman said, "since we have been reporting unsatisfactory readiness conditions since February 1962, and we have found unsatisfactory situations as late as December 1964, and because of the nature of the problems contributing to this condition which I have outlined here to a degree, we believe we are safe in assuming that there has not been a material change between December and now." [14]

"Mr. Gutmann, your report very decisively points out the deficiencies and weaknesses in the Army matériel readiness," Senator Smith said. "Would you, for the committee, identify the officials whom you feel are responsible and should be held accountable for these deficiencies and weaknesses?"

Gutmann submitted a list of the names of the people for the record "from a captain at the company level through the division level to the 7th Army or 8th Army . . . right to the Secretary of the Army." [15]

General Creighton W. Abrams, Jr., Vice Chief of Staff of the Army, and Major General F. V. Chesarek, Assistant Deputy Chief of Staff for Logistics, conceded the accuracy of the testimony and reports by the GAO auditors and by the Stennis subcommittee staff. While admitting that there were many shortages, the two generals asserted that "the Army is in the best peacetime condition in its history."

On the one hand they said the $623,000,000 cut from the Army budget by Secretary McNamara was needed to buy helicopters, trucks, ammunition, spare parts and a wide range of other basic items in "the considered judgment" of the military men. However, they avoided criticizing the Defense Secretary for these cuts by assuming the responsibility because "we were not able to offer sufficient compelling evidence" that the material was essential.[16]

General Abrams insisted that Army combat readiness had improved considerably since the inspections by Gilleas and French, and that more improvements were being made.

"The fact that Mr. Gilleas and Mr. French checked up on you did not have anything to do with the correction of the situation?" Chairman Stennis asked.

"I would have to be frank to say that this added impetus to it," General Abrams answered.

"Suppose Mr. Gilleas and Mr. French never had made these visits and we had never gotten into this inquiry," Stennis said. "What do you think would be the situation today as to these conditions compared with what it is?"

"The action might not be as expeditious as it has been," General Abrams replied, "but on the other hand I must say that this is the direction in which we have been trying to point this whole program." [17]

Later, General Abrams identified the Defense Supply Agency as the agency with responsibility for insuring the flow of repair parts under the new, more centralized operations instituted by Secretary McNamara.[18] Somehow the supply-control studies had failed to produce parts increasingly needed in Vietnam.

While arguing that the shortages had not created any critical problem, General Abrams hurried to add: "I do not want to convey the impression that we do not have problems with respect to either repair parts or maintenance. We do. However, we are perfecting our reporting system and attacking our deficiencies." [19]

The two generals were reluctant to criticize any decisions by the Defense Secretary's office, and Committee Counsel Kendall pushed them to explain why they were willing to accept a $30,000,000 reduction in the budget for needed aircraft repairs and repair parts.

"There was a request by the Army for $66 million, an adjustment of $30 million [by the Defense Secretary], and an approval of $36.7 million," Kendall pointed out.

"This is a difference of opinion between ourselves and the OSD [Office of the Secretary of Defense] analysts as to the applicability of the stocks of the spares at hand," General Chesarek answered.

"Have you been hurt by it, or, prospectively, will you be hurt by it?" Senator Stennis pressed. "Now you are not here to justify what the Department of Defense did. We want to know from the Army what the Army's needs are, and the reasons for them. If somebody overruled you, you don't have to agree with them."

"The unfortunate part, sir, will be—the answer to your question will be known a year or two from now," General Chesarek replied.

"You are here to give a judgment about it," Senator Stennis prodded him. "This is certainly in your field."

"We believe we needed that money for spare parts," General Chesarek continued. "We asked for it twice."

"Did you believe you needed it?" Stennis continued to press.

"We still believe it." General Chesarek finally came out with his opposition.[20]

The severe shortage of trucks was something that could have been predicted, and yet cuts in funds left the Army with a fleet of ancient vehicles that should have been replaced. "It should have been done and was not," was the explanation General Abrams gave.[21]

The Office of the Defense Secretary cut the ammunition budget from $471,000,000 to $344,000,000, and the two generals said they were willing to accept the cut even though they had felt more money for ammunition was needed.

"I personally would feel much better if we had more money in ammunition," General Chesarek said in an effort to keep his difference with the Defense Secretary on the mildest note.[22]

Comment by several committee members indicated displeasure with the difficult task of prying dissent out of the Pentagon witnesses, and it was Senator Strom Thurmond, the South Carolina Republican, who hit the point with force.

"Now, I may be wrong, but I have got an impression from listening to these statements here by you gentlemen that you are trying to defend the position taken by the Defense Department," Thurmond said. "The Army asked for over $600 million that they didn't get. In my opinion they need it. That money, in my judgment, should have been granted and should have been used to have filled this shortage of equipment. And yet you come over here and you try to explain it away, this, that, and the other. That frankly doesn't appeal to me . . . I think you uniformed people in the service are going to have to begin to stand up, if it means you get no further promotions, if it means you don't get any other position that you might want." [23]

General Abrams said he hoped they hadn't "created a bad impression here.

"Some of the charts . . . show that the Army is not in a good position on some of these items," General Abrams said. "But it does also show what the procurement program is and so on . . . we are not trying to defend anything." [24]

Later, Gilleas and French made an investigation of the Army divisions in Europe where they found equipment shortages and a lack of spare parts, but they said they "were impressed by the fact that they [the shortages] were not so numerous as those which were found to exist among U.S. divisions." [25]

After listening to the reports and examining the classified figures, Senator Margaret Chase Smith described the shortages as "more than shocking and it is very discouraging." [26] Because of the necessary national security classification of specific figures, Senator Smith, Chairman Stennis and other members of the subcommittee were restrained from using specific details to warn the public and their colleagues in the House and Senate of the need for greater preparedness.

Senator Stennis gave several speeches in which he sounded a general warning that the Pentagon needed to be prodded into spending more money to carry on the fighting in Vietnam without sacrificing the preparedness of the divisions in the United States and in Western Europe. He ordered his staff to prepare a formal report on the shortages and the responsibility for them in the hope that this might jolt the public with solid facts. The critical report was approved by the members of the Senate Preparedness Subcommittee, and in late July was submitted to the Defense Department for elimination of any facts or figures that might be considered of a highly classified nature.

Even as the Preparedness Subcommittee was taking testimony of the shortages, Defense Secretary McNamara was assuring the Senate and House Appropriations Committees that no more funds were needed. He said that our war reserve stocks and equipment levels were such that all active divisions would be able to engage in combat for sustained periods of time.[27]

"The fiscal year 1966 Defense budget request now before the Congress would provide all the funds we need at this time to continue the strengthening of our overall military posture and to carry out whatever combat operations our forces are called upon to perform during the next twelve months," McNamara informed House Appropriations Committee Chairman George H. Mahon, the Texas Democrat, on June 9, 1965.[28]

The Defense Secretary admitted no serious problem, and explained that "the decline in our defense expenditures from a high of $51.2 billion in fiscal year 1964 to an estimated $49 billion in fiscal year 1966 simply reflects the substantial completion of the buildup started in 1961.

"While our fiscal year budget request does not include all of the forces or force modernization recommended by the military departments and individual Service chiefs, the Joint Chiefs of Staff agree that the program supported by this budget will increase our overall combat effectiveness and will provide effective forces in a high state of readiness for the defense of the vital interests of the United States," McNamara told the House Appropriations Committee.[29]

In his appearance before the appropriations committees, Secretary McNamara stressed that he was spending more than the previous Defense Secretary. The regular annual appropriations for defense since 1962 average about $9 billion a year more than the average of regular Defense appropriations during the 1958 to 1961 period under budgets submitted by the Eisenhower Administration. Procurement of tactical aircraft for the Air Force had increased from about $360 million in fiscal 1961 to about $1 billion in fiscal 1966. Procurement of Army helicopters alone rose from 286 in 1961 to 935 in 1965 and the appropriation for fiscal 1966 carried an additional 1,008.[30]

The facts on increased procurement could not be disputed, but there were many Democrats and Republicans on the Armed Services and Appropriations Committees who did not share McNamara's optimistic viewpoint about the United States defense posture. They were willing to give the Defense Department more money if it was necessary to fulfill the commitments in Vietnam and also be prepared for trouble at home or in any other parts of the world. The Democrats made certain that their report placed the responsibility for the budget cuts on the Defense Secretary, and carried his assurances that he needed no more money even in the face of the escalation in Vietnam, which had not been anticipated as a part of the initial planning for fiscal 1966.

Three Republican members of the House Appropriations Subcommittee on Defense Spending submitted additional views in the appropriations report to express their grave misgivings about McNamara's refusal to take more money. "The major areas of concern involve Vietnam, Advanced Weapons Development and overall policy," stated Representative Glenard P. Lipscomb, of California, Representative Melvin R. Laird, of Wisconsin, and Representative William E. Minshall, of Ohio.

"In response after response from principal witnesses, the devastating point was made that the budget was inadequate, that it did not take into consideration the increased activities in Viet Nam, and that no budgetary adjustments occurred after the escalation began," the Republicans stated. "This means that while our international prestige and thousands of American servicemen were committed in this area of the world, the fiscal requirements to back them up were not forthcoming.[31]

"It should not be forgotten that the fiscal year 1965 'guidelines' [used in forming the 1966 budget initially] were formulated at a time of apparent detente and mellowing, at a time when a test ban treaty was negotiated and at a time when Secretary McNamara was predicting we could pull our 'advisers' out of Viet Nam within a year or so," the Republicans commented. "Budget 'guidelines' based on these premises do not lend themselves to the demands of a war situation. . . . We would also caution very strongly that equipment and material priorities for Viet Nam must not be permitted to so deplete active force inventories as to impair the readiness of our forces not committed to Viet Nam." [32]

This was the conflict between McNamara and Congress in the summer of 1965 when Senator Stennis personally handed a copy of the highly critical Senate Preparedness Subcommittee report to the Defense Secretary. Senator Stennis said he believed that McNamara should be doing more about boosting spending and improving the combat readiness of the Army, but the Defense Secretary simply rejected the criticism by rolling off the figures showing he was spending much more money and buying more material than had been bought under the Eisenhower Administration.

Senator Stennis and his Preparedness Subcommittee members expected that the Defense Department would examine the report, eliminate the figures that might be a breach of national security, and return it within a few days or at most a few weeks. Instead, the Pentagon stamped the whole report with a national security classification and refused to clear any of it for publication. And as the months rolled by with the report bottled up, the Senate Preparedness Subcommittee found that it was difficult to obtain the same measure of cooperation that had existed prior to the writing of the critical report on Army combat readiness. Chairman Stennis and his staff members did not receive answers to questions they asked at the Pentagon, and written replies to requests for information were often two to four months in coming. The investigations by Gilleas, French, Sam Shaw and others ran into new barriers in obtaining information from the divisions, and efforts were made by the Defense Secretary's office to have all documents for the Senate subcommittee sent to the Pentagon for examination to determine if the facts were consistent with the positions being taken by the Defense Secretary and the other political secretaries.

There were more investigations and some of the Preparedness Subcommittee members made personal trips to examine Army divisions in Vietnam and in other areas. All expressed concern, but the Defense Secretary continued to paint a rosy picture.

The funds that McNamara rejected in the late fall of 1965, he requested in January, 1966. The $13.1 billion he requested was to buy more helicopters, more aircraft, more clothing, more equipment and more spare parts. That supplemental appropriation was to bring total Defense Department spending for fiscal 1966 to more than $60 billion. It set off a frantic buying spree to spend the money for the needed equipment as quickly as possible, and there were serious questions asked about the high prices the Pentagon was forced to pay as a result of delays followed by crisis buying.[33]

The Defense Secretary contended that his programs were well planned and well executed. He was irritated with his critics who wrote about shortages, and he called a press conference to pour out statistics and to explain that the military forces were in much better shape to meet the commitment of more than 200,000 men then in Vietnam than we had been to conduct the war in Korea. McNamara scoffed at the newspaper reporters and congressional critics who indicated that he was responsible for the shortages, but he was willing to admit only one error—cutting back the helicopter purchases in 1965.

McNamara's disputes with Congress intensified in early 1966, and it appeared that he would be in for a showdown on many counts and under less favorable circumstances than had existed during earlier clashes. More and more Senators and Representatives were ready to question the Defense Secretary's judgment and challenge the facts he presented on military matters.

McNamara's job was a difficult one at best. The business of determining the level of strength for military forces would always be a mixture of scientific research and educated guesses. It was inevitable that there would be different opinions on what constitutes a properly balanced military force and what constitutes a proper degree of combat readiness. Secretary McNamara dominated the decisions in the defense field more than any man in Defense Department history, and there were many who were uneasy about his judgment. They believed that even the man whom some regarded as "the best Defense Secretary in history" should be subject to constant critical analysis. Even the most careful and competent audit of Defense Department decisions might not unearth serious flaws, but in Congress it was argued that there must be the right to search and to comment critically. Unfortunately, it might take a major war to test fully the effectiveness of the McNamara strategy.

34

WIDENING CREDIBILITY GAP

> *"There are many honest people in the Government; if they make mistakes they will admit them. . . . If important mistakes are not recognized and corrected we may well end up with our country weakened to the point that we could not win a war if it should occur."*—ADMIRAL HYMAN RICKOVER

REPRESENTATIVE Gerald Ford, as Republican House Leader, declared, in a press conference in April, 1966, that Defense Secretary Robert S. McNamara was engaged in "shocking mismanagement" of the Pentagon. He outlined a broad range of decisions by the Defense Secretary, and made specific reference to "shortages" in equipment and weapons because of what he called "poor planning."

Although he relied for the most part upon information obtained through the investigations of a half dozen Senate and House committees, Ford found himself under an almost immediate attack for "irresponsibility" by those who believed McNamara's claims that "cost effectiveness" studies had saved billions of dollars.

Ford had expected denials and a counteroffensive from the Pentagon, but he was visibly jarred when Senate Minority Leader Everett Dirksen told a press conference, "I have seen no evidence of shocking mismanagement" at the Pentagon. Questioning of Dirksen at a press conference brought his admission that he had not read a series of reports by Senate and House committees, and had made no effort to examine the information then being compiled for several more critical reports on Pentagon operations.

The wily old Illinois Republican understood the political difficulty of being heard above the one loud voice of the Pentagon press office. He wanted no part of a serious political battle against the multi-billion-dollar force of the defense establishment. Political necessity forced him to read some of the congressional reports on Pentagon activities and the critical speeches by Senator John Stennis, a Democrat, but even then Dirksen kept his criticism of McNamara in the lowest possible key. He shied away from Representative Ford's "shocking mismanagement" and said he preferred to call McNamara's decisions "misjudgments" or "serious misjudgments."

While quiet Republican applause greeted Ford's aggressive stand, only a few would take a forceful public position. Some of those who did back Ford publicly found themselves subjected to bitter attacks. They were forced to question the political wisdom of criticizing the man who had sold himself as the Prophet of Cost Effectiveness.

Fortunately for Gerry Ford, a whole series of Senate and House reports were issued in April and May, 1966, highly critical of Defense Secretary McNamara. Nearly all the reports were unanimous, signed by all the Democratic and Republican committee members. And in most instances, it was Democratic chairmen and Democratic committee members who took the most aggressive position—whether the reports dealt with the lack of combat readiness of Army divisions, the "significant shortages of equipment" in Reserve units, announced phase-out of the B-58 supersonic bombers, or the reluctance of McNamara to move forward with a nuclear-powered surface fleet and the Nike X missile defense system.

In an appearance before the Senate Appropriations Committee on

August 4, 1965, Defense Secretary Robert S. McNamara was asked, "How many divisions do we now have that are well equipped, ready to go into combat?"

"All divisions are well equipped, and all divisions are ready to go to combat," the Defense Secretary answered. "We have sixteen."

"Are you telling this committee that the sixteen divisions are [so] well equipped that they have all they need?" asked Senator Allen Ellender, a Louisiana Democrat, with a touch of incredulity. Senate investigations, still unpublished, had raised serious questions about the combat readiness of some divisions.

"Yes, sir," the confident McNamara replied, "without any qualifications whatsoever." [1]

Contrary to the confident testimony by Defense Secretary McNamara, the investigations of the Senate Preparedness Subcommittee showed that some of the Army divisions were only 50 percent combat-ready by the Defense Department's own standards, some were 75 to 80 percent combat-ready, and some were in what was termed a "training status."

Chairman John Stennis, of Mississippi, wrote a report in the fall of 1965 calling attention to facts inconsistent with Secretary McNamara's contentions that all sixteen Army divisions were combat-ready. That report was submitted to the Defense Department for examination and for deletion of those specific details that might violate national security. Instead of deleting information that might be helpful to an enemy, the Pentagon slapped a security classification on the whole report.

Barred from making the report public, Chairman Stennis made speeches during the fall and winter of 1965 warning that it appeared that the Defense Department was taking material "out of the hide" of Army divisions in Europe and the United States to fight the war in Vietnam. He and other members of the Armed Services Committees of the House and Senate urged the Defense Department to seek more funds to sustain the combat readiness of Army divisions in the United States and Europe during the escalation.

Defense Secretary McNamara continued to assert that the Army divisions were fully equipped and combat ready, and he rejected the demands that he take more money to purchase helicopters, ammunition, weapons and equipment.

Investigators for the Stennis subcommittee and other committees ran into more and more trouble obtaining information from the Defense Department. Requests for information were delayed for two, four and six months. When the information arrived it was frequently incomplete or was so dated that it was no longer of value in trying to ascertain the state of readiness of the Army divisions.

Instead of permitting the congressional investigators to proceed with the long-standing practice of obtaining information directly from the field commanders, the Defense Department required that all documents be first submitted to the Pentagon for "review and coordination," prior to being furnished to the Senate or House committees.

"This has delayed the subcommittee's work," a report released in May, 1966, stated. "It is important to point out that all military officials in the field have cooperated splendidly with the subcommittee's efforts. Their refusal to furnish documentation directly reflects their compliance with orders issued from the Pentagon." [2]

The report dealt specifically with combat readiness of four Army divisions within the United States. They were the 4th Infantry Division, Fort Lewis, Washington; the 5th Infantry Division (mechanized), Fort Carson, Colorado; the 1st Armored Division, Fort Hood, Texas; and the 2d Armored Division, also of Fort Hood. In each instance the subcommittee stated that the division was "not combat-ready" and would not be combat-ready until some late date in 1966.

Chairman Stennis and members of his subcommittee were sympathetic with the problem of a huge escalation in Vietnam, but they were concerned because they believed the Defense Secretary had not given the Congress an accurate picture. In the report, the Preparedness Subcommittee stated:

"The Congress has been repeatedly informed in the past, as have the American people, that the United States possesses sixteen Active Army divisions which were combat ready and able to engage an enemy in sustained land combat. Of concern to the subcommittee is the premise that if these were accurate when made, then the impact upon the combat readiness of the remaining Army divisions in the United States would be minimal at best when one considers that we have deployed only three and one-half Army divisions to South Viet Nam. Moreover, these divisions are not engaged in what the military terms 'sustained' combat but in a condition of 'intermittent' combat."

The report stated that a few weeks prior to McNamara's testimony "these divisions were reporting shortages of major items of equipment." While there had been "some improvement" in the equipment situation between the summer of 1965 and May, 1966, the subcommittee found that there are "a number of items of major equipment which are still in short supply. . . .

"Our Army and National Guard Reserve components have been structured in such a manner as to provide combat support and combat service support units for rounding out the Active Army when the latter is committed to combat," the report said. "However, because selected units of that type structured within these Reserve components have not been called to active duty, the Active Army, of which these divisions form a part, has been used, contrary to its intended purpose, as a personnel and equipment pool for units deploying to Viet Nam and as an expansion of the training base. This report portrays the deterioration in the combat readiness of these divisions as a result of such action." [3]

In a letter to Senator Richard Russell that accompanied the report, Chairman Stennis said it was fortunate that there was time to gear up production facilities because the war was with a small undeveloped country.

He declared that in July, 1965, there were "serious deficiencies and inadequacies in Army readiness," and stated that the commitment in South Vietnam had "shown how delicately we are balanced between military strength and weakness in the light of our worldwide commitments.

"The fact that a relatively small and underdeveloped country such as North Viet Nam has been able to tie us down and make necessary such a substantial commitment of our military resources should show us what we can and must expect if similar wars of aggression against small and helpless nations should occur at other points around the world. This makes it imperative that we take a new and sober look at the extent of our worldwide commitments and make a hard and realistic appraisal of what level of effort and response would be required if two, three, or more contingencies or outbreaks should occur simultaneously. It should be more than obvious that the United States cannot alone protect the free world against the aggressive and expansionist designs of Communist nations indefinitely." [4]

Equal controversy arose over Defense Secretary McNamara's efforts to reduce the aggregate strength of the Army Reserve components —the United States Army Reserve and the Army National Guard—

by about 150,000 men, to eliminate all units from the United States Army Reserve and to restructure the units in the Army National Guard as the sole remaining Army Reserve component.

As usual, Secretary McNamara was selling his move as "cost effective" and one that would create efficiency and a superior military force. The Congress was skeptical when McNamara first pushed for the merger and reorganization in 1965, and the Senate Committee on Appropriations amended the Defense Appropriations Act for fiscal 1966 to disapprove the merger plan and continue the Reserve and National Guard as separate organizations. The amendment was intended to make it mandatory that the Reserve be maintained with a strength of 270,000 and the National Guard at a strength of not less than 380,000. The Senate was unanimous in its final action on the legislation containing this amendment.

In the face of this action by Congress, Secretary McNamara announced that he would inactivate 750 guard units with personnel strength of about 55,000. McNamara's announcement came late in the session. On the final day of the session, the Senate Armed Services Committee unanimously adopted a resolution asking the Secretary of Defense to delay inactivation of the Reserve units until early in 1966, after there had been an opportunity to study the impact of the move. McNamara defiantly refused, and disbanded the Reserve units, including all the Reserve combat divisions.[5]

At the same time, McNamara announced that approximately 25 percent of the remaining strength of the Reserve and National Guard —about 150,000—would be designated as a "Selected Reserve Force (SRF)." The units in this smaller, select group were to have one hundred percent personnel manning, more equipment, and increased training schedules.

In 1966, the Stennis Preparedness Subcommittee conducted an investigation of the McNamara merger and wrote a stingingly critical report on the readiness of the Selected Reserve Force, the Reserve Enlisted Program (REP) training and backlog, and the inactivated Reserve units.

McNamara's merger and deactivation operations were a mess, in the view of the Stennis subcommittee. The subcommittee declared McNamara's "defiance" in deactivating the 750 Reserve units "has resulted in a needless loss of trained manpower from a paid drill status, has resulted in excessive assignment of displaced personnel in other units as overstrength, and has made it difficult, if not impossible, for the USAR [Reserve] to achieve the congressionally mandated strength of 270,000 at the end of fiscal year 1966." [6]

The deactivation of Reserve training units had resulted in a lack of Army training centers for enlistees under the Reserve enlistment program, and there was a backlog of 127,000 untrained personnel projected for June 30, 1966, which would grow to more than 139,000 by June 30, 1967. The Stennis subcommittee challenged "the wisdom of planning and programing" by McNamara that had created such a backlog that the Reserve enlistment program had become a virtual haven from the draft.

McNamara had predicted that a large percentage of the members of the deactivated Reserve units would voluntarily join the National Guard drill paid units. This was another McNamara prediction that went wrong. "Only 783, or less than 1½ percent of the total, of the 55,220 members of the USAR units inactivated last fall voluntarily joined ARNG drill paid units." The subcommittee said these figures rendered "suspect" McNamara's predictions that 111,000 members of the Reserve would join the Guard voluntarily if his total proposed merger was approved and implemented.

Even McNamara's Selected Reserve Force failed to measure up to standards, according to the Stennis subcommittee report. The subcommittee pointed to "significant deficiencies in personnel, equipment, and training, all of which would have to be supplied from already overburdened Active Army and Reserve sources if the SRF should be mobilized in the immediate future."

The proposals for elimination of all drill paid units from the Reserve was viewed by the Senate Preparedness Subcommittee as having "serious disadvantages and drawbacks, including loss and displacement of trained and skilled personnel and other turbulence which will result in a significant reduction in readiness and military preparedness.

"These disadvantages are not, in our opinion, either balanced or outweighed by the alleged benefits which would flow from the proposed merger," the Senate subcommittee said with unanimity.[7]

Also, the Stennis subcommittee blamed "significant shortages of equipment" on Defense Secretary McNamara for his cuts in the Army Reserve equipment budget for fiscal years, 1964, 1965 and 1966. The Army requests for procurement of equipment and missiles totaled $9,962,800,000 in the three years. The Defense Department approved only $7,432,900,000 in those three critical years—a cut of $2,529,900,000.

Again the Stennis subcommittee questioned the credibility of the Defense Department in connection with shortages. The Senate subcommittee noted that it had found a shortage of uniforms existed in the Active Army and the National Guard units. "As a result we found that a number of ARNG [National Guard] enlistees were forced to attend drills in civilian clothes," the report stated.

The Pentagon was notified of the evidence of shortages, and the subcommittee began an investigation to determine the scope of the problem. That same day the Secretary of Defense directed that uniforms be airlifted by Reserve transport planes to units to supply the shortages, and an unidentified Pentagon spokesman was quoted as saying it was a problem of distribution and not of shortages.

Although the Pentagon did not present details to the Stennis subcommittee, the report summarized: "The fact that there were shortages has been clearly established, both by visits to the field by members of the subcommittee staff and by testimony of [Lieutenant] General [J.L.] Throckmorton, [Chief, Office of Reserve Components, Department of Army], and it is clear that it was not merely a problem of distribution." [8]

The report commented critically on the fact that even the Selected Reserve Force had a lower priority than the military forces of foreign nations receiving equipment under the military aid program. "While not opposed to military assistance as such, the subcommittee believes that the requirements of our own Reserve components should come first, particularly at a time when we are engaged in a shooting war and the mobilization of our Reserve components is entirely possible, if not probable."

Senator Richard Russell, Senator Stennis and Representative F. Edward Hébert, of Louisiana, were only a few of the experienced men in Congress gravely concerned by what McNamara was doing to the whole Reserve program. They were disturbed by his defiance of the unanimous views of key committees of Congress, irritated by the inaccurate and misleading information that was distributed by the Pentagon, and frustrated by the difficulty of getting the attention of the public, which tended to listen to the "one voice" of the Pentagon. The Senate Preparedness Subcommittee warned:

"We believe that in time of heightened international tensions, and when we are engaged in actual hostilities, a major reorganization of the Army Reserve components with its inevitable turbulence, loss of readiness and loss of trained manpower is both unwise and undesirable. We also doubt the wisdom of further reducing the level of our Reserve Forces. We believe that the force level recommended by the Secretary of Defense is inadequate and would present a high degree of risk which would be minimally acceptable at best.

"In light of the fiscal year 1967 budget presentation which indicates that all of the units now in the USAR are needed under contingency plans, we do not believe that it would be prudent to break up these units based upon the very dubious hope that large numbers of the displaced personnel will voluntarily transfer to the ARNG. Active duty training opportunities for all reserve personnel are now very limited, and we do not believe that our national security or defense posture would be served by deliberately discarding trained manpower and further overloading the already heavily taxed Army training centers." [9]

This report was not by an extremist group of any sort. It was from a committee that included liberals and conservatives in both the Democratic and Republican political parties. In addition to Senator Stennis, the Democrats were Senator Henry M. Jackson, of Washington; Senator Howard Cannon, of Nevada; and Senator Robert C. Byrd, of West Virginia. The Republicans were Senator Leverett Saltonstall, of Massachusetts; Senator Margaret Chase Smith, of Maine; and Senator Strom Thurmond, of South Carolina.

House Armed Services Committee efforts to investigate McNamara's decisions ran into general harassment and a wall of censorship. Under the best circumstances it was difficult for the subcommittee to persuade high military officers to express their frank disagreement with the Defense Secretary, and this problem was compounded by McNamara's policy of sending a representative from his office to be present—even during closed testimony. When the testimony was concluded, representatives of McNamara's office obtained copies of the transcripts to determine if anything had been said that might embarrass the Defense Secretary.

The House Armed Services Committee members were unanimous in feeling witnesses should not be under undue coercion and that information, including classified information, should be made available in executive sessions. It objected to the fact that occasionally the channels of information were "blocked by action within the Department of Defense."

"Documents are stamped 'Secret' which in the opinion of the committee do not contain material that is of a classified nature," the committee complained. "It is quite evident that classifying action is taken in these instances by the Department of Defense for the sole purpose of protecting decisions already arrived at and preventing open and free discussions and debate as to whether the decisions are sound." [10]

The House committee was particularly critical of the Defense Department's actions in connection with the phase-out of the B-52 bombers and the B-58 supersonic bombers and the failure of the Defense Secretary to move forward with contract definition on the Advanced Manned Strategic Aircraft (AMSA) as a follow-on for the aging bombers.

McNamara did not consult with the Joint Chiefs of Staff prior to his announcement of the phase-out of the B-58 supersonic bombers, and even General John P. McConnell, Air Force Chief of Staff, learned of the phase-out in a memorandum from the Defense Secretary's office. The House Armed Services Committee resented statements by Defense Secretary McNamara and other Defense spokesmen that "created the impression" that the Joint Chiefs of Staff did not favor moving ahead with a contract definition on the AMSA and were thus in agreement with McNamara.

"Every effort was made to obfuscate the true position of the Joint Chiefs of Staff and to mislead the Congress and the public into the belief that only the Chief of Staff of the Air Force favored this course of action," the House Committee charged.

The House subcommittee further charged that the Defense Secretary's office had gone so far as to use a security review of the transcript of the testimony of General McConnell to delete a statement that "described the current true position of the Joint Chiefs of Staff."

General McConnell had testified that the McNamara-sponsored FB-111 (the bomber version of the TFX) "as presently conceived is not capable of covering the more distant targets in the U.S.S.R. and Communist China.

"The Joint Chiefs of Staff consider that concept formulation for a follow-on bomber should be completed at the earliest possible time," General McConnell had testified. He said the Joint Chiefs wanted to move into the contract definition phase as quickly as possible so the plane might be operational in fiscal 1974 if it was decided that the full-scale system development was essential.

"The Joint Chiefs of Staff have no alternative to recommending full-scale follow-on bomber development in order to protect the offensive striking power of the United States by preserving an option for an I.O.C. [operational capacity] in fiscal year 1974," General McConnell had quoted from a position paper of the Joint Chiefs of Staff.

The Defense Department had axed testimony contradicting McNamara on grounds that national security was involved, and the House Armed Services Committee was furious:

"His [McConnell's] testimony showed clearly that the Joint Chiefs of Staff unequivocally supported AMSA and in this position was in complete agreement with the committee."

It was charged that the Defense deletions would have presented a "shocking distortion of the true situation, since it would not reveal the present position of the Joint Chiefs of Staff with respect to the need for a follow-on bomber." [11]

McNamara called a news conference to deny any effort to mislead the public or Congress. He said that "confusion" was created because Representative F. Edward Hébert's subcommittee had quoted a Joint Chiefs position for the fiscal 1968 budget, and he had been talking about the 1967 fiscal year budget.

Hébert declared that this was "no excuse for the cover-up of testimony. . . . It is the Defense Secretary who is trying to create confusion in the public mind on an issue that is quite simple," Hébert said. "The question is simply this: You either want to go ahead with a bomber or you don't. Mr. McNamara has made his position clear ever since he took office, and he just doesn't want to go ahead with a manned bomber. The Joint Chiefs of Staff and the Air Force have wanted to go ahead with a manned bomber. It doesn't make any difference if we are talking about 1962 or 1967, or 1968 or 1972. Mr. McNamara has been trying to give the American people the impression that the Joint Chiefs of Staff were backing him in his decision not to go ahead with a manned bomber. This simply was not accurate." [12]

Representative Porter Hardy, a Virginia Democrat, Representative Alton Lennon, a North Carolina Democrat, and Representative Rivers, expressed their resentment that McNamara had tried to give the impression his decision to cut the contract definition money "was backed by our professional military men."

"We want the American people to see who is responsible for these decisions," Hardy said. "It is Mr. McNamara. It is not the Joint Chiefs of Staff."

There was equal controversy over whether the Defense Department should move forward with the Nike X missile defense system. Congress and the Joint Chiefs of Staff believed that such an antiballistic-missile missile program was essential since it was recognized that the Soviet Union had a long-range missile system capable of inflicting the most serious damage on cities in the United States.

McNamara balked at moving into a program that might cost $12 to $20 billion over a ten-year period if fully implemented. He said he saw no reason to hurry into the program because of the Soviet threat, and offered the opinion that there was plenty of time to later consider preproduction activities on a smaller system as a defense against the Chinese Communists.

The Senate and House Armed Services Committees wanted action. Committee members argued that it was not necessary to formulate plans on the full Nike X system in the summer of 1966, but that it was essential that work be started immediately to move from pure research and development into preproduction activities. There was no reason for further delay in achieving some measure of protection for the nation against ballistic-missile attack.

"Any delay in initiating a production base will inevitably produce a comparable delay in operational hardware deployed on the site," the House Armed Services Committee stated in providing authorization of $14.4 million for a start. "There appears to be little doubt that the U.S.S.R. can inflict unacceptable damage to the United States by employing long-range missiles" the report said. "Providing funds now for the necessary preproduction activities of the Nike X program is the first step in strengthening the Nation's defense against a threat that is real today and will grow in danger in future years." [13]

New intelligence reports that the Soviet Union was building a missile defense system put new pressure on such a system for the United States.

"After about nine years of research and development effort, the Nike X system has progressed to such an extent that the committee believes it can afford significant protection against many types of ballistic missile attack," the report said.

"Recent advances in technology and concepts of deployment permit a blanket of protection for the whole United States against a relatively small number of attacking missiles, and a tighter protection against heavier attacks for 25 major cities, at a five-year cost of $8.5 to $10 billion. . . . Because of its building block or modular design concept, the Nike X system lends itself to the initial deployment of a light defense for a small number of cities and a later addition of more extensive coverage as circumstances require."

That House report called the construction of "transcendent importance" and stated it had information "that the Joint Chiefs of Staff are unanimous in supporting the funding of preproduction activities this year.

"Even a modest ballistic missile defense might save millions of American lives in the event of an enemy attack." [14] The report concluded its effort to convince McNamara he should throw aside his "cost effectiveness" charts and apply standards of "military effectiveness."

Admiral Hyman Rickover stressed "military effectiveness" when he appeared before the Joint Committee on Atomic Energy and the House Armed Services Committee to urge a nuclear surface fleet for the Navy. The Navy had three nuclear-powered ships—the aircraft carrier *Enterprise*; the guided-missile cruiser *Long Beach*; and the guided-missile frigate *Bainbridge.* All had been authorized for construction prior to the time McNamara became Defense Secretary in 1961, and all have been in action long enough to determine superiority over conventionally powered ships was provable and accepted.

The Navy wanted a nuclear fleet. The Atomic Energy Commission supported a nuclear-powered Navy. And there was enthusiastic support from the Joint Committee on Atomic Energy and the Armed Services Committees of the House and Senate. However, even in the last months of 1965 and early 1966, Defense Secretary McNamara was undecided as to whether a new aircraft carrier should have nuclear power. Also, he had held up funds that had been appropriated to start work on another guided-missile frigate and rejected suggestions that still another guided-missile frigate be built.

Under pressure, the Defense Secretary finally approved using nuclear power in the new aircraft carrier, but he balked at nuclear-powered frigates. Instead, he approved two conventionally powered destroyers. He claimed that his "cost effectiveness" studies indicated that it cost less for the same firepower to build conventional destroyers. He used essentially the same logic he had used three years earlier in opposing nuclear power for the aircraft carrier, *John F. Kennedy*. The fact that the *John F. Kennedy* was being constructed with conventional power in a nuclear age was still irritating to Rickover and members of the Joint Committee, who characterized it as a waste of millions on a ship that would be obsolete by the time it was in action.

Admiral Rickover and the members of the Joint Committee believed that if there had been any reason for reluctance in using nuclear power in the *John F. Kennedy,* that reason had long ago been demolished. In 1964, the nuclear fleet had conducted a spectacular 30,000-mile trip around the world without dependence upon fuel tankers and supply ships. Such a feat would be impossible for a conventional fleet requiring frequent support from tankers.

The success of that voyage had been buttressed by the performance of the nuclear ships in moving from the United States to Vietnam in record time, and in the unparalleled operations off Vietnam.

"We have the technology today to build a powerful nuclear-powered naval fleet unequaled in history," Admiral Rickover testified before the Joint Committee on Atomic Energy. "But if we are confined to continuing to make paper studies rather than building ships, we may end up when a war comes with many studies and no ships."

The wily Admiral, close to retirement, did not have to exhibit the same care that younger officers did in dealing with McNamara, but even then he drove his points home without mentioning the name of the Defense Secretary.

"I believe you are aware that I do not favor cost-effectiveness studies as much as some do," Rickover testified. He said that there was the same difficulty in gaining recognition for the value of nuclear propulsion in new fleet escort ships—cruisers, frigates and destroyers—that there had been in getting recognition of the value of nuclear power for submarines ten years earlier. Admiral Rickover said that there were the same arguments of opposition by those who had objected to moving the Navy from sailing ships to steam power.

Admiral Rickover declared those who opposed nuclear power for submarines failed "to comprehend that we were talking about a significantly different weapon. . . . Most of the submarines could make only twelve knots for one hour. The nuclear submarines gave unlimited high submerged speed.

"Today we have the same problem in getting analysts to use imagination in appraising the increased military effectiveness of nuclear-powered surface warships," Admiral Rickover said. He pointed out that even on cost, differences were not so great as McNamara indicated, but stressed the military effectiveness of the nuclear carrier.

"The new two-reactor carrier will carry about twice as much aviation fuel as a conventional carrier," Rickover explained. That means the ship will be able to support twice as many air strikes as a conventional carrier. "Also, she will carry 50 percent more ammunition than a conventional carrier. If she were accompanied by nuclear escorts, . . . she and her escorts would be available for practically unlimited operations." [15]

He pointed out that a conventional carrier requires an extra oiler to carry the oil from an advanced-base storage tank to the carrier at sea, and added that "of course tankers would also be required to get the oil to the advanced base.

"Further, you would need escorts for the oilers and tankers, too, particularly in time of war," Rickover told the Joint Committee on Atomic Energy, to demonstrate the extra costs that had not been taken into account by McNamara. "This starts adding up, sir." [16]

Rickover explained that many studies had been made by the Navy, and that recommendations for a nuclear surface fleet failed to move the Defense Secretary to action.

"Some of the studies submitted by the Navy are objected to, but reasons for the objections are not given," Rickover testified. "The people are simply told to make another study. . . . It is my impression that the Navy's rationale is ignored because we do not compute a quantitative value for the increased value of military effectiveness nuclear propulsion provides. We point out the specific military advantages of nuclear propulsion and relate them to specific experiences in war. However, we do not provide a calculated numerical value for increased effectiveness.

"In the cost-effectiveness studies performed by the analysts, they compute numerical values for the effectiveness of nuclear power. However, before they make the calculation, they make certain simplifying assumptions in order to be able to do the arithmetic. These assumptions just happen to eliminate from consideration the principal military reasons for wanting nuclear power in the first place. The analysts generally start their calculations with the assumption that oil for the conventional ships is readily available whenever and wherever it is needed, and that the logistic support forces will not be subject to attack."

Rickover declared that if the Navy could be assured that it would never be asked to perform missions where it would be difficult to get oil to our ships, then there would be no need for nuclear propulsion. "However, the Navy cannot afford to count on such a euphoric situation, since the history of war is replete with examples of major military defeats that were brought about by the inability of military forces to maintain a supply of propulsion fuel to the forces in combat." [17]

Following an extensive inquiry, the Joint Committee warned that "Congress must be alert to assure that the reluctance of the Department of Defense to invest in nuclear powered surface warships does not cause our Navy to lapse into obsolescence." The Joint Committee rejected the "cost effectiveness" studies as containing "a fundamental weakness that makes their conclusions wrong—they are based on false assumptions and do not place proper emphasis on military effectiveness." [18]

The Joint Committee recommended that Congress change the Department of Defense authorization for fiscal year 1967 "to require the two new destroyers to be nuclear-powered ships." The Senate and House Armed Services Committees followed through with language designed to force McNamara to act. The authorization bill stated that, "Not withstanding the provisions of any other law, the Secretary of Defense and the Secretary of the Navy shall proceed with the design, engineering and construction of the two nuclear powered guided missile frigates as soon as practicable." [19]

The House Armed Services Committee put emphasis on Admiral Rickover's complaint about the lack of action by the Defense Secretary on the nuclear-powered frigate that had been authorized in 1965. Congress had appropriated $20 million for long leadtime procurement. The Defense Secretary refused to release the funds to the Navy. As Rickover charged to the committee: "No matter how effective it [the nuclear frigate] might be as a warship—[it] is thus far only a paper ship, a paper tiger." [20]

In its report, the House Armed Services Committee pledged itself to live up to its responsibility under the Constitution of the United States, and quoted Article I, section 8, relating to the powers of the Congress "to raise and support Armies, . . . to provide and maintain a Navy; to make Rules for the Government and Regulation of the land and naval Forces."

In a most unusual demonstration of lack of confidence in Defense Secretary McNamara, the House Armed Services Committee report commented derisively of "the almost obsessional dedication to cost effectiveness" in a decision-maker "who . . . knows the price of everything and the value of nothing." [21]

The House Committee said there could be no doubt about "much brilliance" on the civilian side of the Pentagon, and added: "But the committee is quite willing to question whether this brilliance is reflected in the direction of our military planning. There is a great deal of talent, but one wonders whether there isn't also much misdirected purpose. There can be no greater weakness in men in positions of public responsibility, whether in Congress or the Department of Defense, than that they be incapable of reflection or self-examination." [22]

On June 30, 1966, the Senate-House conference committee agreed that a nuclear-powered, guided-missile frigate should be started immediately, despite the opposition and foot-dragging by Defense Secretary McNamara. In an attempt to force McNamara to give priority to the construction of the nuclear escort vessel, the Senate-House conferees wrote the law with this provision:

"No contract for the construction of either of the conventionally powered guided missile destroyers authorized by this Act shall be entered into until the contract for the construction of the nuclear powered guided missile frigate authorized by this Act has been entered into, unless the President finds that such a contracting sequence would not be in the national interest." [23]

It was about as strongly as Congress could state its belief that the overwhelming evidence demonstrated the need for nuclear power. On other matters, Congress tried to overrule McNamara by insisting that money be provided to move forward with Nike X antiballistic missile system, and the Advanced Manned Strategic Aircraft. There was also unanimous approval of language stating that "the Secretary of Defense shall not direct or approve a plan to initiate or effect a substantial reduction or elimination of a major weapon system until the Secretary of Defense has reported all the pertinent details of the proposed action to the Congress of the United States while the Congress is in session." [24]

But even as the Armed Services Committees pledged "to play the tune to which the legitimate power of the Congress will march back up Capitol Hill," there were many who doubted if Congress would ever be heard more than momentarily over the voice of the power-laden Pentagon.

The loud voice of the Pentagon press office made the astounding claim on July 11, 1966, that McNamara's cost reduction program had saved $14 billion in the five-year period ending July 1, 1966. News releases stated that McNamara had saved $4.5 billion in fiscal

1966 and that his skillful scientific management would be saving the taxpayers $6.1 billion in fiscal 1969. Voluminous packets of graphs, mimeographed sheets and printed material prepared by the Pentagon press office were sent to the Congress, to the newspapers and to key business executives all over the nation to announce this marvelous achievement.

Defense Secretary McNamara appeared in person on a television press conference at the Pentagon to proclaim the wonders he had fashioned for the American taxpayers. He was flanked by a colorful array of slogans and pictures that simplified and dramatized his fiscal magic. The nation's press reported the $14 billion in "savings" with a straight face, and McNamara's favorite columnists and editorial writers again proclaimed "Super Mac" was the best thing that had ever happened to the Defense Department.

Even from his admirers there had been concessions that he might have made a "mistake" on the TFX award to General Dynamics, a blunder in blocking nuclear power for the carrier *John F. Kennedy* and a few dramatic misjudgments on the course of events in Vietnam. But his ardent fans declared that no one could argue with the merit of the $14 billion in "savings."

Before the television cameras, McNamara had emphasized that his claims of savings had been "audited" by an outside accounting firm. He said he wanted to assure the public of an independent judgment to verify the authenticity of his claimed savings.

Despite what looked like a great show for the taxpayers, there was considerable skepticism among the members of at least one congressional investigating committee. For a year a House Armed Services subcommittee headed by Representative Porter Hardy had been engaged in a detailed analysis of some of the major cases of claimed savings for fiscal 1964 and 1965.[25]

Committee Counsel Jack Reddan and his staff were aided by a ten-man General Accounting Office team in an analysis of about $4 billion of the claimed savings in the two years. On the basis of a detailed study of some of the largest claims of savings—claims ranging from $1 million to as much as $150 million—they concluded that McNamara's figures could not be justified.

This didn't mean that the much-publicized cost reduction program had not resulted in some savings of significance, but it did mean that the claims were so exaggerated that they were ridiculous. Harold H. Rubin and the other GAO witnesses related that about one-third of the claimed savings simply did not meet the basic criteria that McNamara had set for himself. The Defense Department contended that it claimed savings only on those decisions initiated after July 1, 1961, when McNamara launched his intensified management activity, whereas, in fact, a good many of the largest claims of savings involved actions that had been launched in the Eisenhower Administration—two, three, four or five years before McNamara had been named Defense Secretary.

The Defense Department credited the Navy with "savings" of $1.6 million in fiscal 1964 on the basis of six engineering changes in the A-6A aircraft on the production line at the Grumman Aircraft Engineering Corporation, Bethpage, New York. The changes did not come from new intensified management in the Defense Department, but originated with the contractor. The engineering changes had been recommended under the Eisenhower Administration and had been approved by the Navy prior to July 1, 1961. In a three-year period, the Defense Department had claimed savings of $7.4 million on these engineering changes.

In testimony before the House Armed Services Committee in February, 1965, McNamara made brief reference to this specific "saving."

"Within the limits of human frailty," Mr. McNamara said, "the claimed savings were completely audited and therefore are representatives of the results we have actually achieved."

The Hardy subcommittee commented caustically: "There was no evidence indicating that auditors even questioned the fact that four of the proposals were approved prior to the effective date of the cost reduction program." In addition, the changes had originated with the contractor and would not measure up to the criteria. Also, there were many other change orders on the A-6A that more than increased the cost of the airplane much more than the amount of the so-called "savings."

"In view of the facts developed by the subcommittee as to the true nature and history of this claimed savings, it is sincerely hoped that this is not a representative case," the Hardy subcommittee said.

There were other instances in which it was contended that McNamara was taking credit for "savings" on the basis of what the Hardy subcommittee characterized as "normal course of business decisions." The Defense Department claimed to have saved $149.7

million in fiscal years 1964 and 1965 as a result of a decision by the Marine Corps to modernize the M-48 tanks rather than purchase new Army M-60 tanks.

The Defense Department formula was used in a manner that gave the older M-48 tanks scrap value. To make the claim of $149.7 million on 507 tanks, the Defense Department computed the cost of 507 new M-60 tanks at $103,317,686 and added to it $83,655,000 as the "cost of ammunition and parts for M-60 tanks had they been bought."

From this total, they simply subtracted $37,194,093, which was the figure set as the "cost of modernization and scrap value of M-48 tanks."

The Hardy subcommittee concluded that this decision was normal and what should have been expected in the normal course of business. It certainly wasn't a saving attributed to more intensive management. The subcommittee also criticized McNamara's formula that gave the M-48 tanks "scrap value" and measured the "savings" by comparing them to the price of the newest, most modern M-60.

The Defense Department gave only reluctant cooperation to Hardy's investigators, but by the time the hearings opened on July 14, 1966, the investigators had a number of solid case histories to demonstrate that McNamara's "real accomplishments fall considerably short of the results publicly claimed." Chairman Hardy also believed that the evidence demonstrated that "some cost reduction actions have had an adverse effect on our national defense structure in terms of degraded combat potential."

As he opened his hearings, Chairman Hardy voiced his approval of the idea of emphasizing a cost reduction program but warned: "Great care must always be exercised to keep such a program in proper balance and perspective.

"Remember the tale about the farmer who saved money by putting green glasses on his cows and feeding them sawdust?" Hardy commented. "The experiment might have been a success, except that just when the cows had developed a taste for this diet, they died of malnutrition."

Hardy said that he wasn't suggesting that a Defense Department with a $58 or $59 billion budget was suffering from malnutrition, but that he wished to warn against an obsession with the cost reduction program that might deprive the military of some of the punch needed for an extra edge over the enemy.

In the course of two weeks of hearings, the Hardy subcommittee explored details on more than a dozen cases which the chairman said constituted "phony" claims of savings that tended to undermine the whole cost reduction program. In most of the cases, it was Defense Secretary McNamara or those in his immediate office who came in for the scathing criticism from subcommittee members.

A decision to cancel procurement of Bullpup A missiles provided the basis for a claim of a $40 million savings for fiscal 1964. The Hardy subcommittee members pointed out that simultaneous with the cancellation of Bullpup A, the Air Force pushed forward with expenditures of $24 million for Bullpup B—another version of the same weapon. Eventually, more than the $40 million was spent on Bullpup B.

"The term 'savings' is very loosely interpreted and applied in this case," the subcommittee stated in its official report. "There is considerable doubt as to the validity of the entire saving claimed for Bullpup procurement cancellations and similar transactions involving other weapons."

In fiscal year 1965 the Defense Department claimed $27.5 million was saved as a result of a decision restricting spending for aircraft spare parts from one fund under control of the Army Aviation Command. But the directive permitted the furnishing of the aircraft spare parts out of another fund.

"In effect, the required spare parts were merely taken out of one bin, rather than the other," the Hardy subcommittee said. "In preparation of the claim of savings, only one side of this transaction was considered; the half that reflected the reduced spending. The remainder which increased requirements for funds under another category was ignored."

Few alleged savings seemed more incredible than the $39 million the Defense Department credited itself with having saved in connection with the Sparrow missiles program. The Air Force canceled its entire fiscal 1965 procurement of a new model of Sparrow. McNamara ordered the Navy to transfer the older surplus Sparrow missiles to the Air Force to take care of an inventory requirement. This was fine with Hardy, who regarded it as reasonable good management to make proper use of the existing inventory of missiles.

But the investigators were surprised at the book juggling that resulted in the Air Force's claiming a $39 million savings on the basis of the canceled program. The Air Force was not required to reimburse the Navy on the interdepartmental transfer of weapons. Also, the transaction was handled as if the Sparrow missiles transferred from the Navy had no value. The Navy lost nothing, but the Air Force gained an inventory that permitted it to claim a $39 million savings.

"The missile had a military value," the Hardy subcommittee said. "It also had a dollar value and the cost of the missile is the only proper basis for valuation. Considering this offsetting cost in relation to canceled procurements, the $39 million claim is a gross overstatement of actual savings accomplished by the missile transfer."

The Army had been working for four years on a new M-470 projectile and had finally come up with tests indicating that it had the characteristics needed to replace and improve upon the standard type M-107 projectile. However, under pressure from McNamara's office, the M-470 program was canceled on the ground that the old M-107 projectile might be improved by using a new super propelling charge.

The Army did not want to cancel the new M-470 project until the M-107 had been fully tested with the stronger propellant charge. Defense Secretary McNamara disagreed, the M-470 program was canceled, and the Defense Secretary declared "a savings estimated at $50 million over a five-year period will result from elimination of procurement of the new M-470."

The M-107 did not live up to the McNamara predictions. Tests disclosed that "the unmodified M-107 projectile, when propelled by a supercharge, departed from cannon tube in a tumbling action and did not reach the intended target." The M-107 continued to be one problem after another, and the Hardy subcommittee concluded:

"Since the decision was made to cancel M-470 projectile in 1963, the Army had no alternative but to carry on with the M-107 development. . . . Although the Army's 11 years of effort have not produced a weapon which would give our combat troops the increased capability they required, DOD [McNamara's office] has not hesitated to clothe this failure in the shining garb of a claimed multimillion-dollar-cost-reduction item and present it to the public as evidence of management excellence." [26]

Defense Department witnesses testified that under the McNamara formula they were to credit a 25 percent "savings" on all contracts that were in the competitive bid category. They said they would make this arbitrary claim of savings even though they did not take the low bid. In fact, it was testified that even failure to stay within the high bid would not invalidate a claim that there were "savings" if a competitive bidding procedure was used initially.

Chairman Hardy and Representative Otis Pike, a New York Democrat, found this to be highly questionable grounds for claiming savings. It simply meant that once a bidding procedure was used, the claims of savings escalated with the cost.

Representative Pike asked if the Defense Department was claiming savings of 25 percent on the F-111 (the TFX) contract which went to the high-bidding General Dynamics Corporation. Figures initially given to Congress showed that General Dynamics had been the high bidder by more than $400 million, but even as Pike was asking the question, other committees had received information indicating that the F-111 was going to cost about double the initial figure.

The TFX did not qualify for the 25 percent "savings" claim because it was not classified as a competitive bid contract, testified Major General Robert G. Ruegg, Assistant Deputy Chief of Staff for Systems and Logistics for the Air Force. However, he said the F-111 did qualify for a claim of 10 percent "savings" since it was classed as an incentive contract.

"Does the ten percent apply as a savings even if the cost of the contract, say, doubles that [initial cost figures]?" Pike asked.

"Yes, it does," General Ruegg replied.

"So the more the contract costs, once you apply the percentage, the more you save?" Pike came back again.

"I want to add something," broke in Assistant Air Force Secretary Robert H. Charles.

"Are you going to make it worse?" Chairman Hardy quipped.

"I hope not," Charles said. "The point here is that if this contract had been cost plus fixed fee our belief is that it would have been ten percent higher than it actually is today."

"You can't prove it," Hardy declared.

"You can't prove it either way," Charles admitted.

Pike found it almost unbelievable, and he observed: "It is going to be a savings no matter what the contract costs, whether it doubles or triples, no matter what happens to it, it is awfully hard to explain savings to the taxpayers."

The doubts of the New York Democrat were shared by most other members of the subcommittee, Democrats and Republicans. What they had discovered was a far cry from the fully documented and audited "savings" that McNamara had led the Congress and the public to believe he had achieved.

The Hardy subcommittee challenged McNamara's claim that his so-called savings had been audited. Hardy declared the accounting firm had only engaged in "a management survey" that merely sampled the techniques of the Defense Department.

The limited scope prescribed by McNamara "was not sufficient to permit an audit of the program details or to enable the firm to attest to the reasonable accuracy of the reported savings," the Hardy subcommittee stated.[27]

Although the Hardy subcommittee members were concerned about the unjustified claims of savings, there was more concern over evidence they said showed that McNamara's pressure to meet the cost reduction quotas had "degraded the combat potential of the Armed Services."

"The evidence also strongly suggests that these actions [which degraded military capability] would not have been taken by the services had it not been for inordinate pressure from the OSD [McNamara's office] to report large savings," the report stated.

It was related that there were "sharp conflicts between military services and the Secretary of Defense" with respect to certain military requirements.

"Generally, in such cases military judgments have bowed to civilian dictates. The subcommittee has evidence that the OSD, in exercising its dominant power, has at times taken unnecessary risks and committed the services to unwise and precipitous course of action."

The Hardy subcommittee accused the Defense Secretary of what they considered unjustified use of national security classifications to prohibit the subcommittee from making public key documents that gave the clearest picture of how the U. S. military capability had been degraded.

"We have made repeated attempts to have the balance [of the documents] declassified," the subcommittee complained. "Our efforts have been unsuccessful. OSD has taken the position that public disclosure would result in 'comfort to our enemy,' but undoubtedly the enemy derives more comfort from our attenuated military capability resulting from the combat use of inferior weapons.

"Public disclosure of the facts could do much to bring about an improvement in the decisionmaking [*sic*] process responsible for the above condition. . . . A skeptic might question whether disclosure in such a situation could adversely affect the national defense or merely the public image of the decisionmakers."

The Defense Department secrecy didn't bar disclosure of all the cases involving what the Hardy subcommittee called "degraded military capability." One of the most significant of these cases involved a claim of $32,575,000 in savings in fiscal 1965 on the basis of McNamara's decision that the Navy and Marine Corps could accomplish their missions with fewer F-4 aircraft.

The Defense Secretary cut the number of aircraft in each squadron from twelve to fourteen. He did it against the advice and repeated protests of the Navy Department. The Defense Secretary reasoned that increased firepower in the F-4 made it possible for twelve planes to do the job of fourteen. The professional military men in the Navy said it was an erroneous judgment.

Also, the Defense Secretary decided to continue the less capable F-8 aircraft on some classes of carriers rather than replace them with the F-4. He also cut the number of F-4's assigned to training missions.

"Increased effectiveness and larger size of the F4H-1 are not considered valid reasons for reducing fighter squadron allowances from 14 to 12," the Navy insisted. The Navy Department memorandum argued that the Navy and Marine Corps aircraft force numbers were already at the lowest safe number and that a cut in the number "would negate gains in technology and combat effectiveness."

The Defense Secretary continued to disregard the warnings of the professional military men through 1965, when he made further cuts in aircraft procurement. He did increase the procurement in 1966 as a result of losses in Vietnam.

"The Navy had foreseen a threat that the civilians in the Pentagon apparently did not see or if they did see it, they ignored it," the Hardy subcommittee said. "It was developed during the hearings that the price of the aircraft that the Navy was not allowed to buy in fiscal year 1965 would have been substantially less than the price paid for them the following years.

"The time and money lost should be charged against the savings claimed if, indeed, there is a saving at all," the Hardy subcommittee voiced in a unanimous view.[28]

Even if the majority of the people in the nation still had great confidence in Secretary McNamara, there were many men of experience in Congress who had the most serious reservations about his claimed accomplishments.

35

THE PROBLEMS OF CENTRALIZED POWER

"The men who create power make an indispensable contribution to the Nation's greatness, but the men who question power make a contribution just as indispensable, especially when that questioning is disinterested, for they determine whether we use power or power uses us."—PRESIDENT JOHN F. KENNEDY

IN the twenty years following World War II the cost of complicated military hardware went up and up. It seemed likely that defense spending would continue to dominate the federal budget and the danger of the military-industrial complex would be a constant problem.

The trend of four reorganizations had been toward a greater centralization of power all in the name of greater efficiency and better planning. Under Robert S. McNamara, the Office of the Secretary of Defense, once envisioned as a small planning unit to coordinate the three services, had become a huge department by itself. Through administrative action, the functions of military intelligence, supply and audit were centralized in the Office of the Secretary of Defense.

Under tighter centralization, the Defense Secretary dominated the balance of force and controlled the missions of the Army, Navy and Air Force. He dominated the contracts for weapons for the services whether it was the selection of the General Dynamics version of the TFX warplane for the Navy and Air Force or the selection of the FB-111 modification of the TFX as the manned bomber to replace the B-52. The Defense Secretary dominated the decision to reject nuclear power for the aircraft carrier, the *U.S.S. John F. Kennedy,* and to delay the plans on the other nuclear surface warships.

It was the Office of the Defense Secretary that controlled the decision to cut the procurement of helicopters. It was in the Office of the Defense Secretary that the decision was made to phase out the Springfield Armory even as the Vietnam war was escalating. The Defense Secretary willingly took the criticism and the credit for the actions in closing down activities at 862 bases.

The broad discretion lodged in the hands of the Secretary of Defense made him more than the boss of a mighty military power. In his hands was an economic weapon over the biggest business corporations in America with the indirect political power that this entailed. Few defense corporation executives would risk his ill will.

United States Senators and Representatives could be aided or ruined by the Defense Secretary's reactions to their pleas on base closings or on the award of defense contracts.

The Defense Secretary had the power to make or break careers of military men whether they aspired to an attractive command or wished to gain or hold an appointment to the Joint Chiefs of Staff.*

Within the world of higher education, the Defense Secretary had authority to award lucrative research contracts, and also designate appointment of academic leaders to prestige committees and commissions.

All this power is augmented with a tremendous propaganda weapon —the Pentagon press office. This multimillion-dollar operation is backed by research facilities that could not be purchased for a billion dollars a year. This is coupled with the authority to order top military men to concur with the decisions of the political level or decline comment. Through subtle as well as direct control over press access to high political appointees and key military officials, the Secretary of Defense has facilities to exert an indirect power over many newsmen by giving or withholding the exclusive interviews.

Consolidation of functions for supply and common services has gone forward steadily under the McNamara regime, creating huge bureaus with authority over the various services—the Defense Supply Agency, the Defense Intelligence Agency and the Defense Contract Audit Agency. Establishment of agencies with full Pentagon responsibility had cut into the power of the Army, Navy and Air Force and eliminated some of the competition that has so often been spoken of derisively as "service rivalry."

While the trend squelches disputes between the various services, it also reduces the sense of competition that has driven the Army, Air Force and Navy to excel in trying to outshine sister services. This competition may have been destructive in some respects, but it also helped to maintain an esprit de corps that had some value as a morale

* Within the ranks of Defense Department employees, the widespread use of lie detectors and personality tests has, in the opinion of Congressional critics, "seriously circumscribed" the liberties of career employees on matters "which have little or nothing to do with their jobs or national security." "From the reports coming to this subcommittee, I believe there is now being created in the Federal Service a climate of fear, apprehension and coercion which is detrimental to the health of the service and is corroding the rights of Federal employees," said Senator Sam Ervin, the North Carolina Democrat who heads the Senate Constitutional Rights Subcommittee.

builder in the biggest centralized bureaucracy in the history of the world. When the service competition is gone, one significant motivation for excellence will have vanished.

Because of the difficulty of retaining the independent thinking and an inquisitive drive for excellence in the Pentagon bureaucracy, the Defense Department found it necessary to go outside the government bureaucracy for the experts to develop and manage the complicated weapons systems. This process developed its own problems. The Pentagon could farm out its duties to manage weapons development, but the possibility of unreasonable profits were a constant problem where there was laxity in policing three or four tiers of subcontractors. Also, while the work of some of the "think factories" might be worth the cost, the Aerospace story demonstrates that too much independence and too little supervision can result in creation of an unruly Frankenstein that pays little attention to normal security rules or reasonable salary patterns.

Experienced executives of defense-connected industry can be of value to the Pentagon and its huge management problems. Also, industry may find great benefit in hiring high-ranking military officers or key Pentagon civilians for top jobs in private industry. However, the heavy flow of men between defense-connected industries and the government certainly creates a great potential for "conflicts of interest" and a "favoritism" in decision that can be costly to the American taxpayers. These officials are the embodiment of the problem of a "munitions lobby" or the "military-industrial complex" that caused President Eisenhower to sound a warning as he left office.

In the report of the House Armed Services Committee on the "Department of Defense Reorganization Act of 1958," Chairman Carl Vinson and his committee warned:

"It was never intended, and is not now intended that the office of the Secretary of Defense would become a fourth department within the Department of Defense, delving into operational details on a daily basis. The Secretary is supposed to make plans." [1]

If one accepts the thesis that Defense Secretary McNamara is a unique individual who has a sound grasp and deep knowledge of details in what is now a $50 billion-a-year operation, we must ask if the overwhelming centralization he has achieved would have been an equal blessing in the hands of the ordinary men who have served as Defense Secretary in the past.

If one accepts the thesis that Defense Secretary McNamara has been a nonpolitical and economy-minded administrator, we must still ask what might be done if the present centralized Pentagon power fell into the hands of politically motivated or vindictive dictator types.

If one accepts the thesis that Defense Secretary McNamara is so purely motivated and so sound in his judgment that he does not need the curb of Congress, we must ask if normal political patterns give us any assurance that we will always have men of such sterling qualities that they can be trusted to operate without the restraint of congressional investigations.

Admiral Arleigh Burke, a former Chief of Naval Operations, warned that abandonment of the Source Selection Board posed "a danger of destroying the integrity of our military procurement." Admiral George Anderson, a victim of his dissent on the TFX contract, warned: "There are no infallible judgments with respect to national security. . . . Such self-deceptions are a preamble to defeat."

Admiral Anderson, a former Chief of Naval Operations, told a National Press Club audience that he was well aware that top military officers must be responsive to the civilian authority, but warned that civilian authorities should not try to muzzle "the forceful expression of contrary views in proper channels or frank response to congressional inquiry. . . ."

Admiral Anderson scoffed at "the myth" that the admirals and generals are "villains opposed to progress and refugees from new ideas." He noted the warnings of Colonel Charles de Gaulle on the weaknesses in the Maginot Line; Admiral James O. Richardson's caution against leaving the U.S. fleet exposed at Pearl Harbor; and the case of Lieutenant William S. Sims, who, before World War I, took his case for gunnery reform directly to the President.

Hanson Baldwin, *The New York Times* military analyst, was willing to give McNamara credit for "instituting some much-needed management reforms" at the Pentagon, but added that the Defense Secretary must also "share the blame" for creating a bureaucratic "overcentralized organization" that hampers new ideas and speedy development.

This distinguished writer cited McNamara's decision against the nuclear carrier, and directed attention to the testimony of Vice Admiral Hyman Rickover criticizing the Defense Secretary's office for asking for "more studies, [and] more analyses: to the point that we don't build ships."

There was corroborative comment from John C. Reis, a member of the Department of Political Science at the United States Air Force Academy, in his book entitled *The Management of Defense*. Weighing recent Pentagon changes in historic perspective, Reis said: "Fantastic though it may seem, defense reformers have succeeded in turning the calendar back sixty years and are ready to face the demands of 'modern warfare' with a bureau system similar to one that failed to meet the test of the Spanish-American War!" [2]

These were responsible critics, and they had support in Congress, where there was respect for "cost effectiveness" as a goal but disillusionment with it as a propaganda slogan. Many had learned that it was essential to look behind the promotional claims and examine performance in detail. However, many have not learned the lessons of our military history, or been impressed with the danger of centralized power in the hands of either military officers or civilian political appointees.

After World War II, there was a continuous chain of investigations of Defense Department spending, starting with the Republican Eightieth Congress in 1947 and moving through the problems of preparedness in connection with the Vietnam war of 1965 and 1966.

Congress must continue to assert its right to investigate and to criticize the corruption, mismanagement and waste that will inevitably invade an establishment that spends $50 billion each year. No system of organization or reorganization will provide permanent solutions in managing such a mammoth war machine. No man, or small group of men, is infallible in the decisions of the balance of service missions or the selection of complex weapons systems. Over a period of years, the ideas of many men of divergent viewpoints will be needed to test our progress and our defense posture.

The power of the Pentagon is a useful power, an essential power, in the world in which we live. But it is a dangerous power, which carries within it seeds for destruction of our political institutions and our whole way of life. It needs constant examination, constant investigation, and constant criticism from within and from without the walls of the Pentagon. It needs to be curbed periodically. Above all it requires dissent.

Debate will continue on the proper balance between the Defense Department and the various services. Controversy exists over the proper roles of the Army, Navy and Air Force, and the proper balance of forces for nuclear deterrent purposes and for limited warfare.

There has been some inclination to represent all controversies and dissent as bad, disruptive and indicative of continued inefficiency. It is significant that dissent is usually frowned upon by the incumbent Administration and encouraged by the political party that is out of power. Republicans were among those who encouraged military dissent in the "revolt of the admirals" against Truman Administration policy in the late 1940's and the dissent of General Douglas MacArthur against Mr. Truman's policies in the Korean War 1950-'51.

When President Eisenhower came to power a large number of influential Democratic Senators, including Senator Richard Russell of Georgia and Senator Stuart Symington of Missouri, took the lead in criticizing Air Force policies. Senator John F. Kennedy and General Maxwell Taylor (Army Chief of Staff) were among the sharpest critics of the Eisenhower Administration for what they considered over-reliance on "nuclear deterrent" and budget restrictions which they contended had created a "missile gap."

While Kennedy and General Taylor had been loud dissenters against Eisenhower Administration policies they were less than encouraging to dissenters after Kennedy entered the White House in 1961. Defense Secretary MacNamara instituted many "cost effectiveness" reforms, but in the process appeared to be heavy-handed in crushing dissent.

Today the public is faced with a defense budget so complicated that it is difficult to reach definitive conclusions on the performance of a Secretary of Defense. We can view a few rather shocking cases that give us cause for concern, but on the whole we must rely upon future investigations by the Senate and House committees to determine if these are isolated instances or symptoms of serious weakness.

Although they slip in under many disguises, the major enemies of proper defense have always included the following:

(1) Political favoritism that results in poor quality or corruptible civilian appointments at the highest levels.

(2) Political influence on contracts that corrupts procurement policies and wastes defense dollars.

(3) Military and Civil Service bureaucracy that tends to promote mediocrity and to punish dissenters.*

(4) Bureaucratic stodginess and devotion to tradition that causes unreasonable resistance to change.

* Widespread and unjustified use of the polygraph and personality testing has created fear and a more than normal reluctance to dissent. The Defense Department gave 14,270 lie-detector tests in fiscal 1964—more than ten times the 1,155 tests given by the FBI in the same period of time. It took sharp Congressional criticism to force the Defense Department to cut the number of polygraph tests to 11,634 in fiscal 1965 and 6,294 in fiscal 1966.

(5) The military-industrial complex as represented by the political-industrial lawyers and scientists who float in and out of Defense agencies and big defense industries.

(6) Defense public-relations experts who exaggerate our condition of preparedness for political gain, and in the process deceive themselves as well as Congress and the taxpayers into overlooking serious defense weaknesses.

(7) The energetic pacifists and the misguided idealists who prematurely push for major disarmament steps on the theory that this will assure the Communist world that our desire for peace is real.

(8) The out-and-out corrupters who deliver shoddy or defective weapons or matériel and recognize nothing but the fast-buck motive.

(9) The overcentralization that creates bottlenecks and reliance upon too few men, and the lack of centralization in areas where it interferes with proper standardization and buying efficiency.

This book has been an attempt to trace these basic problems that have persisted through history. I will not attempt simple answers. There are no easy answers as to what constitutes the proper function of any of the three service organizations or the proper area for domination by a Defense Secretary.

Likewise, there can be no clear definitive line as to what constitutes proper dissent by professional military men and when they have gone beyond the proper role by questioning or even hampering the operations of a civilian Defense Secretary.

There is no man and no small group of men brilliant enough to provide all the answers when complex weapons systems and a $50 billion annual Defense Department budget are involved. Also, no magic formula is to be found in the possession of our scientific experts, our professional military men, or our politically appointed secretaries. All have their functions, but these can be given no comprehensive and final definition. The answer to proper military preparedness lies in constant awareness of the fact that there are no definitive answers, and in the recognition of the obvious deterrents to efficient military preparedness.

To overcome the problems of keeping our war machine up to date, an Administration must seek the following:

(1) Competent, experienced defense-motivated civilian secretaries who possess the integrity to operate within the law, and the wisdom and restraint to avoid use of their lawful power for political or personal gain.

(2) Experienced professional military men and technical experts who display the industry for real achievement, and the courage to express themselves in opposition to old, out-moded ideas or unrealistic new ideas.

(3) A fair system of competitive bidding to enable us to get the best buy possible for our defense dollars.

(4) A truly competitive system for the development of weapons systems so we are certain we have explored reasonable alternatives and are taking advantage of the best technology available.

(5) A system administered to encourage dissent within the chain of command, and that permits dissent outside the chain of command to promote a constant examination and reexamination of all important decisions.

(6) Strict enforcement of laws and regulations dealing with conflicts of interests, delivery of defective weapons or matériel, pay-offs or other corruption.

(7) Constant congressional examination of the administration of the defense buying and the preparedness posture.

When any one of these points is compromised, there is real reason for public concern over our state of preparedness. Even when the compromises are not apparent there is a need for healthy public skepticism about the self-serving declarations of either political appointees or high military officers.

There can be no doubt that the problem of Pentagon power is the overriding problem of our day. It will continue to be the major problem as long as there is the need for maintaining this huge war machine for our protection against foreign enemies.

Certainly, in today's world we could not consider eliminating or even seriously curbing our military might. It would be thoroughly unrealistic to consider placing our trust in the good faith or the agreements the Communist leaders may sign. Unfortunately, it will be necessary to continue to build, and experiment, and spend more billions for newer and newer weapons that we hope we will never be required to use. That fact poses these questions:

Are we, as a people, bright enough and deep enough to understand and control the power of our war machine?

Do we have an understanding of the need for dissent, criticism, and constant checks on this power?

Can we provide the mechanism to spread that power and control it so it will serve as a protection for a free society of free institutions?

Such attractive slogans as "increased efficiency" and "cost effectiveness" usually mask the moves to centralize power. Although these moves may be initiated in Washington, the responsibility for continuing centralization must be shared by every American citizen who fails to understand the ever-present seeds of authoritarianism. That authoritarianism can make inroads only when our citizens are so careless, so short-sighted and so lazy in their thinking that they permit centralized power to overwhelm free institutions.

Do not try to duck your responsibility.

Do not try to blame it on your Congressman or your Senator because he hasn't given you sufficient warning of the problem. It is likely that he has warned you at several stages before giving up in frustration because you would not listen.

Do not try to blame your lack of information on your newspaper editor when you refused to read the long stories of explanation or the editorials. It is likely that he has given you many warnings on the dangers of centralized power before bowing to your preference for comics, gossip and superficial color.

Accept your responsibility for knowing the dangers of centralized power, of knowing the value of dissent and freedom. The future of our government depends upon you and how you shoulder this responsibility. Your attitude and your actions will determine whether we are an unusual people who know the value of freedom, or whether the United States of America will be remembered simply as an interesting experiment in self-government that failed.

APPENDIX AND NOTES

Appendix A

Expenditures, Fiscal Years 1925-1964

Year	Expenditures		
	Department of the Army (formerly War Department)	Department of the Navy	Department of the Air Force
1925	$ 370,980,708	$ 346,142,001	----------
1926	364,089,945	312,743,410	----------
1927	369,114,122	318,909,096	----------
1928	400,989,683	331,335,492	----------
1929	425,947,194	364,561,544	----------
1930	464,853,515	374,165,639	----------
1931	486,141,754	353,768,185	----------
1932	476,305,311	357,517,834	----------
1933	434,620,860	349,372,794	----------
1934	408,586,783	296,927,490	----------
1935	487,995,220	436,265,532	----------
1936	618,587,184	528,882,143	----------
1937	628,104,285	556,674,066	----------
1938	644,263,842	596,129,739	----------
1939	695,256,481	672,722,327	----------
1940	907,160,151	891,484,523	----------
1941	3,938,943,048	2,313,057,956	----------
1942	14,325,508,098	8,579,588,976	----------
1943	42,525,562,523	20,888,349,026	----------
1944	49,438,330,158	26,537,633,877	----------
1945	50,490,101,935	30,047,152,135	----------
1946	27,986,769,041	15,164,412,379	----------
1947	9,172,138,869	5,597,203,036	----------
1948	7,698,556,403	4,284,619,125	----------
1949	7,862,397,097	4,434,705,920	$ 1,690,460,724
1950	5,789,467,599	4,129,545,653	3,520,632,580
1951	8,635,938,754	5,862,548,845	6,358,603,828
1952	17,452,710,349	10,231,264,765	12,851,619,343
1953	17,054,333,370	11,874,830,152	15,085,227,952
1954	13,515,388,452	11,292,803,940	15,668,473,393
1955	9,450,383,082	9,731,611,019	16,405,038,348
1956	9,274,300,874	9,743,715,334	16,749,647,622
1957	9,704,788,331	10,397,223,998	18,360,926,051
1958	9,775,877,444	10,913,287,404	18,436,830,585
1959	10,284,059,445	11,720,053,749	19,083,326,404
1960	10,293,993,401	11,642,486,702	19,065,244,298
1961	11,102,620,707	12,214,297,075	19,777,722,554
1962	12,425,939,098	13,260,183,267	20,839,825,719
1963	12,782,038,071	14,092,991,160	20,822,869,577
1964	13,406,914,629	14,652,424,948	20,749,576,521

Interest on the public debt	Other	Total expenditures by major purposes	Interfund transactions (deduct)	Total expenditures
$ 881,806,662	$ 1,464,175,961	$ 3,063,105,332	------------	$ 3,063,105,332
831,937,700	1,588,840,768	3,097,611,823	------------	3,097,611,823
787,019,578	1,498,986,878	2,974,029,674	------------	2,974,029,674
731,764,476	1,639,175,204	3,103,264,855	------------	3,103,264,855
678,330,400	1,830,020,348	3,298,859,486	------------	3,298,859,486
659,347,613	1,941,902,117	3,440,268,884	------------	3,440,268,884
611,559,704	2,125,964,360	3,577,434,003	------------	3,577,434,003
599,276,631	3,226,103,049	4,659,202,825	$ 21,294	4,659,181,532
689,365,106	3,149,506,267	4,622,865,028	24,369,110	4,598,495,918
756,617,127	5,231,768,454	6,693,899,854	49,298,113	6,644,601,741
820,926,353	4,775,778,841	6,520,965,945	23,958,245	6,497,007,700
749,396,802	6,596,619,790	8,493,485,919	71,877,714	8,421,608,205
866,384,331	5,704,858,728	7,756,021,409	22,988,139	7,733,033,270
926,280,714	4,625,163,465	6,791,837,760	27,209,289	6,764,628,471
940,539,764	6,549,938,998	8,858,457,570	17,233,572	8,841,223,998
1,040,935,697	6,222,451,833	9,062,032,204	6,763,273	9,055,268,931
1,110,692,812	5,899,509,926	13,262,203,742	7,255,331	13,254,948,411
1,260,085,336	9,880,496,406	34,045,678,816	8,817,329	34,036,861,487
1,808,160,396	14,185,059,207	79,407,131,152	39,417,630	79,367,713,522
2,608,979,806	16,473,764,057	95,058,707,898	72,705,896	94,986,002,002
3,616,686,048	14,262,279,670	98,416,219,790	113,282,721	98,302,937,069
4,721,957,683	12,574,435,216	60,447,574,319	121,532,724	60,326,041,595
4,957,922,484	19,305,128,987	39,032,393,376	109,014,012	38,923,379,364
5,211,101,865	15,874,431,605	33,068,708,998	113,476,853	32,955,232,145
5,339,396,336	20,180,029,420	39,506,989,497	32,576,510	39,474,412,987
5,749,913,064	20,427,444,299	39,617,003,195	72,966,260	39,544,036,935
5,612,654,812	17,588,084,620	44,057,830,859	87,546,409	43,970,284,450
5,859,263,437	19,012,727,036	65,407,584,930	104,383,636	65,303,201,294
6,503,580,030	23,756,285,980	74,274,257,484	154,459,602	74,119,797,882
6,382,485,640	20,913,201,820	67,772,353,245	235,352,928	67,537,000,317
6,370,361,774	22,612,578,594	64,569,972,817	181,235,203	64,388,737,614
6,786,598,862	23,985,513,486	66,539,776,178	315,378,243	66,224,397,935
7,244,193,486	23,725,946,561	69,433,078,427	466,763,865	68,966,314,562
7,606,774,062	25,203,401,856	71,936,171,353	566,997,267	71,369,174,086
7,592,769,102	32,017,030,764	80,697,239,466	354,904,091	80,342,335,375
9,179,588,857	27,052,072,193	77,233,385,451	693,972,652	76,539,412,799
8,957,241,615	30,117,238,211	82,169,120,163	653,952,709	81,515,167,454
9,119,759,808	32,773,715,105	88,419,422,997	632,656,417	87,786,766,581
9,895,303,949	35,561,991,141	93,155,193,898	513,396,839	92,641,797,059
10,665,858,127	38,873,222,190	98,347,996,414	663,621,619	97,684,374,795

Appendix B

Military Procurement by States for 1963, 1964, and 1965

(Amounts in thousands)

STATE	FISCAL YEAR 1963	FISCAL YEAR 1964	FISCAL YEAR 1965
	Amount	Amount	Amount
Total, United States	$28,107,882	$27,470,379	$26,631,132
Not distributed by State	2,874,642	3,053,272	3,363,052
State total	25,233,240	24,417,107	23,268,080
Alabama	194,990	190,681	165,176
Alaska	103,476	101,545	74,175
Arizona	285,751	173,825	176,857
Arkansas	39,114	29,731	39,284
California	5,835,670	5,100,650	5,153,639
Colorado	444,196	389,511	249,151
Connecticut	1,048,449	1,126,054	1,180,111
Delaware	47,483	30,424	38,239
District of Columbia	238,120	222,947	247,576
Florida	583,237	782,591	633,332
Georgia	423,290	520,169	662,417
Hawaii	45,206	52,112	72,213
Idaho	8,634	7,804	11,724
Illinois	486,067	429,201	421,899
Indiana	486,759	537,940	604,925
Iowa	130,406	103,392	133,951
Kansas	331,687	289,045	229,051
Kentucky	55,725	40,476	42,749
Louisiana	195,341	181,427	255,834
Maine	58,409	31,531	68,771
Maryland	606,365	547,936	584,333
Massachusetts	1,060,165	1,032,062	1,178,729
Michigan	633,047	591,290	532,897
Minnesota	273,757	217,941	259,500
Mississippi	186,039	155,911	152,188
Missouri	686,111	1,349,071	1,060,781
Montana	79,349	16,422	69,375
Nebraska	33,559	33,921	42,708
Nevada	13,143	6,361	19,142
New Hampshire	51,174	64,857	52,400
New Jersey	1,251,608	917,561	820,309
New Mexico	61,642	71,486	84,137
New York	2,500,146	2,496,438	2,229,473
North Carolina	258,987	273,516	288,408
North Dakota	64,855	192,025	48,997
Ohio	1,345,686	1,028,946	863,113
Oklahoma	111,204	122,489	119,803
Oregon	41,777	29,104	39,624
Pennsylvania	887,452	883,065	988,811
Rhode Island	46,970	38,173	86,323
South Carolina	57,747	51,621	81,580
South Dakota	80,630	23,308	21,062
Tennessee	183,478	193,564	197,287
Texas	1,203,123	1,294,431	1,446,769
Utah	427,679	340,040	191,173
Vermont	12,258	14,012	32,202
Virginia	484,989	690,852	469,097
Washington	1,041,581	1,085,696	545,607
West Virginia	162,201	87,327	90,312
Wisconsin	219,427	177,217	203,003
Wyoming	125,081	49,408	7,867

Appendix C

Contracts Negotiated and Advertised for Bids from 1951 through 1965

FISCAL YEAR	Total Net Value (millions)	FORMALLY ADVERTISED PROCUREMENT		NEGOTIATED PROCUREMENT	
		Millions	Percent	Millions	Percent
1951	$ 30,823	$ 3,720	12.1	$ 27,103	87.9
1952	41,482	4,479	10.8	37,003	89.2
1953	27,822	3,089	11.1	24,733	88.9
1954	11,448	1,789	15.6	9,659	84.4
1955	14,930	2,386	16.0	12,544	84.0
1956	17,750	2,815	15.9	14,935	84.1
1957	19,133	3,321	17.4	15,812	82.6
1958	21,827	3,115	14.3	18,712	85.7
1959	22,744	3,089	13.6	19,655	86.4
1960	21,302	2,978	14.0	18,324	86.0
1961	22,992	2,770	12.0	20,222	88.0
1962	26,147	3,412	13.1	22,735	86.9
1963	27,143	3,538	13.0	23,605	87.0
1964	26,221	3,889	14.8	22,332	85.2
1965	25,281	4,660	18.4	20,621	81.6
Total, 1951-65	357,045	49,050	13.7	307,995	86.3

Source: "Military Prime Contract Awards and Subcontract Payments or Commitments, July 1964 - June 1965," Office of the Secretary of Defense.

Appendix D

Defense Personnel, Military and Civilian, by States for Fiscal Year 1965

	ACTIVE DUTY MILITARY PERSONNEL		CIVILIAN EMPLOYEES	
	Number, June 30, 1965[1]	Estimated annual pay and allowances[2]	Number, June 30, 1965	Estimated annual payroll[2]
United States total	1,041,244	$7,780,791,000	940,763	$6,774,018,000
Alabama	24,016	130,342,000	33,268	227,683,000
Alaska	30,892	137,571,000	6,281	57,311,000
Arizona	21,244	104,506,000	7,176	48,100,000
Arkansas	9,898	53,634,000	3,961	29,065,000
California	212,859	983,125,000	138,777	1,046,581,000
Colorado	35,421	163,031,000	14,450	100,550,000
Connecticut	3,695	23,089,000	3,132	23,460,000
Delaware	7,222	43,086,000	1,236	7,745,000
District of Columbia	19,850	142,486,000	29,040	229,850,000
Florida	69,969	361,772,000	25,154	166,116,000
Georgia	93,980	396,437,000	33,563	223,527,000
Hawaii	40,184	182,799,000	18,964	120,789,000
Idaho	5,410	30,506,000	433	3,036,000
Illinois	47,427	219,320,000	28,124	200,111,000
Indiana	8,506	41,052,000	12,466	83,269,000
Iowa	1,445	8,066,000	630	3,744,000
Kansas	29,757	172,835,000	4,728	31,949,000
Kentucky	48,901	171,979,000	12,050	79,133,000
Louisiana	34,334	127,801,000	6,531	44,290,000
Maine	12,246	64,521,000	1,687	10,498,000
Maryland	51,435	253,749,000	41,103	342,742,000
Massachusetts	30,450	153,458,000	22,809	172,010,000
Michigan	19,899	104,764,000	11,614	83,094,000
Minnesota	5,167	23,892,000	2,105	12,899,000
Mississippi	21,302	104,898,000	6,194	41,676,000
Missouri	28,518	103,612,000	17,101	113,513,000
Montana	9,526	50,413,000	1,030	6,366,000
Nebraska	16,404	101,366,000	3,999	24,914,000
Nevada	7,565	40,086,000	2,656	18,154,000
New Hampshire	7,714	41,374,000	8,147	62,235,000
New Jersey	36,857	165,783,000	25,085	170,601,000
New Mexico	21,507	110,630,000	11,110	75,042,000
New York	35,097	173,826,000	44,628	342,113,000
North Carolina	86,815	344,414,000	10,478	63,389,000
North Dakota	12,306	59,066,000	1,386	8,155,000
Ohio	18,639	110,833,000	37,252	332,930,000
Oklahoma	33,991	161,249,000	25,606	168,584,000
Oregon	4,955	25,722,000	3,420	23,273,000
Pennsylvania	15,593	76,592,000	66,382	509,561,000
Rhode Island	6,550	37,886,000	8,808	56,053,000
South Carolina	50,197	185,320,000	15,302	98,540,000
South Dakota	6,573	34,362,000	1,344	8,865,000
Tennessee	18,428	90,144,000	6,178	44,832,000
Texas	165,099	798,445,000	60,051	398,522,000
Utah	4,642	23,555,000	19,335	138,504,000
Vermont	287	1,581,000	74	399,000
Virginia	88,811	443,878,000	79,582	540,152,000
Washington	45,556	210,507,000	22,301	156,825,000
West Virginia	528	2,513,000	1,126	6,867,000
Wisconsin	4,204	21,593,000	2,311	11,922,000
Wyoming	4,579	24,703,000	595	4,479,000
Undistributed	24,794	142,619,000		
Washington, D.C., metropolitan area	62,246	353,364,000	79,558	594,520,000
District of Columbia	19,850	142,486,000	29,040	229,850,000
Maryland	13,189	65,602,000	16,017	133,566,000
Virginia	29,207	145,276,000	34,501	231,104,000

[1]Excludes naval personnel assigned to fleet units and to other afloat and mobile activities.
[2]Fiscal year 1965.

Source: Directorate for Statistical Activities, Office of the Secretary of Defense, Sept. 14, 1965.

NOTES

Chapter 2

1. For a history of the struggle for proper balance between the civilian and military administration of the Defense establishment, see: Tracy Barrett Kittredge, *Naval Lessons of the Great War* (New York, Doubleday Page & Co., 1921) pp. 13-24.
2. Charles O. Paullin, "Naval Administration 1789-1911," *Proceedings of the United States Naval Institute,* p. 65.
3. Admiral Stephen B. Luce, *Proceedings of the United States Naval Institute 1902.*
4. *Report of the Secretary of the Navy, 1861* (Washington, D.C., Government Printing Office, 1861).
5. *Report of the Secretary of the Navy, 1863* (Washington, D.C., Government Printing Office, 1863) p. xi.
6. Luce, *op. cit.*
7. Richard N. Current, Frank Freidel and T. Harry Williams, *A History of the United States* (*since 1865*) (New York, Alfred A. Knopf, 1959) p. 246.
8. Kittredge, *op. cit.*, p. 20.
9. Navy General Orders Number 9, September, 1909.
10. Elting E. Morison, *Admiral Sims and the Modern American Navy,* (Boston, Houghton Mifflin Co., 1942) p. 84.
11. The definitive biography of Admiral Sims is: Morison, *op. cit.*
12. All of the Sims reports may be found in the Sims Papers.
13. Morison, *op. cit.*, pp. 86-88.
14. *Ibid.*, p. 100.
15. Charles Lee Lewis, *Famous American Naval Officers* (Boston, L. C. Page & Co., 1924) p. 333.
16. Morison, *op. cit.*, pp. 104-05.
17. *World's Work,* July 1917, p. 337.
18. *World's Work,* August 1919, p. 390.

Chapter 3

1. The Huntingdon Horses investigation may be found in the transcript of the testimony: House Report Number 2 (Report of the Committee on Government Contracts), 37th Congress, 2nd Session, pp. lvi-lviii, 507-12.
2. Senate Executive Document Number 67, 37th Congress, 2nd Session, pp. 25-27.
3. House Report No. 2, p. 55.

4. Ripley to Hagner, July 16, 1861, Ordnance Reports, Series 1, Vol. III.
5. Howard A. Meneely, *The War Department, 1861* (New York, Columbia University, 1928) p. 270.
6. House Report No. 2, pp. lvi, 78.
7. *Ibid.*, pp. lxi-lxiv.
8. *Congressional Globe* (February 26-May 2, 1862), Vol. 60, 37th Congress, 1st Session [*sic*], p. 1886.
9. Meneely, *op. cit.*, p. 273.
10. House Report No. 2, pp. 37-38, 40.
11. Report of the Committee on the Conduct of the War, Part III, pp. 45-46, 251.
12. House Report No. 2, pp. 4-41, 51.
13. Report of the Committee on the Conduct of the War, pp. 48-49.
14. House Report No. 2, p. 41.
15. *Ibid.*, pp. lxi-lxiv.
16. Report of the Committee on the Conduct of the War, Part III, p. 53.
17. House Executive Document Number 94, 37th Congress, 2nd Session, pp. 25-26.
18. Meneely, *op. cit.*, p. 271.
19. Meneely, *op. cit.*, p. 271.
20. Full opinion quoted in Meneely, *op. cit.*, p. 263.
21. *Congressional Globe*, p. 1888.
22. Mark Sullivan, *Our Times, Vol. V* (New York, Charles Scribner's Sons, 1933) pp. 210-18.
23. *Ibid.*, p. 221.
24. For a full history of Josephus Daniels' tenure as Secretary of the Navy see:
    Tracy Barrett Kittredge, *Naval Lessons of the Great War* (New York, Doubleday Page & Co., 1921).
25. Sullivan, *op. cit.*, pp. 156-59.
26. *Ibid.*, pp. 223-26.
27. Richard N. Current, Frank Freidel and T. Harry Williams, *A History of the United States* (*since 1865*) (New York, Alfred A. Knopf, 1959) p. 372.
28. Sullivan, *op. cit.*, p. 207.
29. Arthur M. Schlesinger, *Political and Social Growth of the American People, 1865-1940* (New York, The Macmillan Company, 1941) p. 432.
30. Current, *op. cit.*, p. 387.
31. *Ibid.*, p. 376.
32. Kittredge, *op. cit.* (The full book covers the investigation.)
33. *Ibid.*, p. 45.
34. *Ibid.*, p. 47.
35. *Ibid.*, pp. 55ff.
36. Daniels to Page, December 19, 1919, found in Kittredge, *op. cit.*, p. 65.
37. Kittredge, p. 2.
38. Sullivan, *op. cit.*, *Vol VI*, p. 204 (date 1935).
39. *Ibid.*, pp. 203-04.

Chapter 4

1. Colonel Flint O. DuPre, USAFR, *U.S. Air Force Biographical Dictionary* (New York, Franklin Watts, Inc., 1965) p. 169.
2. Isaac Don Levine, *Flying Crusader: The Story of General William Mitchell, Pioneer of Air Power* (London, Peter Davies, 1943) p. 67.
3. Levine, *op. cit.*, p. 215.
4. *Ibid.*, pp. 150-90.
5. *Ibid.*
6. Major Alfred F. Hurley, USAF, *Billy Mitchell, Crusader for Air Power* (New York, Franklin Watts, Inc., 1964) p. 93.
7. Hurley, *op. cit.*, p. 88.
8. *Ibid.*, p. 93.
9. *Army-Navy Journal,* October 11, 1924, p. 1420.
10. Levine, *op. cit.*, pp. 256-57.
11. Roger Burlingame, *General Billy Mitchell, Champion of Air Defense* (New York, McGraw-Hill, 1952) pp. 145-46.
12. *Army-Navy Journal,* September 12, 1925, pp. 25, 27.
13. Burlingame, *op. cit.*, p. 148.
14. *Army-Navy Journal,* September 19, 1925, p. 49.
15. *Ibid.*, p. 54.
16. *Ibid.*, p. 63.
17. Hurley, *op. cit.*, p. 99.
18. *Ibid.*, p .103.
19. Levine, *op. cit.*, p. 260.
20. Burlingame, *op. cit.*, p. 165.
21. Hurley, *op. cit.*, p. 107.
22. Burlingame, *op. cit.*, p. 164.
23. Richard N. Current, Frank Freidel and T. Harry Williams, *A History of the United States (since 1865)* (New York, Alfred A. Knopf, 1959) pp. 527-50.
    Arthur S. Link, *American Epoch* (New York, Alfred A. Knopf, 1961) pp. 472-81.
24. *Information Please Almanac, 1966,* p. 600.
25. Current, *op. cit.*, p. 537.
26. *Ibid.*, p. 537.
27. *Ibid.*, p. 540.
28. *Ibid.*, pp. 540-41.

Chapter 5

1. *The New York Times,* December 7, 1941, p. 1.
2. Richard N. Current, Frank Freidel and T. Harry Williams, *A History of the United States (since 1865)* (New York, Alfred A. Knopf, 1959) p. 548.
   Arthur S. Link, *American Epoch* (New York, Alfred A. Knopf, 1961) p. 502.
3. Senate Report Number 440, Part 6 (Report of the Special Committee In-

vestigating the National Defense Program), 80th Congress, 2nd Session, p. 1.

Current, *op. cit.*, p. 560.

Link, *op. cit.*, pp. 504-05.

4. Senate Report 440, p. 2.
5. Link, *op. cit.*, p. 509.
6. Senate Report 440, p. 285.
7. *Ibid.*, p. 286.
8. *Ibid.*, pp. 286-87.
9. *Ibid.*, p. 295.
10. *Ibid.*, p. 293.
11. Navy Library, telephone interview. February 7, 1966.

Chapter 6

1. Hearings of the Senate Select Committee to Investigate the National Defense Program, Vol. 3, p. 5356.
2. *Ibid.*, p. 5116.
3. *Ibid.*, p. 5119.
4. *Ibid.*, p. 5122.
5. *The New York Times,* November 13, 1958, pp. 1, 33.
6. *The New York Times,* May 26, 1944, p. 10.
7. *The New York Times,* May 27, 1944, p. 17.
8. *Idem.*
9. *The New York Times,* December 3, 1946, p. 33.
10. *The New York Times,* December 4, 1946, p. 63.
11. *The New York Times,* December 7, 1946, p. 34.
12. *The New York Times,* May 29, 1948, p. 30.

Chapter 7

1. Senate Report No. 440, Part 6 (Report of the Special Committee Investigating the National Defense Program), 80th Congress, 2nd Session, p. 130.
2. *Ibid.*, p. 119.
3. *Ibid.*, pp. 114-15.
4. *Ibid.*, p. 115.
5. *Ibid.*, p. 119.
6. *Washington Post,* December 20, 1946, pp. 1, 14.
7. Senate Report No. 110, Part 8, January 2, 1947.
8. *Washington Post,* August 22, 1947, p. 13.
9. *The New York Times,* July 3, 1946, p. 1.
10. *The New York Times,* July 27, 1946, p. 1.
11. *The New York Times,* July 4, 1947, p. 1.
12. *The New York Times,* September 7, 1959, p. 15.

Chapter 8

1. Senate Report No. 440, Part 6 (Report of the Special Committee Investigating the National Defense Program), 80th Congress, 2nd Session, p. 244.
2. *Ibid.*, p. 245.

3. *Ibid.*, p. 246.
4. *Ibid.*, p. 247.
5. *Ibid.*, p. 248.
6. *Ibid.*, p. 248.
7. *Ibid.*, p. 249.
8. *Ibid.*, p. 250.
9. *Ibid.*, p. 253.
10. *Ibid.*, p. 255.
11. *Ibid.*, p. 257.
12. *Ibid.*, p. 258.
13. *Ibid.*, p. 261.
14. *Ibid.*, p. 262.
15. *Ibid.*, p. 371.
16. *Ibid.*, p. 372.
17. *Ibid.*, p. 373.
18. *Ibid.*, p. 375.
19. *Ibid.*, pp. 376-77.

Chapter 9

1. Hearings of the Senate Committee to Investigate the National Defense Program, p. 26760.
2. *Ibid.*, pp. 27083-88.
3. *Ibid.*, pp. 27020-26.
4. *Ibid.*, p. 27029.
5. "Congress and the Nation, 1945-1964," *Congressional Quarterly*, 1965, p. 1693.
6. Hearings, pp. 27146-48.
7. Senate Report No. 440, Part 6 (Report of the Special Committee Investigating the National Defense Program), 80th Congress, 2nd Session, p. 269.
8. *Ibid.*, p. 271.
9. *Ibid.*, p. 272.
10. *Ibid.*, p. 273.
11. *Ibid.*, p. 274.

Chapter 10

1. Senate Report No. 440, Part 6 (Report of the Special Committee Investigating the National Defense Program), 80th Congress, 2nd Session, p. 282.
2. *Ibid.*, p. 283.
3. *Idem.*
4. "Congress and the Nation, 1945-1964," *Congressional Quarterly*, 1965, p. 240.
5. *The New York Times,* June 16, 1946, p. 35.
6. *The New York Times,* May 5, 1946, p. 1.
7. *Ibid.*, p. 8.
8. *The New York Times,* May 9, 1946, p. 16.
9. "Congress and the Nation," *op. cit.*, p. 249.
10. *Ibid.*, p. 247.

11. Senate Report No. 440, p. 308.
12. *The New York Times,* May 23, 1949, p. 1.
13. "Congress and the Nation," *op. cit.*, pp. 254-55.
14. *Ibid.*, p. 255.
15. *Ibid.*, pp. 255-57.

Chapter 11

1. Senate Report 1232 (Interim Report of the Subcommittee on Investigations of the Senate Committee on Expenditures of the Executive Departments), 81st Congress, 2nd Session, pp. 29, 30.
2. Hearings of the Subcommittee on Investigations of the Senate Committee on Expenditures of the Executive Departments, 81st Congress, 2nd Session, p. 1.
3. Senate Report 1232, p. 2.
4. *Ibid.*, p. 2.
5. *Ibid.*, pp. 7, 8.
6. *Ibid.*, pp. 9-11.
7. *Ibid.*, p. 11.
8. *Ibid.*, p. 13.
9. *Ibid.*, p. 12.
10. *Ibid.*, pp. 12-14.
11. *Ibid.*, p. 8.
12. *Ibid.*, pp. 16, 17.
13. *The New York Times,* April 18, 1950, p. 7.
14. Hearings, p. 504.
15. Senate Report 1232, pp. 8, 9.
16. *Ibid.*, p. 14.
17. *Idem.*
18. Hearings, pp. 290-92.
19. *Ibid.*, pp. 313-15.
20. *Ibid.*, pp. 535-39.
21. Senate Report 1232, p. 14.
22. *Ibid.*, pp. 15, 22.
23. Hearings, pp. 477-83.
24. Senate Report 1232, p. 14.
25. *The New York Times,* April 27, 1950, p. 1.
26. *The New York Times,* May 26, 1951, p. 34.
27. *Ibid.*, p. 34.
28. Senate Report 1232, p. 21.
29. *Ibid.*, p. 6.
30. *Ibid.*, pp. 23, 24.
31. *Ibid.*, p. 25.
32. *Ibid.*, p. 31.

Chapter 12

1. "Congress and the Nation, 1945-1964," *Congressional Quarterly,* 1965, p. 265.
2. *Facts on File,* 1950, p. 220C.
3. *Ibid.*, pp. 100H-J.

4. *Ibid.*, p. 205B.
5. "Congress and the Nation," *op. cit.*, pp. 261-62.
6. *Ibid.*, p. 262.
7. *Ibid.*, p. 261.
8. *Facts on File,* p. 308H.
9. "Congress and the Nation," *op. cit.*, p. 267.
10. *Facts on File,* p. 340N.
11. *Ibid.*, p. 366A.
12. *The New York Times,* June 26, 1950, p. 2.
13. *Ibid.*, p. 1.
14. "Congress and the Nation," *op. cit.*, p. 258.
15. *Ibid.*, p. 316.
16. *Facts on File,* p. 220D.
17. "Congress and the Nation," *op. cit.*, p. 269.
18. *Facts on File,* p. 275C.
19. *Ibid.*, pp. 330D-J.
20. *Ibid.*, p. 330L.
21. "Congress and the Nation," *op. cit.*, p. 269.
22. Richard N. Current, Frank Freidel and T. Harry Williams, *A History of the United States (since 1865)* (New York, Alfred A. Knopf, 1959) p. 660.
23. "Congress and the Nation," *op. cit.*, p. 269.

Chapter 13

1. Hearings of the Special Subcommittee on Procurement of the House Committee on Armed Services, 82nd Congress, 2nd Session, p. 3147.
2. *Idem.*
3. House Interim Report of the Special Subcommittee on Procurement of the House Committee on Armed Services, 82nd Congress, 2nd Session, pp. 2, 3.
4. Hearings, p. 3143.
5. *Washington News,* February 9, 1952; *Life,* February 18, 1952, p. 47.
6. *Washington News,* February 9, 1952.
7. Hearings, pp. 3141, 3142.
8. *Ibid.*, pp. 3147-50.
9. *Ibid.*, pp. 3153-57.
10. *Ibid.*, pp. 3158, 3159.
11. *Ibid.*, pp. 3153, 3159.
12. *Washington News,* February 9, 1952.
13. *Ibid.; Cleveland Plain Dealer,* February 9, 1952.
14. *Shreveport Journal,* February 5, 1952.
15. *Washington News,* February 11, 1952.
16. House Interim Report, pp. 1, 3, 4.
17. "Congress and the Nation, 1945-1964," *Congressional Quarterly,* 1965, p. 272.
18. New Orleans *Times-Picayune,* February 8, 1952; *Cleveland Plain Dealer,* February 9, 1952; *Washington Post,* February 14, 1952.
19. Drew Pearson, in the *Washington Post,* February 14, 1952.

Chapter 14

1. Richard N. Current, Frank Freidel and T. Harry Williams, *A History of the United States* (*since 1865*) (New York, Alfred A. Knopf, 1959) p. 666.
2. *Ibid.*, p. 670.
3. "Congress and the Nation, 1945-1964," *Congressional Quarterly*, 1965, p. 275.
4. *Ibid.*, p. 274.
5. Current, *op. cit.*, p. 666.
6. *Ibid.*, 667.
7. "Congress and the Nation," *op. cit.*, p. 275.
8. *Idem.*
9. *Ibid.*, p. 176.
10. *Idem.*
11. *Ibid.*, pp. 279-80.
12. *Ibid.*, p. 286.

Chapter 15

1. Senate Report No. 856 (Report of the Committee on Government Operations made by its Permanent Subcommittee on Investigations), 84th Congress, 1st Session, p. 9.
2. Hearings before the Senate Special Subcommittee on Government Operations, pp. 107-18, 123-43.
3. See: Hearings of the Special Senate Investigation on Charges and Countercharges Involving: Secretary of the Army Robert T. Stevens, John G. Adams, H. Struve Hensel and Senator Joe McCarthy, Roy M. Cohn, and Francis P. Carr.
4. For full text of letter see: *Ibid.*, p. 1249.
5. *Ibid.*, p. 1263.
6. See Hearings of the Senate Select McCarthy Censure Committee.
7. Senate Report No. 856, p. 35.

Chapter 16

1. Senate Report No. 1380 (Report of the Committee on Government Operations made by its Permanent Subcommittee on Investigations), 84th Congress, 2nd Session, p. 11.
2. Hearings before the Permanent Subcommittee on Investigations of the Committee on Government Operations, 84th Congress, 1st Session, p. 1.
3. Senate Report No. 1380, p. 11.
4. *Ibid.*, p. 12.
5. *Ibid.*, p. 2.
6. *Ibid.*, p. 21.
7. *Ibid.*, p. 22.
8. *Ibid.*, pp. 22-23.
9. Hearings, pp. 149-50.
10. Senate Report No. 1380, p. 13.
11. *Ibid.*, p. 14.

12. *Ibid.*, p. 3.
13. *Ibid.*, p. 2.
14. *Facts on File, 1957*, p. 142.
15. Report of the House Committee on Government Operations, August 4, 1957, 85th Congress, 1st Session, p. 1.
16. See full report, *ibid.*

Chapter 17

1. Senate Report No. 1444 (1956 Annual Report of the Committee on Government Operations made by its Subcommittee on Investigations), 84th Congress, 2nd Session, p. 16.
2. Hearings before the Senate Permanent Subcommittee on Investigations of the Committee on Government Operations, January 16, 1953, p. 92.
3. Senate Report No. 1444, p. 17.
4. *Ibid.*, p. 18.
5. *Ibid.*, p. 19.
6. *Ibid.*, p. 18.
7. Hearings, July 21, 1955, p. 18.
8. *Ibid.*, pp. 28-31; Senate Report No. 1444, p. 20.
9. Senate Report No. 1444, p. 20.
10. *Ibid.*, p. 21.
11. Hearings, July 25, 1955, pp. 83-86.
12. *Ibid.*, July 26, 1955, pp. 95-96.
13. Senate Report No. 1444, p. 24.
14. *Ibid.*, p. 24.
15. "Congress and the Nation, 1945-1964," *Congressional Quarterly*, 1965, p. 1735.

Chapter 18

1. Hearings before the Subcommittee on the Air Force of the Senate Committee on Armed Services, 84th Congress, 2nd Session, p. 1.
2. Senate Document No. 29 (Report of the Subcommittee on the Air Force of the Committee on Armed Services), 85th Congress, 1st Session, p. 122.
3. *Ibid.*, see table on p. 123.
4. *Ibid.*, see table on p. 123.
5. *Ibid.*, p. 106.
6. *Ibid.*, p. 37.
7. *Ibid.*, p. 11.
8. Hearings, p. 19.
9. *Ibid.*, p. 21.
10. *Ibid.*, pp. 1498, 1809, 1848.
11. *Ibid.*, pp. 105, 116, 219-20.
12. *Ibid.*, pp. 244, 258, 263, 268-69, 273.
13. Senate Document No. 29, p. 10.
14. *Idem.*
15. Hearings, pp. 1120-22.
16. *Ibid.*, p. 1357.
17. *Ibid.*, p. 109.

18. Senate Document No. 29, p. 55.
19. *Ibid.*, p. 95.
20. *Ibid.*, p. 96.
21. *Idem.*
22. *Ibid.*, p. 127.
23. Hearings, p. 1724.
24. *Ibid.*, p. 1469.

Chapter 19

1. House Report No. 917 (Thirteenth Report by the Committee on Government Operations), 88th Congress, 1st Session, p. 4.
2. *Ibid.*, p. 4.
3. *Ibid.*, p. 5.
4. *Ibid.*, p. 6.
5. *Ibid.*, p. 54.
6. *Ibid.*, pp. 74-75.
7. Report of the Subcommittee for Special Investigations of the House Committee on Armed Services (August 12, 1965), 89th Congress, 1st Session, pp. 6-7.
8. *Ibid.*, pp. 6, 39-40.
9. *Ibid.*, p. 7.
10. *Ibid.*, pp. 7, 33.
11. For full text of the Air Force policy statement see: *Ibid.*, pp. 11-13.
12. *Ibid.*, p. 39.
13. *Ibid.*, pp. 2-3.
14. *Ibid.*, p. 51.
15. *Ibid.*, p. 52.
16. *Idem.*
17. *Ibid.*, p. 54.
18. *Ibid.*, p. 55.
19. *Ibid.*, p. 56.
20. *Ibid.*, p. 61.
21. *Ibid.*, p. 62.

Chapter 20

1. House Report No. 234 (Second Report by the Committee on Government Operations), 86th Congress, 1st Session, p. 19.
2. *Ibid.*, p. 26.
3. *Ibid.*, pp. 10-11.
4. *Ibid.*, p. 74.
5. Clark R. Mollenhoff, *Washington Cover-Up* (New York, Doubleday, 1962) p. 146.
6. House Report No. 234, p. 86.
7. *Ibid.*, p. 83.
8. Presidential Press Conference, September 27, 1956.
9. Hearings of the Special Subcommittee on Government Information of the Committee on Government Operations (January 22, 1959), p. 3973.
10. House Report No. 1224 (Thirteenth Report by the Committee on Government Operations), 86th Congress, 2nd Session, p. 2.

11. Clark R. Mollenhoff, *Washington Cover-Up* (New York, Doubleday, 1962) p. 151.
12. House Report No. 234, p. 81.
13. House Report No. 1224, pp. 3-4.

Chapter 21

1. General Maxwell D. Taylor, U.S. Army (Ret.), *The Uncertain Trumpet* (New York, Harper & Brothers, 1959) pp. x-xi.
2. *Ibid.*, p. 45.
3. Report of the Preparedness Investigation Subcommittee of the Senate Committee on Armed Services, 86th Congress, 2nd Session, p. 1.
4. *Ibid.*, p. 2.
5. *Idem.*
6. *Ibid.*, pp. 2-3.
7. *Ibid.*, p. 22.
8. *Idem.*
9. *Ibid.*, pp. 15-17.
10. *Ibid.*, p. 23.
11. *Ibid.*, p. 4.
12. *Ibid.*, p. 5.
13. *Ibid.*, p. 6.
14. "Congress and the Nation, 1945-1964," *Congressional Quarterly*, 1965, p. 306.

Chapter 22

1. Report of the Subcommittee for Special Investigations of the House Committee on Armed Services, 86th Congress, 1st Session.
2. "Congress and the Nation, 1945-1964," *Congressional Quarterly*, 1965, p. 308.
3. *Ibid.*, p. 311.
4. *Ibid.*, p. 312.
5. *Idem.*
6. *Ibid.*, p. 41.
7. House Report No. 1257 (Eleventh Report by the Committee on Government Operation), 87th Congress, 1st Session, p. 55.
8. *Idem.*

Chapter 23

1. The primary source for this chapter is: House Report No. 1858, "Illegal Actions in the Construction of the Airfield at Fort Lee, Virginia" (Seventeenth Report by the Committee on Government Operations, June 20, 1962), 87th Congress, 2nd Session.

Chapter 24

1. Report of the Special Preparedness Subcommittee of the Senate Armed Services Committee (Military Cold War Education and Speech Review Policies), 87th Congress, 2nd Session, p. 12.
2. *Ibid.*, p. 18.
3. *Ibid.*, p. 19.

4. "Congress and the Nation, 1945-1964," *Congressional Quarterly*, 1965, p. 318.
5. Report, p. 1.
6. *Idem.*
7. *Ibid.*, p. 17.
8. *Ibid.*, p. 14.
9. *Ibid.*, p. 15.
10. *Ibid.*, pp. 14-15.
11. *Ibid.*, p. 30.
12. Hearings of the Special Preparedness Subcommittee of the Senate Armed Services Committee (Military Cold War Education and Speech Review Policies), pp. 508-09.
13. Report, p. 30.
14. *Ibid.*, pp. 18-19.
15. *Ibid.*, p. 31.
16. *Ibid.*, p. 17.
17. *Idem.*

Chapter 25

1. Senate Report No. 970 (Report by the Permanent Subcommittee on Investigations of the Committee on Government Operations), 88th Congress, 2nd Session, p. 1.
2. *Ibid.*, p. 2.
3. *Ibid.*, p. 4.
4. *Ibid.*, p. 5.
5. *Ibid.*, p. 8.
6. *Ibid.*, p. 14.
7. *Ibid.*, chart, p. 13.
8. *Ibid.*, p. 14 and chart, p. 28.
9. *Ibid.*, chart, p. 26.
10. *Ibid.*, p. 18.
11. *Ibid.*, chart, p. 26.
12. *Ibid.*, p. 23.
13. Hearings of the Permanent Subcommittee on Investigations of the Senate Committee on Government Operations, p. 508.
14. Senate Report No. 970, pp. 75-76.
15. *Ibid.*, p. 92.
16. *Ibid.*, p. 93.
17. *Ibid.*, p. 94.
18. *Ibid.*, p. 100.
19. *Ibid.*, p. 103.
20. *Ibid.*, p. 107.
21. Hearings, pp. 566-67.
22. Senate Report No. 970, p. 108.
23. *Ibid.*, chart, p. 109.
24. *Ibid.*, pp. 140-41.
25. *Ibid.*, p. 144.
26. *Ibid.*, pp. 152-53.

27. *Ibid.*, pp. 154-55.
28. *Ibid.*, pp. 153, 155.

Chapter 26

1. Report of the Subcommittee for Special Investigations of the House Committee on Armed Services (August 12, 1965), 89th Congress, 1st Session, pp. 13-14.
2. *Ibid.*, p. 14.
3. *Ibid.*, p. 16.
4. *Ibid.*, p. 17.
5. *Ibid.*, p. 18.
6. *Idem.*
7. *Ibid.*, p. 19
8. *Idem.*
9. *Ibid.*, p. 20.
10. *Ibid.*, p. 21.
11. *Idem.*
12. *Idem.*
13. *Ibid.*, p. 22.
14. *Ibid.*, p. 24.
15. *Ibid.*, pp. 22, 25.
16. *Ibid.*, p. 2.
17. *Ibid.*, p. 3.
18. *Ibid.*, p. 2.
19. *Ibid.*, p. 32.
20. *Ibid.*, p. 34.
21. *Ibid.*, p. 36.
22. *Ibid.*, p. 36.
23. *Ibid.*, pp. 37, 40.
24. *Ibid.*, p. 40.

Chapter 27

1. "Congress and the Nation, 1945-1964," *Congressional Quarterly*, 1965, p. 311.
2. House Report No. 1406 (Authorizing Appropriations for Aircraft, Missiles, and Naval Vessels), Committee on Armed Services, 87th Congress, 2nd Session, p. 3.
3. *Ibid.*, p. 4.
4. *Idem.*
5. *Ibid.*, p. 1.
6. *Ibid.*, p. 3.
7. *Ibid.*, p. 5.
8. *Idem.*
9. *Ibid.*, pp. 6-7.
10. *Ibid.*, p. 7.
11. *Ibid.*, p. 8.
12. *Ibid.*, p. 9.
13. "Congress and the Nation," *op. cit.*, p. 315.

14. *Ibid.*, p. 323.
15. *Ibid.*, p. 327.

Chapter 28

1. Primary source for this chapter is: TFX Contract Investigation Hearings before the Permanent Subcommittee of the Senate Committee on Government Operations, 88th Congress, 1st Session, Parts 1, 2, 3, 5, 10.
2. *Congressional Record,* 88th Congress, 1st Session, February 28, 1963, speech by Senator Clifford Case of New Jersey, p. 3051.
3. Hanson W. Baldwin, "The McNamara Monarchy," *Saturday Evening Post* (March 9, 1963), p. 8.
4. Blackburn Memorandum of March 1, 1963, quoted in TFX Contract Investigation, Part 5, pp. 1203-07.
5. Letter, Campbell to McClellan, April 26, 1963, quoted in TFX Contract Investigation, Part 3, p. 883.

Chapter 29

1. Report of the Subcommittee for Special Investigations of the House Committee on Armed Services (Employment of Retired Commissioned Officers by Defense Department Contractors), 86th Congress, 1st Session, p. 10.
2. *Ibid.*, p. 11.
3. *Ibid.*, p. 3.
4. *Ibid.*, p. 9.
5. Primary source for Gilpatric role is: TFX Contract Investigation Hearings before the Permanent Subcommittee of the Senate Committee on Government Operations, 88th Congress, 1st Session, Parts 2, 4, 10.
6. Nomination of Roswell L. Gilpatric, Hearing before the Senate Committee on Armed Services, 87th Congress, 1st Session, January 17, 1961, p. 2.
7. Primary source for Korth role is: TFX Contract Investigation Hearings before the Permanent Subcommittee of the Senate Committee on Government Operations, 88th Congress, 1st Session, Parts 4, 6, 7.
8. Nomination of McCone, Korth and Harlan, Hearings before the Senate Committee on Armed Services, 87th Congress, 2nd Session, January 18, 1962, p. 4.
9. See text of speeches: *Congressional Record,* speech by Representative H. R. Gross of Iowa, July 24, 1963, p. 12585. *Congressional Record,* speech by Senator Milward L. Simpson of Wyoming, July 28, 1963, pp. 19768-70.
10. Presidential Press Conference of October 31, 1963. See *The New York Times,* November 1, 1963.
11. *Congressional Record,* August 16, 1966, pp. 18657-71.

Chapter 30

1. Report of the Joint Committee on Atomic Energy (Nuclear Propulsion for Naval Surface Vessels), December, 1963, 88th Congress, 1st Session, pp. 36-37.
2. *Ibid.*, pp. 24-25.

3. *Ibid.*, p. 3.
4. *Ibid.*, p. 7.
5. *Ibid.*, p. 8.
6. Hearings before the Joint Committee of Atomic Energy (Nuclear Propulsion for Naval Surface Vessels), 88th Congress, 1st Session, pp. 20-21.
7. *Ibid.*, p. 24.
8. *Idem.*
9. Report, p. 25.
10. Hearings, p. 163.
11. Report, p. 4.
12. *Ibid.*, p. 3.
13. *Ibid.*, p. 4.
14. Hearings, p. 171.
15. *Ibid.*, p. 131.
16. *Ibid.*, pp. 131-32.
17. *Ibid.*, p. 133.
18. Report, p. 16.
19. Hearings, pp. 178-79.
20. Report, p. 17.
21. Hanson W. Baldwin, "Slow-Down in the Pentagon," *Foreign Affairs* (January, 1965), p. 262.
22. Representative L. Mendel Rivers, Navy Day Speech, New Orleans, Louisiana, October 27, 1965.

Chapter 31

1. Primary source for this chapter is: "Collected Documents Summarizing the Case for Retention of Springfield Armory, 1965," made a part of the record of the Senate Preparedness Subcommittee of the Armed Services Committee, March 22, 1966.
2. *Ibid.*, Section I.
3. *Ibid.*, Section II.
4. Undated Memorandum to Representative L. Mendel Rivers from Representative Edward Boland, p. 7. (Copy in possession of the author.)
5. "Collected Documents," *op. cit.*, Section V.
6. *Ibid.*, Section IX.
7. News Release No. 808-65, dated November 16, 1965, issued by the Department of Defense, Office of the Assistant Secretary of Defense (Public Affairs). (Copy in possession of the author.)
8. Opening statement by Senator John Stennis, Chairman of the Senate Preparedness Subcommittee of the Armed Services Committee, March 22, 1966. (Copy in possession of the author.)
9. Statement of Senator Edward Kennedy before the Senate Preparedness Subcommittee of the Armed Services Committee, March 22, 1966. (Copy in possession of the author.)
10. Statement of Representative Silvio Conte before the Senate Preparedness Subcommittee of the Armed Services Committee, March 22, 1966. (Copy in possession of the author.)
11. Statement of Hon. Cyrus R. Vance, Deputy Secretary of Defense, before

the Senate Preparedness Subcommittee of the Armed Services Committee, March 22, 1966. (Copy in possession of the author.)

Chapter 32

1. Appellee's Appendix (No. 10140 in the United States Court of Appeals for the Fourth Circuit), United States of America, Appellee v. William Hermann Godel, Appellant, pp. 29-30.
2. *Ibid.*, pp. 30, 34.
3. Appellant's Appendix (No. 10140 in the United States Court of Appeals for the Fourth Circuit), United States of America, Appellee v. William Hermann Godel, Appellant, p. 214a.
4. Appellee's Appendix, p. 30.
5. *Ibid.*, p. 36.
6. Appellant's Appendix, pp. 108a, 180a.
7. Appellee's Appendix, pp. 35-36.
8. Appellant's Appendix, p. 111a.
9. *Ibid.*, p. 112a.
10. Appellee's Appendix, p. 26.
11. *Ibid.*, p. 28. Appellant's Appendix, p. 114a.
12. Appellee's Appendix, pp. 16-19, 20, 22.
13. Appellant's Appendix, pp. 31a-33a.
14. *Ibid.*, pp. 27a-28a.
15. Appellee's Appendix, pp. 4, 6-7, 11-12.
16. *Ibid.*, pp. 13-15.
17. Statement of Senator John J. Williams before the United States Senate, June 2, 1965, pp. 1-2. (Copy in possession of the author.)
18. *Ibid.*, pp. 2-3.
19. *Ibid.*, p. 4.
20. *Ibid.*, Insertion I, p. 1.
21. *Ibid.*, Insertion II, pp. 1-2.
22. *Ibid.*, p. 1.
23. *Ibid.*, p. 2.
24. *Ibid.*, p. 3.
25. *Ibid.*, p. 4.
26. *Congressional Record,* July 18, 1966, pp. 15262-63.
27. *Ibid.*, July 25, 1966, p. 16090.
28. *Washington Post,* September 16, 1965.

Chapter 33

1. Hearings before the Preparedness Investigating Subcommittee of the Senate Committee on Armed Services (Investigation of the Preparedness Program, May 13, 21; June 2, 3, and 30, 1965), 89th Congress, 1st Session, p. 2.
2. *Ibid.*, p. 2.
3. *Ibid.*, p. 4.
4. *Ibid.*, p. 6.
5. *Ibid.*, p. 7.
6. *Ibid.*, p. 14.
7. *Ibid.*, p. 15.

8. *Ibid.*, p. 19.
9. *Ibid.*, p. 18.
10. *Ibid.*, p. 28.
11. *Ibid.*, p. 32.
12. *Ibid.*, p. 42.
13. *Ibid.*, p. 43.
14. *Ibid.*, p. 49.
15. *Ibid.*, p. 51.
16. *Ibid.*, p. 113.
17. *Ibid.*, p. 129.
18. *Ibid.*, pp. 130-31.
19. *Ibid.*, p. 133.
20. *Ibid.*, pp. 143-44.
21. *Ibid.*, p. 147.
22. *Ibid.*, pp. 150-51.
23. *Ibid.*, p. 154.
24. *Ibid.*, pp. 157-58.
25. *Ibid.*, p. 183.
26. *Ibid.*, p. 197.
27. House Report No. 528 (Department of Defense Appropriation Bill, 1966), 89th Congress, 1st Session, p. 5.
28. *Ibid.*, p. 6.
29. *Ibid.* p. 7.
30. *Ibid.*, pp. 4-5.
31. *Ibid.*, p. 60.
32. *Ibid.*, pp. 62-63.
33. Senate Report No. 1047 (Supplemental Defense Appropriation Bill, 1966), 89th Congress, 2nd Session, p. 3.

Chapter 34

1. Report of the Preparedness Investigating Subcommittee of the Senate Armed Services Committee (on Combat Readiness), 89th Congress, 2nd Session, May 4, 1966, pp. 2, 3.
2. *Ibid.*, p. 2.
3. *Ibid.*, pp. 2, 3.
4. *Ibid.*, p. iv.
5. Report of the Preparedness Investigating Subcommittee of the Senate Armed Services Committee (Investigation of the Preparedness Program: Personnel training, equipment and readiness status of Army Reserve components), 89th Congress, 2nd Session, May 15, 1966, p. 2.
6. *Ibid.*, pp. 2, 3.
7. *Ibid.*, p. 3.
8. *Ibid.*, p. 11.
9. *Ibid.*, p. 13.
10. House Report No. 1536 (Authorizing Defense Procurement and Research and Development, and Military Pay), 89th Congress, 2nd Session, May 16, 1966, p. 10.
11. *Ibid.*, pp. 11-13.

12. *Des Moines Register,* May 6, 1966, p. 1.
13. House Report No. 1536, p. 19.
14. *Ibid.,* p. 17.
15. Hearings before the Joint Committee on Atomic Energy (Naval Nuclear Propulsion Program), 89th Congress, 2nd Session, January 26, 1966, pp. 10, 11.
16. *Ibid.,* p. 10.
17. *Ibid.,* p. 15.
18. *Ibid.,* p. v.
19. House Report No. 1536, p. 2.
20. *Ibid.,* p. 49.
21. *Ibid.,* p. 9.
22. *Ibid.,* p. 10.
23. Conference Report, No. 1679 (Authorizing Appropriations for Defense Procurement and Research and Development for Fiscal Year 1967), 89th Congress, 2nd Session, p. 8.
24. *Ibid.,* p. 11.
25. Hearings, July 13, 14, 18, 19, 20 and 22, 1966, and Report, September 12, 1966, of the Special Investigations Subcommittee of the House Armed Services Committee (on Examination of Department of Defense Cost Reduction Program), 89th Congress, 2nd Session.
26. Report, p. 33.
27. *Ibid.,* p. 41.
28. *Ibid.,* p. 36.

Chapter 35

1. House Report No. 1765 (Report of the House Armed Services Committee on the Department of Defense Reorganization Act of 1958), p. 7.
2. John C. Reis, *Management of Defense, Organization and Control of the U.S. Armed Services* (Baltimore, The Johns Hopkins Press, 1964) p. 192.

INDEX